D0699278

# Tree Improvement
Applied Research and Technology Transfer

# Tree Improvement

## Applied Research and Technology Transfer


*Editor*

Sunil Puri

Professor and Head

Department of Forestry

Indira Gandhi Agricultural University

Raipur 492 012

India



Science Publishers, Inc.

U.S.A.

**SCIENCE PUBLISHERS, INC**
Post Office Box 699
Enfield, New Hampshire 03748
United States of America

Internet site: *http://www.scipub.net*

*sales@scipub.net* (marketing department)
*editor@scipub.net* (editorial department)
*info@scipub.net* (for all other enquiries)

ISBN 1-57808-027-4

© 1998 Copyright reserved

All rights reserved. No part of this publication may be reproduced, stored in a retrieval system, or transmitted in any form or by any means electronic, mechanical, photocopying or otherwise, without the prior permission from the publisher. The request to reproduce certain material should include a statement of the purpose and extent of the reproduction.

Printed in India

SD
399.5
T74
1998

# Preface

Forestry is entering a new age in which genetically improved forest crops are being grown in scientifically planned cropping systems. The reason for this change is the ever more pressing need to grow wood in plantations as exploitation reduces the natural forests. Today the need is not only to grow trees but to produce the same amount of wood on an ever decreasing timber growing land. It is one avenue by which wood volume and value could be increased. Tree improvement is the application of knowledge of genetic variation in tree species coupled with appropriate application of genetic principles, reproductive physiology and orchard management to produce trees capable of better performance in a specified biological zone. The goal of tree improvement is to understand and maintain an adequate genetic resource while improving tree growth rate, disease resistance, stem, wood, fibre quality, etc. The need is to select and develop trees and forests that are managed for production purposes so as to reduce pressure on the remaining natural forests and to provide raw materials in forms more suitable for commercial use and the needs of human society.

During the last four decades studies were directed towards increasing the efficiency, quality and cost effectiveness of all phases of tree improvement programme, and of the consequences of planting improved seedlings. These efforts in tree improvement have taught us the importance of delivering genetically improved trees as rapidly and consistently as possible. Simultaneously efforts are focussing on ways to reduce the time between tree selection and seed production, and on ways to protect trees, seeds and cones from damaging agents, such as adverse weather, insects and diseases. Improved techniques will enable us to "tailor make" seedlots for specific planting sites and to capitalize on the latest selections.

Practical benefits are already being realized at a few places where tree improvement is more advanced. More recently many tropical and sub-tropical countries have initiated similar programmes for genetic improvement. In all existing programmes the current issue is the development of a strategy that allows rapid exploitation of existing genetic variability, while at the same time providing continuing genetic gains, maintaining flexibility for future changes, and minimizing the risks of monoculture, genetic uniformity and loss of variability. The present book is an attempt to expand and accelerate work on tree improvement programme as well as to provide general direction and possible technical plans for the future work. The book addresses the need for providing improved seeds for reforestation/afforestation and developing required scientific knowledge and technology for operational tree improvement. The topics covered are on breeding strategies, population genetics and geographic variation, genetic diversity and conservation, propagation and biotechnology. Under these broad topics, 21 chapters have been written by experts in their respective fields. Since the contributing authors are associated with applied tree improvement programmes in geographically dispersed countries such as the United States, Canada, Argentina, Brazil, Italy, Greece, Kenya, Korea, Australia, Bangladesh and India, the book has a global coverage. Stress is given on examples of progress through tree improvement and difficulties arising for application of tree improvement programme. Emphasis is also given on why and how certain things should or should not be done. Some of the chapters and at places within chapters general concepts and principles necessary to manipulate operational tree improvement programmes are emphasized with specific examples. The book will be useful to anyone interested in improving forest trees.

Many researchers have contributed their support, time and creative analysis to this book. To all of those contributors, special thanks are offered. In addition the help of Miss Kusum Lata Verma in finalizing the drafts of chapters is gratefully acknowledged. Special thanks to my wife, Dr. Geeta, for the advice and support provided in completing this task. Lastly, I am confident that the conclusions and recommendations presented in this book will contribute in improving a major resource—the world's forest trees.

February, 1998 SUNIL PURI

# Contents

# A. BREEDING STRATEGIES

# 1

# Incorporation of New Information and Technology in Breeding and Deployment Strategies for Black Spruce

*Y.S. Park*[1], *G.W. Adams*[2] *and T.J. Mullin*[3]

**ABSTRACT**

The development and evolution of breeding strategies for black spruce in the Maritimes, Canada is discussed. Emphasis is on the biological factors influencing breeding work, the basic framework of the strategies and the integration of clonal production techniques. First-generation improvement began in the early 1970s with seedling seed orchard procedure with plus-tree selection in wild stands. The second-generation breeding strategy followed by selecting the best 400 families which were then subjected to polycross tests to determine their general combining ability; a partial diallel mating system was followed to produce the next generation breeding population. In this paper, the development of a breeding and clonal deployment strategy incorporating the latest information and technology is presented. Simulation techniques and a recently developed generalized computer program, known as POPSIM, are discussed citing examples. The clonal deployment strategy is also discussed.

[1]Canadian Forest Service, Atlantic Forestry Centre, PO Box 4000, Fredericton, New Brunswick E3B 5P7, Canada.

[2]J.D. Irving, Limited, Sussex Tree Nursery Sussex, New Brunswick E0E 1P0, Canada.

[3]Genesis Forest Science Canada Inc., C.P. 64, Succursale Haute-Ville, Québec, Québec G1R 4M8, Canada.

# 1. INTRODUCTION

## 1.1 Background

Intensive tree improvement efforts for six conifer species have been underway in the three Maritime provinces (New Brunswick, Nova Scotia and Prince Edward Island) of Canada since the late 1970s. Most reforestation planting stock now originates from first-generation seed orchards, most of which have been genetically rogued. Second-generation seed orchards of black spruce (*Picea mariana* (Mill.) B.S.P.) and jack pine (*Pinus banksiana* Lamb.) have been established and are beginning to produce seeds (Simpson, 1995). Breeding strategies have been developed for the major commercial species in the Maritimes (Fowler, 1986) and these are evolving as new information becomes available and technological advances are made. The development and evolution of strategies for black spruce is discussed as a case study. This includes biological factors influencing breeding work, the basic framework of the strategies and the integration of clonal production techniques.

The range, economic importance and extent of reforestation with black spruce has been described by Morgenstern and Park (1991). Briefly, black spruce is distributed across North America in cool-temperate and boreal forests where it is highly valued for the production of pulp and paper products. Black spruce is a pioneer species, frequently regenerating after forest fires. Consequently, this species performs well in plantations established after clear-cutting. The widespread natural occurrence, high economic value and use in reforestation have made this species a good candidate for tree improvement.

## 1.2 Review of First-Generation Improvement of Black Spruce

Range-wise provenance studies were established in the Maritime provinces in the early 1970s which aided in the delineation of three overlapping breeding zones (Park and Fowler, 1988). These tests also indicated that there would be little advantage in using non-local sources of black spruce for reforestation in the region. Three breeding programs were initiated, one each for the three provinces. There have been exchanges of breeding material among the three programs. Over 2000 plus-trees were located (Simpson, 1992; Nitschke, 1990; MacKinnon, personal communication) using the five-tree comparison method. The emphasis of tree improvement efforts was on growth rate. Parent-progeny correlations based on wild selections have been found to be low in growth rate (Morgenstern *et al.*, 1975). This, in combination with a precocious flowering habit, resulted in the adoption of a first-generation breeding strategy based on low selection intensity seedling seed orchards and open-pollinated family tests.

The first-generation seedling seed orchard procedure started with plus-tree selection in wild stands. In New Brunswick, a total of 1200 unrelated plus trees were selected over a 10-year period. Seedlings from the open-pollinated seeds of the plus-trees were used to establish both seedling seed orchards and family tests. The seedling seed orchards were planted using single tree plots at a narrow spacing (1 × 2 m), and each family was represented by about 100 trees randomized within the orchards. The family tests were usually established at five locations using 10 randomized blocks of four-tree-row plots. The family tests provided information on family performance for roguing of seed orchards. In addition, the family test plantations were used to select the best 400 trees for second-generation breeding. Combined family and within family selection was used to select individuals to form the second-generation breeding population. These selections were propagated by grafting.

Estimates of heritability and genetic gain for height after 15 years have been obtained for two family test series in New Brunswick including over 300 families. This is nearing half rotation in the Maritime provinces. Individual narrow-sense heritabilities for height are in the 0.2–0.3 range while family heritabilities are estimated to be approximately 0.8 (Mullin *et al.*, 1995). Estimates for breast height diameter are similar. These estimates are in the same range as those reported by Boyle (1986) in northern Ontario but substantially higher than those reported by Nelson and Mohn (1991) in Minnesota, USA. Genetic gain for family roguing to leave the top 25 per cent of families in the seedling orchards is estimated to be 15 per cent for volume at age 15.

### 1.3 Advanced-Generation Seed Production

In New Brunswick, a multi-generation breeding strategy for black spruce as outlined by Fowler (1986) has been adopted. The second-generation breeding strategy begins with the best tree from each of the best 400 families, i.e., a 400-tree breeding population. These 400 parents are subjected to a polycross test to determine their general combining ability (GCA) values. At the same time, these 400 parents were single-pair mated to produce 200 full-sib families to select the best 400 trees, i.e., four best trees per family, forming a breeding population for the third-generation improvement. Similarly, for each ensuing generation, polycross tests will be used to determine GCA values of parents, while a partial diallel mating system will be used to produce the next generation breeding population. In each generation, new clonal seed orchards are established, which are subsequently rogued on the basis of a polycross test. These clonal seed orchards provide genetically improved seedlings stock for reforestation.

The initial development of breeding strategies for black spruce was based on the experience with other species and on currently available information on genetic and other biological characters. Therefore, we must recognize the need for flexibility to accommodate new information and technological advances. During the past 16 years, since the beginning of black spruce breeding program in New Brunswick, more detailed genetic information became available and many new technological advances were made. Hence, the development of a breeding and clonal deployment strategy incorporating the most recent information and technology is presented.

## 2. BIOLOGICAL FACTORS INFLUENCING BREEDING STRATEGIES

### 2.1 Genetic Variability

One of the most important factors influencing the development of breeding strategies is genetic variability. Provenance testing in the Maritimes has indicated that genetic variation for growth rate at the provenance level is clinal (Park and Fowler, 1988). Within a region, allozyme studies have shown this species to have high outcrossing rates with large within-population components of variation and less variation among populations (Boyle and Morgenstern, 1986). Quantitative genetic parameter estimates of growth characteristics, as previously described, have mainly been concerned with additive variance which could be captured in seed orchard-based tree improvement programs. Results obtained to date indicate that investment in black spruce tree improvement is economically viable (Mullin, 1994). Studies have also indicated substantial levels of non-additive genetic variation for growth rate which could be exploited using clonal production instead of traditional seed orchards (Mullin *et al.*, 1992).

An additional trait which is likely to be of importance in tree improvement programs for black spruce in the Maritimes is wood density. At the time of plus-tree selection in New Brunswick, disks were taken when the trees were felled for cone collection. Alternatively, wood cores were extracted, from the plus-tree and comparison trees, for relative density determination. The average relative density of plus-trees selected for height was virtually identical to the average of comparison trees at just over 0.40.

### 2.2 Methods of Propagation

Black spruce is a monoecious species with separate seed and pollen cones. Seed cones are borne in the upper portion of the tree crown and pollen cones are usually found lower in the crown on less vigourous branches although some overlap usually occurs. Caron and Powell (1989) studied plantations of different ages and found that they began to produce seed cones at the age of 7 and pollen cones at the age of 10. Cone-bearing is prolific once the trees become sexually mature. Black spruce is one of the least periodic of the spruces with cone crops being produced as often as several years in a row.

Seeds of black spruce usually exhibit high germination rates (over 90%) with no stratification being required. Seedlots may be stored at sub-freezing temperatures for over ten years without any serious loss of germination success.

The potential of rooted cuttings as a production technique for black spruce has been recognized for over 20 years (Rauter, 1971). Rooting success is commonly over 90 per cent when the donor stock is juvenile (Rauter, 1985), but declines as donors mature. Rauter (1971) found that after four years, rooting had declined to 62 per cent on average with considerable clonal variation. In addition, lower growth rates, longer rooting periods and increased topophysis may be experienced when older donors are used (Rauter, 1985). This has serious implications when considering clonal production because the potential to root individual clones is lost during the lengthy testing period required to identify superior clones. Hedging and serial propagation may be used to delay the onset of maturation. Operational production of black spruce rooted cuttings as a means of bulking up elite controlled crosses has been undertaken in northern Ontario (Rogers, 1990), Quebec (Campagna, 1990) and more recently in New Brunswick (Adams, 1995). A major consideration for using this type of production technique is the increased cost compared to the seedlings.

This must be weighed carefully against potential incremental gains (Mullin, 1994).

A major advance in the propagation of black spruce is the development of somatic embryogenesis over the last ten years (Adams *et al.*, 1994). Somatic embryogenesis (SE) has been demonstrated to be successful across a broad range of black spruce genotypes, and demonstration plantations of plants produced by SE have been established over the last 4 years in New Brunswick (Adams *et al.*, 1994). Production costs are still high using this technique because of labour intensity. However it has a major advantage in that samples of embryogenic clonal lines may be cryogenically preserved, theoretically indefinitely, in liquid nitrogen (Lelu *et al.*, 1993) in a juvenile state. This circumvents the maturation problem encountered with rooted cutting donors. Somatic embryogenesis could be employed as a direct production technique if an automated system is developed to reduce costs. In the near future, however, this method holds great promise as a step preceding a rooted cutting program by preserving clonal lines in a juvenile state during clonal testing.

### 2.3 Techniques for Accelerating Breeding Cycles

The amount of time required to complete a breeding cycle sparked an interest in developing accelerated breeding techniques in the mid 1980s (Greenwood *et al.*, 1988). The annual growth cycle of black spruce begins in late May in the Maritimes and is complete by early August. Accelerated growth procedures in greenhouse, including manipulating day length and providing chilling periods, were developed to obtain two flushes of growth per year on grafted trees in pots (Greenwood *et al.*, 1991). After two years of accelerated growth treatments, black spruce grafts are 1–1.5 m in height and have well developed crowns which are capable of bearing seed cones. Using these techniques, breeding has been conducted on grafts after as little as 28 months from grafting (Adams and Kunze, 1993). Compared to the time it takes to complete a breeding cycle in grafted parents in a breeding orchard in the field, a minimum of 2 years is saved by accelerated growth.

Induction of seed cones using gibberellin $A_{4/7}$ ($GA_{4/7}$) has been very successful for black spruce, commonly improving production by threefold or greater (Greenwood *et al.*, 1994). Pollen cone production tends to be improved as well but not as dramatically. The most efficient method of application is by stem injection during the growth cycle prior to the initiation of seed and pollen cones (Greenwood *et al.*, 1994), although for small trees, foliar applications are also successful (Greenwood *et al.*, 1991).

## 3. BREEDING STRATEGIES FOR CLONAL DEPLOYMENT

### 3.1 Clonal Deployment in Production Forestry

Deployment of clonally propagated trees in production forestry is of great interest in many breeding and reforestation programs worldwide. This is primarily due to improvements in vegetative propagation techniques, such as the refinement of the procedures for rooting of cuttings and major advances in somatic embryogenesis as discussed above. In particular, clonal selection and deployment is receiving attention as an intensive forest management tool for increased wood production. It also provides flexibility by allowing tailoring to changing product goals or environments, especially in high-value plantation forestry, by deploying specialized clones for specific requirements. Another advantage of clonal deployment is that genetic diversity can be carefully programed into clonal plantations by mixing known genotypes.

Tree improvement programs are generally long term, spanning several generations. Progressive improvement is obtained in each generation through controlled mating and recurrent selection. Clonal forestry itself is not a tree-breeding method. It is, rather, an effective means of mass propagating and deploying genetically improved material. Therefore, a sound breeding plan is a prerequisite for any successful clonal forestry program. Here, an operational breeding and clonal deployment strategy for black spruce to take advantage of recent advances in the vegetative propagation technology is presented.

The breeding strategy described here is based on the second-generation breeding plan for the New Brunswick Tree Improvement Council (NBTIC), a cooperative tree breeding program; however, the plan is further modified to take advantage of currently available cloning techniques. These procedures have been adopted by J.D. Irving, Limited, a forest products company in the Maritimes region of Canada. The initial breeding population is the same population described in Park *et al.* (1993), and the material used here represents the first set of parents out of a total of 400 selections to begin the second-generation breeding program of the NBTIC.

## 3.2 Overview of Breeding and Clonal Deployment Strategy

An overview of the breeding strategy is presented in Fig. 1. The set of parents used in the breeding plan consists of 80 clones, representing the best tree from each of the 80 best of 400 families in family tests based on 10-year field height (1). All the parents are polycrossed with a standard polymix and the progeny tested to determine the general combining ability (GCA) of each parent (2). Based on a 3-year result of a polycross progeny test in a nursery, the parents are ranked according to their GCA values (3). This ranking is a basis for forming four 20-tree sublines (4 and 5). One of the four sublines consists of the best 20 GCA parents, called the elite subline (5). In the other three sublines (4), the remaining parents are assigned uniformly across the sublines using their GCA ranking. For generation advancement, a two-tiered mating scheme is employed, an assortative mating for regular sublines based on their GCA rankings (6), while a disconnected diallel mating is performed within the elite subline, where the assignment of parents for the mating will be random (7). Progenies from both the matings will be planted in a full-sib family test which will serve as material for the next generation selection as well as providing performance information for reforestation stock production (8).

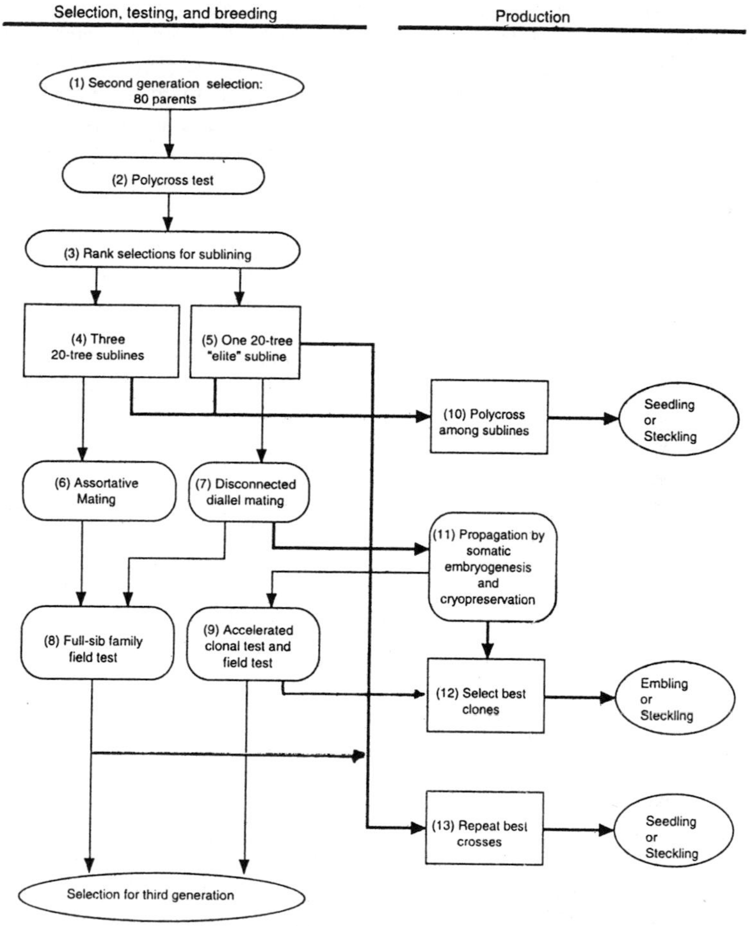


Fig. 1. A flowchart of the breeding and clonal deployment strategies of black spruce in the Martimes, Canada. Solid lines represent material flow, and shaded lines represent information flow (modified from Park *et al.*, 1993).

Additionally, the progeny produced by the disconnected diallel mating will be subjected to a clonally replicated progeny test using an accelerated testing procedure (Sulzer *et al.*, 1993) (9). The production of planting stock is carried out using three methods. The main method of stock production is by controlled pollination to produce full-sib families or polycrosses among selected parents of the sublines (10). Since these controlled-crosses are not likely to provide a sufficient quantity of seeds, the resulting seeds may be bulked, seedlings raised and vegetatively multiplied by serial rooting of cuttings. Also, a portion of seeds for each family produced by the disconnected diallel mating within the elite subline will be subjected to *in vitro* propagation using somatic embryogenesis (11). Most of the embryogenic tissue mass is cryopreserved, while only a portion of the tissue will be used to produce emblings, i.e., propagules produced by SE. The emblings will be subjected to accelerated nursery and field testing (9). Information from these tests is used to identify the best clones, which are retrieved from cryo-storage to produce emblings (12). Since automated embling production and planting systems are not available now, a small number of emblings can be vegetatively multiplied by rooting of cuttings. Also, using the information from both full-sib family (8) and accelerated clonal (9) test, the best specific crosses may be identified, and the crosses may be repeated (13). Like the previous stock production procedures, a small quantity of the resulting seeds will be vegetatively multiplied for reforestation.

The breeding strategy proposed here is focused on controlled breeding followed by vegetative propagation. The potential for genetic gain from breeding and deployment of clonal propagules is expected to be greater than conventional open-pollinated seed orchard breeding and planting of seedlings. This is mainly due to elimination of some inefficiencies of seed orchard breeding, e.g., pollen contamination and asynchrony of flowering, as well as capturing a greater portion of additive and non-additive variances. Production strategies based on controlled pollination and vegetative multiplication offer greater flexibility to change the genetic composition of reforestation stock, as new information becomes available, than conventional seed orchards. In the following sections, we describe operational details of the strategy leading to clonal deployment.

### 3.3 Sublining of Breeding Population

All eighty initial parents of the second-generation selections are divided into sublines, as suggested by van Buijtenen and Lowe (1979), by assigning 20 trees to each of the four sublines. The assignments of parents to sublines are based on the GCA rankings for 3-year height from a polycross test in a nursery. One of the sublines is formed by assigning the best 20 to develop the elite subline, similar to that described by Williams and Lambeth (1992). The main reason for developing the elite subline is to use the best parents intensively in the production of planting stock. For the remaining three sublines, the assignments are evenly distributed so that the mean ranking of the sublines is the same. The management of multi-generation breeding populations using sublines will allow for flexibility while achieving progressive genetic gain. In any multi-generation breeding program, inbreeding is an inevitable consequence, and the use of sublines makes coancestry control convenient by confining inbreeding within each subline. Inbreeding is eliminated in the production population by crossing among different sublines. It is also possible to develop groups of highly specialized sublines, such as sublines that are of high wood density or suitable for specific planting zones.

### 3.4 Controlled-Pollination Schemes for Operational Deployment

Operationally, all the selections are maintained in clone banks. Furthermore, the multiple ramets of a clone can be grafted and maintained in containers for respective sublines. Maintaining grafted clones in containers facilitates controlled pollination, cone induction treatments and control of growing season in a greenhouse.

### 3.4.1 Controlled Polycrossing

As shown in Fig. 1, (10), polycrossing among sublines can be carried out soon after the formation of sublines. The breeding value of each parent in the sublines is determined by a preceding polycross test in the nursery, and the ten best-GCA parents from each of the sublines are selected for use in controlled polycrossing. There are two alternatives for utilizing the elite subline. One is that full-sib crosses can be made with the resulting progeny being bulked for vegetative propagation. This gives precise control of the full-sib family mix. The other is to divide the parents into two groups of 10 trees, each group being an opposite sex, and controlled polycrossing will be carried out between the groups. Polymix pollen from each 10-tree group in the elite sublines may also be used for polycrossing the parents of the three regular sublines for planting stock production. Again, as a stock production method, in each regular subline, a 10-best-tree polymix will be prepared by mixing an equal volume of pollen from each of the 10 best trees. These polymixes are used to pollinate 5–10 best seed parents of different sublines. An example of a controlled polycrossing scheme is presented in Fig. 2. Since the controlled polycrossings are carried out in a breeding hall with a limited number of parents, only a small quantity of seeds will be obtained. Therefore, it is necessary to raise seedlings from the resulting seeds and vegetatively multiply the young seedlings using serial rooting of cuttings. These young seedlings may be maintained for three years as donor plants.

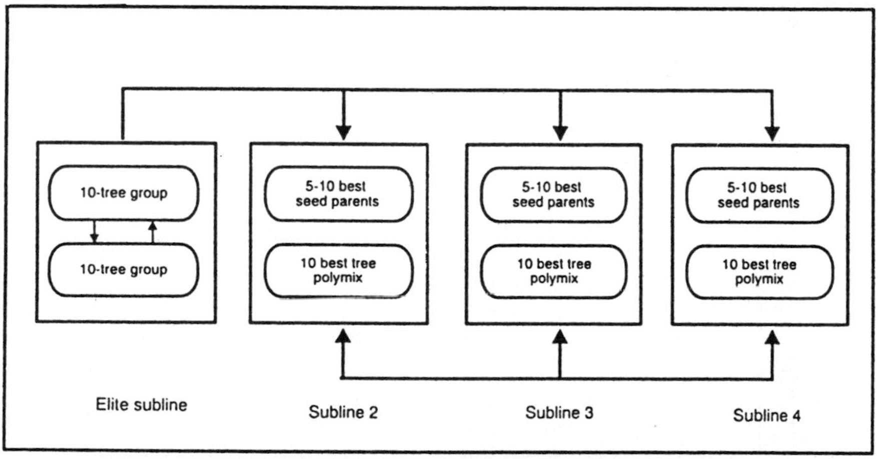


Fig. 2. An example of controlled polycross scheme among sublines and within the elite subline. The resulting seeds are vegetatively multiplied to produce planting stock (from Park *et al.*, 1992).

The improvement attained in this scheme is equivalent to a conventional rogued seed orchard, but without the inefficiencies associated with wind-pollinated seed orchards, such as pollen contamination, non-synchronous flowering, non-random mating, and possible selfing. Since the initial phase of this strategy is based on 3-year nursery test results, the scheme may have to be revised as new information becomes available from the periodic evaluation of polycross tests in the field, especially if there are significant rank changes among parents. Thus, this scheme is readily adaptable to changing needs and more flexible than conventional land-based seed orchards.

### 3.4.2 Disconnected Diallel Mating and Clonal Selection

For the elite subline, a disconnected diallel mating scheme will be used to produce offspring populations for progeny testing and planting stock production. Within the elite subline, the parents are divided into five sets of four parents, and half diallel mating will be performed for each of the five sets resulting in 30 full-sib families (Fig. 3). The assignment of parents among and within the sets will be random. Since the mating is random among the parents,

| | A | B | C | D | E | F | G | H | I | J | K | L | M | N | O | P | Q | R | S | T |
|---|---|---|---|---|---|---|---|---|---|---|---|---|---|---|---|---|---|---|---|---|
| A | | x | x | x | | | | | | | | | | | | | | | | |
| B | | | x | x | | | | | | | | | | | | | | | | |
| C | | | | x | | | | | | | | | | | | | | | | |
| D | | | | | | | | | | | | | | | | | | | | |
| E | | | | | | x | x | x | | | | | | | | | | | | |
| F | | | | | | | x | x | | | | | | | | | | | | |
| G | | | | | | | | x | | | | | | | | | | | | |
| H | | | | | | | | | | | | | | | | | | | | |
| I | | | | | | | | | | x | x | x | | | | | | | | |
| J | | | | | | | | | | | x | x | | | | | | | | |
| K | | | | | | | | | | | | x | | | | | | | | |
| L | | | | | | | | | | | | | | | | | | | | |
| M | | | | | | | | | | | | | | x | x | x | | | | |
| N | | | | | | | | | | | | | | | x | x | | | | |
| O | | | | | | | | | | | | | | | | x | | | | |
| P | | | | | | | | | | | | | | | | | | | | |
| Q | | | | | | | | | | | | | | | | | | x | x | x |
| R | | | | | | | | | | | | | | | | | | | x | x |
| S | | | | | | | | | | | | | | | | | | | | x |
| T | | | | | | | | | | | | | | | | | | | | |

Fig. 3. Disconnected diallel mating scheme for the elite subline to produce progeny for both full-sib and clonal testing for deployment and generation advancement. The parents are assigned randomly within the subline (from Park *et al.*, 1992).

it is expected to provide sound estimates of both GCA and SCA from progeny testing.

In conjunction with progeny/clonal testing, the progeny derived from the elite sublines is used for clonal selection and deployment. After making the disconnected diallel matings (Fig. 1, (7)), a portion of the available seed cones is harvested while immature, and the immature zygotic embryos will be propagated by somatic embryogenesis as described by Park *et al*: (1993) and Adams *et al.* (1994). Once somatic embryogenesis is induced, most of the embryogenic tissue will be cryopreserved while a small portion will be used to regenerate plants (emblings) through maturation and germination of somatic embryos (Fig. 1, (11)). Accelerated clonal testing will be carried out with these embling clones (Fig. 1, (9)). If not enough emblings are produced for the clonal test, the emblings can be vegetatively multiplied by rooting of cuttings. Once the clonal testing has determined the best clones, they can be retrieved from cryogenic storage and propagated to produce emblings (Fig. 1 (12)). Once a few emblings are obtained from the selected clones, they can be vegetatively multiplied by using rooting of cuttings for deployment. Early screening of clones may be based on accelerated test results (2–3 years). Field tests will provide long-term evaluation on clonal performance, and these results may be used to make adjustments to production clone composition, especially if there are significant rank changes. Since all clones are cryopreserved, the required adjustments can be made easily. The greatest genetic gain will be obtained from this clonal selection and deploying of vegetative propagules of selected clones as this strategy utilizes total genetic variation.

#### 3.4.3 Repeat Best Crossing

Based on the results of full-sib and accelerated clonal tests involving the elite subline (Fig. 1, (8) and (9)), the parents that produced the best specific combining ability (SCA) pairs will be identified and the crosses may be repeated. The resulting seeds will be used to raise seedlings and, subsequently, vegetatively multiplied by using rooting of cuttings to produce stecklings for deployment. Genetic gain from this strategy depends on the amount of SCA variance, i.e., dominance effect, within the elite subline. With the absence of SCA effects, however, gains from this strategy are likely to be similar to that of controlled polycrossing among the sublines.

### 3.5 Generation Advancement

Generation advancement, or selections for the next generation breeding population, will be carried out from a full- sib progeny test, by selecting 20 clones in each subline. That is, the equal numbers of parents and sublines are maintained from generation to generation. Production of offspring populations for generation advancement/progeny testing will be carried out for each subline by performing controlled matings. As previously discussed, the 30 full-sib families produced by a disconnected diallel mating within the elite subline will be a part of the population where the selection will be made. For each of the regular sublines, a scheme of weighted assortative mating will be used.

The parents are arranged by their GCA ranking, and controlled mating will be performed. For the top eight parents, three crosses per parent will be made among them, and, among the middle eight parents, two crosses per parent will be made. The bottom four parents will be pair mated with any one of the top eight parents. An example of the mating scheme is shown in Fig. 4, and the mating scheme will produce 24 full-sib families. The reason for employing this weighted assortative mating scheme is that greater use of better GCA parents in breeding will result in higher gain (Lindgren, 1986), although the accumulation of inbreeding within a subline is greater.

| | 1 | 2 | 3 | 4 | 5 | 6 | 7 | 8 | 9 | 10 | 11 | 12 | 13 | 14 | 15 | 16 | 17 | 18 | 19 | 20 |
|---|---|---|---|---|---|---|---|---|---|---|---|---|---|---|---|---|---|---|---|---|
| 1 | | x | x | | | | | | | | | | | | | | | | | |
| 2 | | | x | | | | | | | | | | | | | | | | | |
| 3 | | | | x | | | | | | | | | | | | | | | | |
| 4 | | | | | x | x | | | | | | | | | | | | | | |
| 5 | | | | | | x | x | | | | | | | | | | | | | |
| 6 | | | | | | | x | | | | | | | | | | | | | |
| 7 | | | | | | | | x | | | | | | | | | | | | |
| 8 | x | x | | | | | | | | | | | | | | | | | | |
| 9 | | | | | | | | | | x | | | | | | | | | | |
| 10 | | | | | | | | | | | x | | | | | | | | | |
| 11 | | | | | | | | | | | | x | | | | | | | | |
| 12 | | | | | | | | | | | | | x | | | | | | | |
| 13 | | | | | | | | | | | | | | x | | | | | | |
| 14 | | | | | | | | | | | | | | | x | | | | | |
| 15 | | | | | | | | | | | | | | | | x | | | | |
| 16 | | | | | | | | | x | | | | | | | | | | | |
| 17 | x | | | | | | | | | | | | | | | | | | | |
| 18 | | | x | | | | | | | | | | | | | | | | | |
| 19 | | | | | x | | | | | | | | | | | | | | | |
| 20 | | | | | | | x | | | | | | | | | | | | | |

Fig. 4. A weighted assortative mating scheme used within a regular subline for progeny testing and generation advancement. The parental numbers correspond to their GCA rankings (from Park *et al.*, 1992).

From the mating schemes described above, a total of 102 full-sib families, i.e., 30 families from the elite subline and 24 families from each of the three remaining sublines, are available for progeny testing. The progeny test will be established at three different locations. At each location, eight blocks of 4 tree plots will be planted. Thus 96 trees per full-sib family (a total of 9792 trees for all families) are available for genetic testing and selection for generation advancement. The test will be evaluated at 5-year intervals. After evaluation of the test at 10 years, selection for the next generation will be carried out in the test plantations using a combined index selection, which is based on an individual index value that weighs family and individual performance by their respective heritabilities (Falconer, 1981).

### 3.6 Genetic Testing

Genetic testing is an expensive and critical component of any tree improvement program. As described in section 3.4, the genetic test plantations are used for selection of the next generation breeding material. The main purpose of genetic testing, however, is to determine the performance of genetic entities, or bred material, for target planting areas. Three types of genetic testing will be carried out: (1) full-sib progeny testing involving all four sublines; (2) clonally replicated and accelerated nursery tests involving the elite subline; and (3) clonal field testing of the clones used in the accelerated testing in (2) above. The function of full-sib progeny testing in the field is for selection of material for generation advancement already described in the previous section. The main purpose of the latter two test types is to determine the best suited genotypes for rapid deployment in production forestry as well as providing long-term genetic information to fine-tune the breeding and clonal deployment strategy.

The implementation of an effective clonal deployment strategy will require accurate genetic information. Shaw and Hood (1985) showed that the use of clonal replicates in genetic testing should increase the precision of estimates and cumulative genetic gain during each breeding cycle. Furthermore, to predict genetic gains from clonal deployment strategies, it is necessary to obtain both additive and non-additive variances. By using cloned ramets from full-sib crosses in black spruce, Mullin and Park (1992) partitioned non-additive variance into dominance and epistatic variances. Clearly, the efficiency of clonal selection will benefit from detailed information on the magnitude of genetic variances in the cloned population involving the elite subline.

Clonally replicated accelerated nursery and subsequent field tests are conducted for the progeny derived from the elite subline. About 50 immature seeds from each of the 30 full-sib families obtained by the disconnected diallel mating are used to induce somatic embryogenesis. It is expected that about 60 per cent of the explants would become embryogenic lines. Once embryogenic tissue masses are obtained, most of them will be cryopreserved. The remaining tissue will be subjected to somatic embryo maturation and germination protocols to produce about 10–15 emblings per clone.

The accelerated nursery test will be performed using rooted cuttings of the emblings. Early genetic evaluation techniques have been developed for black spruce (Mullin *et al.*, 1995) as a way to improve genetic efficiency within a generation. Genetic correlations of over 0.80 have been obtained between 3-year greenhouse heights and 15-year field heights in retrospective greenhouse studies of open-pollinated black spruce families (Mullin *et al.*, 1995). We use this testing scheme to identify superior clonal lines for quick deployment in the production forest. As mentioned previously, the best performing clonal lines will be retrieved from cryopreservation and propagated to obtain donor plants for vegetative multiplication. Long-term field tests will be established, and these will remain an integral part of the breeding strategies in the Maritime provinces. The information from the later evaluation of the field test will be used to correct any shortcomings based on early test results. For example, if a significant rank change among clones occurs later during the field test, substitutions are made by retrieving appropriate clones from cryopreservation.

## 4. LONG-TERM MANAGEMENT OF BREEDING POPULATION FOR GENETIC GAIN AND DIVERSITY

### 4.1 Simulation Approach to Population Management

The objective of any breeding strategy is to utilize genetic variation to achieve gain through selection. This will require the conservation of as much genetic variation as possible. In each generation, the breeder striving to maximize gain must face the contradiction that selection methods that are efficient for genetic gain are less efficient for preserving diversity. Aggressive breeding techniques designed to accentuate gain such as combined-index selection, positive assortative mating, and even clonally replicated progeny tests, may also accelerate the loss of genetic diversity within the breeding population, with the resulting loss of potential genetic gain in future generations.

Choosing a proper balance between diversity and gain is a complex issue for any breeding program, and becomes even more difficult if one pursues the additional gain that is theoretically possible through clonal deployment. Increasingly, simulation techniques are being used to evaluate the combined effects of various population management factors (King and Johnson, 1993). Recently, a generalized computer program, known as POPSIM, has been developed (Mullin and Park, 1995). The program allows tracking of changes in genetic structure and diversity over several generations in stochastically simulated breeding and production populations. The user specifies initial base population parameters, such as population size, mean of a quantitative trait, variances of genetic and environmental effects, and other options, then POPSIM provides the breeder with a generation-by-generation description of genetic variances, accumulation of inbreeding, effective population size, and cumulative genetic gain, for a breeding and deployment strategies. Options are available that allow division of the breeding populations into sublines, positive assortative mating or any mating design, alternative selection schemes, restriction of coancestry, and various kinds of production populations.

Use of the simulator, POPSIM, can best be illustrated with examples, and we will consider two scenarios, one involving the three regular sublines and the other involving the elite subline. In the first example, we assume that the base population is composed of 60 unrelated trees, and that the mean value of the trait under consideration is 100 units. We also assume that additive, dominance, epistatic, and environmental variances are 75, 25, 25, and 375 units, respectively. Although we used these hypothetical values for illustration purposes, the breeder can use more realistic values based on test results, if available. In the example, two mating designs for generation advancement were compared. One was a non-assortative double-pair mating (20 crosses per subline), and the other was a weighted assortative mating used for each subline described earlier (Fig. 4). Conforming with our progeny test design, 96 trees per cross were evaluated. Selection for generation advancement was based on combined index selection. Summary and control data information of the simulation for the assortative mating are shown in Fig. 5. The comparisions of changes in genetic structure of the breeding populations over five generations are summarized in Table 1, where it can be seen that the mean (total phenotype) of the breeding population increases over the generations as well as accumulation of inbreeding beginning at generation 2, consequently, reducing effective population size. It is also noted that, with assortative mating, the population mean (total phenotype) at each generation is greater than non-assortative mating, but the accumulation of inbreeding is about double with assortative mating.

In the second example, we consider two clonal deployment strategies involving the elite subline. We assume that the mean of the elite subline is higher by 10 per cent than regular sublines, i.e., 110 units, and the same genetic and environmental variances as the regular sublines were assumed. The mating design used was the disconnected diallel that produced 30 full-sib families as shown in Fig. 3. Clonal testing is based on 20 genotypes per cross, and thus a total of 600 clones are evaluated, using 10 clonal replicates (ramets) per clone. A part of the POPSIM output showing the structure of breeding population, deployment of full-sib family mixtures, and deployment of clonal mixtures at generation 0 is shown in Fig. 6. For deployment of full-sib family mixtures, the best 10 families are selected without other restrictions, while for clonal mixtures, the best 20 clones, with one per cross, were selected for deployment. In this example, the genetic gain from the deployment of the 20-best clonal mixture is 15.6 per cent, while that from the deployment of the 10-best full-sib family mixture is 6.2 per cent.

### 4.2 Deployment of Clonal Populations

As indicated earlier, production of planting stock in our strategy is based on vegetatively multiplied populations following sexual breeding and testing. The major concern in deployment of the clonal population is that a narrow genetic base may make clonal populations vulnerable to disease and pests. A general perception is that plantations of clonally propagated trees are more susceptible than seedling forests, which can lead to a disastrous plantation failure. Clonal propagation *per se* does not make a genotype more susceptible. Furthermore, there are differences among tree genotypes in pest resistance, and almost all the economically important traits are genetically independent of pest resistance characteristics (Zobel, 1982). Therefore, it is possible that, by clonal propagation of individuals selected from an improved population, more resistant clones may be developed in combination with improved economic traits.

There is a risk, however, when only a few potentially susceptible clones are deployed in a single plantation. The question of a safe number of clones

```
                    FOREST TREE BREEDING POPULATION SIMULATOR
                               Version 2.0.16

      Copyright (C) 1994-1995, Genesis Forest Science Canada Inc.

 CONTROL DATA FOR SCENARIO # 1 OF  1
   The user has supplied control data in file: normal.rsp
   Progeny and summary data written to drive e:
   Output will NOT be sent to the printer.
   Scenario summaries WILL be written to file normal.001
   Series data WILL be written to file normal.TXT
   Detailed progress and times WILL be displayed.
  MAIN SIMULATOR SETTINGS ...
   1. Seed for random number generator . . . . . . . . . . .  12345
   2. Number of generations for simulation . . . . . . . . .      5
   3. Number of iterations . . . . . . . . . . . . . . . . .     25
  STRUCTURE OF BASE POPULATION (Generation 0) ...
   4. Number of trees in breeding population . . . . . . . .     60
   5. Number of sublines in breeding population  . . . . . .      3
   6. Effective size of breeding populations expressed as  . .   Ns
   7. Mean of trait in base population . . . . . . . . . . .  100.0
   8. Standardized rate of inbreeding depression . . . . . . -2.000
   9. Additive variance in base population . . . . . . . . .  75.00
  10. Dominance variance in base population  . . . . . . . .  25.00
  11. Epistatic variance in base population  . . . . . . . .  25.00
  12. Environmental variance . . . . . . . . . . . . . . . .  375.0
      Heritabilities:     Narrow-sense:   .150  Broad-sense:   .250
  DESIGN FOR POLYCROSS TESTING ...
  13. Number of males represented in polymix . . . . . . . .     20
  14. Number of polycross progeny tested per parent  . . . .     50
  DESIGN FOR GENERATION ADVANCEMENT PLANTATIONS . . .
  15. PAM design (Uniform sublines) totalling   72 crosses.
  16. Number of genotypes tested per cross . . . . . . . . .     96
  17. Number of ramets cloned per genotype . . . . . . . . .      1
  SELECTION METHODS ...
  18. Selection of breeding population:
        Combined index selection
        with up to    1 trees per FS family and32000 HS relatives,
        and up to    3 progeny per parent.
  19. Selection of seed orchard populations:
        UNTESTED orchards selected by combined index selection,
        and TESTED orchards based on PX-test,
        to select  24 trees,
        with up to    2 per cross and 32000 HS relatives,
        and up to    2 from a common parent.
  20. Deployment of full-sib family mixture:
        The best  12 families will be selected
        with up to 32000 half-sib relatives,
        and up to    2 from a common parent.
  21. A mixture of selected clones will NOT be deployed.
 TIMING:
    First iteration started:  1995.05.26 at 16:50:01.87
    Last iteration completed: 1995.05.26 at 16:53:52.89
```

Fig. 5. A sample printout of the POPSIM program showing simulation control parameters invoving the three regular sublines.

Table 1. Comparision of simulated structure of the breeding population up to fifth generation under two mating schemes, Generation advancement was simulated from three regular sublines (20 trees per subline) using combined index selection from the progeny test resulting from non-assortative and weighted assortative matings (see text)

| | Generation | | | | | | | |
|---|---|---|---|---|---|---|---|---|
| | 0 (base) | | 1 | | 2 | | 5 | |
| | Mean | Variance | Mean | Variance | Mean | Variance | Mean | Variance |
| **NON-ASSORTATIVE MATING** | | | | | | | | |
| Additive effects | 0.1 | 78.1 | 4.7 | 74.1 | 9.0 | 71.3 | 20.8 | 64.5 |
| Dominance effects | 0.2 | 24.1 | 2.2 | 23.1 | 3.8 | 23.6 | 7.5 | 24.5 |
| Epistatic effects | 0.1 | 24.4 | 3.2 | 23.3 | 5.8 | 22.2 | 13.6 | 22.3 |
| Environmental effects | 100.4 | 382.3 | 143.7 | 133.3 | 144.0 | 116.2 | 144.1 | 130.6 |
| Total phenotype | 100.8 | 515.3 | 153.8 | 134.0 | 162.6 | 125.5 | 186.0 | 128.3 |
| Average inbreeding (F) | 0.000 | 0.000 | 0.000 | 0.00 | 0.013 | 0.001 | 0.051 | 0.002 |
| Effective population size ($N_s$) | 60 | | 40 | | 30 | | 17.3 | |
| **WEIGHTED ASSORTATIVE MATING** | | | | | | | | |
| Additive effects | –0.2 | 77.0 | 7.4 | 76.9 | 15.0 | 77.0 | 37.0 | 82.3 |
| Dominance effects | 0.0 | 24.4 | 2.4 | 24.2 | 4.1 | 25.3 | 6.5 | 26.3 |
| Epistatic effects | –0.2 | 25.3 | 2.5 | 26.3 | 5.5 | 25.5 | 13.9 | 20.7 |
| Environmental effects | 100.7 | 370.6 | 144.7 | 127.8 | 144.2 | 134.5 | 144.1 | 121.6 |
| Total phenotype | 100.3 | 504.0 | 157.0 | 127.1 | 168.9 | 137.9 | 201.4 | 132.9 |
| Average inbreeding (F) | 0.0 | 0.000 | 0.000 | 0.000 | 0.023 | 0.002 | 0.100 | 0.003 |
| Effective population size ($N_s$) | 60.0 | | 34.2 | | 22.8 | | 11.1 | |

F is inbreeding coefficient; $N_s$ is 'status effective number'. (Dr Dag Lindgren, Swedish Univ. Agric. Sciences, pres. comm.).

1 RESULTS FOR SCENARIO # 1 AFTER 25 ITERATION(S)

GENERATION 0

BREEDING POPULATION of 20 trees:

| Effect | Mean | (Std. Dev.) | Variance | (Std. Dev.) |
|---|---|---|---|---|
| Additive effects | -.3699E-01 | (2.110 ) | 75.17 | (25.80 ) |
| Dominance effects | -.4914E-02 | (1.279 ) | 25.27 | (9.356 ) |
| Epistasis effects | -.2739 | (1.118 ) | 23.06 | (5.143 ) |
| Environmental effects | 111.0 | (3.769 ) | 379.7 | (102.5 ) |
| Total phenotype | 110.6 | (4.633 ) | 521.2 | (148.7 ) |
| Average Inbreeding (F) | .0000 | (.0000 ) | .0000 | (.0000 ) |
| Effective pop'n size | 20.00 | (.0000 ) | | |

Deployment of Full-sib FAMILY MIXTURE ( 10 best families):

| Effect | Mean | (Std. Dev.) | Variance | (Std. Dev.) |
|---|---|---|---|---|
| Additive effects | 5.788 | (2.068 ) | 48.12 | (15.57 ) |
| Dominance effects | 1.041 | (1.779 ) | 23.70 | (8.604 ) |
| Epistasis effects | -.1681 | (1.116 ) | 22.28 | (5.033 ) |
| Environmental effects | 110.4 | (.3932 ) | 38.57 | (4.644 ) |
| Total phenotype | 117.1 | (2.561 ) | 123.7 | (19.39 ) |
| Average Inbreeding (F) | .0000 | (.0000 ) | .0000 | (.0000 ) |
| Cumulative gain % | 6.208 | (2.263 ) | | |

Deployment of CLONAL MIXTURE ( 20 best clones):

| Effect | Mean | (Std. Dev.) | Variance | (Std. Dev.) |
|---|---|---|---|---|
| Additive effects | 9.000 | (2.895 ) | 45.38 | (14.23 ) |
| Dominance effects | 3.978 | (2.177 ) | 22.49 | (12.09 ) |
| Epistasis effects | 4.225 | (1.912 ) | 21.31 | (8.615 ) |
| Environmental effects | 117.4 | (1.110 ) | 29.13 | (8.466 ) |
| Total phenotype | 134.6 | (3.071 ) | 41.19 | (16.88 ) |
| Average Inbreeding (F) | .0000 | (.0000 ) | .0000 | (.0000 ) |
| Cumulative gain % | 15.64 | (2.707 ) | | |

Fig. 6. A sample output of the POPSIM program showing structure of the elite subline at generation 0, along with deployment of 10 best family mixture and of 20 best clonal mixture based on the disconnected diallel crossing.

to ensure the health of the plantation is a difficult one, because the pathogen-host system is complex, and thus model building is difficult and predictions are unreliable. Several approaches, however, have been used to quantify this problem, and there is a general consensus that planting 7–25 clones appears to provide a robust and perhaps optimal strategy (Zobel, 1993). Once an appropriate number of clones has been decided upon, two commonly used configuration types may be employed: (1) Mosaics Of Monoclonal Stands (MOMS) and (2) Widespread Intimately Mixed Plantations (WIMPs). In MOMS, clones are kept together in blocks while WIMPs are clonal mixtures.

The issue of deployment is also relevant to genetically improved seedlings, since genetic gains must be obtained by reducing genetic diversity at some level. It is, however, generally accepted that, compared to natural stands, seed orchard seeds are genetically sufficiently diverse (Hamrick, 1991). Clonally multiplied populations resulting from our controlled-polycross and repeat crossing, consisting of half-sib and full-sib family mixtures, are not expected, from a point-of-view of diversity, to be drastically different from those derived from intensively rogued seed orchards. It may be argued that deployment of relatives in plantations will lead to consequences similar to those of a monoculture; however, the potential for adverse effects in family mixture plantations is not likely to be serious. Many natural stands of forest trees grow as pure stands and the individuals in such stands are often related (Park *et al.*, 1984). Thus, the control of coancestry in a production plantation can be somewhat more relaxed compared to coancestry control in breeding populations for generation advancement.

## REFERENCES

Adams, G.W. 1995. J.D. Irving Limited-Tree improvement summary. *In*: Proc. 25th Meet. Can. Tree Improv. Asso. Aug. 28–1 Sept., 1995. Victoria, B.C. 133–134.

Adams, G.W. and Kunze, H.A. 1993. From selection to seed production: a case-study by J.D. Irving Ltd. using second generation black spruce and jack pine. *In:* Can. Tree Imp. Assn., Tree Seed Working Group News Bulletin 20, 2 pp.

Adams, G.W., Doiron, M.G., Park, Y.S., Bonga, J.M. and Charest, P.J. 1994. Commercialization potential of somatic embryogenesis in black spruce tree improvement. *For. Chron.* **70**: 593–598.

Boyle, T.J.B. 1986. Ten-year height growth of open-pollinated black spruce families in Ontario. For. Can. Petawawa National Forestry Institute, Inf. Rep. PI-X-61. 24 pp.

Boyle, T.J.B. and Morgenstern, E.K. 1986. Estimates of outcrossing rates in six populations of black spruce in central New Brunswick. *Silvae Genet.* **35**: 102–106.

Campagna, M. 1990. Softwood seedling production by cuttings. *In*: Proc. Northeastern States, Federal and Provincial Nurserymens Conf. July 24–27, 1990. Montreal, Quebec. 3 pp.

Caron, G.E. and Powell, G.R. 1989. Patterns of seed-cone and pollen-cone production in young *Picea mariana* trees. *Can. J. For. Res.* **19**: 359–364.

Falconer, D.S. 1981. Introduction to Quantitative Genetics. 2nd ed., Longman, London and New York. 438 pp.

Fowler, D.P. 1986. Strategies for the genetic improvement of important tree species in the Maritimes. For. Can. Maritimes Region, Inf. Rep. M-X-186. 30 pp.

Greenwood, M.S., Adams, G.W. and Gillespie, M. 1988. Shortening the breeding cycle of some northeastern conifers. *In*: Proc. Twenty-first Can. Tree Imp. Assn. Meeting. Aug. 17–21, 1987. Truro, N.S. Part 2. 43–52.

Greenwood, M.S., Adams, G.W. and Gillespie, M. 1991. Stimulation of flowering by grafted black spruce and white spruce: a comparative study of the effects of gibberellin A4/7, cultural treatments, and environment. *Can. J. For. Res.* **21**: 395–400.

Greenwood, M.S., Adams, G.W. and Kempton, S. 1994. Using recent advances in the control of conifer reproductive development to increase genetic gain. *In*: J. Lavereau (Ed.) Proc. 24th Meet. Can. Tree Improv. Asso. August 9–12. Fredericton, N.B. Natural Resources Canada. 19–26.

Hamrick, J.L. 1991. Allozyme diversity of natural stand versus seed orchard loblolly pine. *In*: S. Magnussen, J. Lavereau and T.J.B. Boyle (Eds) Proc. 23rd Meet. Can. Tree Improv. Asso. Chalk River, Ontario. (Abstract) pp. 24.

King, J.N. and Johnson, G.R. 1993. Monte Carlo simulation models of breeding population advancement. *Silvae Genet.* **42**: 68–78.

Lelu, M.A., Klimaszewska, K.K., Jones, C., Ward, C., von Aderkas, P. and Charest, P.J. 1993. A laboratory guide to somatic embryogenesis in spruce and larch. Forestry Canada, Petawawa National Forestry Institute Inf. Rep. PI-X-111. 57 pp.

Lindgren, D. 1986. How should breeders respond to breeding values? *In*: Proc. Joint Meeting of IUFRO Working Parties on Breeding Theory, Progeny Testing, and Seed Orchards. Williamsburg, Va. N.C. State Univ. Tree Improv. Coop. Raleigh, N.C. 361–371.

Morgenstern, E.K., Holst, M.J., Teich, A.H. and Yeatman, C.W. 1975. Plus-tree selection: review and outlook. Environ. Can., Can. For. Serv. Pub. 1347. 72 pp.

Morgenstern, E.K. and Park, Y.S. 1991. Breeding of *Picea mariana* (Mill.) B.S.P.: seed orchard and clonal approaches. *Silva Fennica* **25**: 280–285.

Mullin, T.J. 1994. Evaluating the economics of alternative breeding and deployment strategies for northeastern conifers. *In*: J. Lavereau (Ed.) Proc. 24th Can. Tree Improv. Assn. Meeting, Aug. 9–12, 1994 Fredericton, N.B. Natural Resources Canada. 82–105.

Mullin, T.J., Adams, G.W., Simpson, J.D., Tosh, K.J. and Greenwood, M.S. 1995. Genetic parameters and correlations in tests of open-pollinated black spruce families in field and retrospective nursery test environments. *Can. J. For. Res.* **25:** 270–285.

Mullin, T.J., Morgenstern, E.K., Park, Y.S. and Fowler, D.P. 1992. Genetic parameters from a clonally replicated test of black spruce (*Picea mariana*). *Can. J. For. Res.* **22:** 24–34.

Mullin, T.J. and Park, Y.S. 1992. Estimating genetic gains from alternative breeding strategies for clonal forestry. *Can. J. For. Res.* **22**: 14–23.

Mullin, T.J. and Park, Y.S. 1995. Stochastic simulation of forest tree breeding populations: a user's guide for POPSIM version 2.0. Can. For. Serv. Inf. Rep. M-X-195. Fredericton, New Brunswick, Canada. 34 pp.

Nelson, C.D. and Mohn, C.A. 1991. Genetic variance of early height growth and expected gains from selection in a Minnesota population of black spruce. *Can. J. For. Res.* **21**: 11–19.

Nitschke, P. 1990. Nova Scotia Tree Improvement Working Group—Seventh Annual Report. Nova Scotia Dep. Nat. Res. 19 pp.

Park, Y.S. and Fowler, D.P. 1988. Geographic variation of black spruce tested in the Maritimes. *Can. J. For. Res.* **18**: 106–114.

Park, Y.S., Fowler, D.P. and Coles, J.F. 1984. Population studies of white spruce. II. Natural inbreeding and relatedness among neighboring trees. *Can. J. For. Res.* **14**: 909–913.

Park, Y.S., Pond, S.E. and Bonga, J.M. 1993. Initiation of somatic embryogenesis in white spruce (*Picea glauca*): genetic control, culture treatment effects, and implications for tree breeding. *Theor. Appl. Genet.* **86**: 427–436.

Park, Y.S., Simpson, J.D., Adams, G.W., Morgenstern, E.K. and Mullin, T.J. 1993. An updated breeding strategy for black spruce (*Picea mariana* (Mill.) B.S.P.) in New Brunswick. *In*: Y.S. Park and G.W. Adams (Eds) Workshop on Breeding Strategies of Important Tree Species in Canada. Fredericton, New Brunswick. August 18, 1993. Can. For. Serv. Info. Rep. M-X-186E Fredericton, NB. 41–54.

Rauter, R.M. 1971. Rooting of *Picea* cuttings in plastic tubes. *Can. J. For. Res.* **1**: 125–129.

Rauter, R.M. 1985. Current status of macropropagation. *In*: L. Zsuffa, R.M. Rauter and C.W. Yeatman (Eds) Proc. Nineteenth Meeting Can. Tree Imp. Asso. Part 2. Aug. 22–26, 1983. Toronto, Ontario. 58–74.

Rogers, D.L. 1990. The black spruce clonal program: recent developments and future directions. *In*: Proc. Ann. Meeting Black Spruce Clonal Forestry Program. Feb. 6, 1990. Timmins, Ontario. Ontario Ministry of Natural Resources. 1–6.

Shaw, D.V. and Hood, J.V. 1985. Maximizing gain per effort by using clonal replicates in genetic tests. *Theor. Appl. Genet.* **71**: 392–399.

Simpson, J.D. 1992. Plus-tree selection in New Brunswick. New Brunswick Tree Improvement Council, Technical Rep. No. 5. 17 pp.

Simpson, J.D. 1995. Thirteenth Annual Report of the New Brunswick Tree Improvement Council. New Brunswick, Canada.

Sulzer, A.M., Greenwood, M.S., Livingston, W.H. and Adams, G.W. 1993. Early selection of black spruce using physiological and morphological criteria. *Can. J. For. Res.* **23**: 657–664.

van Buijtenen, J.P. and Lowe, W.J. 1979. The use of breeding groups in advanced generation breeding. *In*: Proc. 15th Southern For. Tree Improv. Conf. 56–65.

Williams, C.G. and Lambeth, C.C. 1992. Genetic improvement using an elite breeding population. *In*: Proc. IUFRO meeting on Tropical Tree Breeding. Cali, Columbia.

Zobel, B.J. 1982. The world's need for pest-resistant forest trees. *In*: H.M. Heybroek, B.R. Stephan and K. von Weissenberg (Eds) Resistance to Diseases and Pests in Forest Trees. Pudoc, Wageningen, Netherlands. 1–8.

Zobel, B.J. 1993. Clonal forestry in eucalypts. *In*: M.R. Ahuja and W.J. Libby (Eds) Clonal Forestry II: Conservation and Application. Springer-Verlag, Berlin. 139–148.

# 2

# Some Computer-based Tools in Forestry and Genetics

*Federico Mattia Stefanini*[1]

**ABSTRACT**

Some computer-based methods are explained as a valid integration of standard analytical techniques in forestry and genetics. The focus is on the meaningful use of this class of methods, however no attempt is made to cover the whole field either as a spectrum of explained techniques or from the viewpoint of theoretical considerations (statistical, numerical and genetic features). The philosophy of computer-based techniques is stressed by explaining main aspects of computer simulation useful in applied studies and their use in statistical inference (randomization tests, confidence intervals and statistical tests based on simulation and bootstrap techniques). Actual case-studies clarify the fundamental concepts.

## 1. INTRODUCTION

The opportunity to carry out complex and conclusive experiments requires a profound understanding of the biological phenomena, while their quantitative analysis similarly requires deep statistical knowledge. The final answer is only partially obtained by consulting a professional statistician. His know-how must actually be interfaced with the researcher's competence to be really fruitful; otherwise, imprecise communication nullifies the biostatistician's contribution after the consultation (Hyams, 1971).

While a minimal background in statistical science cannot be avoided by the applied researcher, numerical tools can help him to improve the under-

---

[1]Istituto di Selvicoltura, Universita' di Firenze, via S. Bonaventura 13,50145 FIRENZE, Italia.

standing of phenomena without requiring full statistical training. This approach is becoming convenient for the increasing power of computational resources while their unitary cost is decreasing. Moreover, statistical and numerical packages are becoming simpler and more flexible, allowing some difficult analysis to be executed in a semiautomatic manner.

However, even with these new analytical opportunities and tools, some care must be taken. A naive use of computational approach to statistical analysis is destined to be a complete failure, sometimes with the awful side effect of having deceived the researcher in believing he or she possesses the *correct solution.* This trend is also seen in research papers, where sometimes the abuse of computer output, in conjunction with a weak statistical thinking, gives analytic results that are completely wrong.

The intend of this paper is to introduce the reader to the rationale of some numerical tools that are useful in the analysis of forest and genetic experiments. Some basic ideas are exposed, often without a detailed discussion and formalization in order to be an effective introduction to this matter. No attempt is made to outline all the available methods, or the more advanced techniques, and no magic recipe is provided. What is stressed instead is the motivation for the use of numerical approaches. By supporting current statistical techniques with some numerical tools, the researcher is expected to reach a deeper insight into the studied phenomena.

### 1.1 Computing Resources

No special software is necessary to use the techniques described in this paper. Even if the amount of facilities that are available to the user depends on the choice of software, it is better to initially work with a familiar package. It must allow the execution of sequences of instructions, the repetition of blocks of code multiple times and the drawing of values from a random numbers generator. Traditional languages, such as Basic, Fortran, Pascal, APL, are adequate even if it may be necessary to implement some commonly used routines by hand, using a standard source (mathematics: Abramowitz and Stegun, 1972; statistics: Johnson and Kotz, 1969, 1970a, b) or to buy a statistical-numerical library. Otherwise, typical languages that are implemented inside statistical packages are enough, and they have many ready-to-use routines. I used Turbo C++ (Borland), Mathematica (Wolfram Research) and S-Plus (StatSci) to implement the case-studies discussed below. More advice about software can be obtained at the following addresses:

- Wolfram Research Inc., 100 Trade Center Drive, Champaign, Illinois 61820–7237, USA (e-mail: info@wri. com);
- StatSci, 1700 Westlake Ave. N., Suite 500, Seattle, Washington, 98109; and
- Borland International Inc., 1800 Green Hills Road, P.O. BOX 660001, Scotts Valley, CA 95066–0001.

The choice of software can be done by evaluating two main aspects:

(1) the first one is the training period required to make the user competent; high level languages, like S-Plus are simpler (Venables and Ripley 1994); and

(2) the second one is the amount of time demanded to develop a non-trivial application, and the speed of application at run time; my choices reflect the need of high speed in time-critical applications (C++) and the pleasure of using high level languages and environment (see the Mathematica workbook: Wolfram, 1991).

Similar considerations can be made for the hardware. Simple case-studies only need a programmable pocket calculator, but a typical real dataset can be studied only on a low-level desktop computer, i.e. PC 386, 4Mb RAM. I developed the examples below by using a PC 486, 12 Mb RAM, in a Windows 3.1 environment.

The use of a PC belonging to the last generation is recommended, i.e., a 12 Mb RAM and 100Mhz PC, especially if large datasets and sophisticated software, like Mathematica, are used.

## 2. STATISTICAL SIMULATIONS

A computer simulation can be considered a way to produce experimental results by using a model instead of making observations on the real system under study. If the adopted model contains a random component, then a stochastic simulation is given. Each value that belongs to the sample is obtained by simulating the probabilistic mechanism of the correspondent random variable. It follows that simulated-sampled values are not deterministically known in advance.

A stochastic simulation is sometimes called *Monte Carlo* method if it is built to solve a deterministic but intractable problem, as happens in Monte Carlo integration, where a numerical evaluation of a complex integral expression is obtained.

In forestry and genetics, the typical model is stochastic, and it is used to summarize the mechanism that generates data and to forecast data values under general unobserved conditions that are interesting as research goals (future time, unexperimented environmental states, etc.). In this sense, building a model means specifying the probabilistic mechanism to generate observations.

Even if the rationale of the model is not pre-eminent in the following, in actual studies it is. It can express the actual mechanism of considered phenomena, as often happens in genetics, or it can simply constitute a description that is compatible with observed data, a hypothetical postulate about them, as happens when a perfect die is considered. Standard texts in statistics explain how to build and validate a model. Therefore, a computer simulation in forestry and genetics is typically constituted by some form of sampling as the model specifies, making it similar to the observation of a random phenomenon in a field experiment.

Advanced techniques in statistical simulation (not considered here) need an accurate and optimal design to produce results in a small amount of time. An extended discussion of the subject can be found in Ripley (1987), while in the following only one important point will be reported. It is related to the quality of the source of randomness, by which the effectiveness of the simulation depends.

The basic source of randomness for modern computer programs is a routine, called a random numbers generator, but before their advent, tables of random numbers were the main source of randomness. Using a table, a convenient number $d$ of digits is chosen and by some type of random mechanism (dice) a $d$-tuple of digits is drawn from the table, to compose the first random number. By independently repeating this operation $n$ times, an $n$-tuple of values from random variables identically and uniformly distributed is obtained.

Many other distributions are available by means of convenient mathematical transformations. The key concept is the *probability integral transformation* (Casella and Berger, 1990) of the cumulative distribution function (cdf) of a random variable. Let $F(x)$ be the cdf of the random variable $X$ and let $Y$ be a random variable defined as $Y = F(x)$. It follows that $Y$ is uniformly distributed in the interval (0,1) that is $Y \sim U(0,1)$ whichever the chosen distribution $F(x)$ if it is a continuous and strictly increasing function. Thus an observation from the original distribution can be obtained by transforming a value $y$ coming from $Y \sim U(0,1)$ into $x$ by using the transformation $X = F^{-1}(Y)$, where $F^{-1}$ is the inverse function of $F$.

By using a computer the operation is more direct, because common languages have a routine that can be invoked to draw a random number from the uniform distribution in the open interval (0,1), with the number of digits depending on the machine precision. It must be emphasized that many different ways typically exist to generate observations from a chosen distribution that derive from the use of different properties and theorems. They generally differ in the *quality* of the generated distribution and in the amount of necessary computing resources. As example, an observation coming from the Gaussian distribution of mean $\mu$ and variance $\sigma^2$, indicated as $X \sim N(\mu,\sigma^2)$, can be generated by using the Box-Muller approach, the *ratio of uniform* algorithm or the simpler but not optimal method called *sum of 12 uniforms* (a general review in: Ripley, 1987):

$$X = \sigma^2 \left( \sum_{1}^{12} U_j - 6 \right) + \mu$$

where $U_j$ are independent uniform random variables defined in the interval (0,1).

Before building real applications, the quality of randomness generators should be examined because departures of the fundamental generator from the true uniform distribution will result in unpredictable changes that make the simulation irrelevant. Classes of violation and checking methods are exposed in Ripley (1987).

For the most recurrent random variables, there are published routines to draw observations and to calculate relevant quantities related to their cumulative distributions. However, it must be remembered that statistical packages and professional numerical libraries contain optimized routines ready to use. Moreover, extensive publications are available on this subject (a widely cited one is: Johnson and Kotz 1969, 1970a, 1970b) and they must be examined before developing a new implementation of a random variable procedure.

Many different approaches to computer simulation as problem-solvers are available, but in the following only some of them will be discussed according to their usefulness and their relevance in forestry and genetics.

## 2.1 Sampling Distributions, Confidence Intervals and Statistical Tests by Stochastic Simulation

A typical simulation is constituted by a stochastic model whose parameters are completely specified. In a currently used linear model, the structural and the random component must be defined by assigning a vector of values to parameters and a probabilistic characterization to the random component. If the model really corresponds to the actual phenomena, then the real experimentation is reproduced by drawing a sample of dimension $n$ according to model specifications. Let the observed sample $X_j$ be defined as $X_j = (x_1, x_2, ..., x_n)$ where independent and identical drawings are realized. A collection of $B$ independent samples can be obtained similarly, indicated as $(X_1, X_2, ..., X_B)$, by repeating the drawing procedure.

Following this scheme, a sample statistic can be evaluated on each one of the $B$ samples, so that a numerical approximation of the unknown sampling distribution is made available.

It is often interesting to obtain the sampling distribution relative to an estimator $T$ (sample statistic) of a function $\tau$ of model parameter $\theta$, namely $\tau(\theta)$. The estimator $T$ is used for its relevance in the applied field even if it is statistically unmanageable. By repeating the sample drawing from a completely specified statistical model, as above, a numerical assessment can be derived. It corresponds to a numerical assessment of the unknown theoretical distribution, in particular, a numerical approximation based on $B$ samples of dimension $n$, given the assumed model. If $t_j = T(X_j)$ is the value of the statistic calculated on the sample $X_j$, a distribution of numeric values $(t_1, t_2, ..., t_B)$ corresponds to the distribution $(X_1, X_2, ..., X_B)$.

By using the numerically approximated distribution, some other results can be obtained. The set of ordered values assumed by the statistic can be subdivided into three disjoint sets, so that their union corresponds to the whole collection of values. Let the first subset have a maximal value constituted by the $5^{th}$ percentile and the second subset have a minimal value equal to the $95^{th}$ percentile. It follows that the third interval includes the 90% of the whole distribution. It collects the 90% of outcomes under the specified independent and repeated sampling, so it is a confidence interval whose confidence coefficient is 0.9.

One step further, a statistical hypothesis can be tested by considering the $5^{th}$ and $95^{th}$ percentiles as critical values of the test statistic, whose null hypothesis $(H^0)$ corresponds to the assumed model.

In a simple case, a real sample is given, and the value $t_s$ of a convenient test statistic is calculated. The statistical hypothesis fully specifies the model (a parameter value and the random component) so that an approximated sampling distribution akin to the null hypothesis can be derived by simulation. The hypothesis can be tested by assessing the significance of $t_s$, namely if it does represent a common value given the null hypothesis.

The significance assessing is obtained by simulation because the hypothesis definition gives a complete characterization of the random phenomena.

If the chosen test statistic $T$ assumes big values when a departure from the specified model does occur, than the significance of the observed sample statistic $t_s$ can be obtained as: $\frac{ng + 1}{B + 1}$ (Noreen, 1989), where $ng$ is the number of $t$ values that are greater or equal to $t_s$.

On the intuitive ground, if the value $t_s$ related to the actual sample belongs to the right tail (typically 5% of the distribution) than $H^0$ is rejected, because it is unlikely $H^0$ specifies the true model according to the experimental evidence.

## 2.2 A Worked Example: A Simulation of a Simple Quantitative Genetic System

The case-study is a simple quantitative genetic system and a computer simulation is realized within the Mathematica environment to check if some results related to theoretical genetics are effective. A general introduction to the subject is given by Mather and Jinks (1977).

The system under study is made by a natural population of infinite dimension, from which a sample of dimension 100 is randomly collected. A minimal model to explain the nature of a metric trait is $P = G + E$, respectively the phenotypic, the genotypic and the environmental value. The simulation performs a genetic sampling from the population and it adds to each sampled $G$ value, an environmental effect. Environmental $E$ values are obtained by sampling from a normal distribution, so $E \sim N(0, \sigma^2)$. The genetic system is assumed to satisfy the following items:

1) a number of loci $N_g$ is chosen as the genetic basis of the metric trait; loci are not linked;
2) two alleles $i = 1, 2$ per locus $j$ are present in the diploid population; the frequencies $p_{ij}$ of alleles are assigned;
3) the population is in a Hardy & Weinberg (H&W) equilibrium; and
4) the additive value $A$ of omozigotes and the dominance effect $D$ are assigned.

The simulation starts by considering the assigned allele frequencies, using the relation $p_{2j} = 1 - p_{1j}$ for each locus $j$. The joint distribution of alleles on more loci is derived using previous assumptions, that is by the product of single distributions. The genotypic frequencies are calculated using the H&W law.

A random sample of 100 individuals is drawn from the genotypic distribution. For each individual, the correspondent metric value is calculated by adding its $G$ and $E$ values. The first is calculated by adding (with its sign) each additive and dominance genetic effect for $N_g$ loci. The second one is randomly drawn from the distribution described above.

Formally, let $k$ be the individual index, $g$ the genotype related to the locus $j$ for the individual $k$ then:

| | | |
|---|---|---|
| $P_k = G_k + E_k$ | $G_k = \sum_{1}^{N_g} A_j I\{11\}(g) - \sum_{1}^{N_g} A_j I\{22\}(g) + \sum_{1}^{N_g} D_j \; I\{12\}(g)$ | $E_k \sim N(0, \sigma^2)$ |

where 11 indicates one homozygotic genotype, 22 the other one, and $I$ represents the indicator function that takes value 1 if the genotype in locus $j$ is omozigotic of the type indicated into the brace brackets, zero otherwise.

Results are shown in Fig. 1. In the upper part of the figure the three components are reported with a small number of genes and allele frequencies far from 0.5. In the lower part, the genetic component $G$ is diagrammed for 8 genes, where three of them have the same allele frequencies as considered before. Three main conclusions can be derived under the assumed items:

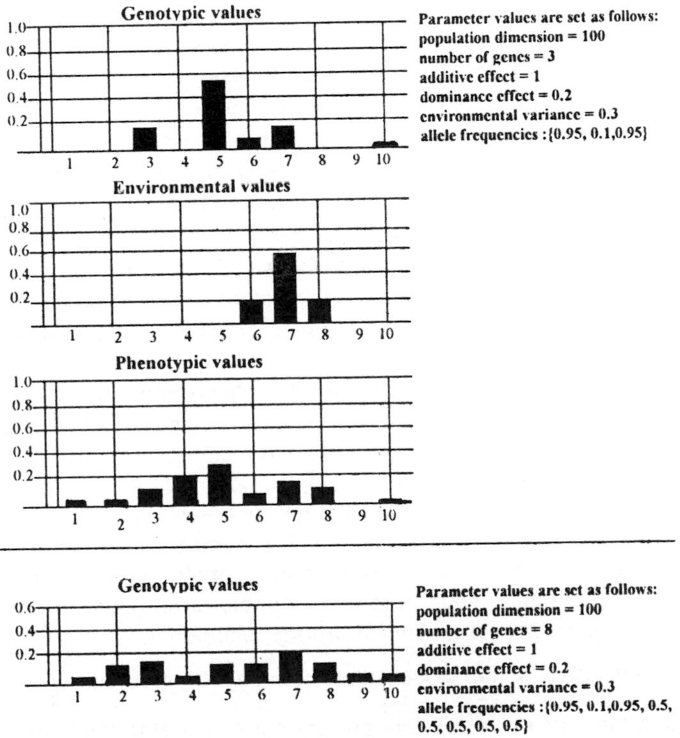


Fig. 1. Simulation of a simple genetic system. Ten class labels are reported on the abscissa and relative frequencies on the ordinata. The full discussion is contained in the text.

1) a small number of genes whose allele frequencies are far from 0.5 causes the distribution of genotypic values to be a bad approximation of the Gaussian distribution;
2) at the same time, an environmental component with substantial variance is enough to bring the shape of the phenotypic distribution near the normal; and
3) by considering more genes, the genetic segregation alone is enough to give a genotypic distribution similar to the Gaussian before the environmental value is added.

## 3. STATISTICAL TESTS BY USING RANDOMIZATION

Randomization tests are used if a statistical hypothesis regards more than one variable at a time. A simple case will be considered, where the null hypothesis asserts that two random variables are unrelated. The rationale of this test is based on a shuffling procedure that ensures no relation holds between variables; thus, it offers the way to build the null hypothesis distribution.

In the shuffling procedure, the original correspondence existing between variables is broken by permutating one set of values (first variables) in respect to the second set (second variable). Then a measure of association among variables is calculated for each permutated dataset. If the considered variables are qualitative, a convenient measure of association is the Pearson's $\chi^2$, because a contingency table summarizes all the available information. It must be recalled that $\chi^2$, is equal to zero if no association is present into a contingency table, and it increases as the association intensifies.

A numeric approximation of the null hypothesis distribution is derived by repeated shuffling and $\chi^2$ assessment. The significance of the original sample can be assessed because if the relation between variables does not exist, the original value of the statistic is not unusual in respect to $\chi^2$ measures obtained on the shuffled data sets.

It must be emphasized that the type of shuffling depends on the structure of the real case-study. If the height and the collar diameter of 6 young Fraxinus plants are $\{(x1, y1,), (x2, y2), (x3, y3), (x4, y4), (x5, y5), (x6, y6)\}$, then one of the possible permutations will be $\{(x1, y2), (x6, y3), (x3, y4), (x5, y5), (x4, y6)\}$.

Using the approximate randomization test (Noreen, 1989, cap.2) not all the possible permutations must be evaluated. The number of permutations quickly grows with the increase of observations in the sample and it becomes prohibitive in real case-studies. Thus, a random sample of all possible permutations is assessed as an approximation of the full distribution.

The significance of the association can be obtained as $\frac{ng + 1}{B + 1}$, where $ng$ is the number of $\chi^2$ values that are greater or equal to the value observed in the original dataset.

According to some authors, in many cases a suitable choice of $B$ is 1000, because this number is almost certain to give the same results as the full distribution of permutations (Manly, 1991) with a probability of a first type error equal to 0.05. Instead, 5000 permutations seen enough to set the first type error to 0.01.

A further development of this technique is based on the stratification of observed values according to a discrete variable that is not conceptually relevant, but that constitutes a significant source of variation. In this case, the shuffling procedure is performed within the set of observations that are homogeneous for the label associated with the stratifying variable. This approach is detailed by means of the following case-study.

### 3.1 A Case-study: On the Independence of Allele Frequencies by Sampling Area

This case-study is of a forest experimentation performed in field (unpublished data). A data set of 8 genetic marker loci and 23 sampled areas is considered, where the overall number of alleles is 21. Sampled areas can be further subdivided according to the values of two qualitative variables, named *dis* (2 levels) and *dir* (4 levels). They are combined according to a full factorial scheme. The aim of the analysis is the evaluation of the putative association existing between allele frequencies and the sampling structure. A statistical test is built to decide if *dir* and *dis* are the significant causes of variation.

A two-step procedure was performed using approximate randomization testing. It is based on random permutations of plants within sampling structure, and the adopted measure of association is the Pearson's $\chi^2$ statistic.

In the first step, the null hypothesis of no relation between sampled areas and allele frequencies at different genetic loci was tested to verify if sampled areas should be considered the stratifying variable of the subsequent analysis. The Pearson's $\chi^2$ of the contingency table *areas by alleles* (Table 1) was computed and the null hypothesis was rejected if the value of the sample statistic belongs to the right tail ($p < 0.05$, $B = 5000$). The value of probability $P$ was calculated as $P = \dfrac{ng + 1}{B + 1} = \dfrac{ng + 1}{5000 + 1}$, with $ng$ the number of values after permutation that are greater than the value of the original sample, and $B$ the number of performed permutations. The null hypothesis of no association between areas and allele frequencies (*area*) was rejected with $P < 10^{-3}$, because of the low value of *ng*.

In the second step, a stratified approximate randomization test was performed using areas as strata. The null hypothesis of no *dis*, no *dir*, no *interaction* effects were tested performing a $\chi^2$ decomposition within strata (area): $\chi^2_{int} = \chi^2_{area} - \chi^2_{dir} - \chi^2_{dis}$, where *int*, *area*, *dir*, *dis* are respectively labels for the *interaction*, the *main area*, the *dir* and the *dist* terms.

The procedure is performed as follows:

- the *area* $\chi^2$ is calculated within each area on a table 8 rows (4 times 2) by 21 columns (the overall number of alleles);

Table 1. Contingency tables at different levels of observation (collapsing). On the top, sampled areas by alleles related to 8 assessed loci are shown when each area is totally collapsed. On the bottom-left is a contingency table of a generic area *j* and its tables that are derived by collapsing according to *dir* and *dis* values (bottom-right)

| $R_j$: Area | Allele frequencies at different loci | | | | | | | | | | | | | | |
|---|---|---|---|---|---|---|---|---|---|---|---|---|---|---|---|
| 1 | 0 | 48 | 0 | 46 | 2 | 46 | ... | ... | 47 | 0 | 0 | 48 | 48 | 0 | 0 |
| 2 | 0 | 48 | 0 | 44 | 4 | 48 | ... | ... | 48 | 0 | 0 | 48 | 45 | 0 | 3 |
| 3 | 0 | 48 | 0 | 44 | 4 | 48 | ... | ... | 48 | 0 | 0 | 48 | 46 | 0 | 2 |
| ... | ... | ... | ... | ... | ... | ... | ... | ... | ... | ... | ... | ... | ... | ... | ... |
| 22 | 0 | 48 | 0 | 48 | 0 | 48 | ... | ... | 48 | 7 | 3 | 38 | 44 | 4 | 0 |
| 23 | 0 | 48 | 0 | 48 | 0 | 46 | ... | ... | 48 | 2 | 0 | 46 | 46 | 0 | 2 |

⇑

| $R_j$ | allele | 1 | 2 | ... | 21 |
|---|---|---|---|---|---|
| Dir 1 | Dis 1 | 1 | 0 | ... | 3 |
| Dir 1 | Dis 2 | 2 | 0 | ... | 0 |
| Dir 2 | Dis 1 | 0 | 2 | ... | 0 |
| Dir 2 | Dis 2 | 0 | 1 | ... | 3 |
| Dir 3 | Dis 1 | 2 | 0 | ... | 0 |
| Dir 3 | Dis 2 | 3 | 3 | ... | 1 |
| Dir 4 | Dis 1 | 1 | 2 | ... | 2 |
| Dir 4 | Dis 2 | 2 | 1 | ... | 1 |

⇒

| allele | 1 | 2 | ... | 21 |
|---|---|---|---|---|
| Dir 1 | 3 | 0 | ... | 3 |
| Dir 2 | 0 | 3 | ... | 3 |
| Dir 3 | 5 | 3 | ... | 1 |
| Dir 4 | 3 | 3 | ... | 3 |

⇑
⇓

| allele | 1 | 2 | ... | 21 |
|---|---|---|---|---|
| Dis 1 | 4 | 4 | ... | 5 |
| Dis 2 | 7 | 5 | ... | 3 |

- by collapsing the appropriate rows (bottom of Table 1), two other contingency tables are computed, one for each factor *dir* and *dist*, and $\chi^2$ components are evaluated;
- the $\chi^2$ related to the interaction is then calculated by difference;
- the four $\chi^2$ components above were added on 23 areas to give four overall statistics related to the original sample; and
- the same $\chi^2$ decomposition was repeated on $B = 5000$ randomly permutated data sets (within area) to obtain the overall distributions of the four statistics taking into account the heterogeneity of the strata.

In this step of the analysis, only the null hypothesis about the *dir* source of variation was rejected.

The total $\chi^2$ statistic is decomposed into three independent pieces so that corrections for multiple tests (Manly, 1991) must not be considered. Table 2 shows the results of the two-step procedure.

Table 2. Results of approximate randomization tests. Null hypothesis about Area and *Dis* were rejected ($B = 5000$)

| Component | Sample $\chi^2$ | *ng* | *Prob.* |
|---|---|---|---|
| *Area* | 1068.5 | 2 | < 0.0006 |
| *Dir* | 518.607 | 0 | < 0.0002 |
| *Dis* | 122.878 | 3598 | < 0.700 |
| *Interaction* | 427.014 | 994 | < 0.200 |

## 4. BOOTSTRAP METHODS

Bootstrap methods are among the most promising computer-based statistical techniques to infer about a population. This approach mainly differs from the standard Monte Carlo one, because instead of specifying a model to be used as a sampling mechanism during simulation, it is based on the actual sample that is considered an approximation of the original population. Therefore, the procedure of sampling from the population is replaced by a repeated sampling scheme from the actual set of observations.

The rationale of bootstrap techniques is based on the *plug-in principle.* It suggests estimating the most important features of the population distribution by means of the correspondent features evaluated on the real sample (Efron and Tibshirani, 1993). In this sense, the set of observed values itself is a non-parametric maximum likelihood estimate of the population distribution, that puts a unitary mass on each observation in the sample. When more variables are jointly considered, the resampling scheme is performed on the entire case, or record, or sampling unit, without breaking the natural association within a sampled unit.

### 4.1 Bootstrapping Confidence Intervals

The basic technique is quite simple, but a minimai amount of formaiism must be given to show a general *non-parametric bootstrap* scheme. At first, the standard error of the population mean estimator is considered.

From the population distribution $F$, a sample $X = \{x_1, x_2, x_3 \ldots, x_n\}$ of identically and independently distributed observations is drawn. The arithmetic mean $\frac{\sum x}{n}$ is a sample statistic that is used as point estimator for the population mean, and it is indicated by using the dot notation: $x_{\bullet} = \frac{\sum x}{n}$. Then, a random sample of size $n$ is drawn with replacement from X, by putting on each observation the same probability of being selected equal to $1/n$. By repeating the bootstrap drawing procedure, $B$ bootstrap *replicates* are obtained $X^* = (X_1^*, X_2^*, \ldots, X_B^*)$, where $X^*$ is a rectangular matrix $n$ by $B$, representing the bootstrap distribution. The behaviour of the point estimator is assessed through its evaluation on each column of $X^*$, thus a numerical approximation $(x^*_{1\bullet}, x^*_{2\bullet}, \dots x^*_{B\bullet})$ of the theoretical distribution is derived, and it is called bootstrap distribution of the estimates. The standard deviation s and the average $x^*_{\bullet\bullet}$ of the bootstrap distribution of estimates summarize the main features of the estimator, and the bias $x_\bullet - x^*_{\bullet\bullet}$, is obtained from the difference between sample mean and mean of the bootstrap distribution of estimates. The scheme above is grounded on the assumption that the variability generated by the bootstrap resampling is comparable to the variability that could be obtained by sampling from the original population.

Now, if the mean estimator is substituted by a generic statistic $T$, to estimate a function $\tau(\theta)$ of the population parameter $\theta$, then a general *non parametric bootstrap procedure* is obtained. The function $T$ applied to the sample $X$ gives the value $t = T(X)$, and the bootstrap distribution of estimates $(t^*_1, t^*_2, \dots, t^*_B)$ is obtained by applying the statistic $T$ on each bootstrap replicate.

Many features regarding the sampling distribution can be evaluated by using it, beginning with its standard deviation. The value of the standard error for the estimator $T$ can be evaluated as $\sqrt{\dfrac{\sum (t^*_j - t^*_\bullet)^2}{B-1}}$ where the dot notation indicates arithmetic averaging. A convenient approximation for the standard error is reached by choosing $B$ equals 50 to 200, because more replicates are seldom necessary.

The *non-parametric bootstrap* procedure described above works with commonly used estimators and population distributions, but it can often be improved, for example to prevent its failure in giving meaningful results within some classes of inferential problems (Young, 1994).

One variant of the fundamental scheme given above is called the *parametric bootstrap.* It could happen that the type of population from which the sample comes from is known, according to previously collected information, such as a long series of experiments, or on a theoretical basis. Thus, the shape of the distribution is known, and the correspondent family of parametric distributions is $\{f(x^*; \theta), \theta \varepsilon \Theta\}$, where $\Theta$ is the set of values that $\theta$ can assume. To fully explicit the available information, an estimate of the parameter $\theta$ is made by using an estimator $\hat{\theta} = \hat{\theta}(X)$ found by standard methods (maximum likelihood, method of moments, etc. (Casella and Berger, 1990). Then the bootstrap distribution $X^*$ is obtained by sampling from the distribution $f(x; \hat{\theta})$. The bootstrap distribution of estimates $(t^*_1, t^*_2, \dots, t^*_B)$ is derived by applying the function $T$ to each replicate. It must be emphasized that the resampling mechanism is specified by a mathematical function instead of being a numeric sample, as in the previous method. The use of the bootstrap distribution of estimates is not modified.

If the interest is focused on the variance of a population estimator, an alternative scheme that often reduces the computation is available, and it is called jackknife variance estimation. Its origin precedes and is related to bootstrap methods (Efron and Tibshirani, 1993). The jackknife algorithm excludes one observation (sampling unit) at a time and it calculates the value of the parameter estimator on remaining observations. It follows that $n$ steps are needed if the sample size is $n$. By using the previously given terminology, the jackknife algorithm produces $n$ replicates, and each replicate has dimension $n-1$ because it is equal to $X^*_{(i)} = \{x_1, x_2, ..., x_{i-1}, x_{i+1} .., x_n\}$ with $i = 1, ..., n$.

The jackknife variance estimator is equal to $var_{jack} = \frac{(n-1)}{n} \sum (t^*_{(i)} - t^*_{(.)})^2$, with $t^*_{(i)} = T(X^*_{(i)})$ the outcome of the $i^{th}$ replicate, and $t^*_{(.)} = \frac{\sum t^*_{(j)}}{n}$.

The jackknife variance estimation is simply calculated, but it often overestimates the correct value, and its performance decreases as the chosen estimator is far from a linear function of the observed values. It can be generalized by excluding more than one observation at a time (Efron and Tibshirani, 1993) so that the quality of its estimate can be improved.

The evaluation of confidence intervals based on bootstrap can be improved by using the *bias corrected accelerated method* (*BCa*) (Efron and Tibshirani, 1993). Its rationale is based on the evaluation of two quantities:

1) the acceleration that assesses that rate of change in the standard error of $T$ with respect to the true parameter value $\theta$, measured on a normalized and automatically chosen scale;
2) the bias-correction that evaluates the median bias of the bootstrap distribution of estimates in normal units.

Let the number of bootstrap replicates be equal to $B$ and $t^{*(\alpha)}$ be the 100 $\alpha^{th}$ percentile of the bootstrap distribution of estimates. The value $\alpha$ is chosen so that the interval $(t^{*(\alpha)}, t^{*(1-\alpha)}) = (t^*_{lo}, t^*_{up})$ has a level of confidence equal to $1-2\ \alpha$.

The acceleration $a$ and the bias-correction $z_0$ are estimated by the following equations:

$$a = \frac{\sum_1^n (t^*_{(j)} - t^*_{(.)})^3}{6\sqrt{\left(\sum_1^n (t^*_{(j)} - t^*_{(.)})^2\right)^3}} \quad \text{and} \quad z_0 = \phi^{-1}\left(\frac{\#(t^*_i < t)}{B}\right),$$

where a is related to a jackknife estimation of variability, $z_0$ is evaluated on the bootstrap distribution of estimates $(t^*_1, t^*_2, ..., t^*_B)$, and $t$ is the value in the original sample. Note the $\phi^{-1}$ is the inverse function of the standard cumulative normal distribution function (quantile function of the cumulative normal), thus $\phi^{-1}$ (0.95053) = 1.65. The *BCa* interval is produced by assessing two values $\alpha_1$, $\alpha_2$ that optimally adjust the original interval by taking into account the particular features of the considered case study. The interval $(t^*_{lo}, t^*_{up}) = (t^{*(\alpha_1)}, t^{*(\alpha_2)})$ corresponds to the $1-2\ \alpha$ confidence interval where:

$$\alpha_1 = \phi\left(z_0 + \frac{z_0 + z^{(\alpha)}}{1 - a\,(z_0 + z^{(\alpha)})}\right) \text{ and } \alpha_2 = \phi\left(z_0 + \frac{z_0 + z^{(1-\alpha)}}{1 - a\,(z_0 + z^{(1-\alpha)})}\right), \text{ with } z^{(\alpha)}$$

the value of the 100 $\alpha$ percentile in the normal cdf. It follows that $a = 0$ and $z_0 = 0$ implies $\alpha_1 = \alpha_2 = \alpha$.

Even though this method can become quite computer intensive when many observations are collected, the BCa method gives very accurate results. It must be pointed out that the resulting intervals are transformation respecting and second order accurate; namely, the *BCa* method has optimal statistical properties.

### 4.2 Statistical Hypothesis and the Bootstrap

It is often necessary to test a statistical hypothesis to reach the goal of the analysis. Its formulation establishes the null hypothesis about a parameter $H_0$ and the alternative hypothesis $H_1$ so that the union of $H_0$ and $H_1$ defines the whole set of values that the parameter can assume. A test statistic is necessary to assess the degree of accordance that the sample shows for the null hypothesis. If $H_0$ is correct the value of the test statistic is typically near zero. It increases in magnitude as much as the sample supports evidence that differs from the null hypothesis assertion.

A two-sample example is exposed to give more details on hypothesis testing by using the parametric bootstrap procedure.

Under two different environmental conditions, correlation coefficients assessed for samples belonging to the same biological population are supposed to be equal, so the correspondent null hypothesis is $H_0$: $\rho_1 = \rho_2$ with its alternative hypothesis $H_1$: $\rho_1 <> \rho_2$.

The difference of correlation values can be algebrically transformed as follows (the double arrow means "imply"):

$$\rho_1 = \rho_2 \Rightarrow 2\,\rho_1 = 2\,\rho_2 \Rightarrow 1 + \rho_1 - \rho_2 - \rho_1\rho_2 = 1 + \rho_2 - \rho_1 - \rho_1\rho_2$$

$$\Rightarrow (1 + \rho_1) - (1 - \rho_2) = (1 + \rho_2) - (1 - \rho_1) \Rightarrow \ldots \Rightarrow 0.5 \ln \frac{(1 + \rho_1)}{(1 - \rho_1)}$$

$$= 0.5 \ln \frac{(1 + \rho_2)}{(1 - \rho_2)} \Rightarrow 0.5 \ln \frac{(1 + \rho_1)}{(1 - \rho_1)} - 0.5 \text{ in } \frac{(1 + P_2)}{(1 - P_2)} = 0$$

The last equation is satisfied if the two parameters are equal, thus an equivalent null hypothesis is: $H_0 : \zeta_1 = \zeta_2$ by having defined $\zeta = 0.5 \ln ((1 + \rho)/ (1 - \rho))$.

By the *plug-in* principle, a convenient test statistic is the difference of estimated sample correlation values $r_1$ and $r_2$, after the transformation $z = 0.5 \ln ((1 + r)/(1 - r))$. Fisher originally suggested to use this $z$ transformation to obtain a random variable that is normally distributed (Fisher log-based transformation, Sokal and Rohlf, 1969).

This property can be exploited to obtain the distribution of the test statistic under the null hypothesis $H_0 : \zeta_1 - \zeta_2 = 0$.

Let $n_1$ and $n_2$ be the dimensions of the two samples, and $T$ be a test statistic defined as $T = z_1 - z_2$. The random variable $z$ has a Gaussian distribution with mean $\zeta$ and variance $1/(n-3)$, that is $z \sim N(\zeta, 1/(n-3))$. Thus, the difference of the independent random variables $z_1$ and $z_2$ has normal distribution too (Casella and Berger, 1990). It follows that $T \sim N(\zeta_1 - \zeta_2, 1/(n_1 - 3) + 1/(n_2 - 3))$.

The null hypothesis distribution is derived by substituting the difference of correlation parameters with zero. Under the null hypothesis the statistic $T$ is distributed as a normal with zero mean and variance $1/(n_1 - 3) + 1/(n_2 - 3)$.

The bootstrap distribution of estimates $(t_1^*, t_2^*, \ldots, t_B^*)$ is obtained by sampling from the distribution $N(0, 1/(n_1 - 3) + 1/(n_2 - 3))$. The null hypothesis is rejected with probability $\alpha$ for the first type error if the sample statistic $z_1 - z_2$ belongs to the tails that globally collect the 100 $\alpha$ % of the numerical distribution.

Due to the correspondence existing between confidence intervals and critical regions of a statistical test (Casella and Berger, 1990), bootstrap methods for confidence intervals can be also used to test statistical hypothesis. Therefore, if the null hypothesis asserts that a parameter value is equal to zero then the null hypothesis is rejected if zero belongs to the confidence interval built around its estimator. Thus, the BCa method can be used to test a statistical hypothesis too. More details on this approach are given in the case study below. It must be pointed out that no assumptions on the nature of the population distribution is made to derive the statistical test.

### 4.3 A Case-study: Assessing the Significance of a Correlation Coefficient in Maize, when Two Environments are Considered

The ability of an individual to modify its phenotype, morphologically and physiologically, in response to changes of environmental conditions is referred as *phenotypic plasticity.* Evidence seems to exist for a genetic regulation of plasticity (Bradshaw, 1965). Phenotypic plasticity can change phenotypic pattern of correlation among traits (Schlichting, 1989), even though conclusive data on changes in genetic correlation structure are not yet available.

The considered case-study deals with a synthetic maize population of wide genetic base (BSLE) from which a random sample of 39 inbred lines (S6) was extracted without any selective constraints. The material was tested in two field conditions: the time of normal cultural condition (spring sowing) and a delayed time to achieve a restrictive cultural condition (summer sowing). A large genetic variability of major morphological and physiological components of yield was demonstrated in a previous study on the population. Within the original set of 14 morphological and physiological characters only tow traits are considered, called FT (tassel flowering time) and PH (plant height). Point estimates of simple correlation coefficients (Pearson's correlation) within the two field conditions are $r_1 = 0.0422$ and $r_2 = 0.3354$. Values of the simple correlation between FT and PH are quite different in the tested conditions, as is expected if phenotypic plasticity is present.

The standard method to derive the 95% confidence interval for a correlation coefficient uses a transformation to obtain the normality. Fisher proposed the transformation $z = \frac{1}{2} \ln \left(\frac{1 + r}{1 - r}\right)$, but Hotelling considered a better transformation for small sample dimensions ($10 < n < 50$, as in this case), $z^* = z - \frac{3z + r}{4(n - 1)}$ (for more details see Sokal and Rohlf, 1969, p. 518–523). The expected variance for $z^*$ is equal to $\sigma^2_{z^*} = \frac{1}{n-3}$. It follows that $(z^*_{lo}, z^*_{up}) = (z^* - 1.96\, \sigma_{z^*}, z^* - 1.96\, \sigma_{z^*})$ is the desired interval in transformed scale.

Correspondent results on the original scale can be derived by using standard tables, or by solving numerically the system of two equations based on $z$ and $z^*$, which in this case gives the final equation $152 z^* - 74.5 \ln \left(\frac{1 + r}{1 - r}\right) + r = 0$, where $z^*$ represents one bound of the interval that must be transformed, so that the interval $(r^*_{lo}, r^*_{up})$ is obtained.

Alternatively, a naive interval can be calculated by means of a *non-parametric bootstrap* procedure. Better outcomes can be derived by using the non parametric bootstrap on a transformed scale, in order to stabilize the variance and to reach the shape of the normal distribution.

An optimal interval can be derived by using the BCa method. The optimality stands on the mechanism inside the BCa method that performs a variance stabilization, a feature that is not present in the *non-parametric bootstrap* alone. All these results are reported in Table 3. According to the correspondence existing between confidence intervals and statistical tests, the null hypothesis of no correlation $H^0 : \rho = \theta$ is rejected for the second environment, but not for the first one.

Table 3. Simple correlation coefficients of FT and PH in two environments, and their statistical evaluation. The symbols $r_{lo}$, $r_{up}$ indicate the inferior and superior confidence limits ($1 - \alpha = 0.95$). Confidence intervals obtained by standard analytical results have degree of freedom equal to 39–2 = 37. Confidence intervals based on the *non-parametric bootstrap* are based on 1000 replicates. BCa confidence intervals are based on B = 2000 replicates. Note the difference among the adjusted $\alpha_1$, $\alpha_2$ and the initial $\alpha$

| Method | First environment | | | Second environment | | |
|---|---|---|---|---|---|---|
| | Point estimate | $r_{lo}$ | $r_{up}$ | Point estimate | $r_{lo}$ | $r_{up}$ |
| *analytical* | 0.0422 | –0.2769 | 0.3528 | 0.3354 | 0.0086 | 0.5791 |
| *n.p.B* | 0.0668 (mean) | –0.2795 | 0.4135 | 0.3385 (mean) | 0.0636 | 0.5617 |
| *BCa* | 0.0642 (mean) | –0.3683 $\alpha 1 = 0.0032$ | 0.3222 $\alpha 2 = 0.9268$ | 0.3312 (mean) | 0.0724 $\alpha 1 = 0.0277$ | 0.5696 $\alpha 2 = 0.9775$ |

Now, the interest is focused on the null hypothesis of no difference between correlation coefficients of two field conditions.

The method based on parametric bootstrap (see the previous paragraph) was applied to test the null hypothesis $H^0: \rho_1 - \rho_2 = 0$, with its alternative hypothesis $H^1: \rho_1 <> \rho_2$. The difference observed in the sample was –0.2932 in the original scale, and –0.3066 in the transformed scale. The difference was not significant, because critical values coming from the bootstrap distribution of estimates were (–0.4595, 0.4561), with B = 5000 replicates.

A different approach was also used to test the same hypothesis of no difference between correlation coefficients, by means of BCa method.

The quantity of interest is $\rho_1 - \rho_2$ that is estimated by using the *plug-in principle* as:

$$d = \sum_{1}^{2} (-1)^{i+1} \frac{\sum (x_{il} - x_{i\bullet})(y_{ij} - y_{i\bullet})}{\sqrt{\sum (x_{ij} - x_{i\bullet})^2 \sum (y_{ij} - y_{i\bullet})^2}},$$ with $i$ the index of environmental condition and $j$ the index of sampled unit within environmental condition, $x$ and $y$ the observed variables.

The confidence interval $(l - \alpha = 95\%)$ for the difference $d$ (see the paragraph above) of estimated correlation coefficients was obtained. Now, some further details are given on calculations based on the BCa method:

1) By using the standard bootstrap technique, $B_1 = 2000$ replicates of dimension $n = 39$ were resampled from the first population, and $B_2 = 2000$ form the second population. Each drawing was independently performed with replacement.
2) The difference between the two groups of replicates was obtained by simply subtracting correlation values in the same position, as if it were a subtraction between two vectors.
3) The jackknife estimate of the acceleration factor was derived by joining the two sets of 39 experimental units by column, so that a matrix of dimension (78 × 2) was built. Jackknife replicates were obtained by leaving out a row at a time and by evaluating the difference d on the other 77 cases. The value of the acceleration factor was $a = -0.000509$.
4) The value of $z_0$ was derived using the vector of differences among bootstrap replicates (1). The number of replicates greater than the original difference in correlation was calculated and then divided by 2000. The resulting value was used to find the quantile of the standard normal distribution corresponding to it, namely $z_0 = -0.115562$.
5) $\alpha_1$ and $\alpha_2$ were equal to $\alpha_1 - 0.006029$, $\alpha_2 - 0.937414$.
6) The resulting interval was $(t^*_{lo}, t^*_{up}) = (t^{*(\alpha_1)}, t^{*(\alpha_2)}) = (-0.7749, 0.0669)$.
7) The null hypothesis of no difference in correlation was accepted because the interval includes the value zero, thus the observed difference does not support a strong evidence against the equality of correlation coefficients.

## 5. SOME FURTHER TECHNIQUES

Modern computer-based tools are not restricted to the techniques exposed here. Advanced methods typically need a sound statistical training that includes numerical methods and optimal programming techniques. Some suggestions for further readings will be considered in the following.

Bayesian inference deals with a set of models in which parameters are considered random variables and where the approach to probability can also be subjective. The wide amount of literature devoted to this particular subject prevents doing a comprehensive exposition of these fields. A concise but complete introduction can be found in O'Hagan (1994), which also describes some numerical techniques (Gibbs sampling, Metropolis algorithms, etc.). One of the typical reasons to make the *Bayesian choice* is related to the existence of previous knowledge about the system under study. The knowledge is represented by a convenient statistical distribution for the parameter of interest, called prior distribution. It includes all the information available before the experiment and its definition is not trivial. After the experiment, the likelihood akin to observations represents a new source of information that must be considered. Through the use of Bayes' theorem, the two sources of information are joined into a unique distribution, called the posterior distribution. It summarizes all what is known about the parameter, thus it expresses the final global amount of information that includes what is derived from the last experimentation.

If the posterior distribution is particularly difficult to work with, some specific numerical technique can be used to obtain a numerical evaluation. Monte Carlo Markov Chain methods (MCMC, Tanner, 1993) are particularly useful for making a numerical approximation for complex posterior distributions. MCMC jointly used with recent compoutational algorithms (EM algorithm, Data Augmentation Algorithm, etc.) have been revealed to be very powerful in the analysis of complex systems (Tanner, 1993).

Some other computer based techniques that are of particular interest for statistic modeling come from the Artificial Intelligence (A.I.) field: Artificial Neural Networks (ANN) and Genetic Algorithms (GA). They can be considered as adaptive algorithms that "learn the right model" by means of actual datasets. In both cases the rationale of their formulation stands on the success that similar algorithms have had in natural systems, where they solve complex non-linear problems. An introduction about this type of technique can be found in Smith (1993) and Goldberg (1989).

## 6. DISCUSSION

The most important principle in the field of computer-based tools is: *don't abuse*. A suitable evaluation on the opportunity to use a specific statistical technique must be always done. It is a principle that must be considered also when commercial statistical packages are used. It is obvious that an assertion does not became correct only because it is on a computer printed output. More attention must be paid if the software is produced by the researcher himself that will use it few times. Moreover, no relevant result can derive by manipulated datasets, even if advanced numerical techniques are used.

It must be remembered that very unusual experiments or complex biological systems need a sound basis in probability and statistical inference (Casella, and Berger, 1990) to be analyzed and modeled, even if computer-based tools are available. A typical example is related to statistical tests. By using a convenient numerical method, the researcher can often select a test statistic that optimally discriminates between the two hypotheses even if the sampling distribution is unknown. This choice is related to the resulting statistical power of the performed test, and it implies an adequate insight into the field of statistical inference.

Further considerations are to be done. When the data comes from a specified population, a Monte Carlo test can be evaluated. The full specification of the population allows us to build the probabilistic mechanism on which a simulated random drawing can be realized. Whatever the test statistic, the correspondent sampling distribution can be always approximated numerically by evaluating the statistic on repeated samples. In some cases a full specification of the population (model) is not available. In these cases it happens that stringent or unrealistic or uncheckable features are assumed to fully specify the population, so that hypothesis rejection could be due to wrong reasons.

By using approximate randomization methods, it is possible to assess the existence of a relation among random variables. The significance of any test statistic can be assessed, whatever the type of population from which the sample is derived, even if the sample is not random or observations arise under unusual conditions. Some authors have shown this method is often as powerful as standard tests when the relative assumptions hold.

Meanwhile, no formal derivation is possible to draw inferences about the population from which the sample was drawn. A great care must be taken while planning the type of shuffling, especially if it could break a temporal connection among variables. This caution comes from the fundamental assumption that all the possible permutations of the data are equally likely. In some cases this assumption may not be correct, but it remains necessary to correctly reject the null hypothesis (Noreen, 1989).

Bootstrap techniques belong to a young field of statistical research, suggesting a wide development in future (Young, 1994). They can become a powerful addition to the statistician's toolkit, especially if they are jointly used with other non-parametric procedures (i.e., density estimation). Bootstrap often outperforms standard methods for error assessment, but in more advanced inferential problems its performances are not completely known. More needs to be known about the bootstrap behavior in small samples.

This field is growing at a fast rate, but many problems in the application of bootstrap are still unsolved (Young, 1994). From a theoretical point of view the bootstrap works, but it can fail if it is naively use together with a particular set of estimators. There is the necessity to find a set of automated procedures to identify the bootstrap breakdown when it happens. Moreover, no bootstrap technique is overall optimal, so robust criteria to choose the best procedure for the case-study at hand must be identified.

## ACKNOWLEDGMENTS

The author thanks G. Vendramin for providing a dataset. The work was partially supported by a grant from the Italian Ministry of Agriculture, in the framework of the National Project "Biotechnologie Vegetali, Area 3".

## REFERENCES

Abramowitz, M. and Stegum, I.A. 1972. Handbook of Mathematical Functions. Dover Publications, New York. 1046 pp.

Bradshaw, A.D. 1965. Evolutionary significance of phenotypic plasticity in plants. *Adv. Genet.* **13**: 115–55.

Casella, G. and Berger, R.L. 1990. Statistical Inference. Wadsworth, Belmont. 650 pp.

Efron, B. and Tibshirani, R.J. 1993. An Introduction to the Bootstrap. Chapman & Hall, New York. 436 pp.

Goldberg, D.E. 1989. Genetic Algorithms in Search, Optimization and Machine Learning. Addison-Wesley, New York. 412 pp.

Hyams, L. 1971. The practical psychology of biostatistical consultation. *Biometrics* **27**: 201–211.

Johnson, N.L. and Kotz, S. 1969. Distributions in Statistics: Discrete Distributions. Houghton Mifflin, New York. 327 pp.

Johnson, N.L. and Kotz, S. 1970a. Distributions in Statistics: Continuous Univariate Distributions I. Houghton Mifflin, New York. 300 pp.

Johnson, N.L. and Kotz, S. 1970b. Distributions in Statistics: Continuous Univariate Distributions II. Houghton Mifflin, New York. 306 pp.

Manly, B.F.J. 1991. Randomization an Monte Carlo Methods in Biology. Chapman and Hall, London. 281 pp.

Mather, K. and Jinks, J.L. 1977. Biometrical Genetics. Chapman and Hall, London.

Noreen, E.W. 1989. Computer-Intensive Methods for Testing Hypotheses. Wiley, New York. 229 pp.

O'Hagan, A. 1994. Bayesian Inference, Kendall's Advanced Theory of Statistics. vol. 2B, University Press, Cambridge. 330 pp.

Ripley, B.D. 1987. Stochastic Simulation. Wiley, New York. 237 pp.

Schlichting, C.D. 1989. Phenotypic plasticity in Phlox. II Plasticity of character correlations. *Oecologia* **78**: 496–501.

Smith, M. 1993. Neural Networks for Statistical Modeling. Van Nostrand Reinhold, New York. 235 pp.

Sokal, R.R. and Rohlf, F.J. 1969. Biometry. Freeman, San Francisco. 887 pp.

Tanner, M.A. 1993. Tools for Statistical Inference. Springer Verlag, New York. 156 pp.

Venables, W.S. and Ripley B.D. 1994. Modern Applied Statistic with S-Plus. Springer-Verlag, New York. 462 pp.

Wolfram, S. 1991. Mathematica. Addison-Wesley, New York. 961 pp.

Young, G.A. 1994. Bootstrap: more than a stab in the dark? *Statistical Science* **9**(3): 382–415.

# 3

# Breeding Strategies in Northern Forests: Three Examples from Eastern Canada

*E.K. Morgenstern*[1]


## ABSTRACT

Black spruce breeding includes family selection in view of the low heritability of height growth, and the updated strategy sees a shift to clonal testing and selection using somatic embryogenesis. The white spruce program is more traditional with emphasis on plus-tree selection and grafted clonal orchards as the stem and crown form are more variable than in black spruce and the heritability of these traits is high. For the Norway spruce, provenance selection is the key to achieve hardiness, good growth, and low susceptibility to the white-pine weevil (*Pissodes strobi*).


## 1. INTRODUCTION

Developing strategies for advanced programs extending over several generations is not a simple task. Strategies based on inadequate base populations and inheritance models can severely restrict genetic gain some generations hence, and/or lead to early loss of vigour due to inbreeding (Nienstaedt and Kang, 1987). Even a carefully developed strategy supported by much research in related disciplines may have to be modified at some future date. A good strategy therefore is one that is flexible enough to accommodate amendments and is well adapted to the organizational structure of the forestry administration supporting the work so that the breeding program can actually be carried out (Namkoong *et al.*, 1980).

---

[1]Genetic Resource Consultants, Pembroke, Ontario, K8A 6W8, Canada.

This chapter discusses strategies developed for three species in the Maritime Provinces of Canada, with emphasis on early generations. The three provinces, New Brunswick, Nova Scotia, and Prince Edward Island, are shown in Fig. 1.

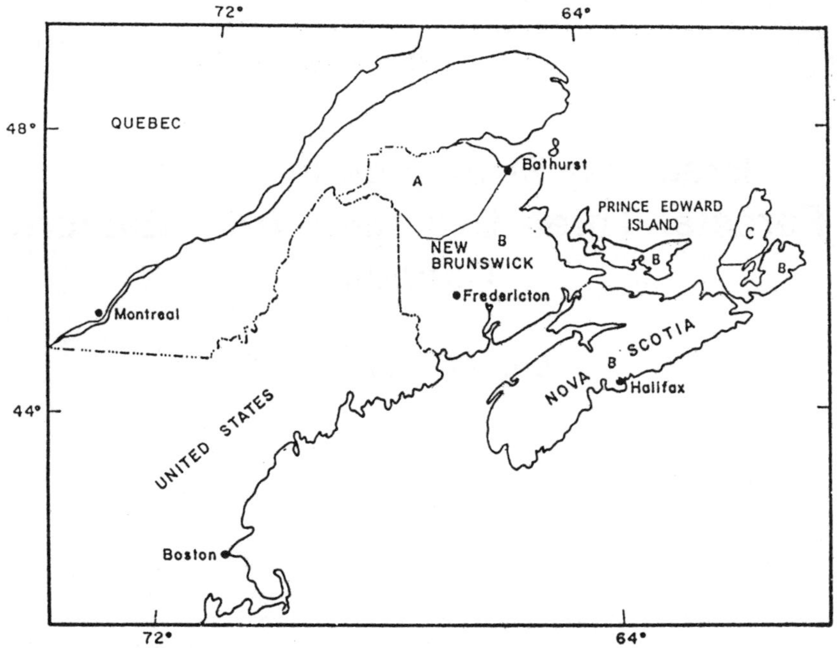


Fig. 1. Map of the Maritime Provinces of Canada. A, B, and C are breeding regions delineated for the breeding of Norway spruce (*Picea abies*). A is the northern region, B the southern region, and C an exclusion zone due to climatic severity.

## 2. BLACK SPRUCE (*Picea mariana* (Mill.) B.S.P.)

Black spruce is one of the most widely distributed species of North American cool boreal forests. It is relatively resistant to insects and diseases, possesses great reproductive capacity by seed and layering, and regenerates well after fire. As a result of its favourable wood density and fibre characteristics, it is an important species for the pulp and paper industry.

### 2.1 Breeding Strategy

The development of a breeding strategy for this species is a story that spans several decades. It is intimately related to the development of research in provenance, population genetics, vegetative propagation and biotechnology.

When breeding began on a small-scale during the 1958–60 period in Ontario, the program imitated procedures pioneered in Sweden: careful plus-tree selection, grafting of scions onto rootstocks, and establishment of clonal seed orchards (Carmichael, 1960). There was little research at that time and experience in tree selection, grafting and other techniques was very limited. The significance of species differences was not recognized and quantitative genetic parameters unknown.

During the next 10 to 15 years it was recognized that plus-tree selection in natural stands with much site variability may be inefficient, considering the traits to be examined. Plus-tree selection must begin in these stands but its intensity must be adjusted to the situation in each species. Black spruce exhibits very little variation in stem and crown form; the bole is straight and the crown compact, with short, thin branches. These traits therefore need not be included in a selection program. The only other major trait observed in the field is height growth, but this has a low heritability and selection for it was considered very inefficient even if measurements are made and comparisons with neighbours are included. It was decided, therefore, that plus-tree selection in the field be performed at a low intensity and be done rapidly by some form of ocular selection (Morgenstern *et al.*, 1975; Coles, 1979).

The emphasis was then shifted to family selection. Theory indicates that when heritability is low, the performance of a group of relatives is more easily evaluated than that of individuals. When a large number of relatives contribute to a family mean, the average phenotype approaches the mean genotype (Lerner, 1958). Family selection in black spruce was therefore anticipated by collecting open-pollinated cones from the selected plus-trees. From these cones, families of half-sibs can be raised and established in family tests (Morgenstern, 1975).

The second characteristic of black spruce that was important for breeding was its capacity to flower at an early age. Observations in plantations with good growth revealed that flowering begins at the age of 6 years from seed (Morgenstern and Fowler, 1969). This provides an opportunity to obtain seed production by means of seedling seed orchards.

With this in mind the strategy of tree improvement during the first generation was as follows (Fowler, 1986). Rapid plus- tree selection was followed by establishment of family tests and seedling seed orchards. The family tests had regular spacing, i.e., approximately 2 × 2 m. The seedling orchards were planted at a much closer spacing, 1 × 2 m, in anticipation of roguing at a later date. Site preparation was minimal and the whole operation was much less expensive than clonal orchards. Measurements in the family tests, repeated two to three times at the age 7–15 years from seed, are then evaluated to identify the best families. The inferior families are subsequently removed (about 90% of all trees) in two or three operations, leaving about 300 to 500 trees per ha. The family tests are left to grow as ordinary plantations but can also be used for breeding in succeeding generations if the need arises (Fowler, 1986). This strategy greatly accelerated first-generation breeding. The first-generation seedling orchards produced enough seed for reforestation within 10 to 13 years since the beginning of the program (Simpson, 1994). An economic analysis indicated that a proper balance between plus-tree selection and family selection had been achieved (Cornelius and Morgenstern, 1986).

## 2.2 Advanced-generation Breeding

The New Brunswick program began in 1977 and second- generation breeding in 1990. From the original 1200 trees selected and 1200 families grown between these two dates, the best 400 families will be identified. Since the original 1200 trees were selected over a 10-year period, several series of tests were planted, and measurement, selection and orchard roguing still continue. From the 400 families mentioned, the best tree of each is vegetatively propagated by rooted cuttings and moved to a breeding garden. Here a polycross test is made to determine general combining ability, and a single-pair mating scheme performed to produce 200 families. These 200 families go to a selection plantation with large plots and few replicates, where the 200 best families are identified, using the polycross test results as additional information. Four trees from each of these 100 families are used to generate the third generation breeding material. This is divided into 20-20-tree breeding groups or sublines (Van Buijtenen and Lowe, 1979) for the purpose of minimizing inbreeding in subsequent generations. Subsequently, for each generation, polycrossing and partial diallel mating will be used to produce the next generation breeding material. Clonal orchards are established to produce seeds. Thus, four generations are turned over within about 50 years (Fowler, 1986).

As expected, the plans made a decade ago have now been modified to incorporate new options provided by research results in quantitative genetics and biotechnology.

In his Ph.D. dissertation, T.J. Mullin estimated complete genetic variances for height growth and survival, i.e., additive, dominance and epistatic genetic variances, from a diallel cross which was clonally replicated by rooting of cuttings. The study showed that epistatic variances are surprisingly high, and this strengthened the case for clonal testing and selection to increase genetic gain. He also devised several selection strategies (Mullin *et al.*, 1992). The biotechnological advances relate primarily to somatic embryogenesis, improved rooting of cuttings, and cryopreservation of embryonic cultures (Park and Bonga, 1993).

An early glance at the updated strategy was provided by Morgenstern and Park (1991). The latest published description (Park *et al.*, 1993) explains how the new ideas will be applied to the on-going New Brunswick breeding program. Then, only the first 80 trees selected in the first generation will be involved. The updated plan anticipates several mating schemes, clonally replicated tests, accelerated greenhouse tests, clonal propagation via somatic embryogenesis, and cryopreservation of embryonic material. Instead of relying on seed production in orchards, it suggests production of stecklings (rooted cuttings) from juvenile seedlings of controlled crosses and of plants through somatic embryogenesis. However, somatic embryogenesis needs to be perfected further to become a viable alternative for the mass production of planting stock. While vegetative propagation is more expensive than traditional seedling production in nurseries, it eliminates the need for seed orchards which are costly to maintain and not always as efficient in generating genetic gain as expected.

Not mentioned here have been the numerous provenance trials, studies of the mating system and of population structure, and of population genetics of black spruce in general. All of these investigations have been of great value in building a knowledge base which is so necessary to create viable breeding plans (Morgenstern and Hall, 1990; Morgenstern and Park, 1991).

## 3. WHITE SPRUCE (*PICEA GLAUCA* (MOENCH) VOSS)

White spruce is one of the most important and common conifers in North America. It is large in size and much of the wood is converted to lumber and it is also used for pulp. Regeneration by planting is not easy due to the growth of grasses and shrubs on the fertile sites.

### 3.1 Breeding Strategy

Considerable background information has been accumulated on this species. White spruce is considered a variable and a promising species for genetic improvement. Substantial provenance differences in height growth have been found (Nienstaedt, 1969). In contrast to black spruce, here the stem and the crown form are very variable and must be included in selection programs along with height growth and perhaps wood density. The stem and crown forms are strongly inherited and therefore can be improved by plus-tree selection in natural stands, where the initial selection is primarily made (Morgenstern *et al.*, 1975; Coles, 1979). Based on this information, two breeding strategies have been developed (Fowler, 1986).

The first strategy was based on fast-growing southeastern Ontario provenances. These were superior to all Maritime provenances tested by about 1970, and were therefore established in two seedling seed orchards in Nova Scotia and one in New Brunswick. Many trees begin to flower when 10 to 15 years old and therefore seedling orchards are a possibility. Although plans for selection and breeding over several generations were made, these were not executed because new provenance experiments in Nova Scotia with larger provenance samples indicated even better performance of native and of Prince Edward Island provenances which exceeded the growth of Ontario provenances.

The actual breeding programs executed in the three provinces used the second plan prepared for native populations (Fowler, 1986). The strategy recognizes the opportunity for improvement of stem straightness, branch size and crown form during the plus-tree selection phase. The relatively high heritability of these traits justifies a greater expenditure for plus-tree selection, to improve lumber quality even in the first generation. The larger branch size as compared to black spruce makes grafting easier and grafted clonal orchards are therefore recommended for the first generation. In the second and subsequent generations, polycross and diallel matings are planned and breeding groups will be established using procedures similar to those described for black spruce. It is expected, that here too, new information and techniques will make it necessary to update the 1986 strategy.

## 4. NORWAY SPRUCE (*PICEA ABIES* (L.) KARST.)

Norway spruce is economically the most important species of northern Europe. In Canada it is a desired species because of its ornamental value and capacity to outgrow white spruce, particularly on somewhat acid, poorer sites. As an exotic species, it presents some problems to the breeder.

### 4.1 Breeding Strategies

In a native species with a large range, breeding is carried out within defined subdivisions of the range, such as breeding regions, seed zones or ecological regions. It is assumed that native populations of trees are phenologically adapted to the regional climate and to native plant competitors, and have low susceptibility to native insects and diseases. But when breeding begins in an exotic species, the situation is entirely different. Provenance studies are then not only helpful but absolutely mandatory (Zobel and Talbert, 1984).

This principle is clearly evident in the Norway spruce, especially since this species is exceptionally variable. Problems encountered when introducing it to eastern Canada include hardiness, growth, and susceptibility to the white pine weevil (*Pissodes strobi* Peck). The best provenances with favourable responses in these three traits in average environments come from mid-elevations of the Sudetan and Carpathian Mountains of Poland, Slovakia, and Romania, or, in cold environments, from Lithuania, Latvia, northeastern Poland, and Bjelarus (Fowler and Coles, 1979). Even if the weevil susceptibility is higher, this trait can be significantly improved within one generation due to its relatively high heritability (Coleman *et al.*, 1987).

The breeding strategy proposed for the Maritime Provinces by Fowler (1986) recognized two breeding regions: a northern and a southern one (Fig. 1). The breeding population was assembled by selection within the provenance experiments. Scions were grafted onto rootstocks to establish clonal seed orchards. In 1986, 100 clones were found for the southern region and 40 for the northern one. These numbers have increased since then.

The breeding plan included intra-provenance polycrosses and disconnected half-diallels to produce seedlings for progeny tests. Since Norway spruce produces few flowers before age 20 to 30 years, accelerated breeding techniques such as treatment with gibberellic acid was anticipated. Vegetative propagation of rooted cuttings from young seedlings is also anticipated. Because of the lower demand for seed from this species as compared to the native species, the breeding program has had a low priority and progress has been slower.

In summary, when the breeding strategies for these species are compared, it is clear that species differences in variability, utilization and genetic parameters are the major contributing factors that determine why these strategies are so different.

**ACKNOWLEDGEMENT**

The development of advanced breeding strategies in eastern Canada was greatly facilitated by Dr. D.P. Fowler, whose experimentation, analytical skills and insights led to the publication of the first comprehensive strategy for all important species in 1986.

**REFERENCES**

Carmichael, A.J. 1960. Report to Committee on Forest Tree Breeding. *In*: Proc. Seventh Meetg. Comm. For. Tree Breedg. Can., August, 1960. Part II. pages B-1 to B-7.

Coles, J.F. 1979. New Brunswick Tree Improvement Council makes impressive strides. *For. Chron.* **55**: 32–33.

Coleman, M.N., Nieman, T.C. and Boyle, T.J. 1987. Growth, survival and stem form of a 22-year old Norway spruce progeny test. Can. For. Serv. Inf. Rep. P1-X-73. 10 pp.

Cornelius, J.P. and Morgenstern, E.K. 1986. An economic analysis of black spruce breeding in New Brunswick. *Can. J. For. Res.* **16**: 476–483.

Fowler, D.P. 1986. Strategies for the genetic improvement of important tree species in the Maritimes. Can. For. Serv. Inf. Rep. M-X-73. 46 pp.

Fowler, D.P. and Coles, J.F. 1979. Provenance trials of Norway spruce in the Maritimes. Can. For. Serv. Inf. Rep. M-X-101. 71 pp.

Lerner, I.M. 1958. The Genetic Basis of Selection. John Wiley & Sons, New York. 298 pp.

Morgenstern, E.K. 1975. Open-pollinated progeny testing in a black spruce breeding program. *In*: Proc. 22nd Northeast. For. Tree Improv. Conf. 1974. 1–8.

Morgenstern, E.K. and Fowler, D.P. 1969. Genetics and breeding of black spruce and red spruce. *For. Chron.* **45**: 408–412.

Morgenstern, E.K., Holst, M.J., Teich, A.H. and Yeatman, C.W. 1975. Plus-tree selection: review and outlook. *Can. For. Serv. Pub.* 1347. 72 pp.

Morgenstern, E.K. and Hall, J.P. 1990. Genetic aspects of black spruce silviculture. *In*: B.D. Titus, M.B. Lavigne, P.F. Newton and W.J. Meades (Eds) The Silvics and Ecology of Boreal Spruces. Can. For. Serv. Inf. Rep. N-X-271. 107–111.

Morgenstern, E.K. and Park, Y.S. 1991. Breeding of *Picea mariana* (Mill.) B.S.P.: seed orchard and clonal approaches. *Silva Fennica* **25**: 280–285.

Mullin, T.J., Morgenstern, E.K., Park, Y.S. and Fowler, D.P. 1992. Genetic parameters from a clonally replicated test of black spruce (*Picea mariana*). *Can. J. For. Res.* **22**: 24–36.

Namkoong, G., Barnes, R.D. and Burley, J. 1980. A philosophy of breeding strategy for tropical forest trees. Commonwealth For. Institute, Univ. of Oxford, Tropical Forestry Paper No. 16. 67 pp.

Nienstaedt, H. 1969. White spruce seed source variation and adaptation to 14 planting sites in northeastern United States and Canada. *In*: Proc. Eleventh Meetg. Comm. For. Tree Breedg. Can., Pt. 2. (1968). 183–194.

Nienstaedt, H. and Kang, H. 1987. Establishing a *Picea glauca* (Moench) Voss base breeding population for the Lake States Region of the United States. *Silvae Genet.* **36**: 21–30.

Park, Y.S. and Bonga, J.M. 1993. Conifer micropropagation: its function in tree improvement programs. *In*: M.R. Ahuja (Ed.) Micropropagation of Woody Plants. Kluwer Academic Publishers, Dordrecht, Netherlands. 457–470.

Park, Y.S., Simpson, J.D., Adams, G.W., Morgenstern, E.K. and Mullin, T.J. 1993. An updated breeding strategy for black spruce (*Picea mariana* (Mill.) B.S.P.) in New Brunswick. *In*: Y.S. Park and G.W. Adams (Eds) Breeding Strategies of Important Tree Species in Canada. Nat. Res. Can. Inf. Rep. M-X-186E. 41–54.

Simpson, J.D. 1994. New Brunswick Tree Improvement Council Twelfth Annual Report. Natural Resources Canada, Fredericton, N.B. 23 pp.

Van Buijtenen, J.P. and Lowe, W.J. 1979. The use of breeding groups in advanced generation breeding. Proc. 15th South. For. Tree Improv. Conf. 55–65.

Zobel, B. and Talbert, J. 1984. Applied Forest Tree Improvement. J. Wiley & Sons, New York. 505 pp.

# 4

# Scientific Exchange of Information for Tree Improvement Programs

*Dietmar W. Rose*[1] *and Luis Ugalde*[2]

## ABSTRACT

Increasing planting programs with improved trees is one element of a strategy to deal with the socio-economic problems of the rural poor. More applied research on promising species and technologies is required for the success of these planting programs. This research needs to identify suitable species and cover as wide a range of species, sites, and treatments as possible. Usable results need to be generated without delay. Accelerated research must rely on scientific networks to effectively coordinate research. Additionally, extension efforts are required for successful transfer of technologies on promising species. Several regional networking efforts are demonstrating the benefits of coordinated tree improvement research. International donors need to enforce increasingly such standardization and coordination of tree improvement research as a condition for funding.

## 1. INTRODUCTION

The increasing crisis of fuelwood and food shortage in developing countries points to the urgency of finding appropriate tree species that can provide the needs of a growing world population.

Many fuelwood research projects initially concentrated on finding promising fuelwood species. Fuelwood plantation programs with some best performing species like the fast-growing Eucalypts have often failed because they did not have the desirable characteristics as fuelwood and did not meet local needs

[1]College of Natural Resources, University of Minnesota, St. Paul, Minnesota, U.S.A.
[2]MIRA Database, Madeleña Project, Turrialba, Costa Rica.

for other tree products such as cattle fodder and fruits. With this recognition, fuelwood research programs expanded their investigations to tree species that could provide fuelwood besides other products. The expansion of research to these multipurpose tree species (MPTS) has increased the potential number of species that need to be investigated, and has increased the complexity of questions for research.

Tree improvement programs thus have an important role in the research of developing countries. This research needs to identify genetic improvements quickly, needs to focus on provenance and family trials, coppicing trials, and biotechnology. The transfer of research findings needs to rely on scientific networks that can accelerate the development of appropriate models by pooling data from many experiments. This collaborative research can focus attention on those species with the greatest promise in diverse environments.

## 2. GROWTH MODELS FOR MPTS

Yield tables have been the forester's most valuable tool for managing forests. They are the basis for prediction of yields at different ages and determination of rotations. Recent efforts in industrialized countries now focus on the development of more flexible stand-growth and individual tree-growth simulation models, e.g., STEMS (USDA Forest Service, 1979). These models permit growth projections for a wide range of management options. The empirical, historical-bioassay approaches are becoming less acceptable because of their inability to predict future production with changing environmental conditions and forest management systems (Kimmins, 1985). These approaches will continue to be useful for short-term yield predictions where time required to establish the bio-assay is not too long.

Newer approaches need to rely on an understanding of the biological and environmental determinants of forest production, and not only on records of past plant growth. Yield or productivity should be related to either simple or complex environmental gradients or to individual environmental factors, e.g., temperature, precipitation, evapotranspiration, and the length of vegetation period. Within an area of relatively uniform climate, soil moisture and soil fertility are gaining increasing use in the prediction of site-yield potential. Other soil, topography, and vegetation parameters should be examined for their potential as yield predictors (Kimmins, 1985).

Species performance in different environments and in different production systems is ideally based on growth and yield models that describe the interaction of stand management and environmental factors such as soil, site, and climate. Several environmental models that attempt to integrate climatic conditions with existing vegetational patterns exist. The underlying hope in using such models is that important agricultural and forestry-crop cultural techniques might be shifted from one part of the world to another with a predictable measure of success. The success of transfer, in addition to the socio-economic, political, and administrative conditions, depends greatly on the relationship of the crop to the environment where it grows or will be grown. Cagaun *et al.*

(1980), points out that it is axiomatic that the closer we are in meeting the environmental requirements of the tree crop, the higher would be the level of successful transfer. Agrotechnology developed in the temperate regions, for example, is not usually directly transferrable to the tropics. The experience of the Benchmark Soils Project suggests that propagation and cultural technology associated with agronomic crops can be expected to be more easily transferred within than across climatic regions (Silva, 1985).

In the development of environmental growth and yield models, climate data play an important role. For modeling growth and yield of trees on a long-term basis as happens in forestry research, the cost and time involved make it doubtful that daily weather observations can be made at a reasonable logistic expense and with an acceptable degree of consistency. The availability of long-term historic climate data from the experiment will provide opportunities to develop environmental simulation models for MPTS that have not been available up to now. For most ongoing MPTS experiments in the world, weather observations during the experiment and on the experimental site are impossible to obtain. Environmental simulation models developed will be more likely to be based on historical climate information obtained from the nearest meteorological station including temperature and rainfall.

If weather station data are used exclusively, the possibilities of fitting functions to describe a climate between weather stations via smoothing and other techniques need to be considered. Large variations can exist over fairly short distances. Research in Australia (Booth *et al.*, 1987), related to climatic analysis using modern developments in interpolation, shows how climatic conditions can be estimated reliably for sites that may be some distance from recording meteorological stations. This study shows that given the latitude, longitude, and elevation of any site, mean monthly values of maximum and minimum temperature can be estimated with an error usually well below 0.5°C. Rainfall is more variable, but mean monthly values can be estimated with an error of less than 10 per cent over most of the country.

Environmental growth and yield models require the collection of large amounts of information. The key end uses of these models for MPTS are:

1) to match species and sites not only for survival but in terms of performance,
2) to quantify the tradeoffs between management systems, e.g., fuelwood versus fodder production,
3) to provide production functions for economic analysis of MPTS production systems, and
4) to facilitate MPTS technology transfer to other locations beyond sites of experimentation.

## 3. MPTS PRODUCTION SYSTEMS

MPTS occur in basically three types of production systems, plantations, natural forests, and agroforestry systems. The development of models and appropriate field measurement guides for *plantation experiments* are relatively easy because much experience exists worldwide in plantation forestry. *Natural forests* present a more difficult problem for modeling because often the history of the stands, i.e., origin and previous management interacations, are not known, and the stands are often mixes of several species. *Agroforestry systems* are the most difficult MPTS systems because of the many combinations of trees, crops, and animals that reduce the likelihood of finding many repeated experiments in diverse environments.

### 3.1 Measurements Required

MPTS produce a variety of outputs depending on the management objectives. Field techniques have to be designed to measure these different outputs and predictor variables so that models that support decision-making can be developed. While models of the commercial stem of trees on the basis of tree diameter, height, and some measure of form or taper are well established, models for other tree components are not because these other components typically have not played a very important commercial role. Salazar and Rose (1984) have developed the methodology to quantify major components of some MPTS production systems that rural populations use to facilitate the comparison and ranking of alternative tree species and production systems.

One question that is difficult to answer is what variables to measure in the field to develop prediction models for products such as fuelwood, foliage, etc. Initially, more variables should be measured in the field than might be required in an acceptable prediction model. Practical considerations dictate the selection of few variables, but could require later data collections on additional variables. Variables that can predict yields may differ between major tree species. Because of the high cost of measurements, projects also need to be familiar with and emphasize proper statistical sampling procedures. For tree characteristics not measured on every tree or on every plot such as crown ratios, deriving local or regional prediction models from subsamples would be necessary. Such models would predict variables that are difficult to measure from predictor variables that are part of a minimum data set for each experiment plot.

### 3.2 Appropriate Models for MPTS

Stand and individual tree growth modeling techniques that work in temperate zones of the world can also be applied in the tropics. Growth and yield models for MPTS can benefit from the modeling experience and the approaches of the temperate forests especially for plantation of single or mixed species. Individual tree models offer the greatest amount of flexibility of predicting growth and yield over wide ranges of management treatments, but require much more data for model construction, testing, and verification.

For temperate-zone forests often plot data for ages less than 10–20 years are not available because models typically attempt to describe commercial timber yields. Few models of the establishment phase of forests exist and, therefore, relatively little work has been done on modeling ingrowth. Growth models for temperate tree species thus are not especially suitable for short-rotation MPTS, but the modeling experiences themselves are relevant to MPTS research. Management and modeling problems faced by foresters in the tropics are also much more complex. Because MPTS systems produce multiple outputs that need to be quantified, growth and yield models need to be developed for each individual component. Management treatment of the tree plots may represent a compromise between producing sufficient biomass and achieving some defined level of another output. Additionally, potentially many MPTS exist in contrast to the rather limited number of species in temperate forests. The potential of many MPTS to coppice introduces further complexity into the growth and yield modeling.

Models of wood and other product yields will most likely be regression-type models, e.g., polynomials and nonlinear models. An excellent summary of growth modeling methodology for temperate forests is contained in Clutter *et al.* (1983). It describes the most common methods for constructing site index curves and growth and yield models for basal area and volumes of trees and stands. What is new for MPTS, is the quantification of these outputs via appropriate measurement procedures. The sheer number of MPTS species, treatments, and MPTS outputs make the development of descriptive summary tables and graphs by key environmental and management factors the first priority to begin to understand key relationships among factors.

### 3.3 Constraints for Modeling MPTS

Although MPTS models are beginning to be developed, much of the information from these experiments that exist worldwide cannot be readily accessed because no uniform standards for measurements have been established and key environmental information is frequently not recorded. Only a few years ago, many MPTS experiments worldwide were duplicating each other because much attention was focused on so-called miracle trees. Furthermore, interdependencies exist among these individual components, i.e., increased production of one may reduce the production of another.

No single country or institution has the resources to collect sufficient data for the development of growth models for even a small number of MPTS and production systems. Many decades were required to develop growth and yield prediction models for major commercial tree species in temperate climates. Model development for tropical species is far more complex, and the time to develop such models is limited.

## 4. NETWORKS FOR RESEARCH ON MPTS

Only by pooling data from well-coordinated experiments will it be possible to develop environmental growth and yield models for MPTS and systems within the next decade. For accelerated model development, research experimentation needs to be coordinated and research findings need to be shared (Rose, 1988). To coordinate research, scientists need to agree to work on what is considered the most important species and production systems. Any experience that already exists needs to be shared.

Expanded tropical forestry research will require efficient transfer of information. MPTS technology transfer can be defined as taking of an MPTS innovation from its site of origin to a new location where succeeding is likely (Cady *et al.*, 1988). MPTS technology transfer can increase the quantity, quality, and variety of MPTS products. It can increase the efficiency with which scarce resources are used and therefore, increases research efficiency. The first step to the efficient exchange and transfer of information on MPTS among scientists is the development of database management systems (DBMS). These systems facilitate the efficient storage, retrieval and transfer of information needed for modeling and decision-making. A key component of these systems are databases of MPTS data or collections of interrelated data on MPTS experiments. Research networks would help in the extrapolation and transfer of results within and between regions and research institutions. With the organization of available data into databases, major gaps in current information on key MPTS can be identified more quickly and efforts that could fill these gaps in the shortest possible time through coordination and cooperation among scientists can be made. Such coordinated experiments will generate information on any species, site, treatment, and production system combination much earlier and much more efficiently.

Key networking features are the existence of a minimum data set, standardized procedures, trial coordination, sharing of information, and the pooling of data for improved and accelerated model development. A *minimum data set* is the essential soil, climate, and MPTS information needed to model MPTS performance. A *benchmark site* is capable of generating the minimum data set for one or more MPTS. A *network of benchmark sites* provides the range of environmental conditions needed to develop and validate MPTS growth and yield models. Research networks can facilitate the testing of MPTS, individually or in association with other crops, over a wide range of environmental conditions and treatments.

Using minimum data sets and standardized procedures for measuring necessary variables ensures that the absolute minimum information for model development and end user decision is collected. Information retrieved from the database can identify priorities for data collection not currently adequately covered by existing systems and avoid duplicating already existing information. Establishment of MPTS information databases will permit improvement in all phases of forest management, e.g., seed procurement and species selection for environmental zones. It can shed light on climatic, biophysical, and social constraints in tree seedling production and establishment, and improve nursery operation and stand-management techniques.

## 5. THE CENTRAL AMERICA MPTS DATABASE

Since 1980 CATIE has been carrying out research projects on MPTS. The MADELEÑA (Tree Crops Production) Project is being coordinated and implemented through agreements between CATIE and the national institutions charged with forestry research in Guatemala, Honduras, El Salvador,

Nicaragua, Costa Rica and Panama. MADELEÑA has initiated many formal and demonstration units for testing fuelwood species and management systems.

To help organize the entry and retrieval of all relevant information generated by the project, the need for a MIS that combines silvicultural, physical, climatic, social, and economic information was identified (Rose, 1985). Since then, uniform standards for implementing MPTS experiments have been established to permit analysis, exchange and transfer of scientific information on MPTS. Technical guides for the establishment, measurement, analysis, and model development of MPTS production systems have also been developed. The microcomputer-based MIRA (Manejo de Información sobre Recursos Arbóreos) system was developed (Ugalde, 1988). This system represents the pioneering work in use of database and management information system technology in the tropical regions of the world for application of silvicultural research. The MIRA System includes the information generated by field research plots since 1980 from all central American countries. The design reflects the most important aspects of the physical, biological, and social environments in which the project work is being carried out. Details on the design and content of this database are presented in Ugalde (1988).

A key goal of MIRA is to provide ready access to the data necessary for development of models that can predict growth and yield of tropical species growing in different environments and under different management systems. Another objective of MIRA is to provide relevant data summaries of information for making decisions at different levels. The design permits the system to provide relevant information for different users: the farmer, the extensionist, national and international researchers, and national planners in the region.

Silvicultural farms were developed to allow the collection of information from a broad range of MPTS systems, such as trees, stems, coppices from plantations or natural forests, and some agroforestry systems like living fences, shade trees, trees on pastures, and wind breaks. The variables in these field forms are the basic and most common variables measured in a plot. The information collected in the silvicultural field forms is the basis to compare different management alternatives for producing different components of biomass in MPTS research. The raw data collected in these forms is useful for different kinds of statistical analysis and for developing yield and growth models.

### Site Description

For the Central American Project, the experimental sites are being established in different environmental zones such as the humid tropics, arid and semi-arid tropics, and the tropical highlands. The hierarchy developed allows clear identification of the location and environment of a measurement at a level as low as an individual branch or foliage on a tree. Forestry regions are the subdivisions of a country. Within the forestry regions individual sites can be identified which have fairly homogeneous physiographic and soil characteristics. The sites within a forestry region are more closely described in terms of climatic, physiographic and general soil information. Lots within sites coincide with major existing stands. Within sites, experiments and demonstration units are established. The sites are described using the system developed by Holdridge (1947) to classify ecological life zones based especially on climatic information (Ewell and Whitmore, 1973).

SOIL DESCRIPTION

Soil Taxonomy was used to classify the soils in the six Central American countries. The pedons were established within experimental sites. The site selection where pedons were located was coordinated by a soil taxonomist in each country and based on guidelines given by the project staff; for some experimental sites more than one pedon was required. Soil samples are being collected from each horizon within the soil profile. These variables may explain the constraints or growth limitations for some species, allowing easier data collection and development of management models.

CLIMATE DESCRIPTION

A major tradeoff between measuring relatively few experiments with detailed weather information (daily measurements) versus measuring many experiments using historic climate information needs to be evaluated. The MADELEÑA Project has selected the latter strategy. Climate information being collected consists of the variables considered most relevant to describe temperature and rainfall. Temperature and rainfall data are obtained from the nearest meteorological station to where experiments are established. The information is being extracted in most cases from annual meteorological reports from each country, and in some cases from other sources like universities and experimental stations that collect information for some specific areas.

## 5.1 Current Status of the MIRA System in Central America

The MIRA database design uses the FoxPro program. This Management Information System (MIS) is based on a relational database management system (DBMS). At present the MIRA system includes three components: Silvicultural, Socioeconomic and Extension (Fig. 1). These databases are installed and in operation in thirty institutions in Central America. The MIRA system records and stores data from thousands of silvicultural sample plots from monitoring of socioeconomic factors, and from extensions related to multipurpose trees. The status of the three database components is as follows:

### 5.1.1 SILVICULTURAL COMPONENT (MIRA-SILV)

Data from the following sources have been recorded and is being stored:

- More than 150 species have been tested under different ecological conditions in the Central American Region.
- About 300 formal experiments exist. More than 800 experiments composed of individual plots have been carried out.

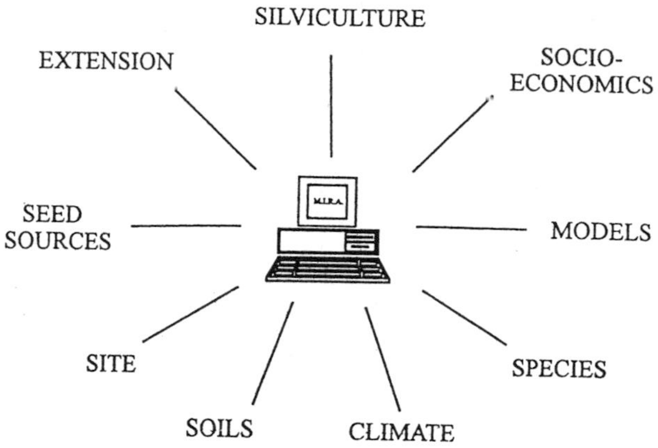


Fig. 1. The Mira System

- More than 14,000 individual plots of trees are available for analysis. More than 43,000 measurements plots means have been calculated from the growth data.
- 327 soil profile descriptions with 1426 horizon analyses, including chemical and physical characteristics, describe growth sites.
- 1400 seed lots are described, showing provenance and source information for the seeds used in the different plots.
- Climatic information for 629 different meteorological stations exists including precipitation and temperature. The MIRA system matches the experimental sites where the Project operates with this data.
- Experimental site description information for 964 sites exists.

5.1.2 Socioeconomic Component (MIRA-SE)

This component was strengthened in the second phase of the Project from 1986–91. The research of the socioeconomic effort has concentrated on the following areas:

*Socioeconomic Information:* It has been collected on nurseries and plantations. Many closely monitored demonstration farms have been established to measure the impact of tree plantations on the economy of small and medium farms.

*Demonstration Farms:* The objective of these farms has been to demonstrate the benefits of trees in plantations and agroforestry systems. Detailed information was also taken on the original financial situation of the farms, and the inputs and outputs of the tree, agricultural and agroforestry systems. The information generated on these farms with considerable participation by the farmers themselves has been registered in the database.

*Production Process:* In the first phase of the project some information was taken on the establishment costs of tree systems and nurseries. This effort has been strengthened during the second phase with the development of a standard methodology and a socioeconomic research plan implemented by an economist hired in each cooperating country of the network. This effort has registered the costs and outputs of about 400 activities for nurseries, site preparation, planting, maintenance, thinning and harvesting activities in tree plantations and some agroforestry systems.

*Marketing:* This effort includes the publishing of price bulletins including 3–8 regions per country. These bulletins detail the prices for the principal agricultural and tree inputs required for establishment and maintenance of plantation and agroforestry systems and also the value of tree products produced. This bulletin has been an invaluable source of information for tree growers and is also providing historical price information. A large part of this information is registered in the database. In addition, several studies have been carried out to identify products and specific markets.

#### 5.1.3 Extension Component (MIRA-EXT)

Extension efforts of the project have concentrated on developing materials and coordinating efforts on a national and regional level. Part of this effort has been the promotion of a simple monitoring system for projects promoting tree planting in the region. The MIRA-EXT system provides standard forms and a computer program for taking and registering data on extension and technical assistance activities carried out with farmers and farmers groups. This database provides valuable information for evaluating the effectiveness of extension efforts and the basis for more in depth social and economic research on the extension process.

Tables 1 and 2 show the experiments and the most promising species identified based on the research carried out by the network in the Central American countries. Analysis shows that some thirty species demonstrate major promise with respect to growth and yield. Figure 2 shows a map of Central America with the research sites.

### 5.2 Impact of the Central American Network

The Madeleña Extension and Research Network has been extremely successful. A key to its success has been the involvement of government and non-government development organizations working together toward a common goal: integrating the forest resource into the economy of small and medium farmers. Another key to its success has been that the Network solicits expression for tree planting information from small farmers and extensionists in the region and facilitates the generation and distribution of appropriate information to satisfy these needs. A few statistics of how well Madeleña is responding to these information requests are that, collectively, extensionists receive more than 5400 man-days of training per year and that eighty extension-oriented publications are printed annually. The Project's most relevant impact is the

Table 1. Number and type of experiments established by the research network of the Madeleña Project in Central America

| Type | Country | | | | | | |
|---|---|---|---|---|---|---|---|
| | Costa Rica | Guatemala | Honduras | Nicaragua | Panamá | El Salvador | Total |
| ACU | | | | | | 1 | 1 |
| ESP | 6 | 33 | 20 | 9 | 16 | 29 | 113 |
| FER | 8 | 10 | 3 | 1 | 4 | 6 | 32 |
| LHM | | | 1 | | | | 1 |
| MCM | | | 1 | 2 | | | 3 |
| PRG | 1 | 2 | | | | | 3 |
| PRO | 20 | 15 | 13 | | 9 | 11 | 68 |
| PSV | | | 1 | | | | 1 |
| RAV | 1 | | | | | 1 | 2 |
| REB | 3 | 5 | 15 | 5 | 2 | | 30 |
| SPA | 2 | 6 | 7 | 15 | 3 | 1 | 34 |
| TIP | | 1 | 5 | 1 | | | 7 |
| VAR | | | 2 | | 1 | | 3 |
| Total | 41 | 72 | 68 | 33 | 35 | 49 | 298 |

ACU : Agroforestry
ESP : Species selection
FER : Fertilization
LHM : Weeding control
MCM : Plantation maintenance
PRG : Progeny tests
PRO : Provenances
PSV : Site preparation
RAV : Thinning
REB : Coppicing
SPA : Spacing
TIP : Type of seedling
VAR : Varieties

Fig. 2. Map of Central America showing research sites and extension areas (Madeleña-3 Project).

Table 2. Promising species selected by the research network of the Madeleña Project in Central America

| Code | Species | Authors | Family |
|---|---|---|---|
| ACACMA | *Acacia mangium* | Willdenow | Leg. Mimosoideae |
| ALNUAC | *Alnus acuminata* | H.B.K. | Betulaceae |
| AZADIN | *Azadirachta indica* | Adr. Jussieu | Meliaceae |
| BOMBQU | *Bombacopsis quinatum* | (Jacquin) Dugand | Bombacaceae |
| CAESVE | *Caesalpinia velutina* | (Britton & Rose) Sta. | Leg. Caesalpinioidea |
| CALACA | *Calliandra calothyrsus* | Meissn. | Leg. Mimosoideae |
| CASSI | *Cassia siamea* | Lam. | Leg. Caesalpinioidea |
| CASUCU | *Casuarina cunninghamiana* | Miquel | Casuarinaceae |
| CASUEQ | *Casuarina equisetifolia* | J.R. Forst. & G. Forst | Casuarinaceae |
| COLUFE | *Colubrina ferruginosa* | Brongn. | Rhamnaceae |
| CORDAL | *Cordia alliodora* | (Ruíz & Pavon) Oken. | Boraginaceae |
| CUPRLU | *Cupressus lusitanica* | Miller | Cuppressaceae |
| EUCACA | *Eucalyptus camaldulensis* | Dehnh. | Myrtaceae |
| EUCACE | *Eucalyptus cinerea* | F. Muell. ex Bentham | Myrtaceae |
| EUCACI | *Eucalyptus citriodora* | Hooker | Myrtaceae |
| EUCADG | *Eucalyptus delgupta* | Blume | Myrtaceae |
| EUCAGG | *Eucalyptus globulus* | Labill. ssp globulus | Myrtaceae |
| EUCAGM | *Eucalyptus globulus* | Labill. spp maidenii | Myrtaceae |
| EUCAGR | *Eucalyptus grandis* | Hill ex Maiden | Myrtaceae |
| EUCASA | *Eucalyptus saligna* | Smith | Myrtaceae |
| EUCATE | *Eucalyptus tereticornis* | Smith | Myrtaceae |
| GLIRSE | *Gliricidia sepium* | (Jacquin) Kunth ex W | Leg. Faboideae |
| GMELAR | *Gmelina arborea* | Roxburgh | Verbenaceae |
| GREVRO | *Grevilea robusta* | A.Cunn. | Proteaceae |
| GUAZUL | *Guazuma ulmifolia* | Lam. | Sterculiaceae |
| LEUCDI | *Leucaena diversifolia* | (Schlechtendal) Bent | Leg. Mimosoideae |
| LEUCLE | *Leucaena leucocephala* | (Lam.) de Wit | Leg. Mimosldeae |
| MELIAZ | *Melia azedarach* | L. | Meliaceae |
| MIMOSC | *Mimosa scabrella* | Bentham | Leg. Mimosoideae |
| PINUCH | *Pinus caribaea* | Morelet var honduren | Pinaceae |
| TECTGR | *Tectona grandis* | L.F. | Verbenaceae |

number of small and medium farmers in Central America that have received and applied information generated by the project to improve their livelihood and the environment.

## 6. OTHER INTERNATIONAL MPTS DATABASE EFFORTS

Other international efforts have led to the development of DBMS that facilitate the exchange and transfer of information on forestry and MPTS research among scientists and regions of the world. The USAID-funded Forestry and Fuelwood Research and Development (F/FRED) Project was designed to help scientists address the needs of small-scale framers in the developing world for fuelwood and other tree products. It provided a network through which scientists exchange research plans, methods, and results on the production and use of trees that meet the household needs of small farmers. F/FRED has developed an Information and Decision Support System (IADSS) to help scientists manage research field data and other information about MPTS in an Asian research network (Cady *et al.*, 1988; F/FRED, 1990). The International Council for Research in Agroforestry (ICRAF) in Kenya is managing a database for agroforestry research. Through its database, ICRAF is attempting to assemble a body of knowledge on the woody perennials of agroforestry systems by systematically collecting, collating, and providing information in an easily accessible form (Von Carlowitz, 1988). The ICRAF database currently contains more several thousand descriptions of 900 or more species. This database is different from MIRA and F/FRED in that it is based on survey questionnaires and not on controlled scientific experiments. It does, however, support agroforestry research planning.

The Division of Forestry and Forest Products of Australia's Commonwealth Scientific and Industrial Research Organization (CSIRO) is a key institution involved in database applications for forestry research (Brown, 1988). Of special relevance is TREDAT, a database of tree performance designed to store and retrieve the results of field trials of species and provenances (Brown, 1988).

## 7. LOOKING AHEAD

Increasing world populations and decreasing resources require vastly expanded tree growing efforts. To avoid species failures in deteriorating environments, expanded tree improvement research is needed in many different environments. Only by pooling data from well-coordinated experiments will it be possible to develop environmental growth and yield models for major MPTS and systems within the next decade. Through the development and acceptance of standardized procedures, MPTS experiments can be coordinated between countries to avoid duplication of effort and to concentrate growth experiments on those species, sites, and treatments that have not been adequately covered. Information gained from these experiments can be easily transferred and shared among cooperating scientists. An established MIS will permit the retrieval of any or all information maintained in the database.

The establishment of scientific networks and database management systems for tropical forestry research can become a reality if international donors are willing to provide the financial support for the initial organization of such networks. Considerable experience with organizing forestry research information in database management systems has been accumulated over the last ten years. More database expertise is available, many organizations, institutions, and individual scientists have the motivation and interest in networking and associated data standardization and sharing of information. Finally, through advances in microcomputer hardware and software technologies, databases have become truly transportable and can be established anywhere in the world. The many benefits associated with scientific networking clearly justify the necessary funding. Such efforts should receive a high priority in development of tropical forestry action plans by national and international organizations.

Existing networks in Central America and Asia should be joined by agreeing to a common minimum data set and measurement standards. At that point, the network should be expanded to other regions of the world to permit global exchange and transfer of scientific information. The availability of networking through Internet has opened the door for universal sharing of data. Data access can be provided through special gateways in the network like Mosaic. The MIRA database for Central America is the best current example for the success of this approach. This scientists' network for Central America should be expanded to South America and to other continents as well (Rose and Ugalde, 1987). Future coordination between the MIRA efforts and F/FRED should be encouraged and supported by international development agencies.

## REFERENCES

Booth, T.H., Nix, H.A. and Hutchinson, M.F. 1987. Grid matching: A new method for homoclime analysis. *Agric. For. Meteorol.* **39**: 241–255.

Brown, A.G. 1988. Database applications in forestry research—An Australian experience. *In*: Workshop on Database Management Applications in Forestry Research. June 20–25, 1988. CATIE, Turrialba, Costa Rica. 11 pp.

Cagaun, B.G., Tsuji, G.Y. and Ikawa, H. 1980. Planning Agroforestry and Fuelwood Production on the Basis of Soil Taxonomy. Univ. of Hawaii, Instit. of Tropical Agriculture and Human Resources Dept., Paper 61.

Cady, F.B., Pak, J.C. and Tabora, R.G. 1988. A user-friendly decision support system for multipurpose tree research information—The F/FRED experience. *In*: Workshop on Data Base Management Applications in Forestry Research. June 20–25, 1988. CATIE, Turrialba, Costa Rica. 8 pp.

Clutter, J.L., Fortson, J.C., Pienaar, L.V., Brister, G.H. and Bailey, R.L. 1983. Timber Management: A Quantitative Approach. John Wiley & Sons, New York. 333 pp.

Ewell, J.J. and Whitmore, J.L. 1973. The ecological life zones of Puerto Rico and the U.S. Virgin Islands. U.S. For. Serv. Res. Pap. ITF-18. 72 pp.

F/FRED Proje `. 1990. IADSS User's Manual. Version 2.0 ed. MPTS Network Research Series. Manul No. 1. Maui, Hawaii, F/FRED GLobal Research Unit.

Holdridge, L.R. 1947. Determination of world plant formations from simple climatic data. *Sci.* **105**: 367–368.

Kimmins, J.P. 1985. Future shock in forest yield forecasting the need for a new approach. *For. Chronicle* **61**(6): 503–513.

Rose, D.W. and Ugalde, L. 1987. Developing a management- information system for a Latin American multi-purpose tree species research network. *In*: Proc. IUFRO Workshop Planning Forestry Research—Role of Multi-Purpose Tree Species in the Life of Rural Farmers. 39 pp. (plus Executive Summary).

Rose, D.W. 1985. Report to USAID/ROCAP to Support Development of a Project Paper for the Tree Cropping and Fuelwood Production Project-Database and Management Information System Component. USAID, Washington, D.C. 27 pp. (plus appendix).

Rose, D.W. 1988. Information Management for Expanded Tropical Forestry Research. Paper Developed for UNDP Task Force Bellagio II Meeting. 25 pp. (plus Executive Summary).

Salazar, R. and Rose, D.W. 1984. Firewood yields of individual trees of *Guazuma ulmifolia* Lam. in pastures in Hojancha, Guanacaste-Costa Rica. *Common. For. Rev.* **63**(4): 271–278.

Silva, J.A. 1985. Soil-Based Agrotechnology Transfer. Benchmark Soils Project. Hawaii Institute of Tropical Agriculture and Human Resources, University of Hawaii. 269 pp.

Ugalde, L. 1988. Effective Information Management in Forestry: An Application to Fuelwood and Multi-purpose Tree Species Research in Central America. Ph.D. thesis, College of Forestry, Univ. of Minnesota. 191 pp. (plus appendices)

USDA Forest Service. 1979. A generalized forest growth projection system applied to the Lake States region. General Tech. Rep. NC-49. 96 pp.

Von Carlowitz, P.G. 1988. Establishing a multi-purpose tree and shrub database—Opportunities, limitations, and problems. *In*: Workshop on Database Management Applications in Forestry Research. June 20–25, 1988. CATIE, Turrialba, Costa Rica. 10 pp.

# 5

# Reproductive Biology of Forest Trees and Its Application in Tree Improvement

*P.D. Dogra*[1] *and R.C. Dhiman*[1]

**ABSTRACT**

Regeneration and genetic diversity of forest trees is regulated by reproductive characteristics of species through seed and vegetative propagation. Vegetative propagation produces high genetic gain by multiplying genetically superior trees into isogenic nursery stock. Reproduction of forest stands through seed is achieved by natural regeneration and by planting seedlings of the desired species. Large quantities of quality seed is needed to meet the planting targets. High genetic quality seed production is being carried out only in a few developed countries at present. Reproductive characteristics of most tree species vary. They need to be developed for immediate needs of operational forestry. Reproductive methods—asexual (cutting, layering, budding and grafting) and sexual (seed) are discussed in the paper citing examples of trees from India.

## 1. INTRODUCTION

Reproductive biology is an important component in forest tree regeneration and in tree improvement where wild populations are used as base gene resources. Tree improvement produces genetically superior trees which have better growth, tree form, site adaptability, wood quality, disease resistance, high productivity and product uniformity. Genetically superior trees are multiplied through techniques based on reproductive characteristics of a species. Genetic diversity in wild forest tree species too is regulated by species reproductive characteristics. Superior intraspecific genetic variation is identified, brought from the wild forests to experimental areas, improved, test evaluated and mul-

---

[1]Forest Research Institute (ICFRE), P.O. New Forest, Dehra Dun, India.

tiplied. This includes outstanding, race, plus-tree, rare genotype, and hybrid tree selection from natural forests. Best genotypes are cloned true to parents on a large scale by developing techniques of vegetative propagation and tissue culture. The operational plantings are, however, always carried out with a mixture of a recommended number of clones to maintain heterozygosity and provide crop security against diseases and pest damage. Micropropagation, however, requires large investments and the cost of plants produced is high. Moreover it is still at an experimental stage for most forest tree species. It is therefore imperative that conventional vegetative propagation be developed for operational forestry.

Use of genetically improved seed or germplasm is not a standard practice for tree planting in India and many other countries because the reproductive materials are not genetically identified, developed, produced, certified or released in any systematic tree breeding program for use of tree growers. Many indigenous tree species are harvested commercially but not genetically developed and multiplied for use in operational plantations. Seeds used are mostly unselected and without any provenance or seed source control. They are often procured through services of village-seed-collectors and other agencies from unknown seed sources. Genetically selected superior seed production is needed on a priority basis in large quantities for plantation work. Information on characteristics of reproductive biology of forest tree species is essential for this purpose. It varies from species to species and even between population and clones within species. Knowledge of breeding systems of indigenous trees, particularly of tropical tree species, is scarce. Some of the tree reproduction and improvement methods which have a vast potential for regeneration in India are discussed in this account.

## 2. REPRODUCTIVE SYSTEMS

Reproductive biology of a tree species consists of two systems of reproduction: the sexual seed propagation (from self and cross- pollination) in which trees produce abundant seeds every year or in cycles of 2–4 years throughout their life span; and asexual (vegetative propagation and apomixis). Each system reproduces genetically different progenies, and both determine the genetic structure of the population. They, thus, form an integral part of the genetic system of the species.

The two sexual and asexual systems are also used in the classification of silviculture practices in forest management. The high forest systems are based on seed (sexual) regeneration (natural, artificial or both); and coppicing (asexual) is used under coppice systems to raise tree crops from short-rotation stool-coppice. Natural regneration through seed in high-forest-systems is achieved under clear-felling, uniform and selection-systems and these are further modified to suit local conditions and crop compositions. In the clear-felling system, the mature crop is removed in one operation and the felled area is restocked mostly by artificial regeneration. In some of its modifications fellings are executed in alternate or continuous strips and felled areas show limited regeneration success from the seeds shed from trees standing on adjacent strips.

Regeneration under uniform system is induced by opening the tree canopy in several operations, i.e., by felling after natural seeding followed by secondary and final fellings. Well distributed, healthy, superior and better-form-trees are retained as seed trees. On appearance of their regeneration, wider openings are created by removing some trees under secondary fellings. Once new tree crop establishes itself the remaining old trees are removed in the final felling. In some forests an adequate stock of seedling/pole crop of the desired species is retained as advance regeneration to form future crop before initiating the first felling after its natural seed fall. For example, this system is applied to *Pinus roxburghii, Cedrus deodara, Abies pindrow, Picea smithiana* and some *Shorea robusta* and tropical moist forests.

Management under selection system is mainly restricted to the high value tree species in irregular forests (mixed and uneven aged single species forests). The crop is removed either as selected single trees or trees in small groups and consequently the resultant crop is always irregular. Mature trees above a certain exploitable diameter are felled and new spaces created for regeneration and growth of new seedlings. This system is applied to *Abies pindrow, Picea smithiana, Cedrus deodara, Shorea robusta*, and in many species of tropical moist forests.

Natural asexual regeneration of some forest tree species is ensured under different coppice systems, mainly: i) simple coppice, ii) coppice with standard, and iii) coppice with reserve (retention of already established seedlings, saplings and poles). New shoots come up from stumps after fellings in *Shorea robusta, Quercus* spp., *Tectona grandis, Acacia catechu, Anogeissus latifolia, Azadirachta indica* and *Dalbergia sissoo* and these shoots are managed for development of the future crop. In the simple coppice system, the entire forest crop is clear-felled whereas in coppice with standard system a part of the old mature forest crop is retained to form the first double storey under which coppice regeneration from stumps of felled trees comes up to form second storey in a double storeyed forest. In coppice with reserve system, well grown saplings and poles already established are retained to form a part of the new crop. Another modification of the coppice system is pollarding (e.g., in *Salix* spp., *Populus* spp. and *Hardwickia binata*) where tree stems are cut back at heights which are safe from cattle browsing of newly emerged shoots. Coppicing power in tree species decreases after harvesting several early coppice rotations. Moreover all stumps do not coppice and a variable number die in every rotation. There is thus a slow erosion of tree gene resources in coppice worked forests. Genetic base of coppice worked forests can be improved through seeds by encourging coppice forests to produce seeds for natural regeneration.

The genetic manipulation and control of superior genetic variability in tree improvement is achieved through the judicious use of both the sexual (self- or cross-pollination) and the asexual reproductive systems.

## 3. ASEXUAL REPRODUCTION

Asexual or vegetative propagation of a tree (genotype) gives rise to isogenic trees. Genetically identical trees raised from a single tree thus belong to a single genotype (clone). Cloning is, therefore, the perpetuation of the same genotype. This is a rapid method of utilizing improved genetic stock. It offers much higher genetical gain than that possible with sexual (seed) propagation and it circumvents all problems of seed orchard establishment. In practical tree improvement programs it is employed for: 1) conservation of rare or outstanding genotypes in clone banks; 2) multiplication of superior genotypes and inducing earlier flowering for use in clonal seed orchards; 3) evaluation of genotypes and their interaction with site/environment through clonal testing; 4) testing for C effects (topophysis) which are long time persistence of age- or position-effect in trees raised from cuttings or grafts; and 5) to capture maximum genetic gain from broad sense genetic heritability.

### 3.1 Asexual-propagation-characteristics

Tree species can be easily raised through cuttings, layering, grafting, budding, coppicing and through root-suckers. The inherent characteristics of vegetative propagation of species, population and clone are different. There is a need to exploit the asexual reproduction potential to capture maximum genetic gain from broad sense heritability to obtain greater uniformity of tree crops, and, to speedily encash gains of tree improvement. As soon as a tree is tested and shown to be genetically superior it can be multiplied and converted immediately into a superior stock through vegetative propagation methods (from stem and root cuttings, budding, grafting and tissues culture). Wider use of vegetative propagation can shorten the time-lag faced in seed reproduction and regeneration.

#### 3.1.1 Cuttings

Rooted cuttings are used for preserving special genotypes, obtaining rapid regeneration, and saving genotypes faced with extinction because of their inability to reproduce viable seed. Few conifers root easily from cuttings but broad leaved species vary enormously in rooting behaviour (Troup, 1921). *Boswellia serrata*, for example, can be cloned easily from large cuttings planted in damp rainy season. Similarly *Albizia lebbeck, Artocarpus chaplasa* and *Dalbergia sissoo* are easy to raise by cuttings. There are other species which are extremely difficult to root, such as, *Juglans regia*. Many others fall in an intermediate category between these two. The major difficulties in use of rooted cuttings in operational planting are: i) age, where cuttings from young trees root readily but cuttings from the same trees on growing old do not root; ii) trees vegetatively propagated from older ones often grow more slowly than those raised from young trees (Talbert *et al.*, 1982); iii) propagules of some species do not grow into normal trees due to C-effects; iv) many tree species show large clonal variability in rooting ability, some clones do not root or root poorly. Superior clones are thus lost in the plantation because of the different degrees of unrootability of some or many clones. The number of clones established successfully must therefore be kept high to keep the broad genetic base intact.

Recent developments using controlled conditions have made propagation of traditionally difficult species to root easily. Modern research and technology have developed feasible methods for mass propagation from rooted cuttings. The species and clones differ in rooting ability but rooting success also varies depending upon the physiological condition of the ortet tree (age, propagule collection period, and cutting position on the tree). Physiologically mature tissues take longer to root, show lower percentage of rooting and develop fewer roots than physiologically juvenile tissues. There is thus a gradual loss of ability to propagate by cuttings with the advancement of age. Cuttings collected from 4-year old *Dalbergia sissoo* plants resulted in 60–90 per cent rooting compared to 10–20 per cent in cuttings collected from 30-year old trees (Gupta *et al.*, 1993). Juvenile stage cuttings of genetically tested trees can be produced by coppicing species which sprout from cut tree stumps. Thus methods of pollarding, coppicing, hedging and pinning down (nursery seedlings for bud sprouts, see Joshi and Dhiman, 1994) must be developed to maintain the juvenile stage. On pinning down one-year old *Pinus roxburghii, Dalbergia sissoo, Acer oblongum, Bauhinia variegata* and *Celtis australis* produced 72, 215, 196, 216 and 390 axillary shoots, respectively, in two harvests. These shoots on setting in propagation units gave over 90 per cent rooting within a month (Joshi and Dhiman, 1994). Thus cuttings can be used to produce plants in large number which can be further induced to develop root system through use of hormones, rooting media, and other nursery practices.

### 3.1.2 Grafting and Budding

Stock and scion cleft- and bud-grafting have been used successfully in conifers and in *Tectona grandis* for establishing seed orchards. Time and type of grafting, stock and scion relationship and graft compatibility must be worked out for each species. Bud-grafts in *T. grandis* flower in 3 years when taken from top 1/3 region of the tree-crown (Kedharnath, 1974). Budding of teak has been practized in India and clone collections established for production of bud-wood in states of Maharastra, Andhra Pradesh, Kerala and Madhya Pradesh. In seed orchards, *in situ* bud-grafting is practized on root stocks planted a year ahead of budding (Keiding, 1972). The grafting of *T. hamiltoniana* buds on *T. grandis* root stocks show approximately 50 per cent success (Hedegart, 1978). Cleft grafting is used to provide stock/scion grafted stock for superior germplasm seed orchard establishement in *Bombax ceiba* (Venkatesh, 1974). The grafts of *B. ceiba* flower within one year after grafting if the scions are selected carefully (Venkatesh and Arya, 1967). Such success stories are available in many other tropical and temperate tree species, but very little work has been done on technology of grafting for seed orchards.

### 3.1.3 Layering

Air layering is practized through induction of rooting on tree branches. Root formation is induced on an intact branch by girdling and hormone application. Air layering is used to obtain roots for species which show poor success with rooted cuttings. Air layers are removed after callus formation and rooted in beds. It is also utilized to produce propagules from tree directly to avoid graft incompatibility for seed orchard establishment. *Casuarina equisetifolia* reproduces by natural layering of lower branches in sandy coasts. Kadambi and Dabral (cited from Champion and Seth, 1968) experimented with air layering on 42 forest tree species of which half rooted with this technique. Layering techniques if developed can be successful in many more hard to root species with the use of modern physiological methods.

### 3.1.4 Root Suckers

Propagation by root suckers is common in many tree species. *Bombax ceiba* trees can be reproduced from small sized root cuttings (Joshi and Dhiman, 1994). *Dalbergia sissoo* has two types of roots, the nutrition absorbing downward growing roots without buds; and sucker producing horizontal roots. The horizontal roots attain considerable length up to 30 feet but remain in the upper shallow region of soil sending up root suckers whenever roots are exposed or damaged. *Diospyros melanoxylon* and *D. tomentosa* throw up root suckers in large numbers. In *D. melanoxylon* root suckering is a characteristic feature of the species and it establishes itself by vegetative propagation after clear felling. Large land patches of sucker reproduction persist and these are difficult to eradicate. The profuse production and tenacity of the suckers to survive ensures their survival and regeneration. There are other species as tenacious in sucker production as *D. melanoxylon*, such as *Butea frondosa* and *Ougenia dalbergoides*. Regeneration of the species through sucker production is particularly common in dry areas where conditions for seedling reproduction are adverse. This is best shown by *Prosopis cineraria*, a species of the desert region, where seedling production is unable to establish itself except along rivers and moist depressions. On the elevated drier grounds where conditions are adverse, *P. cineraria* survives by means of sucker reproduction (Troup, 1921). Several families exhibit the tendency to reproduce by suckers such as Leguminosae, Rosaceae and Bignonaceae.

Damage to roots stimulate sucker formation but this stimulation may also occur without damage. Research in developing techniques for utilizing this unique inherent characteristic of sucker formation in many tree species needs to be undertaken. In field-site-experiments it was observed that *Dalbergia latifolia, D. sissoo, Dichrostachys cineria* and *Azadirachta indica* show copious root suckers formation induced by trenching soil around the trees. In *Dalbergia sissoo*, formation of root suckers is stimulated by exposing and mutilating the horizontal shallow roots. Cost effective field techniques of the types described above must be developed where outstanding genotypes (through induced sucker formation) can occupy large bare land patches to bring them under tree cover. Root cuttings in many tree species are highly successful especially in those where stem cuttings show poor rooting response. Small size root cuttings can produce plants similar to the ones produced from big size stem cuttings.

### 3.1.5 Coppicing and Pollarding

The ability of many tree species to survive and grow after being subjected to cutting, lopping, burning, browsing (or to other injuries) by means of growth of new shoots from top, side and base of stumps or tree stems, is known as the coppicing ability. Many hardwood species sprout from stumps after cutting trees and such sprouts constitute an important source of wood production when managed under coppice systems. *Dalbergia sissoo* coppices vigorously, stumps sprout into masses of shoots, some from cambium around edge of cut surfaces and some from side of stools. The stools often rot and the many shoots produce their own roots giving rise to independent plants. Some of the species which coppice strongly are *Tectona grandis, Shorea robusta*, Dalbergias, Albizzias, *Anogeissus* spp., *Diospyros tomentosa, D. melanoxylon, Syzygium cumini, Butea frondosa*, etc. Those which coppice fairly well are *Pterocarpus marsupium, P. dalbergioides, P. santalinus, Aesculus indica, Terminalia tomentosa, T. bellerica, Quercus incana* and *Hardwickia binata. Hardwickia binata* coppices better if stumps at felling are kept high and then pollarded (Champion and Seth, 1968). Amongst factors that influence coppicing are tree size, cutting season and site characteristics. The genetic coppicing ability of the species is however the most important.

Pollarding is same as coppicing except that new shoots emerge on the top of a short trunk 1–3 m high rather than at the ground level. The number of trees which can be propagated vegetatively is large but only a few, namely *Shorea robusta* and *Quercus* spp., are exploited through coppice for forest use in India. In recent years many multipurpose tree species which coppice or pollard vigorously, like *Casuarina equisetifolia* are managed to produce fuelwood on a large scale. Profusely coppicing species can give wood in short rotation for pulp wood, turnery, fencing, fire wood, farm sticks, etc.

## 4. SEXUAL (SEED) REPRODUCTION

The morphology, development and the time of maturity of reproductive structures and how they function in terms of breeding systems (cross and self pollination) are important. The efficiency of sexual reproduction leading to tree fertility depends upon genetical and environmental factors affecting it. It is important to understand the physiology of floral bud initiation and bud location on the tree; its maturation; receptivity; seed set, seed-production and germination to assess tree fertility. The lack of flower initiation or pollen, is a major hurdle in seed production. Studies on duration of flowering, pollen production, pollination mechanisms, seed-set, seed shed, tree spacing and thinning, fertilizer and irrigation application on flower and seed production; inherent differences between trees and provenances in pollen, fruit- and seed-production; factors affecting pollen production, pollen shed, pollination, fertilization, gene flow, breeding systems (self- and cross-pollination), hybridization, embryology, seed quality, fruit and seed ripening and seed dispersal, are important to tree improvement and to understand genetic structure of populations. With freeze drying techniques, pollen of many tree species can be stored for future use. Strategies for artificial use of stored pollen in tree improvement, increase of seed set, and regeneration needs to be developed and implemented.

Many species like *Dipterocarpus tuberculatus, Shorea robusta, Hopea parviflora, Tectona grandis, Gmelina arborea, Pterocarpus delbergioides, Acacia catechu, Terminalia myriocarpa, Chloroxylon swietenia, Artocarpus hirsuta, Dalbergia sissoo, Pinus wallichiana, Toona ciliata, Acacia* species, *Mesua ferrea* and *Michelia champaca,* generally produce good seed every year (Troup, 1921). In *Pinus wallichiana* good seed years are most frequent (Troup, 1921). Some species produce little or no seeds in between large seed crop years. The years skipped in producing seed vary at species or within species at a population or individual level and some of this may result from climatic damage to crop. Annual synchronization within species of good or bad seeding of all trees may not take place even on the same area and site because populations or individuals differ, perhaps genetically, in these characteristics (Dogra, 1987).

According to Troup (1921), *Cedrus deodara* shows a 3-years interval between good seed year in widely separated localities of Jaunsar (Uttar Pradesh), Bashair and Kulu (Himachal Pradesh). Abundance or failure of seeding in *C. deodara* is sometimes known to be widerspread in north-west Himalayas. Abundant crops however may vary in different provenances (Dogra, 1987). Cones may be produced in lean years on portions of some trees in some stands. A complete lack of cone formation in *C. deodara* over very wide regions is rare (Dogra, 1987).

In *Picea smithiana* and *Abies pindrow* good seed years are repeated only after long intervals. Natural regeneration is therefore not good in these species. In *Pinus roxburghii* there seems to be no regularity in intervals between good and bad seed years as shown by records of different localities. *Shorea robusta* too shows seed-set failures in between good seed years which vary in different regions. Although *Dalbergia sissoo* produces abundant crop of pods every year, *D. latifolia* seeds neither regularly nor abundantly. Thus species within a genus differ in seeding behaviour. The good and bad seed years of a species or of trees within species may thus arise either due to genetic or environmental or both factors and thus affect reproductive biology.

A good seed year in one locality need not be a good one in another. Reliable information for judging the best time for seed collection based on seeding cycles of species and provenances is required. Conifer species, for example, differ from each other in having 1, 2 or 3 year reproductive cycle (Singh, 1978). Pollen (male cones) and ovules (female cones) are produced in abundance in the same year in some conifers of the Himalayas. In *Pinus wallichiana* complete failure to set seed is rare. In *Anogeissus pendula, A. latifolia, Bischoffia javanica* flowers and seed are produced in great quantities in years of drought. *Quercus* species flower in spring and their acorns ripe in June and July. The time at which the fruits ripen, is the best time to collect seeds. Seeds can be collected and stored when produced in plenty and in years of scarcity these can be used provided storage techniques are developed sufficiently to prevent nonviability. Unfortunately, seed storage technology needs to be developed for many forest tree species, especially of tropical trees which posses a major problem because of absence of dormancy or presence of a very short period of dormancy in the seed.

Monsoon is the natural seed germination season for most tropical trees. Seeds of Dipterocarpaceae germinate immediately after being shed just before monsoon. Seeds which germinate on falling on the ground are *Shorea robusta, Artocarpus chaplasha, A. hirsuta, A. heterophyllus, Dipterocarpus tuberculatus, Hopea odorata, H. parviflora, H. wightinana, Sterculia villosa, Chukrasia velutina, Toona ciliata* and *Cedrela microcarpa*. Seeds of many species fall a month or two before monsoon but they germinate only when rains begin. The species whose seed retain viability for some months or for less than a year are *Ailanthus excelsa, Stereospermum suaveolens, Azadirachta indica, Bischoffia javanica, Butea frondosa, Syzigium cumini, Holoptelea integrifolia, Dalbergia latifolia, Casuarina equisetifolia* and *Quercus semecarpifolia.* Tree species which retain seed viability for more than a year are *Xylia dolabriformis, Albizia lebbek, A. chinensis, Adina cordifolia, Cordia myxa, Quercus incana, Michelia doltsopa* and *Melia azederach* (Troup, 1921).

Information on seed ripening periods and dispersal characteristics of a species is important for proper harvesting and storage of fruits and seeds. *Xylia xylocarpa* pods which dehisce on the tree are flat and woody and contain 6–10 seeds. The seed must therefore be collected before dispersal. In *Acacia catechu* seeds cling to pod valves even after dehiscence and can be detached only by beating. In *Albizia lebbek* dehiscence of pods mostly occurs on the ground. In *Quercus* species acorns can be picked from the ground. In *Chukrasia velutina* ripe capsules disperse winged seeds on windy days from December to March and after dispersal the empty capsules hang from trees. In *Dillenia indica* the fruit consists of a stiff tight covering of thickened sepals. The seed must be extracted from green and not from dried fruits for them to germinate properly. Pulp of fleshy fruit like that of *Azadirachta indica, Gmelina arborea* and *Michelia* must be removed during seed extraction. In *Anogeissus latifolia* fruits are collected only when they commence breaking up.

### 4.1 Seed Source

Selection of seeds and its genetic control is exercized through documentation of the source (place) from which the seed is collected. Field tests of provenances or of single tree progenies are used to evaluate and show the inheritance of desired characters. High quality heavy seed production areas or seed stands must be selected for different tree species from its distributional range. In these, poor phenotypes can be rouged out and outstanding trees maintained to intermate and produce improved seeds. Seeds thus collected will be of known origin and have a better genetic quality. Ghosh (1977) converted about 1000 hectares covering 32 species into seed production areas for *Acacia catechu, Adina cordifolia, Bombax ceiba, Chukrasia velutina, Dalbergia sissoo, Gmelina arborea, Michelia champaca, Shorea robusta, Tectona grandis* and

*Terminalia myriocarpa*. This is summarized under the following steps: 1) selection and protection of suitable seed stands from existing wild seed populations; 2) selection of most suitable seed origin and field testing for evaluation; 3) selection of sound seed of known parent origin; 4) identification and documentation of seed stands producing seeds of known genetic performance within specified areas and sites; 5) establishment of clonal seed orchards in suitably isolated areas of a mixture of genotypes to produce genetically predictable seeds; and 6) employment of modern nursery techniques to raise vigorous standard stock from seeds genetically tested for high survival and productivity.

## 4.2 Seed Orchards

For production of genetically improved seeds in large operational quantities seed orchards are necessary. Its concept of seed production is based on features of reproductive biology and selected genetic clones or progenies. Seed orchards produce genetically improved seeds *in mass* using mixed clones or seedlings of progeny-tested elite trees, in suitable mating designs, in isolated locations favourable for cross pollination and good management. Orchards are of two types: clonal and seedling orchards. Clonal orchards are established with vegetative propagules, grafts, cuttings and bud plantlets. These orchards are efficient because clones produce seeds earlier, seed harvesting is easier, show predictable seed production and performance. Seedling orchards are established by planting seedlings, rouging the poorest trees and leaving the best families for seed production. A genetic provenance test plantation can also be converted into a seedling seed orchard.

Tropical forests are more heterogeneous in species composition. Most species are insect, bird or animal pollinated and their seeds mature in a short time. Information on pollination biology of these species needs to be collected. The role of insects, birds and animals needs to be elucidated in pollination, breeding systems, gene flow, and seed dispersal in each of the different species. Methods of establishing seed orchards of tropical species are still to be worked out. Flowering and fruit development conditions are variable and little is known of fruit and seed maturation, processing, and storage of fruit and seeds. Some attempts to establish seed orchards of teak have been made in India and elsewhere (Keiding, 1972; Kedharnath, 1980). Flowering period of one inflorescence in teak is 2–4 weeks in which up to 3000 flowers appear and 300 flowers open each day after sunrise. Optimum fertilization period is 11:30 to 13:00 hours. Teak is cross pollinated by insects and self-incompatibility is high.

For a broad genetic base a mixture of tested clones is used in the making of an orchard. Factors like self-fertilization, lack of flowering, flower abscission, non-synchronous flowering of clones, seed or pollen abortion, lack of pollen or of pollinating agents and incompatiblity which decrease seed production must be examined. Genetic variability in geographically different areas must be taken into account in seed orchard establishment. High adaptability, good performance, disease resistance of genotypes must be assured for certified seeds for sites or regions for which the seed is produced. Careful choice of site of seed orchard in suitable climatic areas with pest and disease control and correct irrigation and manuaring are important for heavy seed production. The location of seed orchard is made on the basis of the superiority of the site, isolation from pollen-contamination and easy accessibility for management. Seed orchards are designated as first, second or more advanced generation orchards depending upon their cycle of improvement.

## REFERENCES

Champion, H.G. and Seth, S.K. 1968. General Silviculture for India, Govt. of India, Delhi.

Dogra, P.D. 1987. Natural variability, genetic control, tree breeding and reproductive potential of wood producing species in India. *In*: S.S. Bir (Ed.) Aspects of Plant Sciences. **9**: 101–135.

Ghosh, R.C. 1977. Handbook on Afforestation Techniques. Govt. of India, Delhi.

Gupta, B.B., Kumar, Adarsh and Negi, D.S. 1993. Vegetative propagation through branch cuttings in *Dalbergia sissoo* Roxb. *Ind. For.* **119**(5): 386–387.

Hedegart, T. 1978. Data sheets on species undergoing genetic improvement 2. Data sheet on *Tectona hamiltoniana* Wall. *Forest Genetic Resources Information* (FAO, Rome) **8**: 39.

Joshi, N.K. and Dhiman, R.C. 1994. Vegetative propagation in operational forestry. *In*: N.K. Joshi (Ed.) Indian Forestry—New trends. Forest Research Institute, Dehra Dun.

Kedharnath, S. 1974. Genetic improvement of forest tree species of India. *Indian J. Genetics and Pl. Br.* **34**A: 367–374.

Kedharnath, S. 1980. Genetic improvement of forest trees. *In*: Proc. Second Forestry Conference, Dehra Dun. 1–17.

Keiding, H. 1972. Seed orchards in *Hevea* and teak. *In*: Proc. Symp. on Seed Orchards. Scandinavian Assoc. Geneticists, Denmark. Forest Tree Improvement **4**: 109–123.

Singh, H. 1978. Embryology of Gymnosperms. Gebruder Borntraeger, Berlin.

Talbert, J. T., Wilson R.A. and Weir, R. J. 1982. Utility of first generation pollen parents in young second generation loblolly pine seed orchards. *In*: 7th North American For. Biol. Workshop. Lexington, Ky.

Troup, R.S. 1921. The Silviculture of Indian Trees. Vol. 1–3. Clarendon Press, Oxford.

Venkatesh, C.S. 1974. Forest tree improvement work in Indian history, organization and present activities. *In*: R. Toda (Ed.) Forest Tree Breeding in the World. Yamatoya Ltd., Tynuoc-ku. Tokyo. 137–145.

Venkatesh, C.S. and Arya, R.S. 1967. Observations on the flowering and fruiting behaviour of semul grafts. *Ind. For.* **93**: 586–587.

seeds for given regions for which the seed is produced. Careful choice of site of seed orchard in suitable climatic areas with pest and disease control and adequate irrigation and manuring are important for higher seed production. The location of seed orchards is made on the basis of the suitability of the site, isolation from pollen contamination and easy accessibility for management. Seed orchards are [illegible] or [illegible] depending upon the cycle of [illegible].

REFERENCES


[illegible]

# 6

# Hastening Seed Production: A Tool for Increasing the Rate of Genetic Improvement in Eucalypt Species

*M.W. Moncur*[1]

## ABSTRACT

The rate of genetic improvement in temperate eucalypt species has been limited by the long generation time as well as poor and erratic seed production. Plant growth regulators have been used successfully to enhance flowering and control vegetative growth in *Eucalyptus*. Application of paclobutrazol by soil drench, stem injection or spraying, enhanced flower-bud numbers and seed production and shortened generation time in *E. nitens* and *E. globulus*. Flower-buds were even induced in seedlings exhibiting juvenile foliage. Applying paclobutrazol to 2.5 year-old plantation-grown *E. nitens* seedlings resulted in a reduction in generation time from eight to five years. Intensive management systems were developed to further reduce generation time. Using grafted material growing in containers, and by applying paclobutrazol at 6 months, it was possible to produce seeds in less than two years from grafting.

Application of paclobutrazol reduced the level of endogenous gibberellic acid (GA) in apical tissue and enhanced the reproductive activity of grafted trees. Grafts maintained in a warm glasshouse over winter did not produce flower-buds, despite the paclobutrazol-induced reduction in GA. A period of cold appears to be near obligate for floral induction in temperate eucalypts. Photoperiod has no apparent effect, while further research is required on effects of water status. These results have been used to develop improved seed production systems for temperate eucalypt species and may be useful with other species of the genus.

[1]CSIRO, Division of Forestry, GPO Box 4008, Canberra City A.C.T., Australia.

## 1. INTRODUCTION

The need for efficient production of high quality seeds of eucalypts is increasing as plantation programs expand. Seed orchards are being increasingly recognized as a way to obtain genetically improved seedlings for reforestation. Phasing out the use of seeds from land races or unselected seeds from natural stands in favour of that from seed orchards is expected to significantly increase volume yields. The genetic gain from premier seedlots of *Eucalyptus grandis*, compared with seeds from unimproved material, was 66 per cent in height and 159 per cent in volume per hectare, at 2.5 years (see this and other examples in Eldridge *et al.*, 1993).

To further improve the genetic resource, controlled-pollinations can be made between selected parents which contain favourable traits. Seeds from these crosses are then planted out and further selections are made. Thus plantation improvement is an ongoing though sometimes protracted process.

A number of factors impede the progress of plantation improvement. The long generation time, and especially the long juvenile phase, of woody perennials is a serious constraint. Considerable effort is being directed to the development of early selection techniques in order to reduce the time taken to select elite material for breeding purposes. Individuals or provenances of some species exhibit precocious flowering. Such early flowering, especially in plants from harsh environments, is usually negatively correlated with growth and is thus of limited use in breeding programs. An ability to induce precocious flowering in seedlings of desired provenances and progenies would increase the potential of genetic improvement by providing a means of reducing the generation time of breeding stock.

A second limitation is the low level of seed production in some species. The amount of seed produced by forest trees varies greatly among species and from year to year. Biennial or even less frequent bearing is not uncommon. Many temperate species, and in particular eucalypts, are difficult to propagate from cuttings or by tissue culture, and until these limitations can be overcome seed is the preferred option for mass production of planting stock. Plant growth regulators have been used successfully to enhance flowering and control vegetative growth. The growth regulator paclobutrazol is now being used as a management tool in many eucalypt seed production areas (Moncur, 1994).

In this chapter, the role of growth retardants to control vegetative growth, improve seed production and reduce generation time in temperate eucalypts, in particular *Eucalyptus nitens* and *E. globulus* is discussed. These are fast growing species used for pulp and other wood products. They are endemic to south-eastern Australia and are widely grown in many overseas countries (Eldridge *et al.*, 1993). Seedlings of these species must be at least 5 or 6 years old before they flower in plantations in Australia. While *E. nitens* is a noted poor seeder, *E. globulus* seeds well but has a tendency towards biennial bearing. The paper will also discuss the effect of environmental variables and cultural treatments on flowering and their interaction with growth retardants.

## 2. APPLYING PACLOBUTRAZOL AS A CULTURAL TREATMENT

### 2.1 Effect of Seedling Growth and Development

Eucalypts have a distinct juvenile phase which can last as long as 10 years in some species (Jacobs, 1955). The juvenile phase of development usually coincides with rapid early vegetative growth and the plants are considered incapable of flowering regardless of growth conditions. There is evidence that cultural conditions which enhance vegetative growth can shorten the juvenile period and result in flowering (see Hackett, 1985). Longman and Wareing (1959) reported that birch seedlings grown in continuous light produced catkins 10–12 months after germination. Their experiments indicated that the attainment of a minimum size was the critical factor, as repeated cycles of growth and dormancy were not so effective. Growing grafts of *E. nitens* under cyclic regimes failed to promote flowering (Moncur and Hasan, 1994).

The effect of paclobutrazol on phase change was investigated. Seedlings of *E. nitens* and *E. globulus* along with seedlings of *E. globulus* (provenance Wilsons Promontory), known for its precocious flowering, were planted. Paclobutrazol was applied as a soil drench in autumn when the plants were 15 months old. Only Wilsons Promontory seedlings had initiated adult leaves by this time. Twelve months later, the application of paclobutrazol had resulted in reduction in vegetative growth in all species but had no effect on the phase change. *E. nitens* seedlings were still juvenile, while *E. globulus* seedlings had commenced phase change. Wilsons Promontory plants produced flower-buds and the number was related to the dose rate of paclobutrazol (Table 1).

Table 1. The effect of paclobutrazol applied at two rates on growth and development of *E. nitens* and *E. globulus* seedlings

| Species/Provenance | Control | | | Low rate | | | High rate | | |
|---|---|---|---|---|---|---|---|---|---|
| | Ht | FB | A/J | Ht | FB | A/J | Ht | FB | A/J |
| *E. nitens* | 1.5 | 0 | 15 | – | – | – | 0.3 | 0 | 0 |
| *E. globulus* | 2.7 | 0 | 50 | 2.0 | 0 | 44 | 1.4 | * | 67 |
| Wilsons P. | 1.2 | 53 | 100 | 0.6 | 360 | 100 | 0.1 | 1233 | 100 |

**Note:** Paclobutrazol was applied 15 months after planting., Measurements were taken at 27 months.
Ht = height increase (m) after paclobutrazol applied.
FB = number of flower-buds per tree.
* one tree produced 48 flower-buds.
A/J = % of trees with adult foliage.

In Tasmania, Hasan and Reid (1995) treated potted 6-month old-seedlings of Wilsons Promontory (*E. globulus*) by spraying with paclobutrazol. They reported that twelve months later the paclobutrazol treatment had no significant effect on the level of vegetative maturity attained, or on the node at which vegetative maturity was attained as indicated by the node at which the first intranode appeared (Table 2). *E. globulus* seedlings from a commercial source

Table 2. Effect of paclobutrazol applied at two rates on height and leaf maturity in seedlings of *E. globulus* from Wilsons Promontory (Hasan and Reid, 1995)

| Treatment | Height (cm) | Mean leaf maturity score | | Node of first intranode |
|---|---|---|---|---|
| | | Main shoot | Lateral shoot | |
| Control | 118.7 ± 1.8 | 2.30 ± 0.12 | 2.44 ± 0.11 | 26.2 ± 0.5 |
| Low | 96.8 ± 3.6 | 2.09 ± 0.13 | 2.28 ± 0.13 | 25.5 ± 0.8 |
| High | 84.2 ± 4.5 | 2.10 ± 0.10 | 2.19 ± 0.09 | 26.7 ± 0.9 |

**Note:** Maturity was based on a subjective assessment of leaf shape and petiole insertion (1 = opposite, sessile, oblong-ovate leaves; 2 = ovate leaves; 3 = ovate leaves, petiole leaves; 4 = lanceolate, petiolate leaves and visible intranodes).

aged between 18 and 22 months and treated at the same time as the Wilsons Promontory seedlings were still in a juvenile leaf phase.

In a trial to assess the effect of timing of paclobutrazol on phase change and early flower-bud induction, potted seedlings of *E. nitens* were treated with paclobutrazol, applied as a soil drench, between 4 and 22 months after planting. Regardless of when the seedlings were treated, all seedlings still had juvenile leaves after 27 months. A small proportion of seedlings that were treated with a high rate of paclobutrazol initiated flower-buds. When treated at 6 months 25 per cent of the seedlings produced flower-buds at age 17 months and these seedlings initiated a second crop at 25 months. In addition 15 per cent of 8 month old seedlings produced flower-buds. In these seedlings 3.2 flower-buds were produced per umbel instead of the usual 7.0 for *E. nitens*, suggesting that the induction was not fully successful. It is thus possible to produce flower-buds in *E. nitens* seedlings while they still exhibit juvenile foliage, but the mechanism controlling induction is far from clear.

## 2.2 Effect on Reproductive Development

To overcome problems of seed production associated with juvenility, the use of grafted material was studied. Grafting has the advantage of being a non-destructive method of capturing a selection, maintaining its maturity and providing a flexible system with which to add and remove selections from the breeding population. Mature scions of *E. nitens* were grafted onto potted seedling stock in spring (August). Paclobutrazol was applied as a soil drench in autumn (March) 6 months later. After growing through winter, the plants produced flower-buds in November/December (14–15 months after grafting). A second crop of flower-buds, from this single application, was also initiated the following year (26–27 months after grafting) (Table 3).

An espalier was established as a part of an intensively managed system for seed production in *E. nitens*, following the development of such a system in France (Cauvin, 1984). In espalier systems flowers develop at 1–2 m above ground instead of the usual 15–20 m. Thus controlled pollinations and seed harvest can be completed in a time-effective and safe manner. Intensive management, including high inputs of nutrients, irrigation and canopy pruning,

Table 3. The effect of a single application of paclobutrazol on 6-month-old grafts of *E. nitens*

| Treatment | Year 1 | | Year 2 | | Year 1 + 2 |
|---|---|---|---|---|---|
| | Pots | FB | Pots | FB | FB |
| Control | 5/10 | 15 | 7/10 | 14 | 29 |
| Low | 10/10 | 64 | 9/10 | 53 | 117 |
| High | 10/10 | 48 | 10/10 | 75 | 123 |

**Note:** Pots = fraction of pots with flower-buds.
FB = mean number of flower-buds per pot with flower-buds.

is required to maintain the bearing potential of the grafts. Pruning keeps the espalier no more than 2 m high and ensures that reproductive shoots receive maximum light.

One-year old *E. nitens* grafts were outplanted into the espalier. After 6 months of growth, branches were trained by tying down to wires running 1 and 2 m above ground level. Grafts were treated with paclobutrazol either by collar drench or stem injection. Over the next 5 years there was regular management input but no further paclobutrazol was applied. The results demonstrated that a single application of paclobutrazol is highly effective in increasing seed output from *E. nitens* grafts in an espalier orchard. The effect of paclobutrazol treatment on flower-bud production was associated with both dose and application method (Table 4). These results (see Tables 3 and 4) confirm the persistent nature of the chemical.

Table 4. The effect of paclobutrazol on umbel production in grafted *E. nitens* grown in an espaliered orchard (Moncur *et al.*, 1994)

| Treatment | Umbels produced per graft | | | | | |
|---|---|---|---|---|---|---|
| | Year 1 | Year 2 | Year 3 | Year 4 | Year 5 | Total |
| TIL | 950 | 161 | 168 | 86 | 130 | 1495 |
| TIH | 1430 | 235 | 351 | 37 | 293 | 2347 |
| CDL | 2501 | 1294 | 994 | 90 | 848 | 5727 |
| CDH | 3551 | 1841 | 1039 | 333 | 897 | 7660 |
| Control | 145 | 160 | 89 | 32 | 57 | 483 |

**Note:** Paclobutrazol was applied as either TI = trunk injection, CD = collar drench, at two rates: L (low) and H (high).

### 2.3 Effect on Generation Time

The application of paclobutrazol results in a qualitative change in flowering status in *E. nitens* (Table 4) and *E. globulus* (Hasan and Reid, 1995; Reid *et al.*, 1995), effectively reducing generation time. To establish the magnitude of the effect of paclobutrazol on generation time *E. nitens* was grown under a range of management regimes. Two and a half-year old *E. nitens* seedlings grown in the field were treated with a single soil drench application of paclobutrazol. Flower-buds were first observed in year 3, flowering in year 4, and mature seed in year 5 (Table 5). By growing *E. nitens* grafts in an espalier seed orchard, generation time was reduced to 4 years. It was reduced further by applying paclobutrazol to either 6 or 18-month old grafts. Following development of floral buds, grafts were transferred to a warm glasshouse at the onset of winter. Depending upon the age, the mature seeds were harvested 1.9 or 2.9 years after grafting. Control trees produced only a few flower-buds by the harvest date.

Table 5. Effect of management practices on generation turnover in *E. nitens*

| | Seedlings | | Espalier | Grafts | |
|---|---|---|---|---|---|
| | Field | Field | | Pots | Pots |
| Age when paclobutrazol applied (year) | – | 2.5 | 2.5 | 1.5 | 0.5 |
| Seed to f.bud* | 6.0 | 3.0 | 3.0 | 2.0 | 1.0 |
| F.bud to flower* | 1.0 | 1.0 | 0.5 | 0.5 | 0.5 |
| Flower to seed* | 1.0 | 1.0 | 0.5 | 0.4 | 0.4 |
| Duration* | 8.0 | 5.0 | 4.0 | 2.9 | 1.9 |

*Years from seed or grafting to seed (Moncur and Turner, 1993).

## 2.4 Effect on Gibberellins (GA)

The application of GA generally inhibits flowering in woody angiosperms. Most notably, $GA_3$ and $GA_{4/7}$ inhibit or suppress flowering in a wide range of fruit trees (Pharis and King, 1985). When the *E. nitens* espaliered orchard (see Table 3) was sampled in September, at the time of floral initiation, the concentration of $GA_1$ in the apical tissue was related to the number of flower-buds produced in December three months later (Fig. 1) (Moncur and Hasan, 1994). In an experiment to test the interaction between paclobutrazol and duration of cold (Table 3) all grafts that flowered had a low quantity of GA. The postulated mode of action of paclobutrazol in stimulating reproductive activity by reducing net biosynthesis of endogenous GA was partially substantiated by the finding that reproductive activity in paclobutrazol-treated grafts partially reverted to the untreated state following treatment with $GA_3$ (Moncur and Hasan, 1994).

A lowered level of endogenous GA is not the sole requirement for induction of floral primordia in *E. nitens* (Moncur and Hasan, 1994). Paclobutrazol-treated material exposed to different periods of cold had similar GA concentrations, although only those grafts exposed to cold produced flower-buds. Likewise for the first flowering in *E. globulus* seedlings, low over-wintering temperatures in Tasmania appeared near obligate (Hasan and Reid, 1995). This function may resemble the vernalization response of annual plants, though its function in a

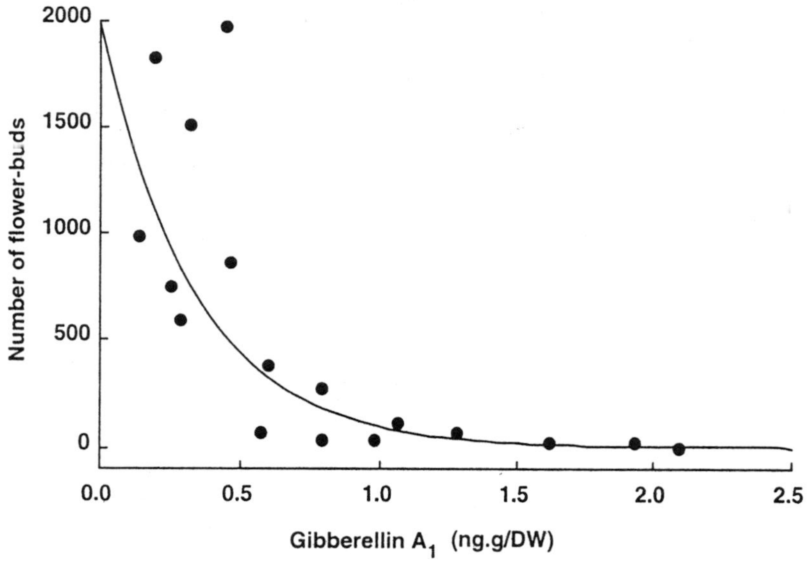


Fig. 1. Relationship between flower-bud production and $GA_1$ in an *E. nitens* espaliered orchard. Concentrations of $GA_1$ was detected in apical tissue by the method of Hasan *et al.* (1994). Regression: $Y = 1990.674 \times 10^{-1.321}X$, $r^2 = 0.798$.

woody perennial species is not clear. A period of cold could result in the destruction of a flowering inhibitor, a change in inter-organ competition, or both.

When gibberellins were applied to eucalypt seedlings, either by soil drench or leaf spotting, the vegetative growth accelerated. Further work needs to be carried out on application of gibberellin to promote fast early growth during the juvenile phase in an attempt to shorten the period to sexual competence.

**2.5 Concerns with Paclobutrazol Use**

Results presented in this paper indicate (Tables 3 and 4) that the effects of paclobutrazol can persist for at least five years. Although paclobutrazol is apparently active in soil for a considerable time (Hasan *et al.*, 1993) it has limited mobility. This was clearly evident in the espalier as untreated grafts growing close to treated grafts did not respond, either vegetatively or reproductively, during the five years following an initial application. Trunk injection produces a short-term effect with no soil contamination, which makes this the preferred method of application.

There has been no evidence to suggest any cause for concern regarding seed production or germination (Griffin *et al.*, 1993; Hasan and Reid, 1995). Controlled crosses have been carried out on paclobutrazol-treated material, as well as with pollen from these plants, without any detrimental effects. Germination and subsequent seedling growth have not been reduced by application of paclobutrazol relative to untreated controls.

### 2.6 Effect of Other Cultural Treatments

Manipulative treatments such as girdling, cincturing, root pruning and espalier training which retard vegetative growth and elevate the levels of assimilates in distal portions of the shoot or branch and enhance reproductive development were studied.

Girdling and root pruning of *E. globulus* and *E. nitens* seedlings had no effect on growth and development. The controls in the espalier orchard (Table 4) did not produce significant numbers of flower-buds without application of paclobutrazol, suggesting that tying down of branches had no effect on floral induction. *E. nitens* grafts have been grown in pots for over two years without producing flower-buds. However, once these grafts were treated with paclobutrazol they produced flower-buds within a year.

Growing *E. globulus* seedlings in small pots effectively promoted floral initiation (Hasan and Reid, 1995). It is not clear whether the flowering was a result of root constriction, water or nutrient stress or other influences. This promotory effect was additive to that of paclobutrazol application.

The results presented in this paper demonstrate that untreated grafts produced flower-buds, although few in number compared to those on treated grafts, indicating that they were sexually competent. Moncur *et al.* (1994) have interpreted the action of paclobutrazol as potentially enhancing the number of apical meristems that become reproductive in mature material within a given year. The induction process in natural environments is slow, with *E. nitens* taking up to five years to initiate flower-buds and up to ten years before a good seed crop is produced. Thus they suggest that paclobutrazol can be considered a rapidly-acting inducer, while extended cold and/or water stress are slow acting inducers.

## 3. ENVIRONMENTAL EFFECTS

Tree breeders wish to shorten the period from seed germination to flowering in any one generation, in order to maximize the number of cycles of selection possible within a given time. An understanding of mechanisms controlling floral induction and subsequent development is a pre-requisite for such manipulations.

*E. nitens* and *E. globulus* produce flower-buds in the leaf axils of new growth in the spring following a cold winter, suggesting that exposure to low temperature or changing daylength may be involved in the flower induction process. It should be noted that *E. globulus* flowers and sets seed well in the equatorial highlands, e.g., Kenya, Rwanda and Ecuador, where there is no extended winter. This may suggest that other environmental variables such as water status may be important in the induction process.

### 3.1 Temperature

The effect of low temperature on induction of flowering is well known. A number of Australian woody perennials are known to require low temperature to initiate flowering (King *et al.*, 1992). There is only one report of a eucalypt responding to cold. *Eucalyptus lansdowneana* initiates flower-buds when plants are transferred from a heated glasshouse (24°C/19°C) to a cold glasshouse (15°C/10°C) for 5 or 10 weeks, then back to the heated glasshouse (Moncur, 1992).

In a series of experiments scions from mature *E. nitens* trees of a single clone were grafted onto *E. nitens* seedling root stock in year 1 and year 2. When grafts were either 6 or 18 months old (in April), they were treated with paclobutrazol by soil drench. Five grafts of each age were then placed in a naturally-lit glasshouse (25/17°C). The remaining grafts were grown outside under Canberra weather conditions. Canberra mean minimum temperatures during May to September are below 5°C. A further five grafts of each age were transferred to the glasshouse in June and September. Grafts were held in these conditions until early December, when flower-bud production is normally completed, and then all grafts were moved outdoor until next December.

Paclobutrazol suppressed height growth and leaf production, but flowering occurred only in the paclobutrazol-treated grafts that were exposed to low temperatures over winter (Table 6). By December (Year 2), all grafts had experienced two winters outdoors and those treated with paclobutrazol produced flower-buds (Table 6). Two 18-month-old and two 6-month-old paclobutrazol-treated grafts that initiated flower-buds in Year 1 were grown in a heated glasshouse (25/18°C) during the second winter. In contrast to the grafts maintained outdoors over the second winter, the grafts in the warm glasshouse failed to produce flower-buds the following spring.

Table 6. Effects of paclobutrazol and duration of cold on flower-bud production of *E. nitens*, treatments of which commenced 6 and 18 months after grafting (Moncur and Hasan, 1994)

| Treatment | Year 1 | | | | Year 2 | | | |
|---|---|---|---|---|---|---|---|---|
| | + P | | Control | | + P | | Control | |
| | Pot | Graft | Pot | Graft | Pot | Graft | Pot | Graft |
| *18 month-old grafts* | | | | | | | | |
| April* | 0/5 | 0 | 0/5 | 0 | 5/5 | 112 | 0/5 | 0 |
| June | 0/5 | 0 | 0/5 | 0 | 5/5 | 20 | 0/5 | 0 |
| September | 0/5 | 0 | 0/5 | 0 | na | na | na | na |
| Outside | 4/5 | 55 | 0/5 | 0 | 3/3 | 92 | 0/5 | 0 |
| *6 month-old grafts* | | | | | | | | |
| April | 0/5 | 0 | 0/5 | 0 | 5/5 | 71 | 1/5 | 12 |
| June | 0/5 | 0 | 0/5 | 0 | 5/5 | 106 | 0/5 | 0 |
| September | 0/5 | 0 | 0/5 | 0 | 5/5 | 107 | 0/5 | 0 |
| Outside | 2/5 | 15 | 0/5 | 0 | 3/5 | 36 | 0/5 | 0 |

**Note:** + P = paclobutrazol applied.
Pot = number of pots out of five with flower-buds.
Graft = mean number of flower-buds, for those grafts which had produced flower-buds.
* = month when grafts were transferred from outside to a warm glasshouse.
na = not available.

The flowering of *E. globulus* seedlings which experienced high winter temperatures was strongly inhibited (Hasan and Reid, 1995). These findings indicate that the effectiveness of paclobutrazol use can be increased by appropriate environmental treatment (in this case, low winter temperatures). Flowering patterns of plantation-grown *E. nitens* were studied over a range of altitudes (40 to 720 m) in Tasmania. A 20-week difference in the date of onset of flowering was observed over the range of altitudes. It was also observed that the duration of flowering decreased as altitude increased.

### 3.2 Photoperiod

In contrast to many tree genera, floral development in eucalypts is not daylength-dependant (Moncur, 1992). Paton (1978) considered that eucalypts were long-day plants relatively insensitive to day length. Scions from mature *E. nitens* trees of a single clone were grafted onto *E. nitens* seedling root stock. In April 1993, when 18 months old, the grafts were treated with paclobutrazol by soil drench and grown outdoors in Canberra. During half of May the grafts were placed under fluorescent lights which extended the natural photoperiod to 16 hours. Grafts were grown under these conditions until December when flower-bud production occurs. There was a significant effect of paclobutrazol on flower-bud production but the additional light had no effect (Table 7).

Table 7. Effect of paclobutrazol and extended lighting on flower-bud production in *E. nitens* grafts

| Treatment | Pots with FB* | FB per pot** |
|---|---|---|
| +L +P | 7/8 | 60 |
| +L –P | 7/8 | 9 |
| –L +P | 6/8 | 62 |
| –L –P | 4/8 | 8 |

**Note:** +L = extended lighting
–L = natural daylength for Canberra (May, 11.2; June 10.8; July 10.9; August 11.6; September 12.6 h)
+P = paclobutrazol added
–P = no paclobutrazol added
* = number of pots out of eight with flower-buds.
** = number of flower-buds per pot that produced flower-buds.

### 3.3 Water Stress

There is some circumstantial evidence that water stress predisposes eucalypts to flower. In particular, *E. viminalis* seedlings grown in France flowered 12 months after experiencing drought conditions compared with 30–36 months or longer under well watered conditions (J. Marien, pers. comm.). In addition, field observations on phenological patterns of *E. diversicolor* in Western Australia suggest that flower-bud initiation may be favoured by summer moisture stress in association with high light intensity (R. Breidahal, pers. comm.).

Some evidence has been gathered to implicate water status as an environmental stimulus which may potentiate the flowering process in *E. globulus* (Hasan and Reid, 1995).

In an initial attempt to quantify the effects of water stress on flowering in eucalypts, grafts of *E. nitens* were established in large pots. When 18 months of age, mild (–3 to –5 bars) to moderate (–5 to –10 bars) water stress was applied by withholding water. Leaf water potentials and weight of pots were taken at regular intervals to develop a watering regime to impose stress. Half of the grafts were treated with paclobutrazol by soil drench. Treatments commenced during winter to coincide with the two months prior to floral initiation.

Paclobutrazol-treated grafts used less water over the two-month period. New growth in spring was delayed by water stress and paclobutrazol. Paclobutrazol-treated grafts produced greater number of flower-buds while the effect of water stress was not significant. Levels of ABA increased with water stress while IAA levels decreased (Hasan, unpublished data). It is probable that water stress reduced or delayed leaf initiation: as these are the sites of floral initiation, flower-bud development was also restricted.

## 4. MANAGEMENT SYSTEM FOR SEED PRODUCTION

Many eucalypt seed orchards start out as field progeny trials. In major breeding programms of *E. nitens* these trials are assessed at 6–8 years of age. The trials are then thinned, using assessment results to choose the small proportion of trees left for future seed production. As trials are usually planted at close spacing, the remaining trees have small crowns with initially-low seed production potential. After 2–3 years, with increased growing space and light interception, the trees reach a size where good seed production is possible. Seed production has been considerably increased by an application of paclobutrazol at the time of selection. Trees are usually 15 m or more by this time and paclobutrazol is applied by stem injection. Methods of application have been documented by Hetherington and Moncur (1994). In this method, where seed trees occupy considerable space, land is not used to its full potential.

If selections can be made at an earlier age, with the aid of molecular markers, the orchard can be assessed and thinned at year 1–3. Paclobutrazol will ensure that the seed is available by year 4–5. However, the problem of under-utilization of land still remains.

A more intensive method would be to take scions from selected trees, graft onto seedling stock, and after establishment, plant out into an orchard. By careful pruning, height can be controlled and lower branching encouraged. Once a good framework has been obtained paclobutrazol can be applied and the first seed crop expected two years later. This method maximizes the use of space and time. As the breeding program advances new genetic material can be incorporated into the design. Generation time will now be limited only by prevailing environmental conditions.

To further shorten generation time, grafts can be established in containers. Once established the grafts are treated with paclobutrazol in autumn, grown through a natural winter to meet cold requirements and then grown under non-stress conditions through to flowering.

Following cross-pollination and successful fertilization, the grafts can be moved to a warm glasshouse to speed up maturation. It is possible to complete the phase from grafting to seed in under two years. When grafts are treated with paclobutrazol at six months of age 300–400 flowers can be produced on each plant. If 50 of these are successfully pollinated and produce 3–8 seeds per capsule a total of 150–400 seeds can be produced per grafted selection. These seeds may well be sufficient for a reasonable assessment of genetic parameters.

Improvement in pollination methods could further increase seed production. Honey bees can be used to pollinate glasshouse-grown crops. Chemical emasculation to prevent selfing in open-pollinated seed production is another avenue of research with potential benefits.

Progress is being made to initiate flower-buds in juvenile seedlings. So far greater success has been achieved with *E. globulus* (Hasan and Reid, 1995) than in *E. nitens* (this paper). The suggestion by Hasan and Reid (1995) that there is a separation of vegetative and reproductive juvenility in *E. globulus* is an important finding. Together with the observation of flower-buds on juvenile field-grown *E. nitens*, it suggests that factors which control the developmental sequence of vegetative and reproductive phase change can be independently manipulated in *Eucalyptus*.

## 5. CONCLUSION

Efficient tree breeding and seed production in orchards depend on early and consistent flowering, neither of which is characteristic of forest trees in general. The promotion of flowering by paclobutrazol constitutes a practical method of promoting flowering for breeding and seed production in at least several eucalypt species. This finding is particularly important in *E. nitens*, because domestication of this species has been limited by shortage of seed (Eldridge *et al.*, 1993). Detailed characterization of the environmental stimuli of flowering, especially in juvenile seedlings, could provide a basis to further enhance the promotive effect of paclobutrazol application.

## ACKNOWLEDGMENTS

The author is grateful for the valuable comments provided by A.G. Brown, C.E. Harwood and L.D. Pryor.

## REFERENCES

Cauvin, B. 1984. Precautions pour 1'hybridation des *Eucalyptus*. *In*: Proc. IUFRO Internaional Conf. on Frost Resistant Eucalypts. Sept. 26–30, 1983. Bordeaux, France. Association Foret-Cellulose, Nangis, France. 509–523.

Eldridge, K.G., Davidson, J., Harwood, C.E. and van Wyk, G. 1993. Eucalypt Domestication and Breeding. Clarendon Press, Oxford. 288 pp.

Griffin, A.R., Whiteman, P., Rudge, T., Burgess, I.P. and Moncur, M.W. 1993. Effect of paclobutrazol on flower-bud production and vegetative growth in two species of *Eucalyptus*. *Can. J. For. Res.* **23**: 648–656.

Hackett, W.P. 1985. Juvenility, maturation and rejuvenation in woody plants. *Horti. Rev.* **7**: 109–155.

Hasan, O., Reid, J.B. and Potts, B.M. 1993. Paclobutrazol induced precocious flowering in eucalypts: a possible role for gibberellins. Research Report No. 8. Tasmanian Forest Research Council Inc., Hobart, Australia. 50 pp.

Hasan, O. and Reid, J.B. 1995. Reduction of generation time in *Eucalyptus globulus*. *Plant Growth Regul.* (in press).

Hetherington, S. and Moncur, M.W. 1994. Management of eucalypt seed orchards with paclobutrazol. *In*: Proc. Australian Forest Growers Conf. Launceston, May 1994. 235–238.

Jacobs, M.R. 1955. Growth Habits of the Eucalyspts. Commonwealth Government Printer, Canberra. 262 pp.

King, R.W., Dawson, I.A. and Speer, S.S. 1992. Control of growth and flowering in two Western Australian species of *Pimelea*. *Aust. J. Bot.* **40**: 377–388.

Longman, K.A. and Wareing, P.F. 1959. Early induction of flowering in birch seedlings. *Nature* **26**: 2037–2038.

Moncur, M.W. 1992. Effect of low temperature on floral induction of *Eucalyptus lansdowneana* F. Muell. & J. Brown subsp. *lansdowneana*. *Aust. J. Bot.* **40**: 157–167.

Moncur, M.W. 1994. Flower induction and enhancement in tropical species. *In*: R.M. Drysdale, S.E.T. John and A.C. Yapa (Eds) Proc. Intern. Symp. Genetic Conservation and Production of Tropical Forest Tree Seed. ASEAN-Canada Forest Tree Seed Centre Project, Muek-lek, Sarabini, Thailand. 173–181.

Moncur, M.W., Rasmussen, G.F. and Hasan, O. 1994. Effect of paclobutrazol on flower-bud production in *Eucalyptus nitens* espalier seed orchard. *Can. J. For. Res.* **24**: 46–49.

Moncur, M.W. and Hasan, O. 1994. Floral induction in *Eucalyptus nitens*. *Tree Physiol.* **14**: 1303–1312.

Paton, D.M. 1978. *Eucalyptus* physiology. 1. Photoperiodic responses. *Aust. J. Bot.* **26**: 633–642.

Pharis, R.P. and King, R.W. 1985. Gibberellins and reproductive development in seed plants. *Ann. Rev. Plant Physiol.* **36**: 517–568.

Reid, J.B., Hasan, O. Moncur, M.W. and Hetherington, S. 1995. Paclobutrazol as a management tool for tree breeders to promote early and abundant seed production. *In*: B.M. Potts, N.M.G. Borralho, J.B. Reid, R.N. Cromer, W.N. Tibbits and C.A. Raymond (Eds) Eucalypt Plantations: Improving Fibre Yield and Quality. Proc. CRC-IUFRO Conf., Hobart. 293–298.

# B. POPULATION GENETICS AND GEOGRAPHIC VARIATION

# 7

# Plus-tree Selection as a Tool in Tree Improvement

*Sunil Puri*[1]

## ABSTRACT

In most forest trees, which are long-lived, predominantly outcrossing, wind pollinated, and generally quite widespread in distribution, population variation accounts for most of the genetic variation. Tree improvement programs must place great emphasis on the exploitation of this variation. Knowledge of the genetic structure of the forest populations is important in determining the efficiency of different selection procedures. Every tree improvement program begins with the identification of individual trees which are above average in quality for some particular traits, and are used to establish a base population for future breeding. Plus-tree selection is the very first stage of a breeding program. The paper reviews the different methods used for plus-tree selection. It also highlights the limitations of methods and means to evaluate the selected trees.

## 1. INTRODUCTION

Tree improvement is a process of managing genetic resources. Through this process the inherent amount and organization of genetic variability in a particular population is managed by recurrent cycles of selection and breeding. The managed population becomes increasingly better suited to produce a desirable end product.

Tree improvement involves three distinct, but related, phases: conservation, selection and breeding, and propagation. As one moves from one phase to the other, decreasing amount of variations are being managed. Therefore, at

[1]Department of Forestry, Indira Gandhi Agricultural University, Raipur 492 012, India.

any one time, more variation is being conserved or selected than is being deployed through propagation.

Selection and breeding are the central activities of a tree improvement program. Selection is the first step which involves selection of desirable genotypes and its breeding and propagation. Breeding involves formulation of mating designs and evaluation of resultant progeny for the next generation. The theory behind tree breeding is relatively simple: from a large number of candidates, select potential 'parent' trees and performance test them by growing their progeny. Once ranked for their performance, the few best parents are selected for commercial use. This approach results in large improvements in crop quality and yields. However, many specialist skills are required to put the tree breeding theory into practice.

Keeping in view the gains one can obtain through tree improvement program, the present paper considers the strategies for selection using the technique of plus-tree selection.

## 2. SELECTION

It is a basic tool used in tree improvement programs. This enables the manipulation of variability in a population in the desired direction. The fact that genes vary in their effects, and that individuals inherit different combination of these genes, provide the basis for selection. Through selection a progressively improved breeding population is created which through successive generations of forest regeneration on different sites can yield cummulative better forest products. This is achieved through cycles of selection, in which genetic variabilities of economic traits are measured, manipulated and delivered so as to improve the population average of the traits over time. An additional consideration is that the rate of genetic progress should be as rapid as possible. Genetic gain ($\Delta G$) per unit time (T) can be formulated as:

$$\Delta G = i\,\sigma_p\,h^2/T$$

where i is the intensity of selection, $\sigma_p$ is the phenotypic standard deviation, and $h^2$ is the heritability of the trait. Maximizing $\Delta G$ requires efficient control of all four factors. Developing an efficient improvement strategy requires genetic knowledge pertaining to the breeding population, its selection methods; criteria and sizes (Comstock, 1977). Indeed, as Guries and Ledig (1977) noted, a breeding strategy inappropriate to the actual population structure of a species will reduce the genetic gain achieved.

It can be safely stated that what should actually be selected is the constellation of genes present in superior individuals of the basic population so that a new population could be built up, comprising largely of superior individuals. Unfortunately, the problem is not so simple as stated above. One cannot directly measure the 'genotype' of an individual, i.e., the potentialities conferred on that individual by the constellation of genes. One has to be content with measuring the external expression of the 'phenotype' of the individuals. The phenotype, however, need not always reflect closely its genetic endowment. For, it is a well known fact that the phenotype is the result of interaction of the genotype and the environment under which the genotype is developing. Therefore, unless, one is in a position to disentangle these two components of the phenotype, which may interact in various ways, it will be difficult to make an assessment of the true worth of the genotype. The identification of the effect of individual genes is formidable because most morphological characters are environmentally sensitive and are subject to polygenic inheritance and some degree of non-additive gene effects. In other words, the observed phenotype (P) is the sum of the genotype (G), the environment (E), and the interaction of genotype and environment (GE):

$$P = G + E + GE$$

The genotype can be further partitioned into additive (A) and non-additive (NA) variation, so:

$$P = A + NA + E + AE + NAE$$

Since breeding value for a trait depends solely on A, if NA and/or E are non-zero and cannot be seprated from A, observation of the phenotype gives no information on genetic variation.

There are other reasons which also contribute to lessen the utility of selection, i.e., to reduce the gain which may be obtained from selection. Most of the characters of economic importance are controlled by a large number of genes (polygenes). There is also considerable interaction among the various genes present in any genotype. The mating system of a population determines the pattern in which gametes unite (Allard *et al.*, 1975), and consequently exerts primary control on the genotypic frequency distribution of subsequent generations. The mating system can be defined by two parameters: (i) the outcrossing rate (t); and (ii) allele frequencies in the outcrossed pollen pool (p). Important questions about variation in the mating systems are: whether t is constant for all genotypes, and whether t and p are changing through time and space (Allard *et al.*, 1975).

The extent of the pattern of gene flow, through the tranfer of pollen and seed, further determine the spatial arrangement of genotypes in forest trees. Restricted gene flow and within population differentiation due to microsite selection pressure cause the formation of neighborhoods, or family clusters, among which allele frequencies will differ. Such population subdivision brings about an excess of homozygotes when trees from the neighborhoods are pooled, a phenomena known as Wahlund's effect (Wahlund, 1928). Restricted gene flow also reduces effective population size. This will increase genetic drift (Kimura and Crow, 1963) and also the level of inbreeding due to mating among relatives.

Differential self-compatibility among genotypes causes heterozygote deficiencies (Brown, 1975). In contrast, differential sexuality among genotypes, a situation often observed in forest trees (Schoen and Stewart, 1987; Cheliak *et al.*, 1987), will result in an excess observed heterozygotes, whilst differential fertility can cause either effect, depending on whether heterozygotes or homozygotes are the more fertile. Polyembryony and post-zygotic selection can also cause an excess of observed heterozygotes (Park and Fowler, 1983). Thus the mating system and the major evolutionary forces of selection, migration, and drift combine to produce the observed allele and genotypic frequencies in populations, their spatial distributions, effective sizes, inbreeding coefficients, and gene flow, all of which may vary within and among populations and over time.

The ability to identify precisely the genes responsible for producing a particular character and the long life span of trees make tree improvement programs difficult, but not impossible, to pursue. One such method, by which information can be obtained, especially when improvement programs are initiated, is the technique of plus-tree selection.

## 3. PLUS-TREE SELECTION

Plus-tree is an outstanding individual which occurs in natural stands, or in even-aged stands, combining as many desirable traits as possible, such as good stem form, good height and dbh, good bole length, less of taper, narrow crown, resistance to pests and diseases, etc. Thus the approach to tree improvement involves the selection of trees from wild populations based on their apparent superiority in one or more traits. Such superior trees occur in very low frequency and a keen eye is needed to locate such trees. Once a right base population has been identified then the plus-tree selection begins. It has to be a continuous process.

Selection of plus-trees has to be based on multiple criteria so as to bring about genetic upgrading in a number of traits. Four broad approaches are available to achieve this. One approach is '*Tandem Selection*'. In this method the improvement is focussed on one character at a time over successive breeding generations. This is not regarded as a suitable method for trees due to their long generation period. The second approach is called *'Independent Culling Levels'*. In this system, a 'candidate' tree is compared to a number of neighboring trees for various characters. The level of merit for each character is fixed and the candidate tree which does not reach this level is rejected regardless of its acceptability in other characters. The rigidity of the selection level will naturally depend on the contribution of the trait in question to the economic worth. This is the most commonly used selection technique. It has a weakness, as Ledig (1974) pointed out, in that comparisons among neighboring trees will be very ineffective if these trees are genetically related. The inbreeding depression associated with, for most economic traits, consanguineous mating requires that efforts be made to avoid the inclusions of relatives in the same breeding population. Based on the assumption that widely separated trees are less likely to be related than neighbors, most parent-tree selection programs requires a certain minimum distance between selections. This distance will also be affected by non-genetic considerations such as accessibility and total available resource in relation to the required numbers of plus-tree selections. In the absence of genetic information, minimum seperation distances have tended to be conservative. A knowledge of the population structure of a species allows a far more realistic estimate of the required seperation. Cheliak *et al.* (1985) recommended a seperation of 65 m for white spruce.

The third approach is the one where an index is used. This provides an objective method that weighs the characters in a systematic manner taking into account relative economic value of each character, genotypic and phenotypic variance of each character and genotypic and phenotypic covariance of each pair of characters. The fourth approach is called '*Base Line Selection*', used where a species, especially hardwoods, tend to occur in uneven-aged or uneven-sized stands, and individual trees may be widely seperated, making direct comparison with neighbors impossible. In this system a candidate tree is selected and compared to a regional average (or baseline) for the species calculated from a composite of measurements taken on a number of trees within the region. To be selected, the candidate must exceed this regional average by some arbitrary amount.

By ocular judgement, candidate trees can first be identified for their overall superiority and then marked with a band of yellow paint at breast height and suitably numbered. Then its superiority can be assessed by actual measurements for certain traits and compared with similar measurements made on five check trees which should be dominants and codominants in the immediate vicinity of the candidate trees. Then for each trait assessed the superiority of the candidate tree over the average of the five check trees can be compared. Sometimes a total scoring system also called the grading system is followed. Here each character is given a score according to its expression in the individual tree. Each character is assigned a score ranging from usually 0 to 5 with 5 as the most desirable expression. If the total score for all the characters judged exceeds a given minimum then the tree is accepted a plus tree and a second band with yellow paint is given to it.

Brown and Goddard (1961) expressed the idea that plus-tree selection should not identify the largest tree, but should identify the tree that has utilized the growing space most efficiently. Crown measurements are made and related to basal area and volume to identify plus-tree. Goddard and Strickland (1969) developed grading standards to select plus trees in Southern pines without the use of check trees. In order to develop grading standards, first dominant and codominant check trees from stands were measured. Multiple regressions were applied to the data, ploting volume over site index, tree age and crown size and developed equations for assessing a candidate tree against the average values of check trees growing under similar conditions. From equations, expected tree volumes were calculated for given crown measurements, site indices and ages. Volume of a candidate tree was then compared to the expected volume of an average tree growing under similar conditions. Dividing the deviation by the standard error of the regression, the growth efficiency units were obtained and used to evaluate the trees.

Stanton and Canavera (1983) selected white birch phenotypes on the basis of three techniques: (i) mean annual volume increment after adjustment by comparison trees, (ii) without this adjustment, and (iii) on the basis of differences between actual and predicted basal area increments regressed on crown surface area. Results indicated significant differences between techniques but none of them produced progenies significantly taller than the controls. Another study by Van Damme and Parker (1987) applied to black spruce used: (i) regression of basal-area increment of crown-surface area, (ii) stem volume on crown radius, and (iii) height on age. Open pollinated progenies from the selected trees at 2 years of age were significantly different but there were no differences among selection methods. In a study of various competition indices applied to improve plus-tree selection, Thomas (1980) also found that this approach is not helpful.

There are other reasons why selection based on crown characteristics may not be effective. Although correlations of growth and leaf characters in young trees and in experiments are often strong, there are reasons why these relationships may not exist in mature stands or may not be easy to assess (Assmann, 1970). Crown measurements may not accurately reflect leaf surface area; there may be differences in leaf arrangement and proportion of sun and shade leaves, and differences in phenology. Also, selection based on crown measurements cannot eliminate or account for differences in microsite. These reasons indicate that selection by this technique may not be promising.

## 4. EVALUATION OF PLUS-TREES

Once a plus-tree is chosen, the selected material should be collected and assembled in one or a few places so that further evaluation and breeding can proceed efficiently. Scions can be propagated in an orchard by grafting or rooting so that the original parent genotype is retained intact. In some instances it may be easier or more desirable to collect seeds instead of (or in addition to) scions and raise the seeds in a plantation or orchard setting. In this method the genes of the selected tree are preserved, but the original genotype is no longer intact. Each seedling contains a different sample of the genes of the selected tree, the other genes coming from whichever tree provided pollen for fertilization. The decision to use clones versus seedlings can have some effect on the level of improvement obtained during the first generation, with clonal orchards generally providing greater oppurtunities for improvement. Irrespective of propagation tecnique followed, the important thing is that the success of tree improvement program depends upon the successful propagation of selected material for the orchard.

Since the plus-trees have been selected based on their phenotype, it is essential to progeny test the plus-tree to know their breeding value and to identify the good genotypes. Thus, progeny testing of plus-trees is an essential component of tree improvement programs. Based on the test results those plus trees which are inferior can be removed from the orchard. A clonal orchard where undesirable clones have been removed or rogued, based on progeny test, is called a rogued seed orchard. A new orchard may be set out using only clones of elite trees (i.e., progeny tested trees), if it is not possible to rogue out the undesirable clones from the first orchard. Such an orchard of progeny tested clones has been referred as 1.5 generation orchard. A second generation clonal orchard will be one where clones are obtained from seedlings selected in the progeny trial experiments raised from controlled matings between first generation selections. Additionally, the progeny test can be used for selcotion of best trees in the best families and these can be cloned to raise a new orchard. The early flowering in the first clonal orchard can be used for making controlled crosses between clones, wherever that is feasible to obtain seeds for rasing two-parent progeny tests. Such test will provide valuable information on general and specific combining abilities.

In tree improvement programs one is always interested to know the genetic gain. Symbolically, the expression of genetic gain is:

$$G = S \times h^2$$

Where G is *gain*, S is *selection differential*, and $h^2$ is *heritability*. Because they are based on estimates that vary from species to species and population to population, neither term on the right side of equation is fixed, and it is possible to alter the level of gain obtained by manipulating S and h. Selection differential is a measure of the average difference between the selected population and the wild population. Its magnitude depends not only on how many (or few) individuals one select, but also on how much variation exists within the wild population. Thus it is possible to change the selection differential for a character by selecting a smaller fraction of the original population. If this reduced fraction represent a significant shift from the population mean, the process will be successful. In practice, there are limits to just how small a fraction can be induced, and *inbreeding depression*, or loss of vigor caused by matings among closely related individuals, could become a serious problem if the breeding population is severely reduced. A viable alternative, at least with forest trees, is to expand the number of stands in which selections are made. This serve the purpose of expanding the base population.

The other alternative is to increase the *heritability estimates*. Heritability is a measure of the proportion of variation in the population that is attributable to genetic differences among individuals. It may be defined as the degree to which a character is influenced by heredity as compared to environment, or as the proportion of genetic variance in phenotypic variance. The larger the heritibility estimate, the greater is the expected tendency for parents to pass their characteristics on to their offspring. For a given population the heritibility estimate could be increased by providing uniform growing conditions. By minimizing differences caused by environmental variation, one can maximize estimates of variation caused by genetic differences. However, heritability estimates are not fixed and may change over time as the trees mature. Different populations possessing different genes yield very different heritability estimates.

Heritability may be calculated by the method of parent progeny regression or by utilizing progeny response which is subjected to analysis of variance. The latter method is generally followed. If the progenies considered are families of half-sibs then the component for progenies estimates one fourth of the additive genetic variance. Once heritability estimates have been obtained for a trait from an adequate sample of populations and environments, it is then possible to predict the response to selection or the expected genetic gain ($\Delta G$).

Any or all the methods described lead to increased gains in tree improvement programs. Current estimates of genetic gain based on the selection of wild trees are in the order of 10 to 20 per cent, depending on the species and trait in question (Wright, 1976; Zobel and Talbert, 1984). It is likely that subsequent generations of breeding and selection will lead to additional gains of at least this magnitude.

The initial step of plus-tree selection is often difficult: experience is limited, genetic theory may not be well understood, and guidelines from other species and regions may be of little value. The difficulties with selecting plus trees should not lead to excessive costs. Plus-tree selection is of course a necessary first step in a selection program but the time and effort spent on it must be controlled. Cost must be related to the genetic gain achieved—the cost-benefit ratio must be positive. There are no general rules, but it is essential that one must know what can be achieved and realize that the point of diminishing return is very quickly reached in some species.

## REFERENCES

Allard, R.W., Kahler, A.L. and Clegg, M.L. 1975. Isozymes in plant population genetics. *In*: C.L. Markert (Ed.) Isozymes. IV. Genetics and Evolution. Academic Press, New York. 261–272.

Assmann, E. 1970. The Principles of Forest Yield Study. Translated by S.H. Gardiner. Pergamon Press, Oxford. 293 pp.

Brown, A.H.D. 1975. Sample sizes required to detect linkage disequilibrium between two or three loci. *Theor. Pop. Biol.* **8**: 184–201.

Brown, C.L. and Goddard, R.E. 1961. Silvical considerations in the selection of plus phenotypes. *J. For.* **59**: 420–426.

Cheliak, W.M., Dancik, B.P., Morgan, K., Yeh, F.C.H. and Strobek, C. 1985. Temporal variation of the mating system in a natural population of jack pine. *Genetics* **109**: 569–584.

Cheliak, W.M., Skroppa, T. and Pitel, J.A. 1987. Genetics of the polycross. I. Experimental results from Norway spruce. *Theor. Appl. Genet.* **73**: 321–329.

Comstock, R.E. 1977. Quantitative genetics and the design of breeding programs. *In*: E. Pollak, O. Kempthorne and T.B. Bailey (Eds) Proc. Int. Conf. on Quantitative Genetics. Iowa State Univ. Press, Ames, Iowa. 705–718.

Goddard, R.E. and Strickland, R.K. 1969. Manual of Procedures Used in the University of Florida Cooperative Forest Genetics Research Programme.

Guries, R.P. and Ledig, F.T. 1977. Analysis of population structure from allozyme frequencies. *In*: Proc. 14th Southern Forest Tree Improvement Conference, Gainesville, Fla. 246–253.

Kimura, M. and Crow, J.F. 1963. The measurement of effective population number. *Evolution* **17**: 279–288.

Ledig, F.T. 1974. An analysis of methods for the selection of trees from wild stands. *For. Sci.* **20**: 2–16.

Lindquist, B. 1951. Forstgenetik in der Schwedischen Waldbaupraxis. Newumann Verlag, Radebeul. 269 pp.

Park, Y.S. and Fowler, D.P. 1983. Inbreeding in black spruce [*Picea mariana* (Mill.) B.S.P.]: self fertility, genetic load and performance. *Can. J. For. Res.* **14**: 17–21.

Schoen, D.J. and Stewart, S.C. 1987. Variation in male fertilities and pairwise mating probabilities in *Picea glauca*. *Genetics* **116**: 141–152.

Stanton, B.J. and Canavera, D.S. 1983. Phenotypic selection in *Betula papyrifera*. *Can. J. For. Res.* **13**: 1159–1163.

Thomas, C.E. 1990. Use of Competition Indices in the Selection of Western Hemlock Plus Trees. Ph. D. thesis, Univ. of British Columbia. 156 pp.

Van Damme, L. and Parker, W.H. 1987. Selection of *Picea mariana* for growing space efficiency. *Can. J. For. Res.* **17**: 421– 427.

Wahlund, S. 1928. Zusammensetzung von Populationen und Korrelationserscheinungen vom Standpunkt der Vererbungslehre aus betrachtet. *Hereditas* **11**: 65–106.

Wright, J.W. 1976. Introduction to Forest Genetics. Academic Press, New York. 463 pp.

Zobel, B. and Talbert, J. 1984. Applied Forest Tree Improvement. Willey and Sons, Toronto. 521 pp.

# 8

# Selection of Superior Trees

*Dale Simpson*[1]

**ABSTRACT**

Selection of superior or plus-trees is the starting point of a genetic improvement program. An examination of population genetic structure will determine what proportion of genetic variation resides within stands and among stands, providing guidance on where to concentrate selection efforts. Characters to be improved should be carefully chosen based on their economic importance and heritability. The heritability of selected traits and the biology of a species contribute to developing appropriate plus-tree selection procedures and breeding plans. The comparison-tree selection procedure is the one most commonly practised, but users should be aware of potential ramifications of family structures that can exist among trees in natural stands. Plus-tree selection programs for white spruce (*Picea glauca* (Moench) Voss) and black spruce (*Picea mariana* (Mill.) B.S.P.) are compared.

## 1. INTRODUCTION

The objective of tree improvement programs is to obtain a significant amount of genetic gain at a reasonable cost while maintaining sufficient genetic variability in the breeding population to ensure future gain (Zobel and Talbert, 1984). This is accomplished by selecting trees possessing phenotypic characteristics deemed of most economic importance and using the trees as parents to produce offspring for reforestation programs and in breeding programs. The more variable a tree species and the more extensive its range, the more likely it is to respond to selection and breeding (Carlisle and Teich, 1976).

---

[1]National Forest Genetic Resources Centre, Canadian Forest Service, Fredericton, New Brunswick, Canada.

Gains obtained from plus-tree selection are controlled by the quality of the trees selected (Zobel and Talbert, 1984) and the means by which the plus trees are used to disseminate their genes such as seedling seed orchards, clonal seed orchards or clonal propagation systems. Estimates of gain from plus-tree selection range from less than 1 per cent (Cornelius and Morgenstern, 1986) to 5 per cent for height growth (Holst and Teich, 1969) or 5 per cent (van Buijtenen and Saitta, 1972) to 10 per cent for volume growth (Porterfield *et al.*, 1975).

The goal of selecting plus trees is to identify superior genotypes. Since the expression of a tree's genotype is modified by environmental factors, phenotypic selection is actually what is practised during plus-tree selection. Thus the genetic 'worth' of each selected tree must be determined from the results of progeny tests. The selection method or procedure used is dependent on the reproductive biology of the species, variation pattern (stand to stand vs. tree to tree) and heritability of characters being selected.

## 2. FACTORS AFFECTING PLUS-TREE SELECTION

### 2.1 Genetic Structure of Tree Populations

Generally, genetic differences exist both between populations (stands) of a tree species and among trees within populations. Genetic differentiation between populations results from evolutionary events such as natural selection, migration and genetic drift. Variation among populations is composed of two portions: (1) variation between geographic regions, and (2) genetic differences between populations within the same region (Stern, 1964). In general, population variation and tree-to-tree differences account for the bulk of the genetic variation found within a tree species growing in natural stands. These two sources of variation may account for nearly 90 per cent of all the observed variation (Zobel and Talbert, 1984).

The genetics of tree populations has been studied for many species in order to determine the degree of relatedness among trees within populations (stands) and among populations. Red pine (*Pinus resinosa* Ait.), for example, is a species that exhibits little variation among trees or populations (Fowler, 1965). Coles and Fowler (1976) reported that family relationships existed among white spruce (*Picea glauca* (Moench) Voss) trees growing within 100 m of each other (neighborhoods) with the average relationship approximating a half-sib (Park *et al.*, 1984). When selecting trees under this condition a sufficient distance must be maintained between plus trees to avoid selecting trees that may be related. Matings among related trees can result in inferior offspring.

Most of the variation within a species resides within populations. This is consistent for species such as: Douglas-fir (*Pseudotsuga menziesii* (Mirb.) Franco) (Yeh and O'Malley, 1980), Sitka spruce (*Picea sitchensis* (Bong.) Carr.) (Yeh and El-Kassaby, 1980), lodgepole pine (*Pinus contorta* Dougl.) (Wheeler and Guries, 1982), western larch (*Larix occidentalis* Nutt.) (Fins and Seeb,

1986), black spruce (*Picea mariana* (Mill.) B.S.P.) (Boyle and Morgenstern, 1987) and tamarack (*Larix laricina* (Du Roi) K. Koch) (Ying and Morgenstern, 1991). These estimates are based on isozyme analyses, which tend to use selection neutral markers.

The preceding studies demonstrate that for these conifer species (except white spruce) over 90 per cent of the genetic variation is indeed contained within populations. This implies that an appreciable amount of genetic gain may be obtained by selecting trees within populations. The quantity of gain captured depends on how effectively plus trees are selected as these trees are only a sample of the total amount of variation present. It is also important to select trees from a large number of stands, because there is genetic variability among stands as well. It is best to maintain a conservative approach by selecting trees from many stands. This will maximize genetic diversity in the breeding population.

## 2.2 Where to Select Plus Trees

### 2.2.1 Wild Stands vs. Plantations

The best stands should be selected from within seed zones or ecological regions (Morgenstern, 1975) because it is expected that a higher genetic gain might accrue from selection in the best stands than in ordinary stands (Squillace, 1967). The stand should be even aged (Brown and Goddard, 1961) to allow for more accurate tree comparisons (Morgenstern, 1975). Selection should be confined to middle-aged stands close to future expected rotation age because selection should lead to the identification of genotypes that perform best under managed plantation conditions. Trees that inherit the capacity for rapid growth at an early age are most desirable.

Plantations offer good opportunities for selecting trees because all individuals are of one age and site differences generally can be identified. Ledig (1973) listed three advantages to selection in plantations rather than in wild stands: (1) plantation trees have grown under uniform spacing and are all the same age, (2) compared to trees in natural stands, plantation trees have been subjected to cultural practices more typical of those that the progeny of plus trees will experience, and (3) adjacent trees in plantations are less likely to be related than they are in natural stands. Selections should not be made in plantations of non-local or unknown provenances younger than rotation age (Ledig, 1973). There is probably little fear of obtaining maladapted trees from selection in mature plantations because evidence from exotics has suggested that one generation of environmental selection can greatly contribute to the creation of acclimated races. None the less, as much information as possible should be obtained about the seed origin.

The size of the genetic base from which the seed was collected that was used to grow the seedlings for the plantation should also be considered. Stand collections of seed are superior to collections from a small number of trees. Seed biology is another aspect. For example, for a species that produces small-sized seed, large areas of plantations could originate from one mother.

If a restricted genetic base is suspected, either eliminate such plantations from plus-tree selection or reduce the number of trees selected in them.

Zobel and Talbert (1984) proposed a list of guidelines to follow when selecting plus trees and they are listed below.

1. Select trees in good quality stands.
2. Locate stands on sites similar to where plantations will be established.
3. Select stands within 20 years of anticipated future rotation age. [Do not select Big, Old trees].
4. Obtain information on the seed source of plantations.
5. Stands should ideally be of a pure species composition due to differential growth rates of different species.
6. Avoid stands that have been highgraded.
7. Select only one tree from small natural stands to avoid trees that are related. This does not apply to plantations.
8. It is not necessary for plus trees to exhibit heavy seed production unless seeds are required for establishing open-pollinated progeny tests and/or seedling seed orchards.

#### 2.2.2 Good vs. Poor Sites

The best phenotypes are found on the best sites (Ledig, 1973), where the expression of genetic diversity is favored (Morgenstern, 1975). Ledig (1973) suggested that trees be selected from sites similar in type to those on which their progeny will be planted. However, Brown and Goddard (1961) reasoned that good phenotypes from poor sites would react more favorably on better sites than the reverse. Superior trees may be those individuals most capable of responding to improved site conditions (Ledig, 1973). The best practice is to select trees on better quality sites, similar to those that will be planted, and where progeny tests will be established.

### 2.3 Potential for Improvement and Choice of Traits

#### 2.3.1 Genetic Gain

Genetic gain may be defined as the average value by which a selected population deviates from the original population. The genetic gain or response to selection is important in order to evaluate costs and benefits of various aspects of a tree improvement program (Morgenstern, 1975). The most reliable way to determine the effectiveness of plus-tree selection is to grow progenies from selected trees and empirically determine the amount of gain achieved (Squillace, 1967). Three factors contribute to the gain obtained or expected: (1) the genetic variance or amount of genetic variation in the population, (2) the accuracy of estimating heritability of the selected traits, and (3) the intensity of selection (Stern, 1964). If mass selection is practised in a plantation, heritability estimates obtained from the progeny data alone may be applicable. But, if selection is practised in wild stands, the heritability estimates should be based upon offspring-parent regressions. Most estimates of heritability are determined from progeny data alone, based on resemblances among trees within families.

These families were usually growing under plantation conditions and therefore, the heritability estimates only apply to selection under such conditions. They would not apply to selection in wild populations (Squillace, 1967).

If heritabilities of desired traits are low, then the intensity of selection should also be low, but if the heritabilities are high the selection intensity should also be high. When the heritability is low, environmental conditions exert a strong influence on the phenotypic expression of the trait(s) being selected, thereby increasing the difficulty of selecting 'genetically superior' plus trees. In this case, it is more efficient and effective to select large numbers of trees and to plant open-pollinated progeny tests. Progeny tests will be more effective in identifying genetically better parent trees because heritabilities of the desired traits will be higher due to the trees growing under more environmentally uniform conditions. Conversely, if heritability is found to be high and one is more confident that the superior quality of selected plus trees is a reflection of their genotype and is less influenced by the environment then fewer trees can be selected. Generally, more time and effort are devoted to selection in the latter case. Even in this case, most genetic improvement programs still require progeny testing of plus trees.

### 2.3.2 Choice of Traits

All traits are under some degree of genetic control but they are also influenced by the environment, e.g., height, diameter at breast height (dbh) and stem form. Variation in resistance to insects and diseases may only become apparent when there is an infestation (Carlisle and Teich, 1976). Traits are chosen based on a combination of their economic importance and degree of genetic control. However, genetic control is the over-riding criterion. It makes little sense to attempt improvement of a trait if it is weakly inherited. Generally little is known about heritability of traits when a tree improvement program is initiated. In this case, reliance should be made on the degree of phenotypic variation observed in the traits of interest, keeping in mind environmental factors that also impact a tree's phenotype. If a large amount of variation is observed it can be assumed that heritability is high. Just because a trait does not exhibit a lot of variation does not preclude selecting for it. The selection strategy chosen can mitigate some of the inefficiency in selecting traits not exhibiting a lot of variation. One means, discussed later, is to rapidly select a large number of plus trees and establish open-pollinated family tests. Future selection in the family tests will be more effective because heritability of the traits will be higher as a result of the trees growing in a more controlled, uniform environment.

Emphasis may be placed on different traits at different points in time during the breeding program. For example, plus trees may be selected for growth rate and stem form in the first generation. If stem form of the resulting progeny is acceptable then emphasis can be placed on other traits such as growth rate and wood quality in the next generation.

Height growth, dbh, volume, and stem straightness are traits most often selected for. These traits are economically important to the forest industry but their heritability, in natural stands, (particularly for height and dbh) is low. Rouse (1987) points out that crooked stems will decrease the quantity of lumber recovered from sawlogs. To illustrate this, a 20-cm diameter log, 5 m long with a 7.5-cm sweep will yield 40 per cent less lumber than a straight log with the same dimensions. Additional traits to consider may include crown form, branch angle, branch diameter, cone production, and wood density.

One has to be careful not to include too many traits. It becomes increasingly difficult to find suitable plus trees the more traits that are being selected for. Kiss (1976) reported that the initial selection standards for Douglas-fir were too high. It soon became evident that trees with all requirements including rapid height and diameter growth, disease and pest resistance, narrow crown, straight stem, short and small diameter branches, thin bark, and good cone production were very rare. As a result, the standards were relaxed and the greatest weight was placed on height superiority and stem form.

Traits may be weakly correlated with each other. If traits are negatively correlated then an improvement in one trait will result in a loss (of improvement) in another. Height growth and the quality traits of stem straightness, crown form, branch angle, and branch diameter were negatively correlated for 7-year-old open-pollinated jack pine (*Pinus banksiana* Lamb.) families (Adams and Morgenstern, 1991). However, by age 14 the negative correlation between height growth and stem straightness diminished to almost zero (Simpson, unpublished data on file). Such relationships can only be determined from analysis of progeny test data but should be considered when selecting trees in progeny tests for the next generation breeding program. Although the heritability of traits on plus trees selected in natural stands will be low, selection should favor plus trees exhibiting rapid growth rates and better than average quality.

## 3. SELECTION METHODS

A number of selection methods have been developed for tree improvement programs. The method chosen for a tree species depends on the type of genetic variation present in the population, the type of stands (natural vs. plantation, even-aged vs. uneven-aged) available for plus tree selection, as well as the intensity of the tree improvement effort.

### 3.1 Comparison-Tree Selection

The comparison-tree method is the most widely adopted method of plus-tree selection. A candidate tree is compared with its nearest neighbors or the average or best dominant trees in a stand; it must be superior in one or more traits in order to be chosen (Morgenstern, 1975) and should not be older than the comparison trees (Brown and Goddard, 1961). This procedure is efficient in plantations and even-aged stands of a single dominant species or when only a few species are co-dominant (Ledig, 1973; Morgenstern, 1975).

The purpose of using comparison trees is to adjust or correct the phenotypic value of the candidate tree for environmental effects common to that stand but distinguishing it from other stands (Ledig, 1973). The use of comparison trees as a correction for environmental effects should increase the genetic gain (Ledig, 1974). One shortcoming is that the comparison trees may be related to the candidate tree and in this case comparison-tree selection becomes within-family selection (Falconer, 1981) and could result in a reduction in genetic gain. For six trees in a stand (plus tree and five comparison trees) to be unrelated, 12 parents, 24 grandparents, and 48 great-grandparents are required. Unless a population has been constantly shrinking, comparison and candidate trees will be related. Ledig (1973) concluded that comparison-tree selection should be analyzed as within-family selection. Within-family selection will result in higher genetic gain than individual-tree selection only if the family relationship is very low and environmental variation among populations is very large relative to genetic and within-population environmental variation (Ledig, 1974).

The fault with comparison-tree selection is not that 'bad' trees are chosen but that 'good' trees are discarded. The effectiveness of this method can be improved by increasing the number of comparison trees and by using comparison trees not immediately adjacent to the candidate tree. This would reduce the average relationship among trees. However, comparison trees distant from the candidate will not occupy the same microclimate and, therefore, fail in their primary purpose of correcting for local environment (Ledig, 1974).

### 3.2 Individual-Tree Selection

The individual-tree selection procedure is also called ocular or mass selection. Trees that are vigorous, healthy, and of good form are rapidly identified. No measurements are taken nor are individual traits rated or scored. The procedure can be used for two situations: when the heritability of traits is considered so low that substantial progress can only be made through selection in progeny tests (Morgenstern, 1975) or when the traits are highly heritable in which case the phenotype is a good reflection of the genotype (Zobel and Talbert, 1984). It is applicable when only a few traits are being selected (Morgenstern, 1975). It can also be considered when selection crews have gained considerable experience using another method (comparison-tree) and thus increase productivity by eliminating the time required to measure and record information collected from the comparison trees.

### 3.3 Base-Line Selection

Base-line tree selection can be used when stands are even-aged and when it is difficult to find comparison trees adjacent to the candidate due to high species diversity. Individuals are located and their value for traits of interest is compared to the average for the region in which the selections are made. The average, called a base-line, may take the form of a regression line or equation (Ledig, 1974). Candidate trees must exceed the base-line by a certain amount in order to be incorporated into the breeding population (Morgenstern, 1975).

The base-line procedure was adopted by Brown and Goddard (1961) to enable selection for growth efficiency. It consisted of a regression of basal area increase versus crown length x crown radius. The measurements needed to relate crown size and growth were relatively time consuming so Brown and Goddard (1961) made them only if the candidate tree met minimum requirements in crown and branch characteristics and was free of damage from insects and disease. Rudolf (1956) developed a similar system whereby a regression of diameter at breast height squared x height versus crown diameter squared x crown length was used. He reasoned that if this relationship is expressed as a percentage, then soil and other site differences can be eliminated, to some extent, as variables. Superior trees had to be at least 20 per cent greater and plus trees at least 50 per cent greater than the average for trees within 20 metres that were of comparable age and species and growing under similar conditions. Ledig (1974) suggested that base-lines could be developed from accumulated comparison-tree data and that estimates of environmental variance indicate that such base-lines could apply over wide areas.

## 4. ECONOMIC CONSIDERATIONS

The selection of plus trees is time consuming and can be expensive. Care must be taken to achieve a balance between finding the 'right' trees and the time and money expended to find them. It is difficult to know when the point of diminishing returns has been reached. One must always bear in mind that trees being selected in natural stands and plantations are identified based on their phenotype. Only after the trees have been progeny tested can the genetically superior ones be identified.

Morgenstern (1983) presented results from a study, conducted in natural stands, of various selection methods. Although the comparison-tree method was the most widely used, he suggested that other methods such as individual-tree (ocular), base-line, and absolute standards should also be considered. It is important that distinctions be maintained between less intensive family/seedling seed orchard selection and more intensive clonal seed orchard selection. Family selection is adopted when the heritability of selected traits is low, there is a low level of variation for these traits and the environmental impacts on the expression of the traits are high. In this case it is best to quickly select large numbers of phenotypically good plus trees and place more effort in the establishment of well-designed, open-pollinated family tests. In contrast, when clonal selection is practised, more time is spent selecting phenotypically superior plus trees. Morgenstern (1983) found 1.6 to 4.1 person days were spent searching for plus trees for family selection versus 4.0 to 9.6 person days for clonal selection. He pointed out that, although these times were high, because most organizations had been selecting trees for 2 to 3 years, the time will be reduced as crews become more experienced. These times would be less if trees were selected in plantations. Funds should be directed where the greatest gains can be made.

## 5. CASE-STUDIES

Tree improvement programs for two tree species, white spruce and black spruce, will be used to illustrate and contrast the various aspects of plus-tree selection discussed previously. The development of genetically improved planting stock is conducted by the New Brunswick Tree Improvement Council in the province of New Brunswick, Canada. The Council was formed in 1976 and membership consists of eight industrial companies, two universities, and the provincial and Federal governments. Plus-tree selection spanned a 10-year period and was conducted primarily in natural stands.

### 5.1 White Spruce

The range for white spruce spans the North American continent, where it grows primarily in Canada. It is used for both pulp and lumber but is most valuable as a lumber species because of the size the trees can achieve. The traits chosen for genetic improvement had to be compatible with both end product uses. Growth rate was deemed to be the principal trait to be improved. Therefore, height growth was chosen as a selection trait. This was closely followed by stem straightness and crown form. Emphasis was directed to selecting trees with a narrow, compact crown on the understanding that such trees were able to utilize photosynthate more efficiently for the production of stem wood by not producing a large, bushy crown. These three traits were chosen as the primary ones to select for. Secondary traits included pruning ability, branch diameter, and branch angle. Pruning ability or capacity to shed dead, lower branches is important for the production of clear lumber. Small diameter, flat-angled branches produce smaller knots with less volume. This is important for the cooking process for pulp production and improves lumber quality.

A plus-tree selection/breeding strategy was developed by considering the genetics and biology. The species is genetically variable among and within populations (Nienstaedt and Teich, 1971). With high heritability for height growth (Teich, 1975) and considerable variation in stem straightness and crown form, a high selection intensity was warranted. Trees grown from seed may not produce commercial quantities of cones until 30 years old (Fowells, 1965) whereas grafts will produce cones 6 years after grafting (Nienstaedt and Jeffers, 1970). Considering these factors, the decision was made to institute intensive plus-tree selection in conjunction with grafting to preserve the trees in clone banks/breeding gardens and to deploy the grafts into clonal seed orchards (Fowler, 1986).

Suitable stands were located using 'local knowledge', aerial photographs, cover-type maps and checking timber cruise data. The most efficient way to cruise a stand for plus trees was in strip fashion with crew members positioned about 50 m apart. Candidate trees were initially identified as having superior height growth, acceptable stem straightness and crown form and free from injury, disease, and insect damage. If a candidate tree warranted grading, then five dominants from within the surrounding stand (50 to 200 m away and on the same site) were selected and marked. These dominants were within 10 years of age and growing in the same competitive situation as the candidate. The candidate tree and the five comparison trees were measured for total height, age, dbh, and height to first live whorl. This information was recorded on a selection form (Table 1). The candidate tree was then scored for each of the quality traits following the procedures accompanying Table 1. If a tree did not score points for two of the principal traits (height, crown, and straightness) then it was rejected. Occasionally, one of the comparison trees scored higher than the candidate tree and thus became the plus tree. Figure 1 shows a white spruce plus tree that exhibits most of the quality traits. Increment cores were collected from about 80 per cent of the plus trees and comparison trees to obtain base-line data on wood density of trees growing in natural stands and to provide a database on wood density of the plus trees.

The 340 plus trees selected were almost 10 per cent taller on average than the comparison trees (Fig. 2). Very few trees were selected that were over 100 years of age because the intended rotation age for managed plantations is 40 to 60 years. Wood density of 275 plus trees and their respective comparison trees was virtually the same, 0.350 vs. 0.349 (Simpson, 1992).

### 5.2 Black Spruce

Black spruce, like white spruce, also spans North America, growing primarily in Canada. It tends to occur on boggy, poorly drained sites but is also found on better drained upland sites (Fowells, 1965). It is a preferred species of the pulp and paper industry because of its consistent fibre qualities.

There tends to be less variation among trees for stem straightness and crown form compared to white spruce. Generally, trees are straight, with narrow crowns and small diameter branches. Emphasis was placed on height growth even though Morgenstern (1973) showed the heritability of height growth to be low. The type of sites where trees were selected was such that variations in microsite alone could have strong effects on height growth; therefore, one could not be confident about selecting superior genotypes. As well, 6-year-old black spruce seedlings can produce cones (Morgenstern and Fowler, 1969). The consensus was that it would be more effective and economic to practise mass selection to quickly identify superior phenotypes, collect cones from them, and plant the resulting open-pollinated seedlings in seedling seed orchards and family tests (Fowler, 1986). Greater genetic gain is anticipated in the second generation due to more effective selection in family tests.

Suitable stands were located and cruised for plus trees in much the same manner as for white spruce but less time per tree was spent searching for plus trees. A candidate tree had to be 10 per cent taller, be at least the average dbh, and be as good as the comparison trees for straightness, crown form, branch angle and size, and pruning ability. To be selected, the candidate tree had to be equal or superior to the comparison trees in eight of nine quality traits: stem straightness, stem taper, crown radius, crown density, branch angle, branch diameter, pruning ability, cone production, and freedom from insect and disease damage (Table 2). After grading, the plus tree was felled and the cones collected. Seedlings were grown and planted in family tests

Fig. 1. Outstanding white spruce plus tree exhibiting many superior characteristics.

and seedling seed orchards. Sometimes trees were selected when there was no cone crop. Although these trees were well marked it was often difficult to relocate them when returning to collect cones. It was more efficient to wait until there was a good cone crop before selecting plus trees. Black spruce cones are semi-serotinous, remaining closed for several months after maturing, thus allowing for a 4- to 6-month selection period. Occasionally a tree exhibiting

Table 1. Plus tree grading form and scoring procedures

**PLUS TREE SELECTION REPORT FOR WHITE SPRUCE**

Co-operator ______________________ County ____________ Tree No.__________

Location ____________________________________________________________

Map No. ________________ Photo No. _____________ Selection Date _________

Latitude _________________________ Longitude __________________________

Cone Collection ____________ Scion Collection ____________ Crew ___________

**Field Data**

| | | Height (m) | Age | Dbh (cm) | Height to 1st live whorl | Ht/Age |
|---|---|---|---|---|---|---|
| Comparison Tree | 1 | | | | | |
| | 2 | | | | | |
| | 3 | | | | | |
| | 4 | | | | | |
| | 5 | | | | | |
| | Mean | | | | | |
| Select Tree | | | | | | |

Stand Description

Forest Type

Density

Condition

Origin

Disturbances

Aspect

Per cent Slope

Moisture Regime

Soil Type

Elevation

Selected Tree Scores

Height __________

Crown __________

Straightness __________

Pruning Ability __________

Branch Diameter __________

Branch Angle __________

Age Adjustment __________

Total Score __________

## DIRECTIONS FOR SCORING

The comparison trees must not be immediately surrounding the select tree and should be in a similar competitive situation to the select tree.

1. *HEIGHT* — scoring is dependent on the percentage the select tree is above the average comparison tree height

| | |
|---|---|
| < 10% taller | 0 points |
| 10–12.5% | 1 point |
| 12.6–15% | 2 points |
| 15.1–17% etc | 3 points |

2. *CROWN* — judged subjectively by comparing the select tree to the comparison trees. Crown radius is average to small for stem size and competition under which tree has grown. It is based on uniformity, density of foliage and dominance.

| | |
|---|---|
| 0 points | same as the comparison trees |
| 1–3 points | slightly to much better |

3. *STRAIGHTNESS* — judged subjectively for the select tree and not compared to the comparison trees. No tree is accepted with spiral grain as indicated by bark configuration, any crook in two planes, or a crook in one plane which will not allow a line from merchantable top to stump to stay within the confines of the bole.

| | |
|---|---|
| 0 points | almost rejected because of above reasons |
| 1–3 points | slight sweep or crook to perfectly straight |

4. *PRUNING ABILITY* — judged subjectively by comparing the select tree to the comparison trees. It is the ability to shed lower branches.

| | |
|---|---|
| 0 points | same as average of comparison trees |
| 1–2 points | better than average |

5. *BRANCH DIAMETER* — judged subjectively by comparing the select tree to the comparison trees.

| | |
|---|---|
| 0 points | same as average of comparison trees |
| 1–2 points | better than average |

6. *BRANCH ANGLE* — judged subjectively by comparing the select tree to the comparison trees.

| | |
|---|---|
| 0 points | same as average of comparison trees |
| 1–2 points | better than average |

If crown, pruning ability, branch diameter or branch angle is (are) poorer than average then deduct 1 or 2 points accordingly.

7. *AGE ADJUSTMENT* — no select tree is acceptable which is more than 5 years older than the comparison tree average. Younger trees are given a bonus of 1 point for each 5 years they are younger than the comparison trees.

Table 2. Plus tree grading form

**PLUS TREE-SELECTION REPORT FOR BLACK SPRUCE**

Co-operator ______________________ County ____________ Tree No.__________

Location ____________________________________________________________

Map No. ________________ Photo No. _____________ Selection Date ________

Latitude __________________________ Longitude ___________________________

Cone Collection ____________ Scion Collection ____________ Crew ____________

**Field Data**

| | | Height (m) | Age | Dbh (cm) | Height to 1st live whorl | Ht/Age |
|---|---|---|---|---|---|---|
| Comparision Trees | 1 | | | | | |
| | 2 | | | | | |
| | 3 | | | | | |
| | 4 | | | | | |
| | 5 | | | | | |
| | Mean | | | | | |
| Select Tree | | | | | | |

Stand Description

Forest Type

Density

Condition

Origin

Disturbances

Aspect

Per cent Slope

Moisture Regime

Soil Type

Elevation

Does the select tree meet acceptable standards for:

| | yes | no |
|---|---|---|
| Stem straightness | | |
| Stem taper | | |
| Crown radius | | |
| Crown density | | |
| Branch angle | | |
| Branch diameter | | |
| Pruning ability | | |
| Cone production | | |
| Free of insect/disease | | |

Acceptable standards should be stand average or better. If 'no' to more than 1 of above *Reject* tree

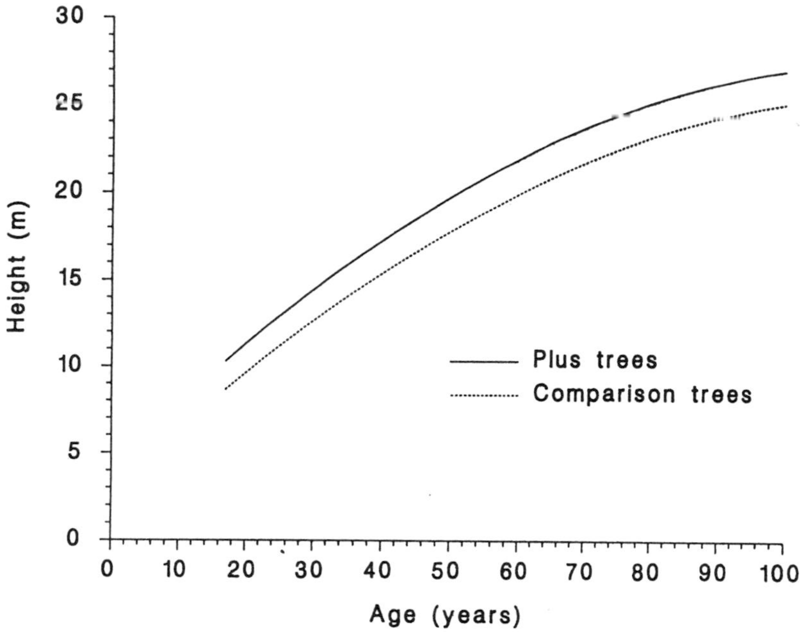


Fig. 2. Height/age curves for white spruce plus trees and comparison trees (Simpson, 1992).

exceptional qualities, usually height growth, was located. In these instances, the tree was left standing, returned to later and climbed to collect scions and cones. The scions were grafted to preserve the genotype of the tree in a clone bank and seedlings grown from the seed were planted in seed orchards and family tests.

A number of crews with several years' selection experience did select plus trees using individual tree techniques. This proved to be quite effective when working in large, uniform, even-aged stands and did improve productivity. When information became available on population structure indicating a high level of variation within stands (Boyle and Morgenstern, 1987), more trees were selected in stands which also increased productivity.

Height growth was the prime trait selected for and the plus trees were about 13 per cent taller than the comparison trees (Fig. 3) (Simpson, 1992). Over 1100 plus trees were selected. Disks were collected from the boles of felled plus trees for wood density determinations and establishment of baseline data. A disk was cut at breast height and another at half the tree height. Just over 30 per cent of the plus trees were sampled in this manner. Wood density of plus trees averaged 0.404. Increment cores were collected from another 7 per cent of the plus trees and their comparison trees that were left standing for various reasons. Wood density of plus-tree increment cores averaged 0.408 and comparison-tree cores averaged 0.404 (Simpson, 1992).

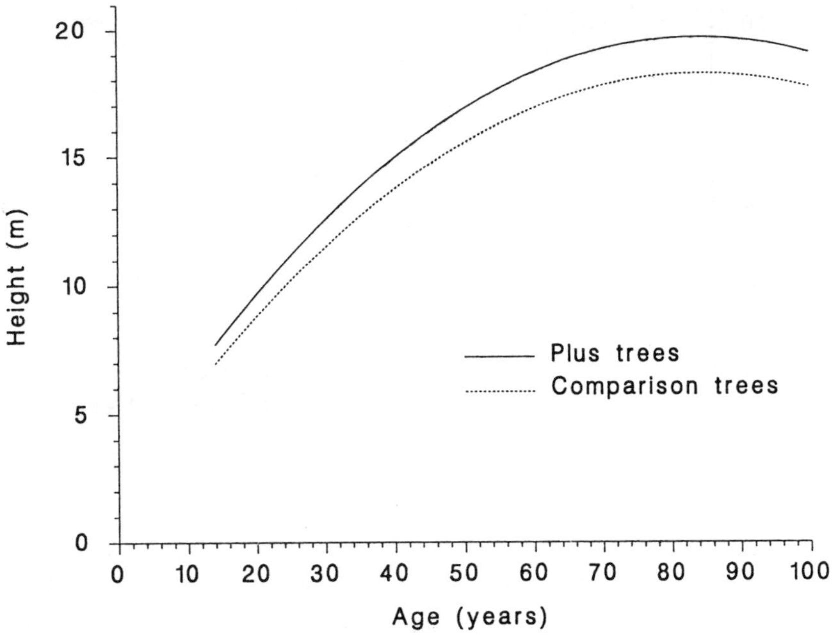


Fig. 3. Height/age curves for black spruce plus trees and comparison trees (Simpson, 1992).

## 6. CONCLUSION

The success of plus-tree selection depends on the variability of the trait(s) being selected, the heritability of the trait(s), and the selection intensity (Morgenstern, 1975) while the method of selection employed depends on the biology of the species being selected (van Buijtenen, 1969).

The steps involved in conducting a plus-tree selection program (Morgenstern, 1975) are given below.

1. Examine the variation pattern of the species to determine at which level to concentrate selection. If experimental evidence indicates stand-to-stand variation is large and tree-to-tree variation within stands is small then selection should be concentrated at the stand level and less effort devoted to selection within stands. It is prudent to select trees from a large number of stands.
2. Decide whether to emphasize high- or low-intensity selection. This decision is based on heritability of traits and the breeding strategy to be employed. High heritability of a trait favors high-intensity selection but low heritability would favor low-intensity selection and increased emphasis on progeny testing a large number of selected trees.
3. Choose the traits or characteristics to be improved by considering those of economic importance and that are suspected or known to be

inherited. As the number of traits increases it becomes increasingly difficult to find the type of tree desired (van Buijtenen, 1969).

## REFERENCES


Adams, G.A. and Morgenstern, E.K. 1991. Multiple trait selection in jack pine. *Can. J. For. Res.* **21**: 439–445.

Boyle, T.J.B. and Morgenstern, E.K. 1987. Some aspects of the population structure of black spruce in central New Brunswick. *Silvae Genet.* **36**(2): 53–60.

Brown, C.L. and Goddard, R.E. 1961. Silvical considerations in the selection of plus phenotypes. *J. For.* **59**: 420–426.

Carlisle, A. and Teich, A.H. 1976. The economics of tree improvement. Proc. 15th Meet. Can. Tree Improv. Assoc., Part 2. 42–56.

Coles, J.F. and Fowler, D.P. 1976. Inbreeding in neighboring trees in two white spruce populations. *Silvae Genet.* **25**(1): 29–34.

Cornelius, J.P. and Morgenstern, E.K. 1986. An economic analysis of black spruce breeding in New Brunswick. *Can. J. For. Res.* **16**: 476–483.

Falconer, D.S. 1981. Introduction to quantitative genetics. 2nd ed. London and New York, Longman Group Ltd.

Fins, L. and Seeb, L.W. 1986. Genetic variation in allozymes of western larch. *Can. J. For. Res.* **16**: 1013–1018.

Fowells, H.A. 1965. Silvics of forest trees of the United States. U.S. Dept. Agriculture, For. Serv., Agriculture Handbook No. 271.

Fowler, D.P. 1965. Effects of inbreeding in red pine, *Pinus resinosa* Ait. *Silvae Genet.* **14**(1): 12–23.

Fowler, D.P. 1986. Strategies for the genetic improvement of important tree species in the Maritimes. Can. For. Serv. Maritimes, Information Report M-X- 156.

Holst, M.J. and Teich, A.H. 1969. Heritability estimates in Ontario white spruce. *Silvae Genet.* **12**(1): 23–27.

Kiss, G.K. 1976. Plus-tree selection in British Columbia. Proc. 15th Meet. Can. Tree Improv. Assoc., Part 2. 24–31.

Ledig, F.T. 1973. The application of mass selection in tree improvement. Proc. 20th Northeast. For. Tree Improv. Conf. 69–83.

Ledig, F.T. 1974. An analysis of methods for the selection of trees from wild stands. *For. Sci.* **20**: 2–16.

Morgenstern, E.K. 1973. Heritability and genetic gain for height growth in a nursery experiment with black spruce. Dept. Environ., Can. For. Serv., Petawawa For. Exp. Sta., Information Report PS-X-44.

Morgenstern, E.K. 1975. Review of the principles of plus-tree selection. *In*: E.K. Morgenstern, M.J. Holst, A.H.Teich and C.W. Yeatman (Eds). Plus-Tree Selection: Review and Outlook. Dept. Environ., Can. For. Serv., Publ. No. 1347. 1–27.

Morgenstern, E.K. 1983. Tree selection techniques in the Northeast: some problems and questions. Proc. 28th Northeast. For. Tree Improv. Conf. 145–153.

Morgenstern, E.K. and Fowler, D.P. 1969. Genetics and breeding of black spruce and red spruce. *For. Chron.* **45**: 408–412.

Nienstaedt, H. and Jeffers, R.M. 1970. Potential seed production from a white spruce clonal seed orchard. U.S. Dept. Agriculture, For. Serv., Tree Planters' Notes **21**: 15–17.

Nienstaedt, H. and Teich, A. 1971. The genetics of white spruce. U.S. Dept. Agriculture, For. Serv., Research Paper WO- 15.

Park, Y.S., Fowler, D.P. and Coles, J.F. 1984. Population studies in white spruce. II. Natural inbreeding and relatedness among neighboring trees. *Can. J. For. Res.* **14**: 909–913.

Porterfield, R.L., Zobel, B.J. and Ledig, F.T. 1975. Evaluating the efficiency of tree improvement programs. *Silvae Genet.* **24**(2/3): 33–34.

Rouse, M.J. 1987. Tomorrow's lumber—today's seedlings. *Can. For. Ind.* **71**: 200–207.

Rudolf, P.O. 1956. Guide for selecting superior forest trees and stands in the Lake States. U.S. Dept. Agriculture For. Serv., Lake States For. Exp. Sta., Sta. Paper No. 40.

Simpson, J.D. 1992. Plus tree selection in New Brunswick. Forestry Canada, Canadian Forest Service-Maritimes, New Brunswick Tree Improvement Council Tech. Rep. No. 5.

Squillace, A.E. 1967. Selection of superior trees. Proc. 9th South. Conf. For. Tree Improv. 7–9.

Stern, K. 1964. Population genetics as a basis for selection. *Unasylva* **18**(2/3): 21–29.

Teich, A.H. 1975. Outlook for selected spruces and pines in Canada: white spruce. *In*: E.K. Morgenstern, M.J. Holst, A.H.Teich, and C.W. Yeatman (Eds) Plus-Tree Selection: Review and Outlook. Dept. Environ., Can. For. Serv., Publ. No. 1347. 28–33.

van Buijtenen, J.P. 1969. Progress and problems in forest tree selection. Proc. 10th South. Conf. For. Tree Improv. 17–26.

van Buijtenen, J.P. and Saitta, W.W. 1972. Linear programming applied to the economic analysis of forest tree improvement. *J. For.* **70**: 164–167.

Wheeler, N.C. and Guries, R.P. 1982. Population structure, genetic diversity, and morphological variation in *Pinus contorta* Dougl. *Can. J. For. Res.* **12**: 595–606.

Yeh, F.C. and El-Kassaby, Y.A. 1980. Enzyme variation in natural populations of Sitka spruce (*Picea sitchensis*). 1. Genetic variation patterns among trees from 10 IUFRO provenances. *Can. J. For. Res.* **10**: 415–422.

Yeh, F.C. and O'Malley, D. 1980. Enzyme variations in natural populations of Douglas-fir, *Pseudotsuga menziesii* (Mirb.) Franco, from British Columbia. 1. Genetic variation patterns in coastal populations. *Silvae Genet.* **29**(3/4): 83–92.

Ying, L. and Morgenstern, E.K. 1991. The population structure of *Larix laricina* in New Brunswick, Canada. *Silvae Genet.* **40**(5/6): 180–184.

Zobel, B. and Talbert, J. 1984. Applied Forest Tree Improvement. New York, John Wiley & Sons.

# 9

# Interactions of Forest Seedling Nurseries and Seed Orchards

*Christopher D.B. Hawkins*[1]

**ABSTRACT**

Selection and breeding with desired growth traits and qualities are the main objectives of tree improvement. Superior genotypes from the testing stage are propagated to establish orchards for the production of seed. Establishment of good seed orchards and raising of forest seedling nurseries are interconnected phases. This paper deals with the implications of seed orchard management on nursery culture; how nursery practices can effect genetic diversity; and how one can deliver genetically diverse and high quality propagules to the field plantation. In order to maximize gains in the field one must consider that selection, breeding, seed production, nursery culture practices and field plantation are continuous processes and should not be treated as discrete entities.

## 1. INTRODUCTION

Techniques to select and breed forest trees with desired growth traits and qualities are relatively recent events compared to the long history of forest utilization (Thompson and Pfeifer, 1992). The three main stages of forest tree improvement are selection, breeding, and testing (El-Kassaby *et al.*, 1992). To achieve the genetic gain (yield), tree improvement programs stress the importance of controlling the genetic composition of seed and thereby planting stock (Johnson *et al.*, 1984).

---

[1]British Columbia Forest Service, Research Branch, Red Rock Research Station, RR#7, RMD#6, Prince George, BC, V2N 2J5, Canada.

Superior genotypes from the testing stage are propagated to establish orchards for the production of seeds. They are managed to promote intermating while preventing pollen contamination (Zobel *et al.*, 1958); subsequently genetic value and diversity of orchard produced seed is expected to remain high through successive generations (Chaisurisri and El-Kassaby, 1993). To meet these objectives, there are several biological requirements when establishing seed orchards: equal representation of female and male gametophytes among clones, synchronous reproductive phenology, random mating, no incompatibility, no selection between fertilization and seed germination, and minimal or no pollen contamination (Eriksson *et al.*, 1973). Most orchards deviate to a lesser or greater extent from this list of ideal attributes (Chaisurisri and El-Kassaby, 1993). There is no guarantee of the physiological quality of seed that will come from a seed orchard because initial parental selection is based on mature tree phenotype (Leadem, 1982). Also, correlations of juvenile to mature attributes are poor at increasingly younger ages (Lambeth, 1980) and poor correlations may cause problems at the nursery.

Seed orchards and forest seedling nurseries are vitally interconnected phases of the reforestation process (Long and Peoples, 1991). Crop variation can be promoted by different nursery cultures. Up to 27 per cent of the observed seedling variation in several species was due to variation among nurseries (Bowden-Green and Rooke, 1980). However, others (Boyer *et al.*, 1987, Mexal and Fisher, 1987) have suggested seed and germination effects are primary causes of seedling size variation. Crop non-uniformity tends to increase with genetic diversity. For many technical reasons (Lang, 1989) related to efficient and effective seedling production, uniform stock is desirable from the nursery. What are the consequences of these opposing objectives on one another?

This chapter will focus on i) the implications of seed orchard management on nursery culture, ii) how nursery cultural decisions can effect genetic diversity, and iii) how the tree improvement objective of delivering genetically diverse, high quality propagules to the field can be met. The nursery examples generally will be from container nurseries in temperate and Boreal climates. However, most of the genetic issues are relevant to bareroot nurseries and warmer climates.

## 2. SEED ORCHARD MANAGEMENT AND NURSERY CULTURE

At the nursery, crop variation begins with the sowing and germination of seeds. Germination responses are likely to be conditioned by environments encountered by the seeds during their development. The first and perhaps the most important explanation for germination variation is the seed source or provenance (Allen, 1961) and family characteristics (Chaisurisri *et al.*, 1992). For example, populations from higher latitudes tend to have earlier and more rapid germination (Roche, 1969). Nutrition of parent trees in the seed orchard can influence seed quality (Allen, 1960) as will the maturity (morphological and physiological) of the seed at the time the cone crop is collected (Bhardwaj and Chakraborty, 1994). Environmental preconditioning during seed development is thought to be a crucial factor influencing seed behaviour (Johnsen *et al.*, 1989).

Pre-treatment of seeds prior to sowing will affect their germination responses. Seed size may also affect germination behaviour and early seedling growth in the nursery. A discussion on some aspects of seed size and germination is included because of the ongoing debate surrounding the issue (Reich *et al.*, 1994) and maternal influence on the trait (El-Kassaby *et al.*, 1992). Developmental processes will not be discussed.

## 2.1 Environmental Preconditioning

Forest tree (seedling) allocation to the field is usually regulated by seed planning zones. The sites of seed and seedling production, respectively orchards and nurseries, are usually not regulated because seed and seedlings are produced at economically favoured rather than at biologically relevant sites. The phenomenon of after effects or preconditioning of progeny due to parent-plant environment is well established though poorly understood (Bjornstad, 1981). Seedlings produced from seed of common parents but at different sites of seed genesis, can have a unique phenotypic expression for each site of seed production when raised in a common environment. This is thought to demonstrate environmental preconditioning (Rowe, 1964). Preconditioning crosses the traditional boundaries of genetics and plant physiology. It adds parent-plant environment as a complicating factor to the familiar genotype plus environment equals phenotype equation (Bjornstad, 1981).

It is important to determine whether after effects (preconditioning) are transient or persist. If they are permanent, nursery and seed orchard management strategies need to account for them. On the other hand, it may be only of academic interest if environmental induced after effects are transient (Lindgren and Wei, 1994). Though no definitive work exists, preconditioning is a major concern when dealing with progeny trials and seed orchards (Rowe, 1964). Observed phenotypic differences are possibly caused by non-genetic physiological differences carried over from parent to offspring (Johnsen and Ostreng, 1994). If this is the case, the effects of preconditioning should decrease over time as the progenies acclimatize to the environment in which they are growing (Ellis, 1992). However if the effects do not diminish with time, it is possible that genes have been permanently activated or deactivated during seed genesis (Johnsen and Ostreng, 1994; Lindgren and Wei, 1994). Plants appear to be most susceptible to preconditioning during seed formation (Rowe, 1964).

Rowe (1964) proposed seeds can be preconditioned specifically by ambient temperature, moisture and light at genesis. He indicated that preconditioning by climate and soil (nutrition) would affect subsequent germination behaviour and early plant development. Other potential preconditioning factors include flowering phenology, date of cone collection, and cone storage durations (El-Kassaby *et al.*, 1992). Preconditioning could be viewed as a special case of genotype and environment ($G \times E$) interaction. Lerner (1958) suggested that environmental effects can vary from ramet to ramet of a clone and this leads to increased within family-variation of the seed produced. He called these C-effects. Preconditioning may also be of practical importance when moving stock to new environments (Rowe, 1964).

Regardless of the practical and theoretical significance of preconditioning, it is of concern in the forest seedling nursery when dealing with seed orchard seed. It cannot be ignored because any factor that influences seed development and maturation has the potential to alter not only its nursery germination behaviour but its post germination development and growth.

### 2.2 Seed Size

The effect of seed size on germination behaviour is variable and somewhat controversial (Chaisurisri *et al.*, 1992; Reich *et al.*, 1994). Ehrenberg *et al.* (1955) observed that phenotypically inferior (minus) trees tended to produce seeds of greater mass than did normal or plus trees of the same stand. Saleem *et al.* (1994) reported better germination for low weight seed of *Celtis australis* but observed better seedling growth from the heavy weight seed fraction. Hellum (1976) observed that heavy white spruce seeds germinated more slowly than their average weight counterparts. Others have reported the size or weight of the seed is not important for the rate of germination or growth in Scots pine (Reich *et al.*, 1994) and Sitka spruce (Chaisurisri *et al.*, 1994). Chaisurisri *et al.* (1994) found clone or the family had a greater effect on germination than did that the seed size. Burgar (1964) reported seed size had no effect on white spruce germination but large seeds resulted in taller and heavier seedlings. It is possible that seed size reflected a stratification of seed parents rather than a seed size effect because the seedlot used was a production lot comprising of many families (Chaisurisri *et al.*, 1994).

Seed size or weight is not a good sorting criteria. Weight of individual seeds can vary with position, size, and position of the fruit on the tree. Seed weight was found to change by as much as 40 per cent annually on the same Douglas-fir tree (Silen and Osterhaus, 1979). Not only are seed size and correlations to germination variable, using them as grading criteria can narrow seed source genetic diversity.

The reported implications of seed size for the nursery are variable and seldom can the role of the family be documented. However, when reported, the effect of seed size appears to be transient (Silen and Osterhaus, 1979). Therefore, discussions on germination and seedling development in the nursery will recognize, that while seed size could be a contributing factor, it probably is of little or no significance.

## 3. NURSERY CULTURE AND SEEDLOT GENETIC DIVERSITY

Nursery practices alter seedlot population genotypes (Campbell and Sorensen, 1984). If the nursery environment is quite different (photoperiod, temperature) from that of seed origin, directional selection (removal of certain families or genotypes) may be promoted. This can decrease the genetic diversity of a seedlot.

Important forest nursery practices affecting crop production include stratification, sowing, germination, fertigation, pest and weed control, lifting, grading or culling, packaging, and storage. These practices or processes can result in directional selection of genotypes within a seedlot (Campbell and Sorensen, 1984). Each practice has a number of alternative approaches. If nursery decisions have been appropriate, a vigorous and uniform crop will result. Nursery practices that maximize seedling recovery and survival after planting will minimize changes in the genetic distribution of the crop (Campbell and Sorensen, 1984).

### 3.1 Seed Stratification

The response to stratification, even by related families, need not be uniform (Long and Peoples, 1991). In fact, seeds from reciprocal crosses, different ramets of the same clone, and different years from the same tree can have considerable variation in their ability to germinate and grow (Perry and Hafley, 1981). Stratification could have an effect on genetic diversity but it will not be considered. Germination should be at its optimum when stratification is done correctly. Ideally, stratification should not exert a selection pressure against specific families provided the families are not bulked.

### 3.2 Seed Germination

Many lots of seeds with nearly identical germination capacity can vary markedly in the onset and rate of germination (Czabator, 1962). At the nursery, it is desirable to have a rapid and uniform rate of germination. Delayed or slow rates of germination places seedlings at a competitive disadvantage (Perry and Hafley, 1981; Long and Peoples, 1991). Much of the observed variation in seedling size is attributable to germination behaviour (Boyer *et al.*, 1987). A great proportion of high quality seedlings at the end of the season will come from seeds that germinated early and rapidly (Long and Peoples, 1991), and received appropriate nursery culture.

Under some circumstances, diversified or variable germination behaviour could be a positive rather than a negative attribute. In natural environments, diversified germination will promote growth of the population when there is risk that any single course of action could induce mortality in all individuals taking that course (Westoboy, 1981). However, this is not the case in a greenhouse.

### 3.3 Grading

At the end of the nursery phase, the nursery crop is graded or culled. Depending on the success of each nursery, culling can result in the removal of few or many seedlings. Culling is based on the phenotype and does not result in an exact genotype culling but it still imposes directional selection and changes the genetic mixture of the seedlot (Campbell and Sorensen, 1984). For example, removal of only small seedlings in a crop with considerable size variation could alter the allelic frequency of the crop (St Clair and Adams, 1993). Culling and inadvertent favouring of certain plant types in the nursery can change the genotype of the crop. This is a mean of directional selection (Campbell and Sorensen, 1984). The grading process likely improves the overall plantation adaptedness and growth capacity of the crop. Any nursery practice that tends to produce seedlings that cannot survive after outplanting fosters directional selection.

### 3.4 Nursery Locale

There are reports of considerable crop variation being directly attributable to nursery location (Bowden-Green and Rooke, 1980; Lang, 1989). The nursery effect is related to day length (photoperiod). Photoperiod can markedly alter vegetative development of woody plants, particularly the timing of growth cessation. This is exemplified when northern provenances are grown in southern nurseries. Some morphological and physiological processes are retarded by the southern photoperiod (Morgenstern, 1976). The flushing phenology of buds is related not only to the present environment but to the environment when the buds were formed in the previous year (Rowe, 1964). High latitude seed sources grown in the south, when planted back at northern latitudes, may have their flushing phenology out of phase from local populations (Hawkins and Hooge, 1988).

Rowe (1964) suggested that a development pattern entrained in one environment can be put out of phase in a new environment. He further suggested that the induced morphogenetic instability is reflected by phenotypic differences. Such differences that appear within the seedling population in the nursery should not be considered irrelevant after planting. In short, nursery environments considerably different from parental origins should not be trivialized, rather, potential impacts of provenance—nursery displacements must be substantiated.

## 4. PRODUCTION OF HIGH QUALITY, GENETICALLY DIVERSE SEEDLINGS

Family composition and seed orchard seedlot construction can be affected by nursery practices. Generally, it is assumed that the family structure of the seedlot leaving the nursery is similar to what it was at sowing. The genetic composition of the planted stock is representative of the parental combinations and there is no directional selection at the nursery (St Clair and Adams, 1993). That is, individuals are removed by a series of random events. This may be a valid assumption under some current seed orchard—container nursery procedures.

### 4.1 Single Sowing

Inherent germination characteristics of each family can affect the representation of individual families in the seedlot after germination (Johnson *et al.*,

1984; St Clair and Adams, 1993). Growth of young seedlings is often influenced by their germination behaviour. This occurs in both single and multiple sow situations.

The following example is of spruce full-sib family germination (Hawkins, 1993). Based on 15-year field rankings (G. Kiss, pers. comm., spruce breeder, BC For. Serv., Vernon, BC), 50, 30 and 20 per cent of the families are respectively from the upper, second and third quartiles. Mean germination of 20 full-sib interior spruce (*Picea glauca, P. engelmannii* and their naturally occurring hybrids) families sown in 415B containers in a greenhouse was 93 per cent with a standard deviation of 3.5, and a range from 85.5 to 97.3 per cent (Table 1). If the families had been pooled in a seedlot, there would be unequal family representation after germination. When germination was examined by quartile, there was no difference in quartile representation before or after germination. However, individual families within a quartile did not have the same before and after representation. Families with the best germination capacities and rapid germination were not necessarily the highest ranked families, for example, family 4 was ranked 88. Families with slow germination rates are not expected to do as well as those which germiate rapidly (Perry and Hafley, 1981; Long and Peoples, 1991). Because of family specific germination rates and capacities, nursery germination procedures did change family composition. This may not maximize the plantation gains possible from these families.

The operational seedlot (Table 1) comprised 29 open pollinated families from the top 50 per cent of 173 interior spruce families (C. Hewson, Provenance Forester, BC For. Serv., Vernon, BC). Six families contributed to about 80 per cent of the seeds. The seedlot had good and rapid germination (Table 1). If the range of family germinations about the mean were similar to that observed for the 20 full-sib families, family representation in the germinated seedlot would not be the same as it was in the presowing seed mixture. Based on family representation by quartile described above, quartile representations likely will be similar before and after germination.

On the other hand, if germination rates and capacities varied significantly by family, family composition in the seedlot could be altered drastically in a single sow situation. Nine open pollinated (pollen from upper quartile) spruce families from the upper quartile were germinated in 1994 at Red Rock Research Station. The results were surprising (Fig. 1). Germination capacity ranged from 61 to 94 per cent. In the previous season at Red Rock, germination capacities of these families, albeit full-sib, ranged from 91 to 97 per cent (Table 1, Fig. 2). When mean family germination was plotted as an exponential function, family differences were marked in 1994 (Fig. 3), especially when compared to 1993 (Fig. 2). Computer controlled greenhouses ensured similar set points were maintained for the two germination periods. Family differences are therefore likely not due to greenhouse environment or nursery treatment. They could be related to seed preconditioning, multiple pollen parents, climate during seed genesis or seed handling.

Regardless of causes, later germinants are not likely at a competitive disadvantage because the cells are far enough apart that seedling to seedling interactions (canopy closure) do not occur until about 100 days after sowing.

Table 1. Nursery germination capacity, start of germination, inflection point (end of the maximum rate of germination), and end of germination for 20 full-sib spruce families and one operational (OP) seed orchard seedlot in 1993 at Red Rock Research Station. Start, end and inflection points calculated as described by Stoehr *et al.* (1994). Seed and 15-year family rankings provided by G. Kiss, spruce breeder, BC Forest Service, Vernon, BC

| Family | Family rank of 173 | Rank quartile | Germination Capacity % | Germination | | |
|---|---|---|---|---|---|---|
| | | | | Start (days) | Inflection Points (days) | End (days) |
| 4 | 88 | III | 97.3 | 10.5 | 18.2 | 19.9 |
| 3 | 25 | I | 97.2 | 12.7 | 20.8 | 23.6 |
| 18 | 46 | II | 96.5 | 11.8 | 19.8 | 22.6 |
| 8 | 60 | II | 96.5 | 11.5 | 20.4 | 23.5 |
| 16 | 94 | III | 96.0 | 10.3 | 18.3 | 19.6 |
| 7 | 31 | I | 95.6 | 13.4 | 19.7 | 21.7 |
| 6 | 20 | I | 95.5 | 11.3 | 18.3 | 18.3# |
| 5 | 6 | I | 95.0 | 10.4 | 19.1 | 20.6 |
| 15 | 15 | I | 94.0 | 12.9 | 20.7 | 23.9 |
| 11 | 3 | I | 93.7 | 13.1 | 19.1 | 22.1 |
| 12 | 2 | I | 93.7 | 13.1 | 19.7 | 23.5 |
| 20 | 4 | I | 93.1 | 13.3 | 21.8 | 26.5 |
| 9 | 116 | III | 92.5 | 11.6 | 19.4 | 22.9 |
| 13 | 83 | II | 91.9 | 14.9 | 20.6 | 23.7 |
| 1 | 11 | I | 91.3 | 14.3 | 20.6 | 25.0 |
| 17 | – | III | 91.3 | 11.9 | 19.3 | 22.5 |
| 10 | 79 | II | 89.0 | 14.6 | 20.9 | 24.3 |
| 19 | 29 | I | 87.2 | 12.1 | 19.6 | 22.0 |
| 14 | 70 | II | 87.1 | 14.9 | 21.1 | 25.1 |
| 2 | 47 | II | 85.5 | 17.5 | 22.8 | 26.9 |
| OP | n/a | n/a | 92.3 | 11.1 | 17.6 | 20.3 |

# Family 6 attained its maximum rate of germination at the end of germination.

The slow growing families will be the ones overtopped during this period rather than the late germinants. This is a function of inherent family growth rate rather than germination behaviour. The family composition of the seed orchard seedlot has also been changed due to the inherent germination behaviour of individual families (Burdon and Sweet, 1976). It would be possible to have a balanced family representation after germination and in planting stock by constructing the seedlot based on family germination capacities. However, it would increase the cost of nursery production (El-Kassaby *et al.*, 1992) as the germination behaviour of each family needs to be known.

Nursery height growth of families can be variable (Hawkins, 1993). Some families germinate rapidly and have a rapid height growth while other rapid germinators display average height growth rates in the nursery. Alternatively,

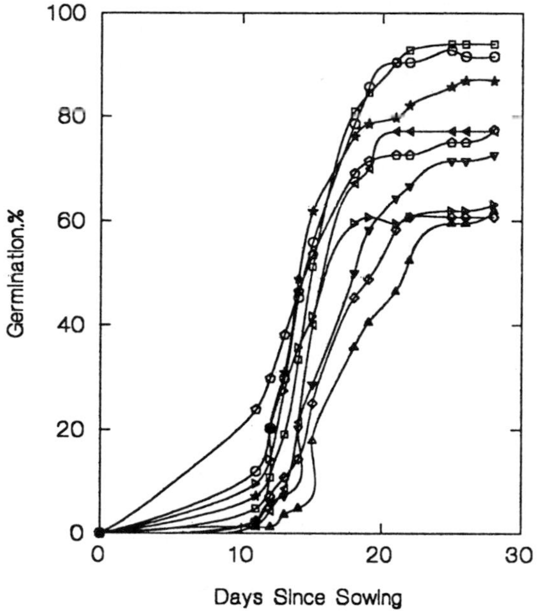


Fig. 1. Mean germination behavior of nine open pollinated spruce families. Seed was collected in 1993 and germinated in 1994 at Red Rock Research Station (C.D.B. Hawkins unpublished data). Family 15 year field rankings by descending germination capacity are 15, 4, 6, 25, 2, 11, 20, 7, 31.

some slow to germinate families have rapid height growth rates while others have slow ones. This invalidates the assumption that seeds from different families in a seed orchard will have similar germination capacities and rates (El-Kassaby *et al.,* 1992). Family germination rates may not correlate to overall 15-year field rankings (Figs. 2 and 3). Families were selected for mature tree phenotype not seed germination and nursery behaviours. Reported differences should come as no surprise.

### 4.2 Multiple Sowing

The impact of germination on the seedlot genetic structure is more complex in a multiple sow situation (El-Kassaby *et al.*, 1992). The first seed to emerge has an advantage. This is often indicated by better height and root collar diameter of those seedlings (Bhardwaj and Chakraborty, 1994). At the end of germination, there may be multiple germinants per cell. Cells will be thinned to one germinant. The usual thinning criteria are to i) remove all germinants but the largest or ii) if all germinants are of similar size, leave the one closest to the centre of the cell.

In the first instance early germinants are favoured over the later ones. For example, there was little difference in germination capacity between families with field ranks of 2 and 25 (Fig. 3). Family 25 is from a slower germinating

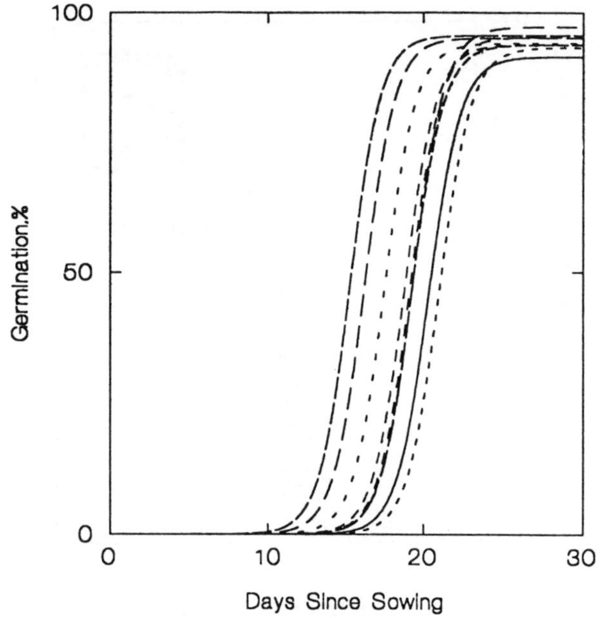


Fig. 2. Exponential germination functions fitted (Stoehr *et al.*, 1994) to nine full-sib spruce families germinated in 1993 at Red Rock Research Station. Seed was collected in 1987 (modified from Hawkins, 1993). Family 15 year field rankings by descending germination capacity are 25, 31, 20, 6, 15, 7, 2, 4, 11.

group and it would be culled if both families germinated in the same cell. Most if not all of the families from the three slower germinating groups would be culled in favour of those from the fastest group regardless of the germination capacity. This germination behaviour is a family characteristic, directional selection is being applied to the crop and genetic diversity may be reduced (Lang, 1989; El-Kassaby *et al.*, 1992). Seedling crops with unknown allelic frequencies also result in this situation (El-Kassaby *et al.*, 1992). In the second instance, seed position in the cell is a chance event if seed weight does not influence its location. Thinning affects all families more or less equally. Therefore, no selection pressure is being applied. Thining adds to the cost of seedling production as does sowing seed that will not become seedling. Now, as in the single sow case, slow growing families in the nursery, even those who emerge rapidly, may be overtopped by the faster growing families prior to canopy closure.

The reduction in representation or complete loss of families from the seedlot is of concern because i) genetic diversity of production plantations will be reduced and ii) expected gains from tree improvement will not be realized (St Clair and Adams, 1993). Again, the conundrum between seed orchard and nursery objectives, that is how to simultaneously maintain genetic diversity and attain crop size uniformity.

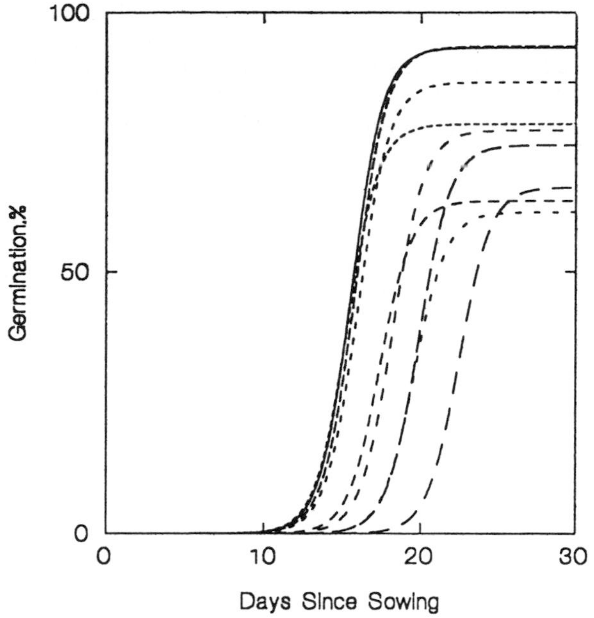


Fig. 3. Exponential germination functions fitted (Stoehr *et al.*, 1994) to nine open pollinated spruce families germinated in 1994 at Red Rock Research Station. Seed was collected in 1993 (C.D.B. Hawkins unpublished). Family 15 year field rankings by descending germination capacity are 15, 4, 6, 2, 25, 11, 7, 20, 31.

### 4.3 End of Season

At the end of the nursery season, the seedlot will be 'graded' based on contractual specifications agreed to before sowing. Generally, seedlings that are short, have small root collar diameters, or are spindly or wimpy (tall without commensurate root collar diameter) will be culled from the seedlot. Some of this stock may be small due to inbreeding or family genetics. Inbreeding may cause weak and aberrant seedlings while slow nursery growth may be a family characteristic. The remainder of the small stock, albeit a small proportion, may result from unsuitable nursery culture. The majority of the culling done for small seedlings could result in directional selection of the seedlot (Campbell and Sorensen, 1984). Wimpy stock may reflect family growth characteristics but in many cases, it reflects poor nursery culture: failure to manage seedling height growth. Removal of wimpy seedlings may result in some directional selection.

Multiple sowing of bulked family seedlots has the potential to reduce genetic diversity through directional selection (El-Kassaby and Davidson, 1990). This results from the need to achieve crop uniformity at the nursery. Bulking of seed orchard seedlots, even though expendient economically, can result in different family compositions after nursery culture compared to that of the sown seed (Johnson *et al.*, 1984). This invalidates an assumption about nursery culture that seedlot genetic distribution is unaltered by culture (St Clair and Adams, 1993). The significance depends on the degree the family contributions have been altered in the seedling crop (St Clair and Adams, 1993). The process probably is significant.

## 4.4 Seedlot Construction

Directional selection in the nursery could be addressed at the seed orchard by collecting and processing seed by family (Perry and Hafley, 1981; Johnson *et al.*, 1984). This is practized on an operational basis by some organizations (Long and Peoples, 1991). Managing seeds of different families and year classes separately will not only address directional selection, it also has the potential to increase the number of plantable seedlings from a seed orchard (Perry and Hafley, 1981). However, the potential benefits of family segregation must be weighed against the extra costs involved in increased handling and record keeping at the seed orchard, nursery, and planting site. Managing by family can also ensure the best genetic material (highest ranked) is used first. When bulked family seedlots are established, a proportion of high performance families remain in seed storage while individuals of lower performing (ranked) families are taken to the field. This has the potential to minimize gain in the plantation.

If families are grown in pure rather than bulked mixtures in the nursery, potential benefits are i) increased seedling quality and crop uniformity, ii) minimized number of culls, iii) enhanced realized gains, iv) ensured genetic composition (diversity) of the seedling crop, v) no imposed directional selection during nursery production, and vi) family specific information with respect to nursery cultural practices. From logistic and economic viewpoints, it is not practical to manage by family in seed orchards and nurseries. A compromise would be to single sow seed and to group families into seedlots according to germination behaviour and nursery growth. In the open pollinated family (Fig. 3), there would be four seedlots based on germination rates. Family specific information will be requisite to group families with like germination and nursery growth behaviours into seedlots. After nursery production, these seedlots comprised of few families can be treated as described below for pure family cultures.

At the end of nursery culture, family segregation can be maintained by planting families in a mosaic of pure blocks (St Clair and Adams, 1993). This offers opportunities of i) controlling the genetic composition of the outplantings, ii) enhancing the gains through preferential planting of better families on better sites, and iii) managing sites for the most appropriate end products. Alternatively, families can be mixed prior to planting. This maximizes seedling recovery and maintains high plantation diversity. The decision to bulk may ultimately come down to questions of biology, degree to which families are diminished or lost, versus logistics and economics, extra costs involved with increased handling and record keeping.

## 5. CONCLUSION

Decisions made by seed orchard management can affect nursery operations. The outcome is usually increased crop variation at the nursery. Nursery decisions to minimize crop variation can result in directional selection of bulked family seedlots. This violates an important assumption about nursery culture. That is, nursery activities do not alter the allelic frequency of the seedlot. Directional selection can be overcome at the nursery by growing families or groups of like behaving families, rather than bulked family seedlots. This approach also has the potential to increase the number of plantable seedlings from a seed orchard. However, growing by family or like family group increases costs at both the nursery and the seed orchards. The decision to bulk or not to bulk families is based on the biological and economic realities of each seed orchard.

Many of the above problems arise because selection, breeding, seed production, nursery culture and plantation forestry are treated as discrete entities. They are not discrete. They are parts of a continuum. In order to maximize plantation gains, all participants must modify their practices so that the negative impacts of their program on others is minimized.

Regardless of overall program modifications, refinement of current nursery practices (operations) could result in i) substantial reductions in the amount of seed used, ii) maintenance of genetic diversity, and iii) field deployment of desired genotypes in known numbers to known locations. Some modifications would reduce costs and others would increase them. Regardless, cultural refinements have the potential to maximize both plantation gain and genetic diversity.

## ACKNOWLEDGEMENTS

This work was supported by the Research and Silviculture Practices Branches of the British Columbia Forest Service. J. Konishi is responsible for spurring my interest on the topic. T. Story prepared the figures and ran statistical analyses. The constructive criticism of G. Dunsworth, M. Carlson, P. Puttonen, T. Story, K. Thomas, J. Weber and E. Stjernberg has been most helpful.

### REFERENCES

Allen, G.S. 1960. Factors affecting the viability and germination behaviour of coniferous seed. IV. Stratification period and incubation temperature, *Pseudotsuga menziesii* (Mirb.) Franco. *For. Chron.* **36**: 18–19.

Allen, G.S. 1961. Testing Douglas-fir seed for provenance. *Proc. Intl. Seed Test. Assoc.* **26**: 388–403.

Bhardwaj, S.D. and Chakraborty, A.K. 1994. Studies on the time of seed collection, sowing and presowing seed treatments of *Terminalia bellirica* Roxb. and *Terminalia chebula* Retz. *Ind. For.* **120**: 430–438.

Bjornstad, A. 1981. Photoperiodic after-effects of parent plant envrionment in Norway spruce (*Picea abies* (L.) Karst.) seedlings. *Rep. Norwegian For. Res. Inst.* **36**(6): 1–30.

Bowden-Green, R. and Rooke, H. 1980. Projected recovery of plantable trees per bed foot. BC For. Serv., Silv. Branch, Unpublished Rep., Victoria, BC. [cited in Campbell and Sorensen, 1984].

Boyer, J.N., Duba, E.S. and South, D.B. 1987. Emergence timing affects root collar diameter and mortality in loblolly pine seedlings. *New For.* **1**: 135–140.

Burdon, R.D. and Sweet, G.B. 1976. The problem of interpreting differences in tree growth shortly after planting. *In*: M.G.R. Cannell and F.T. Last (Eds) Tree Physiology and Yield Improvement. London, Academic Press, 383–502.

Burgar, R.J. 1964. The effect of seed size on germination, survival and initial growth in white spruce. *For. Chron.* **40**: 93–97.

Campbell, R.K. and Sorensen, F.C. 1984. Genetic implications of nursery practices. *In*: M.L. Duryea and T.D. Landis (Eds) Forest Nursery Manual: Production of Bareroot Seedlings. The Hague, Martinus Nijhoff/Dr W Junk Publ. 183–191.

Chaisurisri, K. and El-Kassaby, Y.A. 1993. Estimation of clonal contribution to cone and seed crops in a Sitka spruce seed orchard. *Ann. Sci. For.* **50**: 461–467.

Chaisurisri, K., Edwards, D.G.W. and El-Kassaby, Y.A. 1992. Genetic control of seed size and germination in Sitka spruce. *Silvae Genet.* **41**: 348–355.

Chaisurisri, K., Edwards, D.G.W. and El-Kassaby, Y.A. 1994. Effect of seed size on seedling attributes in Sitka spruce. *New For.* **8**: 81–87.

Czabator, F.J. 1962. Germination value: an index combining speed and completeness of pine seed germination. *For. Sci.* **8**: 386–396.

Ehrenberg, C., Gustafsson, A., Plym-Forshell, C. and Simak, M. 1955. Seed quality and the principles of forest genetics. *Hereditas* **41**: 292–365.

El-Kassaby, Y.A. and Davidson, R. 1990. Impact of crop management practices on the seed crop genetic quality in a Douglas-fir seed orchard. *Silvae Genet.* **39**: 230–237.

El-Kassaby, Y.A., Edwards, D.G.W. and Taylor, D.W. 1992. Genetic control of germination parameters in Douglas-fir and its importance for domestication. *Silvae Genet.* **41**: 48–54.

Ellis, R.H. 1992. Seed and seedling vigor in relation to crop growth and yield. *Crop Growth Regul.* **11**: 249–255.

Eriksson, G., Jonsson, A. and Lindgren D.L. 1973. Flowering in a clone trial of *Picea abies* Karst. Stud. *For. Suec.* **110**: 1–45.

Hawkins, C.D.B. 1993. Genetic-induced variation of container nursery-cultured interior spruce in British Columbia. *In*: J. Laverau (Ed.) Proc. 24th Meet. Can. Tree Improv. Assoc., Fredericton, NB, August 15–19, 1993, Part 2, Ottawa, On, Natural Resources Canada. 115–127.

Hawkins, C.D.B. and Hooge, B.D. 1988. Blackout and postplanting bud phenology in Sxs spruce seedlings. *In*: T.D. Landis (Tech. Coord.) Proc. West. For. Nursery Assoc. Meet., Vernon, BC, August 8–11, 1988, Fort Collins, CO, USDA-USFS, Gen. Tech. Rep. RM-167, 54–56.

Hellum, A.K. 1976. Grading seed by weight in white spruce. *Tree Plant Notes* **27(1)**: 16–17, 23–24.

Johnsen, O. and Ostreng, G. 1994. Effects of plus-tree selection and seed orchard environment of progeny of *Picea abies*. *Can. J. For. Res.* **24**: 32–38.

Johnsen, O., Dietrichson, J. and Skaret, G. 1989. Phenotypic changes in progenies of northern clones of *Picea abies* (L.) Karst. grown in a southern seed orchard. III. Climate change and growth in a progeny trial. *Scand. J. For. Res.* **4**: 343–350.

Johnson J.R., Robinson, G. and Kellison, R.C. 1984. Sycamore seedlings from the nursery—not the same composition as the collected seedlot. *Tree Plant. Notes* **35**(3): 34–35.

Lambeth, C.C. 1980. Juvenile—mature correlation in Pinaceae and implications for early selection. *For. Sci.* **26**: 571–580.

Lang, H-P. 1989. Risks arising from the reduction of the genetic variability of some Alpine Norway spruce provenances by size grading. *Forestry* **62**(Suppl): 49–52.

Leadem, C.L. 1982. Seed testing. *In*: D.F.W. Pollard, D.G. Edwards, C.W. Edwards, C.W. Yeatman (Eds) Proc. 18th Meet. Can. Tree Improv. Assoc. Duncan, BC, August 17–20, 1981. Part 2, Ottawa, ON, Canadian Forest Service. 159–174.

Lerner, I.M. 1958. The Genetic Basis of Selection. New York, John Wiley and Sons.

Lindgren, D. and Wei, R. P. 1994. Effects of maternal environment on mortality and growth of young *Pinus sylvestris* in field trials. *Tree Physiol.* **14**: 323–327.

Long, E.M. and Peoples, B.A. 1991. Nursery management and tree improvement. *In*: Nursery Manage. Workshop Proc., Texas A and M Univ. Austin, TX, Texas For. Serv. Publ. No. **148**: 119–126.

Mexal, J.T. and Fisher, J.T. 1987. Size hierarchy in conifer seedbeds. I. Time of emergence. *New For.* **1**: 187–196.

Morgenstern, E.K. 1976. The seed source environment interaction: a factor in nursery management. *For. Chron.* **52**: 199–204.

Perry, T.O. and Hafley, W.L. 1981. Variation in seedling growth rates: their genetic and physiological basis. *In:* Proc. 16th S. For. Tree Improve. Conf., Blacksburg, VA, May 26–29, 1981. Athens, GA, USDA- USFS, For. Sci. Lab. 200–204.

Reich, P.B., Oleksyn, J. and Tjoelker, M.G. 1994. Seed mass effects on germination and growth of diverse European Scots pine population. *Can. J. For. Res.* **24**: 306–320.

Roche, L. 1969. A genecological study of the genus *Picea* in British Columbia. *New Phytol.* **68**: 505–554.

Rowe, J.S. 1964. Environmental preconditioning with special reference to forestry. *Ecology* **45**: 399–403.

Saleem, M., Bhardwaj, S.D. and Kaushal, A.N. 1994. Effects of seed weight, nitrogen source and split application on growth of *Celtris australis* L. *Ind. For.* **120**: 236–241.

Silen, R. and Osterhaus, C. 1979. Reduction of genetic base by sizing of bulked Douglas–fir seedlots. *Tree Plant. Notes* **30**(1): 24–30.

St. Clair, J.B. and Adams, W.T. 1993. Family composition of Douglas-fir nursery stock as influenced by seed characteristics, mortality and culling practices. *New For.* **7**: 319–329.

Stoehr, M.U., Weber, J.E. and Painter, R.A. 1994. Pollen contamination effects on progeny from an off-site Douglas-fir seed orchard. *Can. J. For. Res.* **24**: 2113–2117.

Thompson, D.G. and Pfeifer, A.R. 1992. Future options for the genetic improvement of conifers. I. Current and near term technologies. *Irish For.* **49**: 27–39.

Westoboy, M. 1981. How diversified seed germination behavior is selected. *Amer. Naturl.* **118**: 882–885.

Zobel, B.J., Barber, J., Brown, C.L. and Perry, T.O. 1958. Seed orchards. Their concept and management. *J. For.* **56**: 815–825.

# 10

# Genetic Improvement Program of *Prosopis* in Northeastern Brazil

*Paulo Cesar Fernandes Lima*[1]

**ABSTRACT**

This paper reports the strategies of the genetic improvement program carried out by EMBRAPA, for the *Prosopis* species. The results obtained with the introduction of species from different ecological zones in the world are presented, as well as the techniques of asexual propagation to establish a clonal seed orchard. Sixteen species of *Prosopis* from several provenances were introduced from Peru, Argentina, Chile, Senegal, Pakistan, Mexico, Cape Verde, Paraguay, Honduras and United States of America, from 1984 to 1994. The best species established in terms of survival and growth were *P. juliflora, P. pallida, P. velutina, P. glandulosa, P. cineraria* and *P. affinis.* Aspects of wood and fodder production and quality of some *Prosopis* species are also presented.

## 1. INTRODUCTION

*Prosopis* naturally occurs in Brazil, in the southeastern areas of the State of Rio Grande do Sul as *P. affinis* and *P. nigra*, and in the extreme south of the State of Mato Grosso do Sul as *P. rubriflora, P. ruscifolia* and *P. friebrigii* (Allen and Valls, 1987; Silva, 1988). Although *Prosopis* occurs naturally in those areas, the principal cultivation and use of the species of this genus are found in the northeastern region, in the semi-arid zone of Brazil. In the mid 1980s the preference for *P. juliflora* increased among other dry farming crops in the region, because of its importance as fuelwood and charcoal, fences, livestock, forage and human nutrition amongst the rural population. Due to its economic

[1]EMBRAPA-CPATSA, Caixa Postal 23, 56300-000 Petrolina, PE, Brazil.

importance for the region and considering the hypothesis of its restricted genetic base (Pires *et al.*, 1988), it is necessary, in short and middle terms, to establish a genetic improvement program to increase the variability among the trees and reduce the risk of inbreeding in the existing population, besides increasing the wood and fodder production by the use of selected trees.

For *Prosopis*, EMBRAPA initiated a genetic improvement program in 1981, through the Agriculture and Livestock Research Center for the Semi-Arid Tropic (CPATSA). This paper reports on the strategies of introduction, evaluation, '*ex situ*' conservation and asexual techniques for *Prosopis* species in a program for genetic improvement of this genus in Northeastern Brazil.

## 2. BASIS OF THE PROGRAM

The main purpose of this project is to introduce, evaluate and select species and provenances of *Prosopis* for different sites; to carry out '*ex situ*' genetic conservation of the best materials and, through asexual propagation establish a clonal seed orchard for commercial seed supply. The program is coordinated by CPATSA, located at Petrolina, State of Pernambuco, at 09°09' latitude south and 40°22' longitude west, at an altitude of 365 m. The program of *Prosopis* is financed by the Brazilian Government, but during four years, January 1987 to December 1990, EMBRAPA received financial help from the International Development Research Center (IDRC).

### 2.1 Area of Study

The program was carried out in the semi-arid zone of Brazil, which represents 75 per cent of Northeastern Brazil (between the latitude of 1° and 18°30' S and longitude 30°30' and 48°20'W). The semi-arid zone represents 13 per cent of the total area of Brazil. Petrolina, where CPATSA is located, is situated in the landscape called 'Depressao Sertaneja'. This landscape comprises 22 per cent of the Northeastern region and it is characterized by a gently undulating area broken by a few rocky hills and a narrow valley with a dissect slope. In general, the soils are shallow Latosols with a low water-holding capacity and a low organic content. They are generally deficient in phosphorous and have pH values ranging from 5 to 7.

According to the Koppen climatic classification, the climate of the region is the BSh type with irregular rainfall, concentrated during 2–4 months of the year, with distinct wet and dry seasonal stations. The annual dry season usually begins in May–April and extends to December. Droughts are frequent. The annual rainfall average varies from 350 to 500 mm and the temperature average is 27°C.

### 2.2 Methodology

The procedures for introduction of species, provenances, progeny trials and '*ex situ*' conservation of *Prosopis* of this program were according to Ferreira and Araujo (1981), Shimizu *et al.* (1982) and Palmberg (1980). The programme had the phases of (a) selecting species and provenances; (b) selecting superior trees within the provenances; and (c) crossing among superior trees for seed production supply.

In the process of selection of superior trees, the first step is to test their ability to survive, grow and reproduce in the environmental conditions of the introduction site. The most used method of selection of forest species in Brazil is the 'independent levels of selection'. It is based on the establishment of a minimum level for each character where all the individuals below that level are discarded without taking into consideration other characters. This method is indicated when genetic correlations between the characters of interest for the selection are positive and significant (Higa *et al.*, 1991).

The main purpose of a base population of *Prosopis* species is to maintain the original genetic variability and to allow races to be formed. Variability can be maintained in different provenances by keeping them separate from each other or by mixing them for recombinations to occur. Although selection eliminates part of this variability, selected trees will be grouped into one population for crosses and selection. The cross system may be of open or controlled pollination.

The methodology for seed collection consisted of getting the seeds from a minimum of 25 randomized mother trees spaced at 50–100 m. In each tree, the same amount of seeds are collected. The provenance seedlot was constituted by mixing seeds of 25 trees. Before storage, the seeds were fumigated to control insects and fungi, and stored at a temperature of 8–10 °C and 30–40 per cent of relative humidity, in a plastic bag. In the region, the presence of *Mimosets mimose* (F), harming seeds of *Prosopis*, is very common.

## 3. *PROSOPIS* INTRODUCTIONS

The references regarding the establishment of the first *P. juliflora* population in Northeast are contradictory. Officially, this species was introduced in Serra Talhada, State of Pernambuco, in 1942, with seeds from Piura, Peru (Azevedo, 1961; Gomes, 1961). Two other introductions were made in 1947 and 1948, in Angicos, State of Rio Grande do Norte, with seeds from Peru and Sudan, respectively (Azevedo, 1955). According to Azevedo (1982a), the seedlings planted at Serra Talhada were destroyed when the planting was young. However on the same site a small population of *P. juliflora* planted in 1942 is still growing probably due to natural regeneration and planting.

Lima and Silva (1991), selecting *P. juliflora* trees for progeny test at Serra Talhada, found some trees with fruits different from the morphological characteristics described for the species. Analyses of the botanical material collected from those trees were identified as *P. affinis*. It suggests that in the seedlot introduced in 1942, there were seeds from *P. juliflora* and *P. affinis* trees, or even, from hybrids of those species. At that time, there was no genetic control in the process of collecting the seeds. According to Gomes (1961), the *Prosopis* seedlot introduced in 1942 from Peru was obtained from stables, after the pods had been given to horses for feeding.

For the genetic improvement program of *Prosopis* in the region, the other point to be considered is the number of trees that originated the whole population of *P. juliflora* in the Northeast. According to Azevedo (1982a), only four trees started the population of Angicos, because of the low survival in the phase of planting. Assuming that the planting at Serra Talhada was destroyed and that only four trees constituted the origin of all *P. juliflora* population of Northeastern Brazil, and that Pires *et al.* (1988) found a low genetic variability for growth characteristics in open pollinated *P. juliflora* progeny trial, it is presumed that there is the existence of a narrow genetic base of this species in the region.

The first *Prosopis* seed introduction by EMBRAPA was made in 1982 with seedlots of *P. tamarugo, P. alba* and *P. chilensis* from Chile, *P. velutina* and *P. glandulosa* var. *torreyana* from USA, and *P. pallida* from Peru. The seeds of *P. tamarugo, P. chilensis* and *P. alba*, from Chile, were collected by Instituto Forestal de Chile (INFOR) and Corporation Nacional Forestal de Chile (CONAF) in collaboration with EMBRAPA.

In 1985, a second introduction was made. *P. alba, P. chilensis, P. argentina, P. torquata, P. nigra, P. flexuosa* and *P. strombulifera* were introduced from Argentina. The seeds were collected by EMBRAPA in collaboration with the Universidad de Catamarca and Estancias del Conlara SA. Table 1 shows the seedlots of *Prosopis* studied by EMBRAPA-CPATSA. Other institutes had sent seeds for testing in the region, like FAO and Danida Forest Seed Centre (DFSC). With these materials, it was possible to start the program and establish trials for selecting species and provenances of *Prosopis* for the region.

### 3.1 Establishment of Species

Ten *Prosopis* trials have been conducted by CPATSA, in order to define the best species and provenances for the region. Three introduction trials of different *Prosopis* species, one provenance test of *P. juliflora*, and two progeny tests of *P. alba* and *P. chilensis* from Chile were established in Petrolina site. The other *Prosopis* trials were established in Pedro Avelino, State of Rio Grande do Norte, Quixada, State of Ceara and in Contendas do Sincora, State of Bahia. All the experiments were set up in a randomized complete block design and *P. juliflora* was used as control.

The seedlings were produced by direct sowing in black polyethylene bags with 8 cm of diameter and 15 cm of height. At the time of planting, a 100g/plant dosage of NPK (5-14-3) was applied. During the first year of establishment, hoeing was carried out on three occasions to prevent weeds from competing with the seedlings. The methodology developed for *Prosopis* seedling production is described by Lima (1993).

### 3.2 Evaluation of Species Performance

Lima (1985 and 1988) and Andrade *et al.* (1993) established *Prosopis* trials in Northeastern Brazil.

Tables 2 and 3 show the survival percentage and height of plants for each species at Pedro Avelino and Petrolina sites, where the first experiments were

Table 1. Species and provenances of *Prosopis* used in the program of CPATSA, Northeast Brazil

| Species | Country | Provenance | Seedlot number | | Latitude | Longitude | Altitude (m) | Rainfall (mm) |
|---|---|---|---|---|---|---|---|---|
| | | | Origin | CPATSA | | | | |
| *P. affinis* | Peru | Piura | * | SF 02/89 | 5°12'S | 80°38'W | 22 | |
| *P. africana* | Senegal | | | SF 02/87 | 14°40'N | 17°26'W | | |
| *P. argentina* | Argentina | Catamarca | * | SF 01/85 | 27°30'S | 64°55'W | | |
| *P. alba* | Argentina | Catamarca | * | SF 02/85 | 27°30'S | 64°55'W | | |
| | Chile | Fundo Refresco, Tirana, Pampa del Tamarugal | INFOR-20-26/82 | SF 12-18/82 | | | | |
| *P. alba* var. *panta* | Argentina | Catamarca | * | SF 03/85 | 27°30'S | 64°55'W | | |
| *P. chilensis* | Argentina | La Rioja | * | SF 07/85 | 29°30'S | 67°00'W | | |
| | Chile | Lampa | DFSC - 1161/83 | SF-01/86 | 37°17'S | 71°53'W | 500 | 306 |
| | | Lampa | INFOR - 43/82 | SF-30/82 | 37°17'S | 71°53'W | | |
| | | Santiago | INFOR - 27-37/82 | SF/19-29/82 | 33°27'S | 70°40'W | 520 | |
| | | Ovalle | CONAF - 38-40/82 | SF-31-33/82 | | | | |
| | | Combarbala | CONAF - 41/82 | SF-34/82 | | | | |
| *P. cineraria* | Pakistan | D.I. Khan | DFSC - 1235/84 | SF 02/86 | 31°15'N | 70°45'E | 330 | 300 |
| *P. flexuosa* | Argentina | La Rioj | * | SF-04/85 | 29°30'S | 67°00'W | | |
| | Chile | Copiado | DFSC - 1457/84 | SF-03/86 | 27°18'S | 70°45'W | 300 | 15 |
| *P. glandulosa* var. *juliflora* | Mexico | La Muralla | DFSC - 1205/83 | SF-04/86 | 26°45'W | 101°32'W | 880 | |
| *P. glandulosa* var. *torreyana* | Mexico | Concepcion del Oro | DFSC - 1211/83 | SF-05/86 | 24°49'N | 101°25'W | 1650 | |

***(Contd)***

*Table 1 Contd.*

| Species | Country | Provenance | Seedlot number | | Latitude | Longitude | Altitude (m) | Rainfall (mm) |
|---|---|---|---|---|---|---|---|---|
| | | | Origin | CPATSA | | | | |
| *P. glandulosa* var. *torreyana* | USA | Texas | | SF-01/83 | 27°31'N | 97°52'W | | |
| *P. juliflora* | Honduras | Comayagua | OFI - 49/83 | SF-08/86 | 14°21'N | 87°37'W | 600 | 880 |
| | Cabe Verde | Trindade | | SF-01/94 | 14°55'N | 23°31'W | | |
| | Mexico | Cananez | DFSC - 1214/ | SF-06/86 | 24°13'N | 104°28'W | 890 | |
| | Senegal | | | SF 01/87 | | | | |
| *P. kuntsei* | Paragaui | | | SF 03/87 | | | | |
| *P. nigra* | Argentina | La Rioja | | SF 05/85 | 29°30'S | 67°00'W | | |
| *P. pallida* | Peru | Ocucaje | DFSC - 1156/83 | SF-07/86 | 14°20'S | 75°40'W | 420 | 35 |
| | | Ica | | SF 01/89 | 14°20'S | 75°30'W | | |
| | | Piura | | SF 43-46 | 5°12'S | 80°38'W | 22 | |
| *P. strombulifera* | Argentina | La Rioja | | SF 06/85 | 29°30'S | 67°00'W | | |
| *P. torquata* | Argentina | La Rioja | | SF 08/85 | 29°30'S | 67°00'W | | |
| *P. velutina* | USA | Texas | | SF 02/83 | 27°31'N | 97°52'W | | |
| *P. tamarugo* | Chile | Pampa del Tamarugal | INFOR-12-19/82 | SF-35-42/82 | | | | |
| | Chile | Fundo Refresco | INFOR - 1-11/82 | SF-01-11/82 | 25°19's | 69°52'W | 1000 | |

*Seeds collected by CPATSA.

Table 2. Survival and height of *Prosopis* species after 12, 36 and 60 months at Pedro Avelino, RN

| Species | Provenance | CPATSA seedlot | Survival (%) | | | Height (m) | | |
|---|---|---|---|---|---|---|---|---|
| | | | 12 | 36 | 60 | 12 | 36 | 60 |
| *P. alba* | Chile | SF 12–18/82 | 91 | 71 | 65 | 0.97 | 1.68 | 2.00 |
| *P. chilensis* | Chile | SF 19–29/82 | 96 | 85 | 56 | 0.80 | 1.93 | 2.12 |
| *P. juliflora* | Brazil | * | 98 | 96 | 89 | 1.02 | 2.01 | 2.96 |
| *P. pallida* | Peru | SF 43–46/82 | 95 | 86 | 77 | 0.76 | 1.70 | 2.54 |

*Seeds from Petrolina, PE.
Source: Andrade *et al.* (1993).

Table 3. Survival, height, diameter at breast height (DBH) and crown diameter of *Prosopis* species at Petrolina, at eight years of age (Trial I)

| Species | CPATSA seedlot | Survival (%) | Height (m) | Diameter at 0.30 m (cm) | DBH (cm) | Crown Diameter (m) |
|---|---|---|---|---|---|---|
| *P. alba* | SF 12–18/82 | 57 | 4.71 | 18.05 | 14.40 | 5.36 |
| *P. chilensis* | SF 19–29/82 | 45 | 3.67 | 13.44 | 7.64 | 3.84 |
| *P. glandulosa* | SF 01/83 | 64 | 2.33 | 10.90 | 6.11 | 3.69 |
| *P. juliflora* | local | 99 | 6.48 | 16.50 | 15.66 | 6.46 |
| *P. pallida* | SF 43–46/82 | 95 | 5.12 | 13.90 | 12.96 | 6.38 |
| *P. velutina* | SF 02/83 | 88 | 3.30 | 11.13 | 4.97 | 4.49 |

established. For semi-arid regions, the resistance to drought is a very important characteristic to be observed in plant selection. All the plants of *P. tamarugo*, from Chile, in both trials, Petrolina and Pedro Avelino, have died. The survival percentage in one year after planting showed the non adaptability of this species to the region. In Pedro Avelino, the plants died six months after planting, and in Petrolina, the survival was 1 per cent at one year of age.

The seedlots which originated the plants of the Pedro Avelino trial are the same which originated the plants of the Petrolina trial. On comparing the performance of trees in both trials, the best growth is observed in plants growing in the Petrolina site, for all species. Maybe the influence of fertility or physical characteristics of the soil have helped the performance of the plants. Both sites belong to the same climatic zone, according to Golfari and Caser (1977).

The survival of *P. velutina* and *P. glandulosa* observed in the Petrolina trial shows the adaptation of these species to this environment. High survival is found in *P. pallida*, coming from Peru, in the sites introduced (Table 3). *P. juliflora* and *P. pallida* had the best average for height and a good survival at Pedro Avelino environment, five years after planting. But trees of those species did not bear flowers and fruits during this period. In this region, it is common to find *P. juliflora* trees bearing fruits at two years of age. In the Petrolina site, *P. juliflora, P. velutina* and *P. pallida* started bearing fruits at around 21 months of age. *P. glandulosa* and *P. alba* started bearing fruits three years after planting and a few plants of *P. chilensis* at five years of age. The pod production of *P. alba* and *P. chilensis* was very irregular during nine years of observation.

Tables 4 and 5 show the results obtained with *Prosopis* planted in Petrolina, in two field trials with different spacing, with 56 and 48 months of age, respectively. *P. pallida* and *P. affinis*, introduced from Peru, showed a good performance in both trials. The survival of the species introduced from Chile was 8 per cent for *P. flexuosa* and 26 per cent for *P. chilensis*. The fruit formation started in the second year after planting. *P. glandulosa, P. juliflora, P. pallida* and *P. cineraria* were the species that showed regular fruit bearing.

Table 4. Survival and height of some species and provenances of *Prosopis* at 56 months of age in Petrolina site (Trial II)

| Species | Provenance | CPATSA seedlot | Survival (%) | Height (m) | Diameter at 0.30 m | Crown Diameter (m) |
|---|---|---|---|---|---|---|
| *P. alba* | Argentina | SF 02/85 | 50 | 3.22 | 10.72 | 5.38 |
| *P. alba* | Argentina | SF 03/85 | 62 | 2.48 | 6.42 | 2.93 |
| *P. chilensis* | Argentina | SF 07/85 | 39 | 2.70 | 7.77 | 3.62 |
| *P. chilensis* | Chile | SF 01/86 | 26 | 2.94 | 7.63 | 3.12 |
| *P. cineraria* | Pakistan | SF 02/86 | 81 | 2.71 | 7.41 | 3.87 |
| *P. flexuosa* | Argentina | SF 04/85 | 67 | 2.44 | 5.96 | 2.81 |
| *P. flexuosa* | Chile | SF 03/86 | 8 | 2.37 | 6.65 | 3.15 |
| *P. glandulosa* | Mexico | SF 05/86 | 76 | 2.46 | 5.15 | 3.08 |
| *P. juliflora* | Brazil | local | 87 | 4.25 | 10.04 | 5.38 |
| *P. nigra* | Argentina | SF 05/85 | 56 | 2.07 | 4.55 | 2.77 |
| *P. pallida* | Peru | SF 01/82 | 79 | 4.48 | 11.04 | 5.81 |
| *P. pallida* | Peru | SF 43–46/82 | 89 | 4.20 | 9.23 | 4.95 |

Table 5. Survival and height of *Prosopis* species at 48 months of age, spaced 3 × 2.5 m in Petrolina–PE (Trial III)

| Species | CPATSA seedlot | Survival (%) | Height (m) |
|---|---|---|---|
| *P. affinis* | SF 02/89 | 100 | 2.84 |
| *P. alba* | SF 03/85 | 96 | 1.63 |
| *P. cineraria* | SF 02/86 | 96 | 1.55 |
| *P. flexuosa* | SF 04/85 | 96 | 1.57 |
| *P. juliflora* | local | 100 | 2.80 |
| *P. kuntsei* | SF 03/87 | 78 | 0.67 |
| *P. nigra* | SF 05/85 | 100 | 1.01 |
| *P. pallida* | SF 43–46/82 | 100 | 2.18 |

Table 6 shows survival, height, crown and diameter at 0.30 m of *P. juliflora* from Honduras, Mexico and Senegal, used for increasing the genetic base of this species in the region. The performances of trees from seeds introduced from Senegal are very similar to Brazil, but trees raised from Mexico and

Table 6. Survival and height of *Prosopis juliflora* provenances in Petrolina – PE at 54 months of age

| Provenance | CPATSA seedlot | Survival (%) | Height (m) | Crown Diameter (m) | Diameter at 0.30 m (cm) | No. of stems at 0.30 m |
|---|---|---|---|---|---|---|
| Honduras | 08/86 | 80 | 1.60 | 4.85 | * | 4 |
| Senegal | 01/87 | 68 | 3.62 | 5.42 | 9.42 | 2 |
| Mexico | 04/86 | 44 | 2.12 | 3.18 | 5.05 | 3 |
| Brazil | local | 44 | 4.06 | 5.83 | 10.14 | 3 |

* Not evaluated.

Honduras seeds showed different characteristics in pod production and pattern of growth. Trees originating from Mexico seedlot produced reddish pods similar in colour to *P. affinis* pods, and trees from Honduras had an initial growth in the first two years with pronounced plagiotropic shoots more or less hortizontal and long thorns.

Although the seedlots are said to be of *P. juliflora*, the morphological characteristics of the provenances do not correspond to the description given by Burkart (1976) for this species. Additional taxonomic studies are necessary on *Prosopis*, mainly on *P. juliflora*. According to Stewart *et al.* (1992), *P. juliflora* links the two centres of diversity in the genus and is the only species native to Central America. It is closely related to the species in South America, including *P. pallida* and *P. affinis*, and in North America, including *P. laevigata* and *P. glandulosa*.

The taxonomy used for some *Prosopis* is uncertain. In most of the literature, *P. glandulosa* is designated as *P. juliflora* (National Academy of Science, 1979). According to Ferreyra (1987), the species denominated *P. juliflora* that grows in Peru do not correspond in morphological aspects to the species denominated *P. juliflora* that grows in Central America.

### 3.3 Wood Production

The data for biomass produced in *Prosopis* is presented in Table 7. The biomass production was found to be the maximum in *P. juliflora* trees: 27.1 tons per hectare. This value is significantly higher compared to the other species introduced in the trial. *Prosopis pallida*, with a yield of 15.7 tons per hectare, is the second species in the rank. There was no statistical difference among *P. chilensis, P. alba, P. glandulosa* and *P. velutina* for wood production. The percentage contribution of leaf biomass to total biomass ranged from 5.6 to 17.3 per cent. Higher percentage of leaves was found in *P. glandulosa*. Analysis of dry matter weight in different diameter classes showed *P. juliflora* and *P. alba* as the species with the lowest percentage of woody dry material in classes under 3.0 cm of diameter.

In all other species more than 50 per cent of their woody dry matter is found in classes under 3.0 cm of diameter. The basic density of the wood found in *Prosopis* planted at Petrolina ranged from 0.66 to 0.91 g/cm$^3$ among

Table 7. Dry wood biomass (ton/ha) of *Prosopis* species at eight years of age by diameter classes in Petrolina–PE

| Classes Stem and branches | *P. alba* | *P. chilensis* | *P. glandulosa* | *P. juliflora* | *P. pallida* | *P. velutina* |
|---|---|---|---|---|---|---|
| < 1 cm | 1.556 (25) | 0.924 (32) | 1.517 (43) | 4.609 (17) | 4.653 (30) | 1.431 (33) |
| 1.1–3.0 | 1.173 (19) | 0.765 (26) | 1.108 (31) | 5.828 (21) | 3.330 (21) | 1.540 (35) |
| 3.1–5.0 | 1.066 (17) | 0.581 (20) | 0.441 (12) | 6.230 (25) | 2.726 (17) | 0.822 (19) |
| 5.1–7.0 | 0.765 (12) | 0.246 (8) | 0.159 (5) | 3.985 (15) | 2.052 (13) | 0.191 (4) |
| 7.1–9.0 | 0.608 (10) | 0.179 (6) | 0.166 (5) | 2.982 (11) | 1.363 (9) | 0.196 (5) |
| > 9.0 | 1.104 (17) | 0.237 (8) | 0.138 (4) | 2.982 (11) | 1.535 (10) | 0.170 (4) |
| Total (ton/ha) | 6.272 c | 2.932 c | 3.529 c | 27.109 a | 15.666 b | 4.350 c |

**Note:** Numbers in parentheses show the mean percentage related to the total. Means followed by the same letter in a row do not differ statistically at the 5% level by Duncan test.

the species. The highest value was found in *P. juliflora*. This value increases the advantage of this species for firewood production.

### 3.4 Fodder Production

The variation in *Prosopis* pod production and pod characteristics like size and protein content is large in the region. According to Azevedo (1982b), the pod production of *Prosopis* in the semi-arid environment ranges from 2 to 3 ton/ha/year and in the humid zones 8 tons has been recorded in Northeastern Brazil.

Lima (1987) studied the correlation between the pod production and the environment in *P. juliflora* cultivated at Petrolina. High temperature, low rainfall and low relative humidity stimulated pod production but varied in yields. In 15-year old trees spaced 10 × 10 m pod production ranged from 5 to 192 kg/tree. The average pod production was 78 kg/tree/year. Felker (1982) found in 5-year old progenies of *P. velutina* pod production ranging from zero to 12.6 kg/tree. In Piura, Peru, Valdivia (1982) concluded that the selected trees of *P. pallida* can produce 60 to 80 kg of pods/tree/year.

Pod production of *P. juliflora* planted in Petrolina during different years of growth is shown in Table 8. In the silvicultural system, as is evident, *P. juliflora* and *P. pallida* showed decrease in pod yield and number of trees producing fruits with age. This is due to narrow spacing and the closure of crown which affected pod production. For *P. velutina* and *P. glandulosa*, the pod yield and number of trees bearing fruits increased with age due to shruby growth.

Table 8. Pod mean yield of *Prosopis* species (g/tree) up to seven years in Petrolina - PE

| Species | Age (years) | | | | | |
|---|---|---|---|---|---|---|
| | 2 | 3 | 4 | 5 | 6 | 7 |
| *P. glandulosa* | 0 | 10.2 | 72.8 | 293.5 | 455.5 | 1359.3 |
| *P. juliflora* | 399.7 | 93.0 | 93.2 | 141.9 | 80.2 | 22.3 |
| *P. pallida* | 361.2 | 232.6 | 346.9 | 1245.6 | 1270.0 | 459.5 |
| *P. velutina* | 23.8 | 84.9 | 601.3 | 1503.0 | 1761.6 | 1742.1 |

Oliveira and Pires (1988) studied the reproductive system and pollination efficiency as the possible cause for low fruit output per inflorescence in *P. juliflora*. They found 269 to 456 flowers per inflorescence. The pollination efficiency in relation to the number of inflorescence and in relation to the number of flowers was 29 and 1.5 per cent, respectively. It is also important to know the pollinating agents, the pollen release period and stigma receptivity to explain the low pollination efficiency in *Prosopis* in the region.

Crude protein (CP) and *'in vitro'* dry matter digestibility (IVDMD) of *Prosopis* species are, in general, superior to some native fodder species (Table 9). The *'in vitro'* rumen fermentation technique is used for estimating relative digestion rates in ruminants and for measuring nutritional value of forages.

Another important point analysed in fodder nutritional status is the tannin level. The determination of tannin content in leaves is important because of its ability to combine with plant proteins in the rumen and its implications in reducing bloat and improving protein utilization. Plant tannins are complex phenolic polymers which vary in chemical structure and biological activity. Two groups of natural tannins are found: hydrolysable tannins, which occur mainly in fruit pods and plant galls, and condensed tannins, commonly found in forage.

Table 9. Data of Crude Protein (CP), '*in vitro*' dry matter digestibility (IVDMD) and tannin content in leaves and pods of *Prosopis* species in Petrolina-PE

| Species | Pods | | Leaves | | |
|---|---|---|---|---|---|
| | CP (%) | IVDMD (%) | CP (%) | IVDMD(%) | Tannin (%) |
| *P. alba* | – | – | 23.27 | 57.06 | 1.97 |
| *P. chilensis* | – | – | 24.03 | 31.63 | 4.37 |
| *P. glandulosa* | 10.36 | 79.65 | 21.24 | 60.16 | 2.25 |
| *P. juliflora* | 7.82 | 74.59 | 18.49 | 59.06 | 1.89 |
| *P. pallida* | 8.08 | 67.91 | 17.83 | 55.55 | 2.01 |
| *P. velutina* | 11.35 | 71.40 | 23.59 | 57.94 | 2.25 |

**Source**: Lima, 1994.

Hydrolysable tannins, but not condensed tannins, are digested by animals (McLeod, 1974). The tannin levels in the leaves of *Prosopis* varied among species (Table 9).

## 4. ASEXUAL PROPAGATION

Self-incompatibility in *Prosopis* results in the formation of outcrossed trees. In order to obtain seedlings with genetically identical characters of the mother tree it is essential to develop asexual propagation techniques.

The technique used at CPATSA consists of selecting trees on the basis of architecture, pod quality, pod production, disease and insect resistance. The main objective is to establish a clonal seed orchard using seedlings raised by rooting cuttings of superior mother trees. Lima (1988b) described the technique developed at CPATSA. Techniques of grafting were carried out, but the success is not satisfactory. Grafting *P. juliflora* onto *P. juliflora*, produced a sucess rate of only 5 per cent. There is a need to examine further graft compatibility between *P. pallida* and *P. juliflora*, and between *P. cineraria* and *P. juliflora*. The success of this process will permit to change population of *P. juliflora* with low pod production onto trees with desired characteristics.

## 5. FINAL CONSIDERATIONS

The process of genetic improvement of *Prosopis* in Northeastern Brazil is in the first stage, with the introduction and selection of species and provenances from natural zones of occurrence for specified sites and uses. The criteria of superior tree selection is based on survival, fast growth and the ability to produce qualitative and quantitative fodder and wood. The fodder quality is evaluated on the basis of protein and tannin content and '*in vitro*' dry matter digestibility.

The genus *Prosopis* shows variability not only in terms of a large number of species, but also in possibility of interspecific crosses (Hunziker *et al.*, 1986). Despite introduction of many species in the past, still a large number of species, provenances, varieties and hybrids needs to be tested.

Among the present introductions the best species for increasing wood yield are *P. pallida* and *P. affinis* from Peru; while for pod production, *P. glandulosa* and *P. velutina* from Mexico and USA, and *P. cineraria* from Pakistan are best.

The process of genetic conservation needs to be carried in a cooperative way, involving the maximum possible number of participants which will provide diversity of genotypes. Although a good technical cooperation exists among the Brazilian institutions, it is necessary to develop relations with international agencies and research and development institutions for exchange of ideas, materials and suggestions. Based on the results of the programme, *P. juliflora* and *P. pallida* should have priority for breeding and genetic conservation. Other species need further studies in order to know their potential.

## ACKNOWLEDGEMENTS

The author expresses his gratitude to Dr Eduardo Assis Menezes for his suggestions on this paper. Gratitude is also extended to IDRC for the financial help to the *Prosopis* programme.

## REFERENCES

Allen, A.C. and Valls, J.F.M. 1987. Recursos forrageiros nativos do Pantanal Matogrossense. Documentos. EMBRAPA CEMARGEM, Brasilia **8**: 1–339.

Andrade, G. de C., Cristo, R.C. de, Henriques, O.N. and Lima, P.C.F. 1993. Introducao e selecao de especies de *Prosopis* na regiao semi-arida do Rio Grande do Norte. *In*: Floresta para o desenvolvimento: Politica, ambiente, tecnologia e mercado. 7 th Congresso Florestal Brasileiro, 17–24 Sptember 1993, Curitiba, Brazil. Sao Paulo: SBS/SBEF, v.1, 134–136.

Azevedo, G. de 1955. Algaroba. Natal. 13 pp.

Azevedo, G. de 1961. Algaroba. Rio de Janeiro:Servico de Informacao Agricola. (Serie SIA, 843) 31 pp.

Azevedo, G. de 1982a. Como e porque a algarobeira foi introduzida no Nordeste. *In*: Algaroba. I Simposio Brasileiro sobre Algaroba, 5–7 October 1982, Natal, Brazil. Natal: EMPARN, (EMPARN, Documentos, 7). 300–306.

Azevedo, C.F. 1982b. Algarobeira na alimentacao animal de humana. *In*: Algaroba. I Simposio Brasileiro sobre Algaroba, 5–7 October 1982, Natal, Brazil. Natal: EMPARN, (EMPARN. Documentos, 7). 283–299.

Burkart, A. 1976. A monograph of the genus *Prosopis* (Leguminosae subfam. Mimosoideae). *J. Arnold Arboretum* **57**(3): 219–249.

Felker, P. 1982. Selecao de fenotipos de *Prosopis* para a producao de vagens e de combustiveis de madeira. *In*: Algaroba. I Seminario Brasileiro sobre Algaroba, 5–7 October 1982, Natal, Brazil. Natal: EMPARN, V.2. (EMPARN, Documentos, 8). 7–24.

Ferreira, M. and Araujo, A.J. de. 1981. Procedimentos e recomendacoes para testes de procedencias. Curitiba, EMBRAP-URPFCS, EMBRAPA-URPFCS. Documentos, 6, 28 pp.

Ferreyra, R. 1987. Estudio sistematico de los algarrobos de la costa norte de Peru. Lima: CONCYTEC/CIID. 31 pp.

Golfari, L. and Caser, R.L. 1977. Zoneamento ecologico da Regiao Nordeste para experimentacao florestal. Serie Tecnica PRODEPEF, Belo Horizonte, n. 10, 116 pp.

Gomes, P. 1961. A algarobeira. Rio de janeiro. Ministerio da Agricultura, Servico de Informacao Agricola. (Serie SIA, 865). 49 pp.

Higa, A.R., Resende, M.D.V. de and Souza, S.M. de 1991. Programas de melhoramento genetico de Eucalyptus no Brasil. *In*: O Desafio. O Desafio da Florestas Neotropicais, Curitiba, Brazil. 86–100.

Hunziker, J.H., Saidman, B.O., Naranjo, C.A., Palacios, R.A., Poggio, L and Burghardt, A.D. 1986. Hybridization and genetic variation of Argentine species of *Prosopis*. *For. Ecol. Mgmt.* **16**: 301–315.

Lima, P.C.F. 1985. Trabajos de investigacion com especies del genero *Prosopis* en la region semiarida del Brasil. *In:* Estado Actual del Conocimiento Sobre *Prosopis tamarugo*. Mesa Redonda Internacional Sobre *Prosopis tamarugo* Phil., 11–15 Junio 1984, Africa, Chile. Rome: FAO. 125–132.

Lima, P.C.F. 1987. Producao de vagens de algaroba. Revista da Associacao Brasileira de Algaroba, Mossoro, Vol. **2**(1): 141–170.

Lima, P.C.F. 1988a. Performance of species of the genus *Prosopis* at 24 months of age in Petrolina. *In:* The Current State of Knowledge on *Prosopis juliflora*. II Inter. Conf. *Prosopis*. 25–29 August, 1986, Recife, Brazil. Rome, FAO. 63–67.

Lima, P.C.F. 1988b. *Prosopis* vegetative propagation through cutting. *In:* The Current State of Knowledge on *Prosopis juliflora.* II Inter. Conf. on *Prosopis,* 25–29 August, 1986, Recife, Brazil. Rome: FAO. 223–227.

Lima, P.C.F. 1993. Seedling production of *Prosopis juliflora* in Northeastern Brazil. *In*: S. Puri and P.K. Khosla (Eds) Nursery Technology for Agroforestry—Applications in Arid and Semiarid Regions. New Delhi, (Winrock- Oxford & IBH series). 75–84.

Lima P.C.F. 1994. Comportamento silvicultural de especies de *Prosopis*, em Petrolina-PE, regiao semi-arida brasileira. Curitiba, Tese Doutorado. Universidade Federal do Parana. 110 pp.

Lima, P.C.F. and Silva, M.A. da 1991. Ocorrencia subespontanea de uma algaroba no Nordeste do Brasil. *Boletin de Pesquisa Florestal* (Colombo) **22/23** : 93–97.

McLeod, M.N. 1974. Plant tannnis—their role in forage quality. Nutrition Abstracts and Reviews, *Farhhan Royal* **44**(11): 803–814.

National Academy of Science. 1979. Tropical Legumes Resource for the Future. Washington, DC. 331 pp.

Oliveira, V.R. and Pires, I.E. 1988. Pollination efficiency of *Prosopis juliflora* (SW) DC in Petrolina, Pernambuco. *In:* The Current State of Knowledge on *Prosopis juliflora.* II Inter. Conf. on *Prosopis*, 25–29 August, 1986, Recife, Brazil. Rome: FAO. 233–239.

Palmberg, C. 1980. Principios y estrategia para el mejor aprovechamiento de los recursos geneticos forestales. *In*: Informe. Curso de capacitacion FAO/DANIDA sobre la mejora genetica de arboles forestales, Merida, Venezuela. Rome: FAO (Estudio FAO: Montes, 20). 27–50.

Pires, I.E., Andrade, G.de C. and Araujo, M. de S. 1988. Genetic variation for growth characteristics in *P. juliflora* progenies. *In*: The Current State of Knowledge on *Prosopis juliflora.* II Inter. Conf. on *Prosopis*, 25–29 August 1986, Recife, Brazil. Rome, FAO. 177–185.

Shimizu, J.Y., Kageyama, P.Y. and Higa A.R. 1982. Procedimentos e recomendacoes para estudos de progenies de essencias florestais. Curitiba, EMBRAPA-URPFCS, EMBRAPA-URPFCS, Documentos, 11. 34 pp.

Silva, M.A. 1988. Taxonomy and distribution of the genus *Prosopis* L. *In*: The Current State of Knowledge on *Prosopis juliflora.* II Inter. Conf. on *Prosopis*, 25–29 August 1986, Recife, Brazil. Rome: FAO. 177–185.

Stewart, J.L., Dunsdon, A.J., Hellin, J.J. and Hughes, C.E. 1992. Wood biomass estimation of Central American dry zone species. Oxford Forestry Institute, Oxford. Tropical Forestry Papers 26. 83 pp.

Valdivia, S. 1982. Assentamento e desenvolvimento rural nas zonas marginais da costa norte do Peru; Piura. *In*: Algaroba. I Simposio Brasileiro Sobre Algaroba, 5–7 October 1982, Natal, Brazil. Natal: Documentos 7. 90–111.

# 11

# Population Variation Studies and Their Application in Tree Improvement Program: An Example with *Cupressus sempervirens*

*Aristotelis C. Papageorgiou*[1]

**ABSTRACT**

Population variation studies are performed in order to describe genetic variation within and between populations. In this article an introduction to gene markers and measures of genetic variation is presented. The application of such studies in tree improvement is examined. There are three main ways of applying results of genetic variation studies in tree improvement: as an assistance for artificial selection, as an assistance for preparing provenance trials and as a control of breeding and sylvicultural activities. An example with the Mediterranean cypress (*Cupressus sempervirens* L.) is presented. Variation and differentiation of natural and artificial populations as well as clone collections are studied. The results and their application in tree improvement are discussed.

## 1. INTRODUCTION

All traits, including those of interest for tree improvement, show variations, either environmental or genetic in nature or even a combination of both. Special experiments (e.g., progeny trials) are needed to separate environmental from genetic factors, and even these laborious and time-consuming trials do not give detailed information on the number of genes involved or the amount of genetic variation within populations. In population studies, geneticists prefer

[1]WWF Greece, Filellinon 26, 105 58 Athens, Greece.

using traits that are controlled only by the genetic constitution of an individual. These traits are called *gene markers* and are defined as qualitative, environmentally stable traits whose mode of inheritance is known. Thus, it is possible to infer the genotype of a tree as a gene marker by observing its phenotype. Before using a trait as a gene marker, it must be identified as such by a procedure called *inheritance analysis* (Hattemer, 1991).

There are several types of gene markers. The most popular are:

*Morphological Traits:* First used by Mendel (1866). They are morphological traits, the expression of which is independent from the environment. They hold little relevance in studies of trees.

*Chemical Markers:* Relative content of secondary compounds such as terpenes. Their environmental and ontogenetic stability has not been established in many cases.

*Isoenzymes:* Enzymes that catalyse similar reactions in the metabolism of an organism. Their structure is directly determined by the genetic information of the DNA. They are often environmentally stable and are widely used, since codominance is widespread at the loci controlling them; alleles can therefore be detected, even in heterozygous condition.

*Molecular Markers:* Several methods to investigate DNA are in use. Restriction-Fragment-Length-Polymorphisms (RLFPs) have been studied in a number of tree species; however, the laboratory techniques for RLFP analysis are rather complicated and expensive, especially since radioactive labelling is required. New methods are based on Polymerase-Chain-Reaction (PCR). One of these methods is the investigation of Random Amplified Polymorphic DNA (RAPDs). Standardization of laboratory procedures is still a problem for these techniques. Their main disadvantage compared to isoenzymes is the absence of codominance and the high costs. After overcoming these problems molecular markers may become a powerful tool for genetic studies.

Gene markers are used for studies concerning the amount of genetic variation in populations. In order to perform *population variation studies* we need, besides a gene marker, *measures of genetic variation* as well. In this article, the ways such studies can be done and their importance for tree improvement will be presented.

## 2. MEASURES OF GENETIC VARIATION

There are different ways to measure genetic variation and choosing amongst them is not simple. The most commonly used ones will be presented here, along with comments about their meaning and importance.

### 2.1 Allelic and Genotypic Frequencies

After the identification of marker gene loci and the experimental analysis of the material, we obtain an array of genotypes for each individual examined.

The number of individuals in a population carrying the same genotype at a certain gene locus is divided by the total number of individuals in the population in order to obtain a *genotypic relative frequency.* Genotypic frequencies are estimated for all genotypes scored at a locus. In the same way we can estimate *allelic relative frequencies* (each genotype contains two alleles in diploid individuals; when they are of the same type, the individual is *homozygote*; an individual with two alleles at a gene locus representing different types is considered a *heterozygote* at this gene locus). Both genotypic and allelic frequencies are also called *genetic structures.* By observing these structures, one has an idea about how common or rare is a genetic variant (genotype or allele) in a population. Genotypic and allelic frequencies are used in order to estimate the parameters presented below.

### 2.1.1 Variation within Populations

Since gene markers are qualitative traits (they score only the existence or absence of a variant), the measures used to estimate genetic variation are not based on the traditional quantitative statistics. The two main questions about variation within population are: how many different variants exist in a population and how frequent (common) are they?

A simple expression of variation is the amount of variants at a gene locus. When alleles are concerned we call this sum *allelic multiplicity* or simply *number of different alleles n.*

This measure is important in order to determine the adaptability of a population, but does not give any information about the frequency of the alleles. Therefore we use an expression called *allelic diversity* in the level of a gene locus (Müller-Starck and Gregorius, 1986), which is also known as the *effective number of alleles* (Crow and Kimura, 1970):

$$V = [\Sigma P_i^2]^{-1}$$

The value '$P_i$' symbolizes the frequency of the 'i'th allele in a population. The allelic diversity becomes 1, when there is no variation at the gene locus concerned (only one allele present in the population). The maximum possible value of 'v' is the number of alleles '*n*' at this gene locus, when they all appear with identical frequencies ($P_i = 1/n = C$).

A derivation of allelic diversity, the term $1 - \Sigma p_i^2$ is one of the most popular measures of allelic variation at single gene loci and reflects the probability that two alleles chosen at random from an infinite population differ in type (Nei and Roychoudhury, 1974). Nei (1973) described it as *gene diversity* and later as *expected heterozygosity* He. Gregorius (1987) proposed the interpretation of

$$\delta_T = 1 - \Sigma P_i^2$$

as a measure of the *total gene differentiation* within an effectively infinite population, which most closely represents the actual meaning of this measure. As mentioned above, $\delta_T$ is indirectly related to the allelic diversity 'v':

$$\delta_T = 1 - \frac{1}{v}$$

### 2.1.2 Differentiation Between Populations

To this measure category belongs mainly the comparison between the genetic structures of two populations and the comparison of the genetic structure of a single population to all others examined.

Pairwise comparisons between populations at the level of their genetic structures are performed through a measure called *genetic distance*. There are many different genetic distances proposed. A simple one for alleles (allelic distance) is $d_o$ proposed by Gregorius (1974):

$$d_0 = \frac{1}{2} \Sigma \mid P_i - P_i' \mid$$

$P_i$ symbolizes the frequency of the i-th allele at a single locus in a population and $P_i'$ the frequency of the same allele in a second population. This genetic distance takes real, non negative values, is symmetric and becomes 0 only when the two populations compared have identical allelic structures, thus containing the same alleles with the same frequencies. $d_0$ becomes 1 only when the two populations have no allele in common. This last property makes, among other reasons, $d_o$ more appropriate than the broadly used genetic distance of Nei (1972). A comparison between genetic distances can be found in Gregorius (1974, 1984).

The genetic distance between a population and the collection of all other populations studied is a measure of *differentiation* (Gregorius and Roberds, 1986):

$$D_j = \frac{1}{2} \Sigma \mid P_i - \overline{P_i'} \mid$$

When $D_j$ is low, the respective population is representative for the collection of all populations. $D_j$ takes its minimum value, 0, when the population referred has an identical genetic structure to the collection of all other populations. $D_j$ becomes 1 when the population referred has no common variant with any other population.

The average of the $D_j$ values of all populations at the level of a single gene locus, weighted for their size, is the *average differentiation* $\delta$, an expression of non similarity (Gregorius and Roberds, 1986). $\delta$ is 0 when the populations are identical to each other and becomes 1, when there is no population with at least one allele common with any other. Nei (1973) proposed the differentiation measure *GST*, which actually expresses Wright's *FST* (1978). Although this measure is widely used, it contains conceptional flaws according to Gregorius (1988).

### 2.1.3 Heterozygosity

The occurrence of two different allele types in a genotype at a gene locus describes a heterozygote genotype. The proportion of heterozygote individuals among all individuals in a population is the *proportion of heterozygotes* at a gene locus. The proportion of gene loci at which an individoum is heterzygous, is called *heterozygosity grade* (Gregorius, 1978).

These measures should not be confused with the term 'expected heterozygosity', which is a variation measure that was presented above. In order to avoid confusion, many geneticists use the term *observed heterozygosity* for the proportion of heterozygotes at a gene locus.

The proportion of heterozygotes among individuals of a population is a parameter often used in forest tree research. Different populations or species have been analysed and characterized according to their heterozygosity. Heterozygous individuals are often considered to have an advantage over homozygotes, because they are expected to be more flexible as far as adaptive traits are concerned. A high proportion of heterozygotes in a population provide a store of genetic reserves and potential plasticity and permit a large proportion of individuals to exhibit combinations of phenotypic properties near the optimum. Therefore, they are associated with high vitality, viability, growth, resistance to air pollution and other traits, being interesting for tree improvement (e.g. Müller-Starck, 1989; Bergmann and Ruetz, 1991). Forest populations show the highest heterozygote proportions among all organisms (including humans). This fact is probably explained by their long life cycle, in which they are exposed to many environmental changes.

The proportion of heterozygotes is not a variation measure; it is a property of the genotypic structure of a population and depends mainly on the allelic variation in the previous generation, the mating system and viability selection (Hattemer, 1994; Papageorgiou, 1995).

Measures of genetic variation are calculated through specially developed computer programmes, such as BIOSYS (Swofford and Selander, 1989) and GSED (Gillet, 1994).

## 3. APPLICATION OF POPULATION STUDIES IN TREE IMPROVEMENT PROGRAMS

The possibilities of applying population studies of genetic variation in tree improvement are examined here. Studies performed are referred by means of isoenzymes. Since the beginning of the isoenzyme marker development, some descriptions of their application in forest tree breeding have been presented (Adams, 1983; Cheliak *et al.*, 1987). In this study, three main application fields are examined.

### 3.1 Assisting Artificial Selection

Trees often show interesting traits only in adult stages. Thus, one is forced wait many years in order to see whether a tree is suitable for certain purposes or not. This hold true especially in traits such as resistance to extreme environmental conditions or pests. Tree improvement procedures would become much more efficient if the desired traits would be expressed in the earlier stages of trees life. *Early selection* would then be possible.

This is possible if an enzyme variant would be correlated with an interesting morphological trait. Although much research has been done in this field and partial success has been reported (Gallo, 1991; Choi, 1993), it is rather improbable for such results to find application in the field. This can be explained by the fact that most morphological traits are controlled by a large number of genes. Yet, research has to continue in the direction of early selection, since in other, better studied organisms, such direct correlations between gene markers and morphological traits have been observed (an overview is given by Bush and Smouse, 1992).

Another application of isoenzyme gene markers as assistance to artificial selection can be seen in the probable relationship between heterozygosity and viability advantages. Many studies have indicated such relationships (e.g., Mitton and Grant, 1980; Moran *et al.*, 1989), but there have been also many exceptions (e.g. Ledig *et al.*, 1983). If such a relationship is proven, then the ability of a provenance to produce a large number of plus trees would be related to the heterozygosity of seeds collected from this provenance. Such information can help breeders concentrate on only a few provenances and save time and money. This application provides a relationship between heterozygosity at the enzyme gene loci studied and the gene loci controlling the traits that tree improvement is interested in. This would be the case, if the evolutionary factors influencing the populations studied affect the whole genome simultaneously; such factors are drift, inbreeding, founder effects, etc. Even selection at one gene locus can affect the rest of the genome (Ziehe and Muller-Starck, 1991).

### 3.2 Assisting the Preparation of Provenance Trials

Tree improvement projects usually begin with provenance and progeny tests. Their aim is to describe the amount of variation within and between provenances. Such trials usually last many years. Population studies of genetic variation cannot replace provenance trials if there is no correlation between morphological traits and isoenzyme variants. However, they can supply important information about genetic variation generally and the evolutionary factors responsible for the genetic structures observed. Such information is very useful, because the existence of genetic variation is the main prerequisite for a successful tree improvement project.

A direct comparison between patterns of genetic variation of morphological traits and isoenzymes gene markers have shown both positive (Guries and Ledig, 1981; Lagercranz and Ryman, 1990), and negative correlations (Rajora *et al.*, 1991). Finally, Lewontin (1984) proved that there is no statistical way to compare the variation patterns between morphological traits and isoenzyme markers. This fact does not reduce the effectivity of genetic variation studies at all. *It is not the direct comparison between gene markers and morphological traits, but the study of the responsible evolutionary factors, which is important for tree improvement.* Such evolutionary factors can be studied only using gene markers. There are two main ways of applying information about genetic variation in provenance trials.

1.When studies of *variation* and *heterozygosity* show clearly that a population has a narrow genetic base and was influenced by genetic drift or inbreeding, then this population should not be chosen as a provenance, since the amount of variation would not be sufficient, even for morphological traits.

2.Patterns of *differentiation* among populations can supply information about gene flow and migration isolation. The investigation of such patterns is closely related to the identification of diversity centres. According to this information, the amount and range of provenances used in a provenance trial can be determined without any loss of time or money.

### 3.3 Controlling Breeding and Silvicultural Activities

Technical mistakes can always happen during a tree improvement project. Labels are switched, records are lost, seeds are accidentally mixed, etc. Such mistakes cause huge errors in statistical procedures and give inaccurate results, which lead to incorrect conclusions and loss of valuable information. The ontogenetic and environmental stability of isozymes makes them an ideal tool to discover and correct such mistakes. The application of isoenzymes in order to control the efficiency of tree improvement activities is described in the following five cases.

A. *Clone identification:* In clone orchards or high yield plantations it can help to classify certain ramets in a clone using the 'exclusion' principle. The genotypes of clones at different gene loci are examined (multi-locus genotypes). This control gains importance for all tree improvement strategies involving micro- or macro-vegetative propagation of plants. The verification of clonal identity is especially important for clonal yield tests on multiple sites and for seed orchards, since clones might be interchanged and the rootstock might overcome the scion (Finkeldey, 1994).

B. *Controlling the validity of controlled crosses:* Such studies are based on the laws of Mendel and the 'exclusion' principle. Multi-locus genotypes are used here as well. This control is mostly used for hybrids between different species, which also gain increasing importance in forest tree improvement (Adams, 1983; Rajora and Dancik, 1992).

C. *Controlling the genetic efficiency of seed orchards:* Such studies are used in order to discover if there have been any undesired side-effects, such as self-pollination (Muller-Starck, 1979; Rudin, *et al.*, 1986), genetic contamination from 'aliens', thus pollen derived from trees not included in the seed orchard (Paule *et al.*, 1993) or non-random spreading of the pollen within the seed orchard (Muller-Starck, 1979; Mejnartowicz and Lewandowski, 1994).

D. *Origin reconstruction:* The reconstruction of origin of planted stands and orchards. Existing references on patterns of genetic variation of original population must exist. These data should show clear differences among original populations. Many studies have already been performed; yet there are many difficulties in performing such controls (Gregorius *et al.*, 1984). When large differences exist between the variation patterns of different interbreeding species, then an application of marker gene loci is possible in order to gain information about the 'genetical purity' of a species (Cheliak *et al.*, 1987).

E. *Broadness of the genetic base:* Material used for large scale afforestations should be controlled through gene markers. An intense reduction of the genetic base through intensive tree breeding or other human activities would derive populations with low adaptability and high vulnerability to environmental changes. A review of anthropogenic influence on genetic variation can be found in Ellstrand and Elam (1993).

## 4. THE CASE OF *CUPRESSUS SEMPERVIRENS*

The Mediterranean or Italian or the common cypress (*Cupressus sempervirens* L.) grows naturally in N. Iran, Syria, Cyprus, Turkey and Greece. Its range is discontinuous, consisting mainly of populations growing over a wide latitudinal, longitudinal and altitudinal range, and in regions with diverse environments.

The Mediterranean cypress has two main varieties, both known since ancient times: the variety *horizontalis*, with a broad crown and wide angles between branches and stem, and the variety *pyramidalis*, with a conical crown form and small angles between branches and stem. The two varieties are interfertile and can yield progenies with different types of crown structures. The variety *horizontalis* is the natural one and can be found mainly in natural stands, but it has also been introduced to many areas. The variety *pyramidalis* is the most widely planted of all cypresses.

Cypress is presently endangered by anthropogenic influences (wildfires, irrational harvesting and grazing) and disease, such as fungi of the genus *Seiridium*. Attacks of such pathogens have already been observed in some Greek stands (Xenopoulos, 1991). Therefore, it is of interest to investigate the resistance of this species to diseases. A tree improvement program in this direction has already started, providing the first resistant clones (Raddi *et al.*, 1990).

The objective of this study was to analyse the genetic variation of the Mediterranean cypress in Greece using isoenzyme gene loci and to study the genetic constitution of Greek resistant clones.

A total of 23 Greek populations and 6 collections of clones resistant to *Seiridium cardinale* have been sampled. The populations represent stands with trees having various crown forms, origin and history. The natural range of the *horizontalis* variety was represented by 14 Cretan populations from a wide altitudal range (150–1800 m) and 4 Aegean islands. Three 'naturalized' populations with intermediate crown forms were sampled from the Peloponnese and the island of Cephallonia and finally two amenity stands from Athens containing exclusively trees of the variety *pyramidalis*, were included in this study. The populations were assigned to two classes, according to their origin: natural (mainly *horizontalis* cypresses) and introduced or ornamental (mainly cypresses having a *pyramidalis* or intermediate form). The comparison between these two classes was performed in order to realise influences caused by the artificial selection for the conical form.

The six collections of resistant clones have been collected from three different progeny trials in southern Greece. The aim of this part of the study was to compare the three plantations for any mistakes in clone labelling, to check the change of genetic variation through artificial selection, to check for any correlation between certain genetic variants and resistance against *Seiridium cardinale* and to control the origin of the clones studied.

Isoenzymes were used as gene markers. Isoenzyme gene loci were identified through inheritance analysis (Papageorgiou *et al.*, 1993). The statistical measures used have been described in the previous sections.

The number of observed alleles at the gene loci used is presented in Table 1. Allele frequencies were estimated, and variation and differentiation measures were calculated. The results indicate high variation within the natural populations and low variation within the introduced and ornamental ones (Table 2). The same tendency was observed for the degree of heterozygosity as well (Table 3). A genetic distance of 0.214 clearly separated the natural from the artificial group.

Table 1. Number of alleles observed at the gene loci examined. In most cases, introduced and ornamental populations have fewer alleles than the natural ones

| Population | PGI-B | PGM-A | PGM-B | NDH-A | 6PGDH-B | MDH-B | MDH-C | GDH-A | LAP-A | alleles / locus |
|---|---|---|---|---|---|---|---|---|---|---|
| Natural | 2 | 2 | 3 | 3 | 3 | 3 | 2 | 4 | 5 | 3.00 |
| Introduced | 2 | 2 | 2 | 3 | 3 | 1 | 1 | 4 | 4 | 2.44 |

Table 2. Allelic diversity (effective number of alleles) observed at the gene loci examined. In most cases, introduced and ornamental populations have fewer alleles than the natural ones

| Population | PGI-B | PGM-A | PGM-B | NDH-A | 6PGDH-B | MDH-B | MDH-C | GDH-A | LAP-A | gene pool |
|---|---|---|---|---|---|---|---|---|---|---|
| Natural | 1.544 | 1.977 | 2.193 | 2.465 | 2.362 | 1.025 | 1.000 | 2.122 | 3.612 | 1.746 |
| Introduced | 1.972 | 1.510 | 1.880 | 1.164 | 2.449 | 1.000 | 1.000 | 1.382 | 2.662 | 1.483 |

Table 3. Heterozyote proportions at all gene loci examined and degree of heterozygosity for the groups of populations studied. Natural populations generally have a higher heterozygoisty

| Population | PGI-B | PGM-A | PGM-B | NDH-A | 6PGDH-B | MDH-B | MDH-C | GDH-A | LAP-A | Heter. grade |
|---|---|---|---|---|---|---|---|---|---|---|
| Natural | 0.321 | 0.525 | 0.404 | 0.605 | 0.635 | 0.025 | 0 | 0.503 | 0.627 | 0.405 |
| Introduced | 0.386 | 0.278 | 0.333 | 0.103 | 0.457 | 0 | 0 | 0.139 | 0.568 | 0.252 |

The results of variation and differentiation studies (Papageorgiou *et al.*, 1994) and the application of allelic profiles (Finkeldey, 1993) have led us to the factors influencing the genetic variation of cypress in Greece.

- The introduced and ornamental populations clearly show symptoms of founder effects, since they derive from the expansion of a small number of introduced individuals.
- The natural population of the high mountains managed to maintain their variation, most probably due to the gene flow.
- The natural populations growing near settlements are very variable as well, but they show symptoms of genetic contamination through the artificial columnar form introduced by humans.

The analysis of genetic variation of the clone collections showed no large differences between their allelic structures and the ones of their original populations. Multilocus genotypes of ramets belonging to the same clone were always identical, which means that no mistakes in sampling and labelling were made. The gene loci PGM-B and LAP showed a possible relation to resistance against *Seiridium cardinale* in two populations. After artificial selection, alleles PGM-B3 and LAP-A5 had significantly reduced frequencies (Table 4). However, this connection between both gene loci and resistance cannot be proven, because the differences observed could be a result of reduced sample size through breeding activities (Papageorgiou and Xenopoulos in preparation). This reduction in size also resulted in a smaller amount of alleles in the clone collections (Table 5).

Table 4. Comparison of allelic frequencies between natural populations (AL and MY) and collections of cones resistant to *Seiridium cardinale*, which are derived from them (AL-R and MY-R). Note the reduction of PGM-$B_3$ and LAP-$A_5$ after artificial selection

| Gene loci | Alleles | AL | AL-R | MY | MY-R |
|---|---|---|---|---|---|
| PGM | B1 | 0.000 | 0 | 0 | 0 |
| | B2 | 0.780 | 1.000 | 0.346 | 0.882 |
| | B3 | 0.220 | 0 | 0.654 | 0.118 |
| LAP | A1 | 0 | 0 | 0 | 0.029 |
| | A2 | 0 | 0 | 0.069 | 0 |
| | A3 | 0.036 | 0 | 0.069 | 0.029 |
| | A4 | 0.304 | 0.583 | 0.310 | 0.529 |
| | A5 | 0.661 | 0.417 | 0.552 | 0.412 |

The fields of application of population variation studies, which were discussed in the previous section, will be discussed further. Isoenzyme gene loci can be applied as an index for *early selection* if there is a clear connection between a trait interesting for tree breeding and an isoenzyme variant. Such a relation was not found for the trait of conical crown form (*pyramidalis*). Pure *pyramidalis* populations were strongly differentiated from natural *horizontalis*

Table 5. Comparison of the number of alleles between natural populations (SY, RO, AL, MY, SA, KO) and collections of clones resistant to *Seiridium cardinale*, which are derived from them (SY-R, RO-R, AL-R, MY-R, SA-R, KO-R). All resistant clone collections contain a smaller amount of alleles

| Gene loci | SY | SY-R | RO | RO-R | AL | AL-R | MY | MY-R | SA | SA-R | KO | KO-R |
|---|---|---|---|---|---|---|---|---|---|---|---|---|
| PGI-B | 2 | 2 | 2 | 2 | 2 | 2 | 2 | 2 | 2 | 2 | 2 | 2 |
| PGM-A | 2 | 2 | 2 | 2 | 2 | 2 | 2 | 2 | 2 | 2 | 2 | 2 |
| PGM-B | 3 | 2 | 2 | 2 | 2 | 1 | 2 | 2 | 3 | 2 | 2 | 2 |
| NDH-A | 3 | 3 | 3 | 3 | 1 | 1 | 2 | 2 | 3 | 3 | 3 | 3 |
| GDH-A | 3 | 3 | 4 | 3 | 3 | 2 | 3 | 2 | 4 | 3 | 4 | 3 |
| LAP-A | 4 | 4 | 4 | 5 | 3 | 2 | 4 | 4 | 5 | 4 | 5 | 4 |
| Total | 17 | 16 | 17 | 17 | 13 | 10 | 15 | 14 | 19 | 16 | 18 | 16 |

ones, but there was no allele existing only in one class but absent in the other. The amount of genetic variation was the factor differentiating them from each other; thus, all variants existing in the *pyramidalis* populations were included, together with others, in the *horizontalis* collections. This difference in the amount of existing alleles was not due to artificial selection, but most probably because of the founding of large stands with material derived by a small group of trees (founder effect).

As far as the resistance against disease is concerned, a direct comparison between collectives of resistant clones and their original populations was performed in order to reveal any connection between isoenzyme variants and the target trait. There have been tendencies which could lead to a hypothetical assumption, but they cannot be applied at an individual level. They could have been caused by other evolutionary factors, such as selection for other environmental facors, mating system, founder effect, etc. More research is needed in order to control the connection between these special alleles and the resistance against *S. cardinale*.

A more promising application of these results to tree improvement is to use them as a *reference for planning provenance trials*. In cypress, this is especially possible, since the evolutionary factors causing the variation patterns observed at isoenzyme loci influence the whole genome simultaneously; thus, we expect to have similar patterns of variation in traits important for tree improvement as well. This is confirmed from provenance trials, as far as crown form and resistance against diseases are concerned (Panetsos, 1994).

Tree improvement for one of the two crown types *pyramidalis* or *horizontalis* requires initial collections of pure subspecies. Artificial selection for the *horizontalis* form should be based on the high populations of the Cretan mountains. Other populations growing near settlements showed a genetic contamination by the *pyramidalis* form and should be avoided. However, when the *pyramidalis* is the target trait for tree improvement, material from abroad (Italy, France) should be imported. Population studies of genetic variation for cypresses growing in other Mediterranean countries are needed. Greek *pyramidalis* stands are in many cases pure, but contain little genetic variation, caused by a reduction of their genetic base, most probably through founder effects.

Artificial selection for resistance against *Seiridium cardinale* is based so far on *pyramidalis* individuals from Italy and France. New provenance tests should be performed in Greece, especially for the natural stands. Indeed, Xenopoulos (1990) found that cypresses from Samos (*horizontalis*) were much more resistant against disease than the ones from the Peloponnese. Since the Samos provenance has high variability as well, it could be a perfect basis for a tree improvement project. Generally, collections of resistant clones should derive from as many families as possible and be planted mostly locally.

The origin of the clone collections was confirmed, as well as the labelling of the clones in the three trials in Greece. The artificial selection for resistance against *S. cardinale* does not change the variation measured initially, but decreases the number of alleles in all populations examined. A large scale planting of this material would produce stands with low adaptability.

According to these facts, a few practical measures are described below.

- Material derived from the Peloponnese stands is not suitable for tree improvement projects, because this source has a narrow genetic base.
- Tree improvement for *pyramidalis* form should be based on material derived from other Mediterranean countries. For the *horizontalis* form, material from the Cretan mountains is proposed.
- Tree improvement for wood production and resistance against *Seiridium cardinale* should be based more on the populations of the Aegean islands, which combine the target traits with high adaptability.
- The number of families consisting the base of artificial selection for resistance against disease should be larger. The number of genetic variants should not be reduced extremely, because this would cause loss of adaptability for the previously mentioned stands. Resistant clones should be planted locally, if possible.

## REFERENCES

Adams, W.T. 1983. Application of isozymes in tree breeding. *In*: S.D. Tanksley and T.J. Orton (Eds) Isozymes in Plant Genetics and Breeding. Part A. Developments in Plant Genetic and Breeding No 1A. Amsterdam, Oxford and New York. Elsevier. 381–400.

Bergmann, F. and Ruetz, F.W. 1991. Isozyme genetic variation in random tree samples and selected orchard clones from the same Norway spruce populations. *For. Ecol. Mgmt.* **46**: 39–47.

Bush, R.M. and Smouse, P.E. 1992. Evidence for adaptive significance of allozymes in forest tree. *New Forests* **6**: 179–196.

Cheliak, W.M., Skroppa, T. and Pitel, J.A. 1987. Genetics of the polycross. 1. Experimental results from Norway Spruce. *Theoret. Applied Genet.* **73**: 321–329.

Choi, W.Y. 1993. Genetische Strukturen bei der Koreakiefer (*Pinus koraiensis* Sieb. *et* Zucc.) und ihre Veränderung durch Zuchtung. Gottinger Forstgenetische Berichte Nr. 15, X + 125 S.

Crow, J.F. and Kimura, M. 1970. Introduction to Population Genetics Therory. Harper and Row, New York, Evanston and London.

Ellstrand, N.C. and Elam, D.R. 1993. Population genetic consequences of small population size: Implications for plant conservation. *Annu. Rev. Ecol. Syst.* **24**: 217–242.

Finkeldey, R. 1993. Die Bedeutung allelischer Profile fur die Konservierung genetischer Ressourcen bei Waldbaumen. Gottinger Forstgenetische Berichte Nr. 14.

Finkeldey, R. 1994. SPINs and GEMs—Genetic markers and their application in forest genetics. *In* : R. Finkeldey and P. Havmoller (Eds) Proc. Regional Workshop on Species Improvement Network (SPIN). Chiang Mai, Thailand, 25–30 July 1994. FAO RAS/91/004. Field Document No 19. Los Ban~os, Phillipines.

Gallo, L.A. 1991. Genetische Analyse metrischer und isoenzymatischer Merkmale bei *Populus tremula, Populus tremuloides* und ihre Hybriden. Forstwiss. Dissertation, Universitat Gottingen.

Gillet, E. 1994. GSED: Genetic Structures from Electrophoresis Data, Version 1.0, User's Manual. Abteilung Forstgenetik und Forstpflanzenzuchtung, Universitat Gottingen, Busgenweg 2, D- 37077 Gottingen, Germany. 49 pp.

Gregorius, H.-R. 1974. On the concept of genetic distance between populations based on gene frequencies. Proc. Joint IUFRO Meeting, SO2.04. 1–3, Stockholm, Session I, 17–26.

Gregorius, H.-R. 1978. The concept of genetic diversity and its formal relationship to heterozygosity and genetic distance. *Math. Biosciences* **41**: 253–271.

Gregorius, H.-R. 1984. A unique genetic distance. *Biom. J.* **26:** 13–18.

Gregorius, H.-R. 1987. The relationship between the concepts of genetic diversity and differentiation. *Theor. Appl. Genet.* **74:** 397–401.

Gregorius, H.-R. 1988. The meaning of genetic variation within and between subpopulaions. *Ther. Appl. Genet.* **76**: 947–951.

Gregorius, H.–R., Hattemer, H.H and Bergmann, F. 1984. Uber Erreichtes und kaum Erreichbares bei der 'Identifikation' forstlichen Vermehrungsguts. *Allgem. Forst- u. Jagdztg* **155**: 201–214.

Gregorius, H.-R. and Roberds, J.H. 1986. Measurement of genetical differentiation among subpopulations. *Theor. Appl. Genet.* **71**: 826–834.

Guries, R.P. and Ledig F.T. 1981. Genetic structure of populations and differentiation in forest trees. USDA. General Technical Report PSW-48. Berkeley, Ca. Pacific Souhwest Forest and Range Experiment Station. 42–47.

Hattemer, H.H. 1991. Genetic analysis and population genetics. *In* : S. Fineschi, M.E. Malvolti, F. Cannata and H.H. Hattemer (Eds) Biochemical Markers in the Population Genetics of Forest Trees. SPB Academic Publishing bv, The Hague. 5–22.

Hattemer, H.H. 1994. Die genetische Variation und ihre Bedeutung fur Wald und Waldbaume, Scheweizerische. *Zeitschrift fur Forstwesen* **145**: 953–975.

Lagercrantz, U. and Ryman, N. 1990. Genetic structure of Norway spruce (*Picea abies*): Concordance of morphological and allozymic variation. *Evolution* **44**: 38–53.

Ledig, F.T., Guries, R.P. and Bonefeld, B.A. 1983. The relation of growth to heterozygosity in pitch pine. *Evolution* **37**: 1227–1238.

Lewontin, R.C. 1984. Detecting population differences in quantitative characters as opposed to gene frequencies. *Amer. Nat.* **123**: 115–124.

Mejnartowicz, L. and Lewandowski, A. 1994. Allozyme polymorphism in seed collected from a IUFRO-68 Douglas-fir test- plantation. *Silvae Genetica* **43**: 181–186.

Mendel, G. 1866. Versuche uber Pflanzenhybriden. *Verh. Naturforsch. Ver.* in Brunn **4**: 3–47.

Mitton, J.B. and Grant, M.C. 1980. Observation on the ecology of quaking aspen, *Populus tremuloides*, in the Colorado Front Range. *Amer. J. Bot.* **67**: 202–209.

Moran, G.F., Bell, J.C. and Griffin, A.R. 1989. The putative Austrian x red pine hybrid: A test of paternity based on allelic variation at enzyme-specific loci. *Silvae Genetica* **29**: 93–100.

Müller-Starck, G. 1979. Estimates of self- and cross-fertilization in a Scots pine seed orchard. *In*: D. Rudin (Ed.) Proc. Conf. Biochem. Genet. Forest Trees, Umea, Sweden. 170–179.

Müller-Starck, G. 1989. Genetic implications of environmental stress in adult forest stands of *Fagus sylvatica* L. *In*: F. Scholz, H.-R. Gregorius, and D. Rudin (Eds) Genetic Effects of Air Pollutants in Forest Tree Populations. Springer Verlag, Berlin-Heidelberg. 127–142.

Müller-Starck, G. and Gregorius, H.-R. 1986. Monitoring genetic variation in forest tree populations. Proc. 18th IUFRO World Congress, Ljubljana, Div. 2, Vol. II. 589–599.

Nei, M. 1972. Genetic distance between populations. *Amer. Nat.* **106**: 283–292.

Nei, M. 1973. Analysis of gene diversity in subdivided populations. *Ann. Hum. Genet.* **41**: 225–233.

Nei, M. and Roychoudhury, A.K. 1974. Sampling variances of heterozygosity and genetic distances. *Genetics* **76**: 379–390.

Panetsos, C.P. 1994 Inherited differences between population and individuals of *Cupressus sempervirens* L. (in Greek w. summary). Ministry of Agriculture, Forest Research Institute, No 17. pp. 19.

Papageorgiou, A.C., Bergmann, F., Gillet, E. and Hattemer, H.H. 1993. Genetic analysis of isoenzyme variation in Mediterranean cypress (*Cupressus sempervirens* L.). *Silvae Genetica* **42**: 109–111.

Papageorgiou, A.C., Panetsos, K.P. and Hattemer, H.H. 1994. Genetic differentiation of natural Mediterranean cypress (*Cupressus sempervirens* L.) in Greece. *Forest Genetics* **1**: 1–12.

Papageorgiou, A.C. 1995. Genetische Untersuchungen zur Zuchtung und Generhaltung der Mittelmeerzypresse (*Cupressus sempervirens* L.) in Griechenland. *Gottingen Research Notes in Forest Genetics* **18**: 190 pp.

Paule, L., Lindgren, D. and Yazdani, R. 1993. Allozyme frequencies, outcrossing rate and pollen contamination in *Picea abies* seed orchards. *Scand. J. For. Res.* **8**: 8–17.

Raddi, P., Panconesi, A., Xenopoulos, S., Ferrandes, P. and Andreoli, C. 1990. Genetic improvement for resistance to canker disease. *In*: Progress in EEC Research on Cypress Diseases. Agrimed Research Programme. Commission of the European Communities, Agriculture, Report EUR 12493 EN. 127–134.

Rajora, O.P. and Dancik, B.P. 1992. Genetic characterization and relations of *Populus alba, P. tremula, P.* x *canescens*, and their clones. *Theor. Appl. Genet.* **84**: 291–298.

Rajora, O.P., Zsuffa, L. and Dancik, B.P. 1991. Allozyme and leaf morphological variation of eastern cottonwood at the northern limits of its range in Ontario. *For. Sci.*: 688–702.

Rudin, D., Muona, O. and Yazdani, R. 1986. Comparison of the mating system of *Pinus sylvestris* in natural stands and seed orchards. *Hereditas* **104**: 15–19.

Swofford, D.L. and Selander, R.B. 1989. BIOSYS-1: A computer program for the analysis of allelic variation in population genetics and biochemical systematics (Release 1.7). Center for Biodiversity, Illinois Natur. Hist. Surv., Champaign, IL. 43 pp.

Wright, S. 1978. Evolution and the Genetics of Populations: The Theory of Gene Frequencies. Vol 2. The University of Chicago Press, USA. 511 pp.

Xenopoulos, S. 1990. Screening for resistance to cypress canker (*Seiridium cardinale*) in three Greek provenances of *Cupressus sempervirens*. *Eur. J. For. Path.* **20:** 140–147.

Xenopoulos, S. 1991. The cypress health state in Greece and new prospect from current research. *In*: A. Panconesi (Ed.) Il cipresso. Comitato Nazionale per le Scienze Agrarie Regionale Toscana. Direzione Generale dell' Agricoltura, Firenze. 61–66.

Ziehe, M. and Müller-Starck, G. 1991. Changes of genetic variation due to associated selection. *In*: G. Müller-Starck and M. Ziehe (Eds) Genetic Variation in European Populations of Forest Trees. J.D. Sauerlander's Verlag. Frankfurt am Main. 259–271.

# 12

# Genetic Improvement of *Sesbania sesban* for Agroforestry Systems

*Peter A. Oduol*[1]


## ABSTRACT

The problems associated with the improvement of multipurpose trees in agroforestry are discussed. The case of *Sesbania sesban*, one of the prominent agroforestry species is explained with respect to genetic variation in provenances (e.g., variation of 197% and 1544% was observed in height and biomass, respectively), selection process for elite ortets for specific traits (potential gains of 40%), their mass production through vegetative propagation as clones and their evaluations in diverse environments using both morphological and physiological criteria are outlined.


## 1. INTRODUCTION

The use of trees in the rural areas of Africa for the provision of food, forage, fuelwood, medicine, poles, fibre, shade and soil improvement is an age old practice. The rise in human population has increased pressure on the woodlands. This natural resource is now being exploited massively, leading to land degradation and loss of genetic resources. There is an urgent need to explore, identify and assess fast growing tree species that can be used in agroforestry. These trees should be able to interact positively within the rural farming practices. It is imperative that tree improvement research efforts should address sustainable farming by providing high quality and productive trees for resource poor farmers. The planting of trees is a long-term investment which requires the use of genetically improved seeds that can give better returns.

---

[1]P.O. Box 43170 Nairobi, Kenya.

### 1.1 Constraints to Multipurpose Trees (MPTs) Improvement

The genetic improvement of multipurpose trees (MPTs) is complex as it requires different objectives, criteria and methods of selection than the traditional breeding programs for plantation forestry species (Owino, 1992; Simons *et al.*, 1994). The numerous problems associated with MPTs improvement have been outlined by Burley and Carlowitz (1984), Owino (1992) and Simons (1992), and these are listed below:

(i) The high number of species involved, currently over 2000 species have been identified and suggested for use in agroforestry.
(ii) There is generally a lack of basic information on the growth of these species.
(iii) The longevity of trees and their prevalence to out breeding.
(iv) The requirement of multiple products and services from these MPTs, calls for the simultaneous improvement of many traits.
(v) The tree species compete with agricultural crops, thus the selected genotypes should be able to interact positively with the crops.
(vi) The requirement of maintenance of a broad genetic base as a biological insurance against catastrophes and also survival in the physical environment where they are grown.

### 1.2 Potentials for Improvement

Tree improvement is the combination of silvicultural operations and tree breeding in the shortest possible time. In order to maximize yield it requires better site preparation as well as the use of genetically superior trees. The differences among trees are the result of three factors (Zobel and Talbert 1984): a) the different environments in which trees grow; b) the genetic differences among trees and c) the interactions between tree genotypes and the environment in which they grow.

The existence of intra-specific variation and high levels of population differentiation were observed in several tree species. For example, significant variation was observed in *Eucalyptus* (Zobel, 1993) and *Prosopis* (Oduol *et al.*, 1986; Felker, 1994). The presence of variation provides the raw material and scope for genetic improvement, and for any successful tree improvement program variation is mandatory.

Through recurrent selection greater gains in yields can be achieved and the selection of propagules from field trees can also lead to gains through vegetative propagation. Thus the ultimate aim is to develop landrace populations which are productive and well adapted over several sites.

## 2. WHY SESBANIA?

*Sesbania* species is widely spread in Africa (Fig. 1) found in the wild and on farmer's fields either deliberately retained or planted. *S. sesban* was selected for this study due to:

i) its wide adaptability;

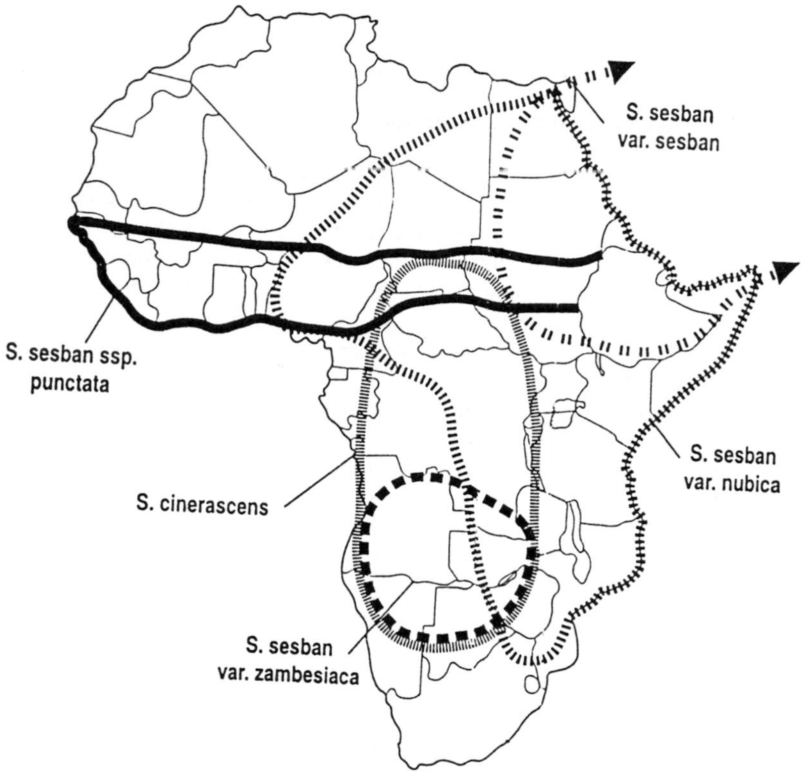


Fig. 1. Approximate ranges of some perennial *Sesbania* species in Africa (after Gillet, 1963).

ii) its ability to produce multiple products and services within a short time. The primary uses include provision of food, fuelwood, fodder, poles, stakes, wood and medicine. Among services are soil conservation and erosion control, soil fertility improvement through mulching and green manuring and N-fixation, leaf fall and provision of shelter and shade;

iii) its compatibility with most agricultural crops; and

iv) its general acceptability by farmers.

Despite considerable interest in this species no research has been done on the genetic variation among its provenances. A series of studies involving the evaluation of phenotypic (morphological) and physiological attributes and their influence on biomass production using provenances and clones of *Sesbania sesban* were initiated.

## 2.1 Provenance Variation

Provenance is defined as the population of a species referred to by its locality of occurence; the place in which any stand of trees (indigenous or exotic) is growing. Provenance studies compare the performance of different origins of trees when grown at one place. The information from provenance tests indicates the amount of genetic improvement which may be expected and can be used to select well-adapted and productive trees for forestry and agroforestry.

## 2.2 Genotype × Environment Interaction

Genotype × environment interaction studies help to ascertain the range of possible sites over which the best selected genotypes can be planted profitably and achieve greater genetic gains. Clonal selection is useful in identifying outstanding genotypes for a single or multiple traits and are used to deploy superior genotypes for direct use (Libby, 1990). It also enables to select widely adapted genotypes. Clonal selection in agroforestry is complex apart from performance they have to be compatible with crops as well as a targeted harvest index (Wood, 1990).

The clones used in the genotype × environment interaction experiment were selected for their apparent superiority in performance, from the provenance trial after 8 months at Maseno, with the following phenotypic characteristics for: (i) poles—straight stem, higher stem dry weight with less branching; (ii) fuelwood—higher stem plus branch weights, and (iii) leaf/fodder—higher leaf weights. The clones were selected from different altitudinal and rainfall zones in order to have a broad genetic base. Five top ranking clones were selected for each category and designated with letters as for poles (P), for fuelwood (F) and for leaves (L).

The selected outstanding ortets from the provenance trial were vegetatively propagated as rooted cuttings using non-mist propagators, whose construction and operational details are given by Leakey (1991). For this study the cuttings were taken from coppicing stumps of the selected trees in the field. The shoots were cut into single node cutting of 5 cm length with a pair of leaves in the nursery. The base of the cuttings were dipped in Seradix '2' powder containing an active ingredient of 0.8 per cent IBA, to enhance rooting (Oduol, 1994).

The objective of this study was to determine growth and yield potentials in *S. sesban* clones when grown under different environmental conditions.

## 2.3 Light Interception

The amount of photosynthetic active radiation (PAR) intercepted by the canopy is of fundamental importance in plant growth and productivity (Caldwell *et al.*, 1986). The relationship between available light energy, photosynthetic activity and dry matter yield in trees have been established by Cannell (1989).

Information on light requirements, interception and transmission potentials for most tropical trees that can be used in agroforestry is lacking. In agroforestry, trees and crops are grown together and each has its own light and water requirements. Trees in farming system create micro climatic changes which are governed by the density of the canopy and the spatial arrangement of the crown characteristics. Thus, knowledge about light interception by canopies is very important in planning tree management in agroforestry.

Clonal responses to light quality could be an interesting determinant of tree form in agroforestry practices as light quality has a major impact on dry matter partitioning in trees (Hoad *et al.*, 1990). Thus it becomes necessary to study light interception in tree crowns in order to understand the photosynthetic processes of trees.

### 2.4 Stomatal Conductance

Increasing demand for wood products suggests the need to increase efficiency of forest operations in order to optimize biomass production. Studies involving water use have received little attention and yet they seem to be very important in plants growing in mixtures. Ong *et al.* (1990) in their studies found that trees compete strongly with crops for water resulting in yield reduction in agroforestry. The use of field measurements of stomatal conductance using sun leaves allows the determination of seasonal water patterns of similar physiological stage of development to be compared.

The aim of this study was to determine whether biomass production is directly related to either: (a) the amount of PAR intercepted by contrasting crowns or (b) Stomatal conductance of individual *Sesbania sesban* clones, grown at Maeno and Machakos.

## 3. MATERIALS AND METHODS

### 3.1 Germplasm Source

The germplasm used in *S. sesban* provenance study was obtained from the International Livestock Research Institute (ILRI) genebank, formerly International Livestock Centre for Africa (ILCA). This included 75 provenances coded as follows: Australia (CS), Burundi (BR), Ethiopia (ET), Hawaii (HW), Kenya (KN), Mali (ML), Niger (NI) and Tanzania (TZ). Other details are outlined by Oduol (1994).

### 3.2 Experimental Sites

The provenance 'trial was conducted at KEFRI/KARI/ICRAF field station at Maseno, Kisumu district, Kenya (Fig. 2); while clonal (genotype × environment interaction) study was conducted on three sites in Kenya: (i) KEFRI/KARI/ICRAF field station at Maseno, (ii) KARI/KWDP field station at Kisii, and (iii) ICRAF field research station at Machakos, whose details are summarized in Table 1. Kisii and Maseno represented the humid highlands of Kenya with a rainfall above 1700 mm. While Machakos is located at the interface of sub-humid and semi-arid zone with rainfall of 700 mm (Fig. 2). Maseno and Kisii are heavily populated with small, intensively managed farms producing food crops and small livestock. *S. sesban* is found growing naturally scattered on farms.

### 3.3 Experimental Design

The provenance trial was planted in a 12 × 7 Alpha incomplete block design, with 3 replications. The layout was row plots of 8 trees with a spacing of 1.5

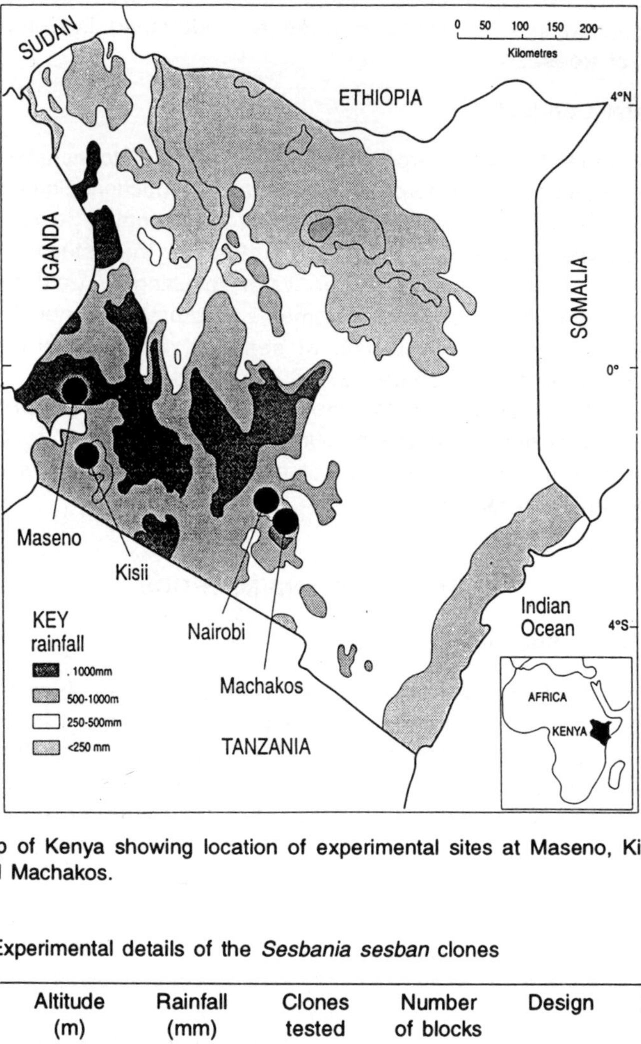


Fig. 2. Map of Kenya showing location of experimental sites at Maseno, Kisii, Nairobi and Machakos.

Table 1. Experimental details of the *Sesbania sesban* clones

| Site | Altitude (m) | Rainfall (mm) | Clones tested | Number of blocks | Design | Plot size (m) |
|---|---|---|---|---|---|---|
| Kisii | 1740 | 2060 | 13 | 6 | RBD | 5 × 3 |
| Maseno | 1500 | 1750 | 15 | 10 | RBD | 5 × 3 |
| Machakos | 1560 | 700 | 15 | 10 | RBD | 5 × 3 |

m between plots and 1 m within rows. Each replicate consisted of 12 blocks with 7 plots per block (each plot represented a provenance).

The spacing in the clonal trial was 2.5 × 2.5 m in a 5 × 3 array (15 cloned individuals from 15 ortets were planted with a single ramet per clone randomized in each block as single tree plots). The gaps for missing trees were planted with different *S. sesban* clones of the same size in order to give equal competition. In both experiments, a single guard row was planted around the perimeter of the whole experimental area at each site.

## 4. ASSESSMENT

The provenances were assessed for height, root collar diameter, crown diameter, number of primary branches on the main stem and biomass production after 8 months of growth in the field. Twelve trees of each provenance were harvested and were partitioned into stem, branches and leaves in order to understand the allometry of the species. The dry biomass was determined by drying at 105 $^{o}$C for 48 hours.

Clones in the genotype × environment interaction trial were monitored for their height growth and biomass production as morphological characteristics. Physiological parameters of light interception and stomatal conductance were measured in two nine-month old average sized trees at Maseno and Machakos. Canopy PAR transmittance was measured using a Ceptometer, (Decagon Devices Inc. Pullman, Washington, USA, 1989) from permanently marked locations within the tree crown, termed lower zone, middle zone and top zone, depending on the height of the tree. At each location four measurements of canopy transmittance were taken, averaged and stored. Thus in a tree twelve measurements were made. To obtain the four measurements per location the Ceptometer was rotated 360$^{o}$ above each location and PAR transmittance readings were taken at approximately 90$^{o}$ intervals. Thus canopy transmittance for each tree was represented by arithmetic mean of 80 sensors × 4 samples per location × 3 locations per tree. Readings were taken on clear days usually between 11.00 and 14.00 h solar time, when the sun angle variation is minimum at the equator. The PAR transmission sampling was done for 4 days per site. The total incoming PAR was measured in open areas at the beginning of each sampling date (average incoming PAR for the 4 days was 695 and 974 u mol $m^{-2}$ $S^{-1}$ at Maseno and Machakos respectively).

Stomatal conductance (gs) was measured using a porometer (LI-COR Inc; LI1600; Steady-State Porometer, Lincoln, Nebraska, USA). The 2 $cm^2$ circular aperture cuvette was used for all measurements on *S. sesban* leaves, in July 1992. Measurements of quantum flux density, humidity and leaf temperature were recorded simultaneously. Diurnal measurements of gs were made on 2 trees (4 replicates per tree) three times during the day (for 3 days at each site), morning (9.00–10.30 h), midday (12.00–01.30 h) and afternoon (15.00–16.30 h) at Maseno and Machakos sites on fully expanded leaves. Early morning measurements were not possible between 07.00 h to 08.00 h due to the presence of dew on the leaves. The General Linear Model (GLM) procedure in SAS for the analysis of un-balanced experiments (Barr *et al.*, 1979) was used.

## 5. RESULTS

### 5.1 General Growth

The overall means for height, root collar diameter, crown diameter and number of primary branches for each provenance are summarized in Table 2. There were considerable differences between provenances in these assessed variables. Height growth of trees varied significantly between provenances by 197 per cent, root collar diameter by 231 per cent, crown diameter by 285 per cent and number of branches by 275 per cent. Fifty four per cent of the tested provenances had heights above the mean of $3.64 \pm 0.81$ m.

Table 2. Range, means, standard error and coefficient of variation for different characteristics of *S. sesban* provenances (n = 75) at Maseno, Kenya

| Character | Range | Mean | ± SE | C.V% | % difference |
|---|---|---|---|---|---|
| Height (m) | 4.87–11.64 | 3.64 | 0.81 | 17 | 197 |
| Root collar diameter (cm) | 5.06–1.53 | 3.69 | 1.09 | 24 | 231 |
| Crown diameter (m) | 3.58–0.93 | 2.76 | 0.68 | 20 | 285 |
| Number of branches (count) | 75–20 | 54 | 12 | 17 | 275 |

* Sample includes 12 plants each from 75 provenances.
SE = Standard error
C.V. % = Coefficient of variation

### 5.2 Biomass Production

Significant differences were observed in biomass production among provenances. After 8 months of growth in the field the average dry mass in the provenances was 1.42 kg $tree^{-1}$, provenance ET6 from Ethiopia registered the highest dry mass of 2.96 kg $tree^{-1}$ while the lowest biomass was recorded in provenance CS73 with 0.18 kg $tree^{-1}$, representing a difference of 1544 per cent (Fig. 3).

There is no clear cut pattern in dry matter partitioning into components of stem, branch and leaf for higher and lower dry mass provenances.

### 5.3 Genetic Gain

The presence of a large variation between provenances indicate that gains can be achieved when a proportion of the population is selected. Increments of 25.8 per cent for height, 34.7 per cent for root collar diameter and 97.2 per cent for tree dry mass can be achieved when a 5 per cent selection is applied among the 75 provenances (Table 3).

### 5.4 Genotype × Environment Interaction

The results indicate significant differences between sites and clones in the assessed variable of height and biomass. Mean height for combined sites was $4.77 \pm 0.22$ m; clone heights at Maseno ranged from 4.50 to 7.11 m, at Kisii

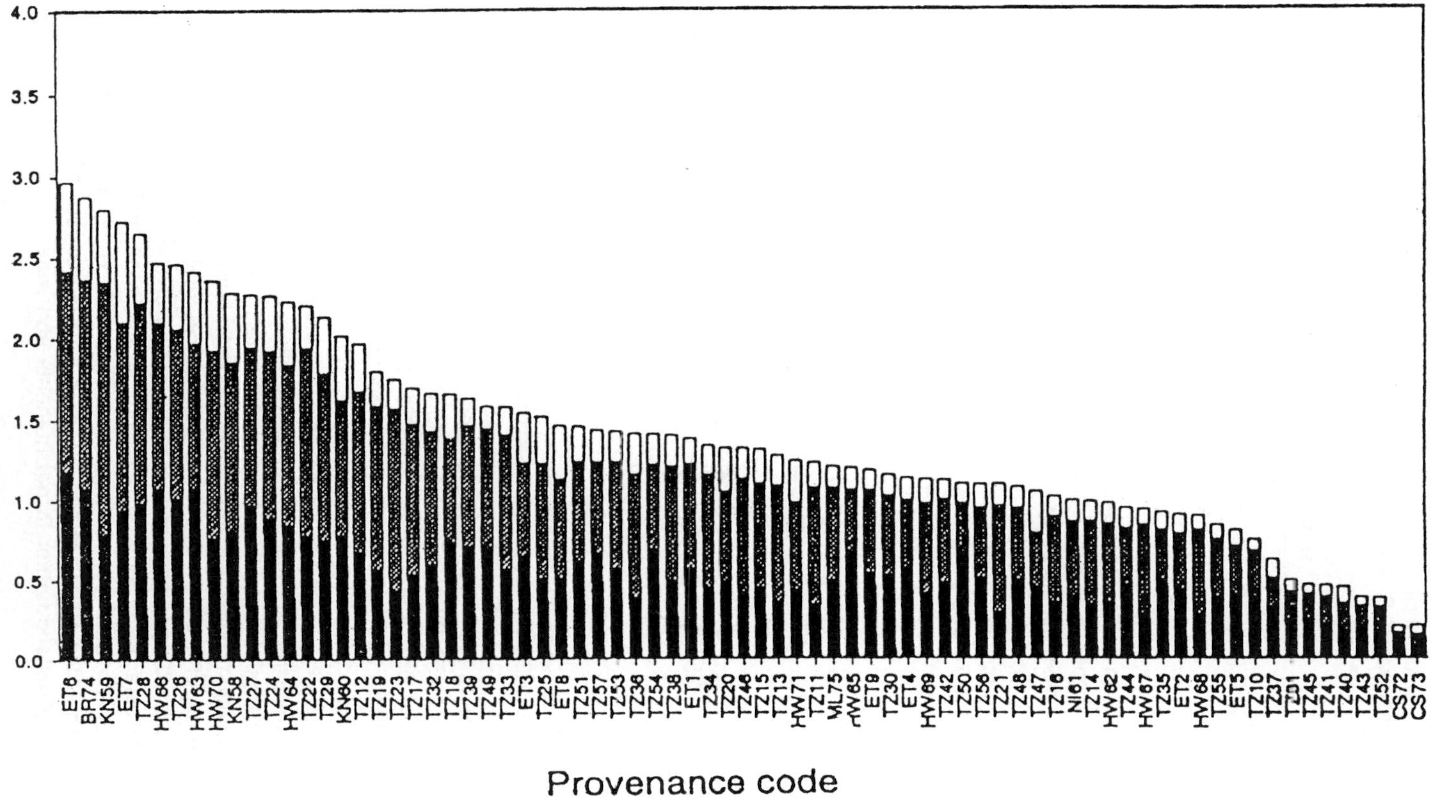


Fig. 3. Variation in total dry mass (kg) of components of stem ■, branch ⊠ and leaf □ of *Sesbania sesban* provenances after 8 months growth at Maseno, Kenya.

Table 3. Mean performance of selected trees (proportion selected 5% of the 75 provenances) of *S. sesban* at Maseno, Kenya

| Character | Mean of selected trees | Population mean | % increase over population mean |
|---|---|---|---|
| Height (m) | 4.58 | 3.64 | 25.8 |
| Root collar diameter (cm) | 4.97 | 3.69 | 34.7 |
| Total weight (kg) | 2.80 | 1.42 | 97.2 |

from 4.03 to 6.35 m and at Machakos from 2.99 to 4.18 m. Clone mean heights were relatively higher at Maseno and Kisii than Machakos (Fig. 4). Dry mass production after nine months of growth differed significantly between clone and sites (Fig. 5). At Maseno (Fig. 5a) mean dry mass yield for stem, branch, leaf, above-ground, root and total tree were 1.75±0.39, 4.82±1.19, 1.67±0.40, 8.24±1.83, 3.59±0.76 and 11.82±2.4 kg tree$^{-1}$ respectively. Total tree biomass at this site varied from as low as 4.92 (7.9 t ha$^{-1}$) to 23.19 kg tree$^{-1}$ (31.1 t ha$^{-1}$).

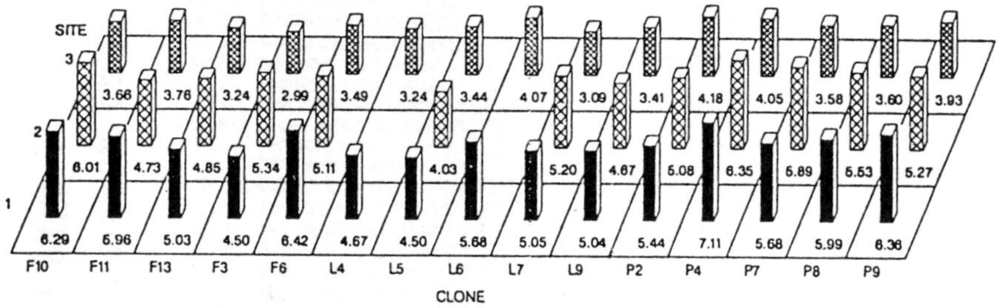


Fig. 4. Variation in height (m) among *Sesbania sesban* clones after 9 months growth (1) Maseno (2) Kisii and (3) Machakos sites in Kenya.

At Kisii stem, branch, leaf, above-ground, root and total tree dry mass were 1.68±0.49, 3.57±1.30, 2.02±0.72, 7.27±2.3, 2.72±0.94 and 9.99±3.01 kg tree$^{-1}$ respectively (Fig. 5b). Total tree dry mass at this site ranged from 3.55 (5.68 t ha$^{-1}$) to 19.96 kg tree$^{-1}$ (31.9 t ha$^{-1}$). At Machakos (Fig. 5c) mean dry mass for stem, branch, leaf, above-ground, root and total tree dry mass were 0.57±0.11, 2.62±0.55, 0.12±0.05, 3.30±0.66, 1.22±0.26 and 4.52±0.87 kg tree$^{-1}$, respectively. Total tree dry mass among *S. sesban* clones at this site ranged from 2.14 (3.4 t ha$^{-1}$) to 8.74 kg tree$^{-1}$ (14.0 t ha$^{1}$).

Root distribution (primary roots) by depth varied between sites. Most of the roots were in upper 0–50 cm depth and confined around the stem at the three sites. At Maseno 89 per cent of the roots were within the depth of 40 cm, while 100 per cent of the roots at Kisii were in this zone and Machakos had 78 per cent of the tree roots in this zone (Table 4). Roots were deeper at Machakos than at the other two sites. This is a resource poor site and hence the roots had to extend further to get nutrients and water.

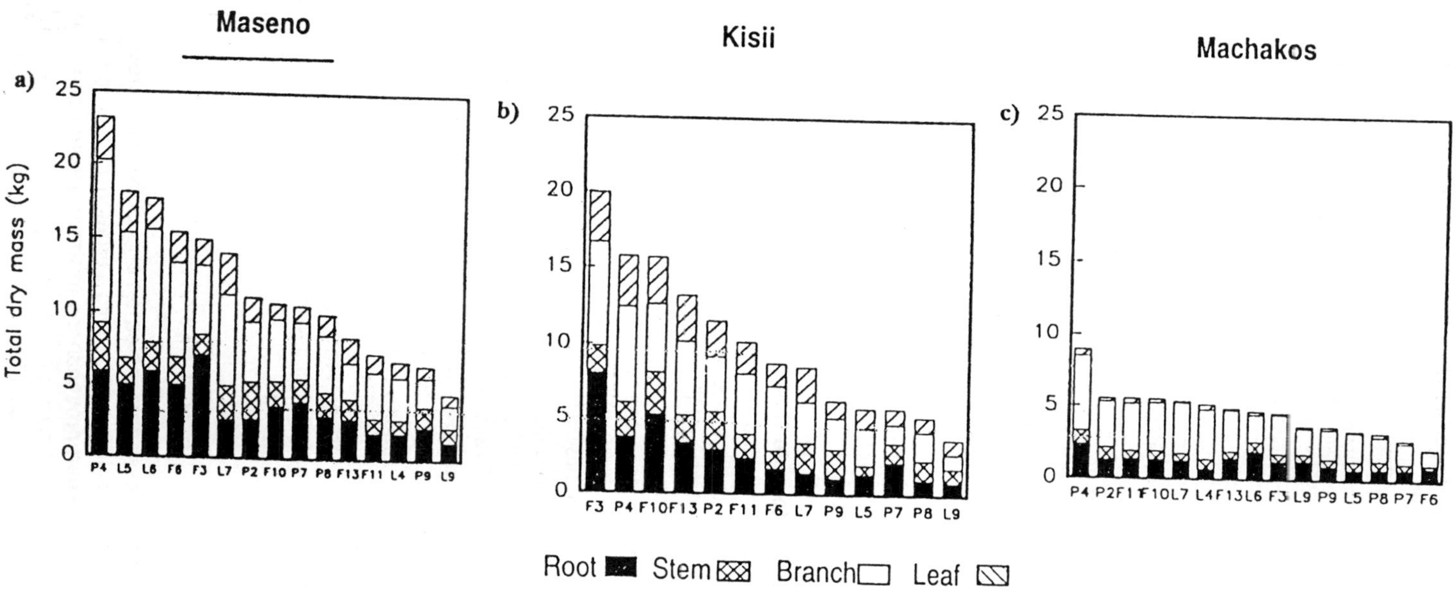


Fig. 5. Variation in dry mass partitioning of components of root, stem, branch, and leaf of *Sesbania sesban* clones at Maseno, Kisii and Machakos.

Table 4. Vertical root distribution percentage in *S. sesban* clones at three sites (Maseno, Kisii and Machakos)

| Site/Depth | 0–10 cm | Top 40 cm |
|---|---|---|
| Maseno | 47 | 89 |
| Kisii | 24–65 | 100 |
| Machakos | 21–57 | 78 |

### 5.5 Light Interception

Significant differences in light interception were observed among clones and between zones within clones (Figs. 6a and b). Light interception among clones and canopy levels varied from 34 to 88 per cent at Maseno (Fig. 6a) and from 13 to 55 per cent at Machakos (Fig. 6b). Light interception at both sites was greater in the middle zone than the top zone. The pattern of light interception was similar among clones selected for fuelwood (F), poles (P) and leaves (L).

### 5.6 Stomatal Conductance

The results for stomatal conductance are presented as averages for the three days (Fig. 7a and b). Significant differences were observed in stomatal conductance among clones at both the sites. Stomatal conductance was high in the early part of the day with almost a linear decline during the day (Figs. 7a and b). It is interesting to note that despite the constancy in environmental conditions, stomatal conductance changed during the course of the day, this may be due to response to changes in the internal conditions of the clones. The results also show that stomatal conductance was significantly greater in the morning than at midday or in the afternoon. At Maseno there were no differences in mean gs between the two afternoon sampling periods (Fig. 7a). Stomatal conductance was higher at Maseno with a range from 1900 to 3500 mmol $m^{-2}$ $S^{-1}$ than at Machakos with a range from 500 to 1500 mmol $m^{-2}$ $S^{-1}$ (Figs. 7a and b). There were differences in stomatal conductances at Maseno between clones selected for fuelwood; F6 and F11 tended to have greater gs in the morning while F3 and F13 had greater gs late in the afternoon. In clones selected for poles P2, P7 and P9 had greater gs in the morning while P8 tended to have high gs at 1200 h and 1500 h, while P4 gs was similar throughout the day (Fig. 7a). Among clones selected for leaves L5 and L7 had greater gs in the morning and L4, L6 and L9 gs were greater at 1700 h.

At Machakos all clones had greater gs in the morning and less in the afternoon, the clones were responding similarly throughout the three sampling periods (Fig. 7b).

## 6. DISCUSSION

The differences in the assessed variables among *S. sesban* provenances at Maseno indicates that there is great genetic variation in this species. These significant differences between provenances in the assessed characters show

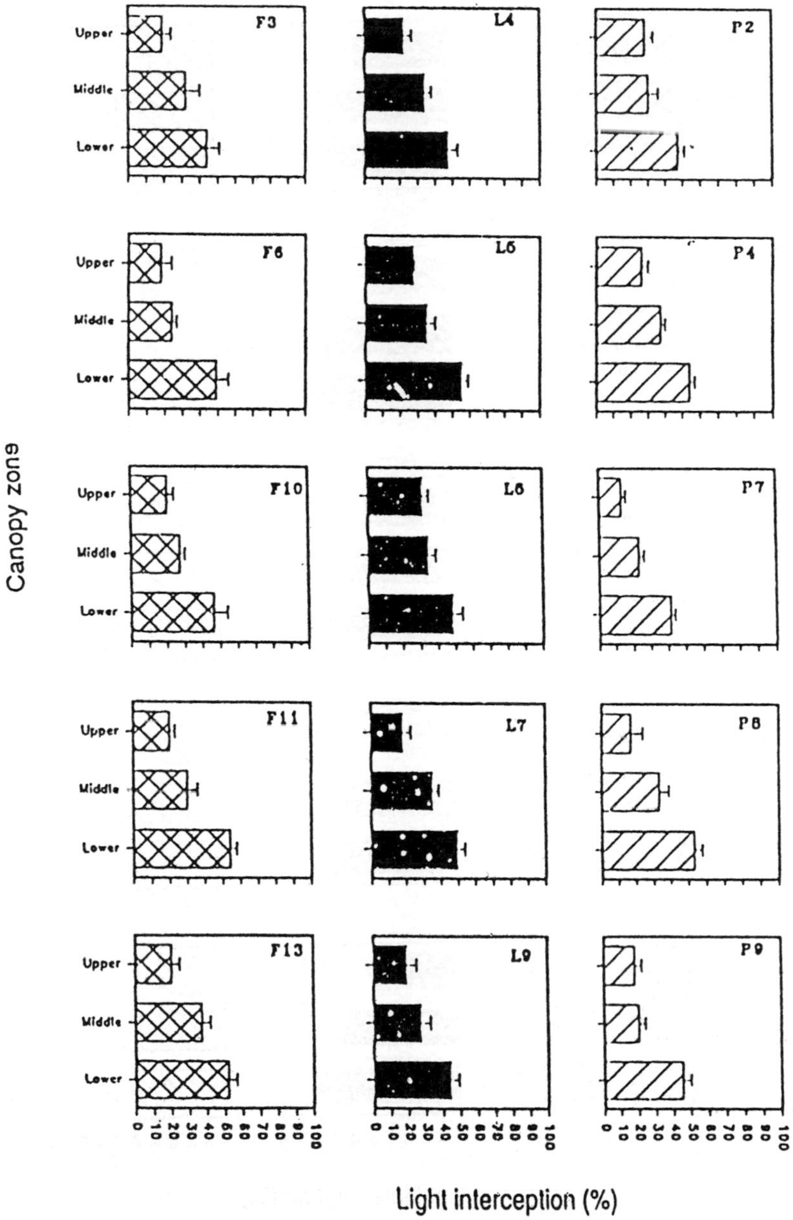


Fig. 6a. Variation in light interception (%) among *Sesbania sesban* clones after 9 months at Machakos, Kenya.
(1 = Lower zone, 2 = Middle zone and 3 = Upper zone)

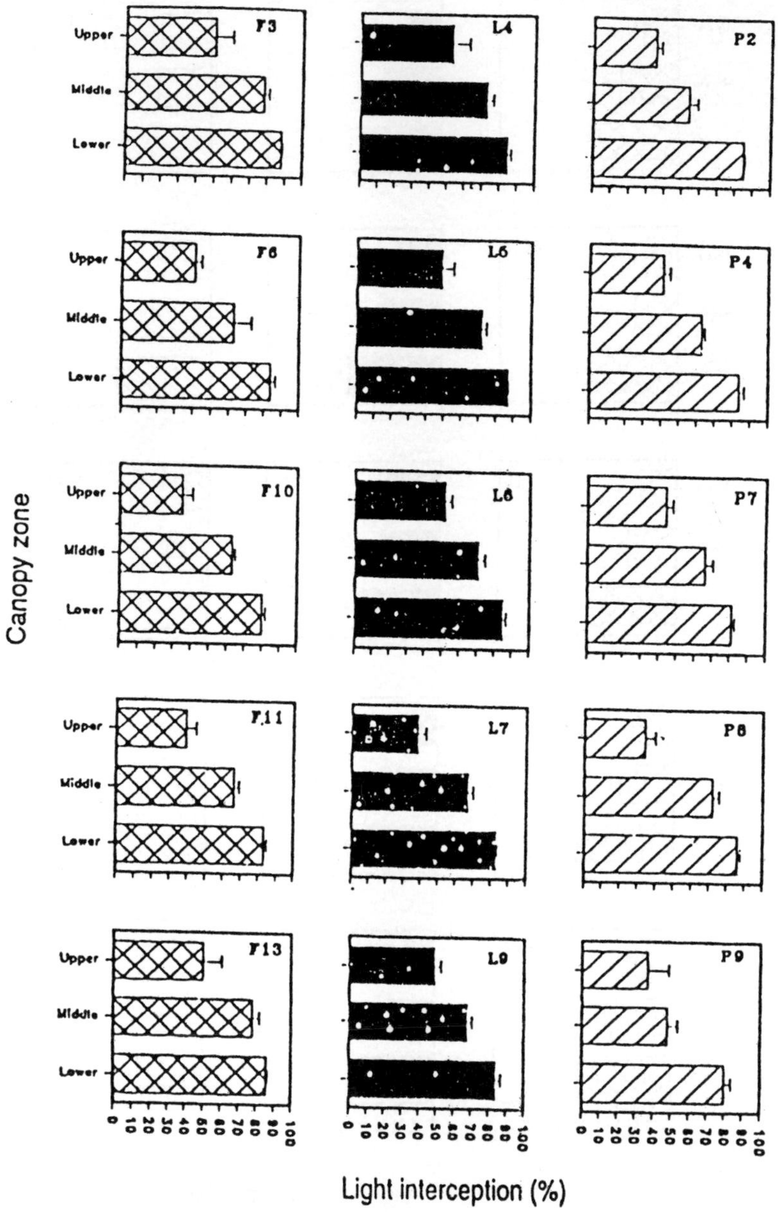


Fig. 6b. Variation in light interception (%) among *Sesbania sesban* clones after 9 months at Maseno, Kenya.
(1 = Lower zone, 2 = Middle zone and 3 = Upper zone)

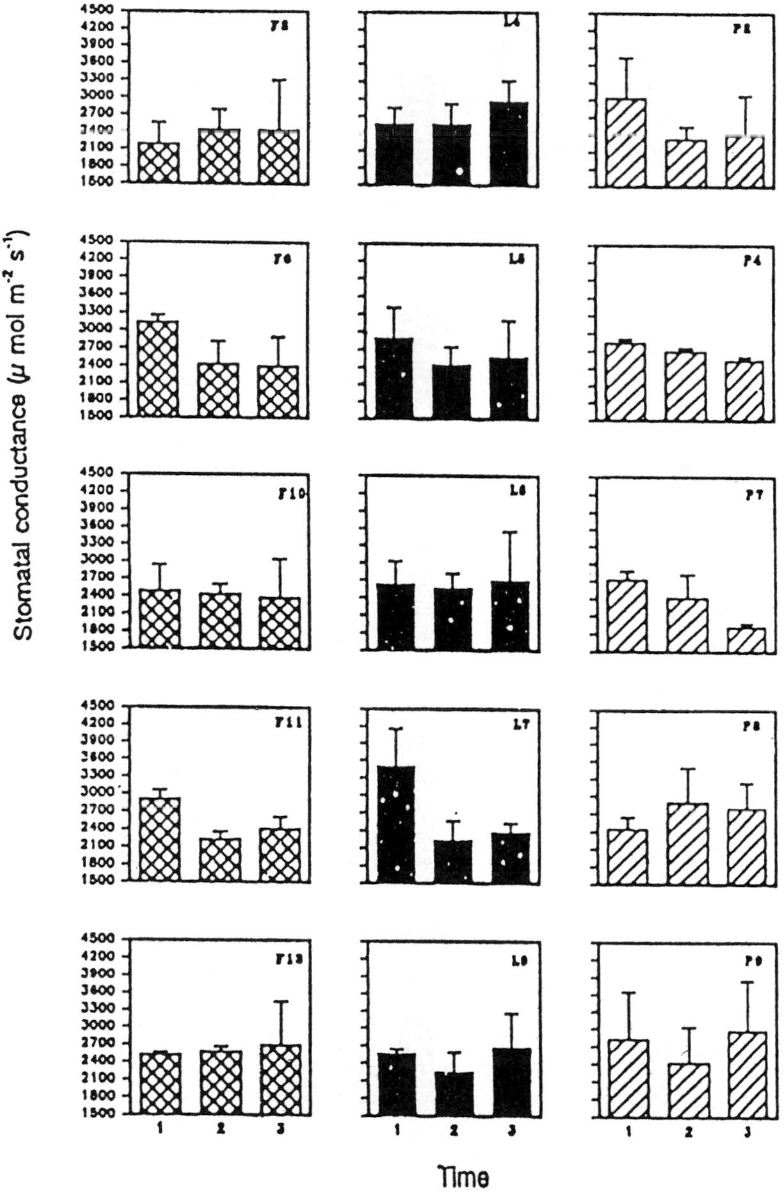


Fig. 7a. Showing stomatal conductance (μ mol $m^{-2}$ $s^{-1}$) for *Sesbania sesban* clones after 9 months at Maseno, Kenya.
(Time 1 = 09.00 h, 2 = 12.00 h and 3 = 15.00 h)

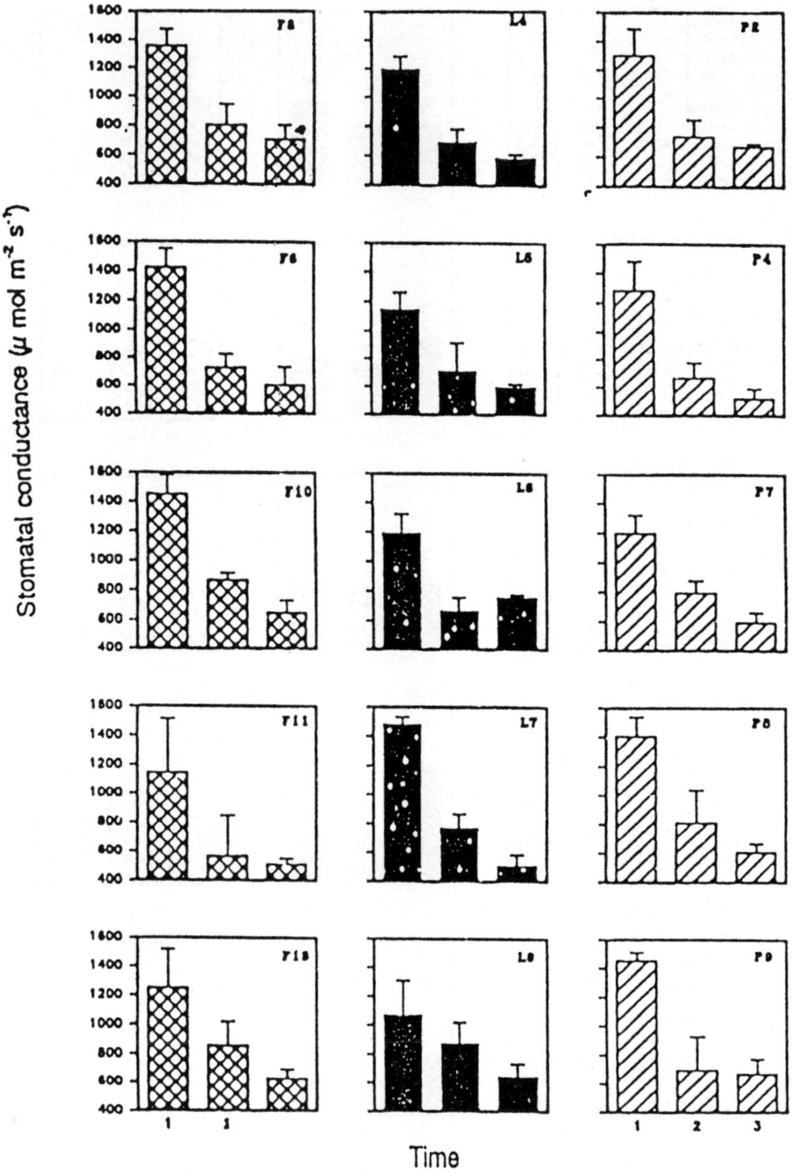


Fig. 7b. Showing stomatal conductance (µ mol $m^{-2}$ $s^{-1}$) for *Sesbania sesban* clones after 9 months at Machakos, Kenya.
(Time 1 = 09.00 h, 2 = 12.00 h and 3 = 15.00 h)

that *S. sesban* has an ecotypic variation making selection at provenance level worthwhile. Variation in height in clones planted at Maseno, Kisii and Machakos was observed. Clones selected for poles had more heights while clones selected for leaf production had consistently lower heights at the three sites. Maseno and Kisii were generally better sites with high rainfall and better soil physical properties than Machakos which normally receives only 700 mm of rainfall and has a prolonged dry period. There were no distinctly superior clones, as clone × site interactions were quite strong. This reflected the inability of some clones to perform satisfactorily at some sites.

Some clones, e.g. P4 and P2, performed consistently well as they were taller across the sites, while clones P8 and F13 were relatively short after eight months. After nine months the clones selected for biomass production varied by 57 per cent in height at Maseno and Kisii and by 40 per cent at Machakos. These significant variations in height and biomass result from non-additivity of genetic and environmental effects. These interactions occurred due to changes in the middle ranks above and below the overall mean. Total dry mass (above and below ground) production was higher at Maseno than at Kisii or Machakos. Machakos experiences a long dry season with soils deficient in nutrients. Root studies revealed niches of exploitation of the soil resources. Roots formed about 30 per cent of the total dry mass at all the sites.

Dry matter partitioning among clones for root, stem, branch and leaf was relatively similar at each site (Fig. 5). The high partitioning of dry biomass to branches and low partitioning to leaf at Machakos represents variation in the phenological phases due to site. Most of the clones at Machakos at the time of harvest were without leaves, while at Maseno and Kisii the clones were still in active vegetative growth. Site rather than genetic variation may have been the major determinant of dry matter allocation.

On the basis of average performance *S. sesban* clones can be classified according to their suitability to site. For example, P4, L5 and L6 clones are suitable for Maseno site, F3, P4 and F10 for Kisii and P4 for Machakos. Some other clones like P2, F11, F10, L7 and L4 could be specifically developed for Machakos due to their similar performance on marginal site. The results suggest that it may be possible to select and develop highly productive single-purpose clones for some sites (Leakey, 1991).

The study reveals how light interception could be used in yield improvement and as a trait to be employed in clonal selection program. There were differences in light interception between sites of Maseno (average 64 %) and Machakos (32 %) sites. This seems to be due to leaf area, as Maseno site tended to have higher leaf areas than Machakos (Oduol, 1994). The low light interception at Machakos was due to the shedding of leaves during the dry season and thus allowing more light through the canopies.

Clones with higher leaf areas were effective to intercept light, for example, P4 and F3 at Maseno and P4 and L4 at Machakos (Fig. 6a and b). The effective reduction in PAR transmission in the clones may explain their fast-growing habits making them succeed in both environments. But effective light interception may not lead to positive response with regard to productivity. For example, if the clone has a lower fine root mycorrhizal network surface area it may not be effective at taking up the nutrients to enable it to maximize productivity. With adequate supply of water and nutrients the clones will use the intercepted radiation efficiently to produce dry matter. These trees with high radiation use efficiency and high reflectivity (light crowns with thin leaflets permitting more radiation to penetrate into the lower canopy) are best in mixed cropping systems (Connor, 1983).

Wide range of response in stomatal conductance indicates the ability of stomata to open or close as the situation dictates and may be due to mechanisms for adaptability and survival (Reich, 1984). The differences in gs is due to gradations of irradiance in the canopy. Moreover in 5–6 m tall trees it was not possible to measure the top leaves which were always sunlit. The difference in gs may also be due to differences in leaf age. The trees assessed were nine months old and had their leaves in various stages of physiological growth. The lower leaves on most trees at Machakos had been shed as the site experiences severe drought. This may have led to low leaf water potential, stomatal closure, and thus reducing photosynthesis and productivity. Salisbury and Ross (1985) found that the stomata tended to close with reduction in leaf water potential. While at Maseno the retention of leaves for more duration may have contributed to high gs and thus to increased biomass productivity in *S. sesban* clones, than at Machakos. The higher value of gs in the morning at Machakos is probably due to good growth conditions so that stomata can maximize $CO_2$ uptake and photosynthesis while minimizing water loss (Wang *et al.*, 1979). Lastly, the use of gs as a selection criteria would only be effective if the different mechanisms to drought avoidance and tolerance employed by the different clones are understood.

## REFERENCES

Barr, A.J., Goodnight, J.H., Sall, J.P. and Blair, W.H. 1979. SAS User's Guide Statistics. SAS Institute Inc.; CARY, North Carolina.

Burley, J. and von Carlowitz, P. 1984. Multipurpose tree germplasm. Proceedings, Recommendations and Documents of a Planning Workshop to Discuss International Co-operation. ICRAF, Nairobi, Kenya. 248 pp.

Caldwell, M.M., Meister, H.P., Tenhunen, J.D. and Lange, O.J. 1986. Canopy structure, light microclimate and leaf gas exchange of *Quercus coccifera* L. in a Portuguese macchia: measurements in different canopy layers and simulations with a canopy model. *Trees* **1**: 25–41.

Cannell, M.G.R. 1989. Light interception, light use efficiency and assimilate partitioning in poplar and willow stands. *In*: J.S. Pereira and J.J. Landsberg (Eds) Biomass Production by Fast Growing Trees. Kluwer Academic Publishers. 1–12.

Connor, D.J. 1983. Plant stress factors and their influence on production of agroforestry plant associations. *In*: P.A. Huxley (Ed.) Plant Research and Agroforestry. ICRAF, Nairobi. 401–426.

Felker, P. 1994. Capturing and managing the genetic variation in *Prosopis* spp. for economically useful characters. *In*: R.R.B. Leakey and A.C. Newton (Eds) Tropical Trees: The Potential for Domestication, Rebuilding Forest Resources. HMSO, London. 183–188.

Gillet, J.B. 1963. *Sesbania* in Africa (excluding Madagascar) and Southern Arabia. *Kew Bull.* **17**: 91–159.

Hoad, S.P., Mclellan, A.J. and Leakey, R.R.B. 1990. Vegetative propagation of *Eucalyptus grandis* W. HILL ex MAIDEN. Institute of Terrestrial Ecology. Final Report to Shell Research Ltd. 77 pp.

Leakey, R.R.B. 1991. Towards a strategy for clonal forestry: Some guidelines based on experience with tropical trees. *In*: J.E. Jackson (Ed.) Tree Breeding and Improvement. Proc. Symp. held at Edgbaston, Birmingham, UK, 8th March 1991. Royal Forestry Society of England, Wales and Northern Ireland. Tring England. 27–42.

Libby, W.J. 1990. Advantages of clonal forestry revisted. *In*: Proc. Joint Meeting of WFGA and IUFRO Working Parties S2. 02–05, –06, –12 and –14. Olympia Wa. 20–24 August 1990, Weyerhaeuser Co., Tacoma, Wa. Sec. 5.13, 13 pp.

Oduol, P.A., Felker, P., McKinley, C.R. and Meier, C.E. 1986. Variation among selected *Prosopis* families for pod sugar and pod protein contents. *For. Ecol. Mgmt.* **16**: 423–431.

Oduol, P.A. 1994. Genetic Assessment of Perennial *Sesbania* Species in Agroforestry Systems. Ph.D. Thesis, University of Edinburgh, 328 pp.

Ong, C.K., Singh, R.P., Khan, A.A.H. and Osman, M. 1990. Agroforestry for the drylands: Recent advances in measuring water loss through trees. *Agroforestry Today* **2**: 7–9.

Owino, F. 1992. Improving multipurpose tree and shrub species for agroforestry systems. *Agroforestry Systems* **16**: 7–13.

Reich, P.B. 1984. Relationship between leaf age, irradiance, leaf conductance, $CO_2$ exchange and water use efficiency in hybrid poplar. *Photosynthetica* **18**: 445–453.

Salisbury, F.B. and Ross, C.W. 1985. Plant Physiology. Wadsworth Publishing Company, Blemont, California. 747 pp.

Simons, A.J. 1992. Genetic improvement of non-industrial trees. *Agroforestry Systems* **18**: 197–212.

Simons, A.J., McQueen D.J. and Stewart, J.L., 1994. Strategic concepts in the domestication of non-industrial trees. *In*: R.R.B. Leakey and A.C. Newton (Eds) Tropical Trees: The Potential for Domestication, Rebuilding Forest Resources. HMSO, London. 91–102.

Wang, S.C., Cowan, I.R., Farquar, G.D. 1979. Stomatal conductance correlates with photosynthetic capacity. *Nature* **282**: 424–426.

Wood, P.J. 1990. Principles of species selection for agroforestry. *In*: K.G. MacDicken and N.T. Vergara (Eds) Agroforestry: Classification and Management. New York: John Wiley and Sons. 290–309.

Zobel, B.J. 1993. Clonal forestry in the *Eucalyptus*. *In*: M.R. Ahuja and W.J. Libby (Eds) Clonal Forestry II. Conservation and Application. Springer Verlag, Berlin. 139–148.

Zobel, B.J. and Talbert, J. 1984. Applied Forest Tree Improvement. John Wiley and Sons, New York. 505 pp.

# C. GENETIC DIVERSITY AND CONSERVATION

# 13

# Minimum Viable Population Size and the Conservation of Forest Genetic Resources

*A. Mosseler*[1]

## ABSTRACT

The concept of minimum viable population (MVP) size is an important issue in tree improvement programs, particularly for the conservation of forest genetic resources. The MVP will maintain the population through innate population dynamics, processes, and requirements and endure a variety of external calamities. However, to be useful to operational forest conservation and management, the concept of MVP size should be based on indicators affecting population survival. The factors affecting population viability like environmental, genetic and demographic stochasticity, are discussed in relation to MVP size and conservation of genetic resources. The approaches to identify MVP sizes are also presented.

## 1. INTRODUCTION

Until recently the management of forest genetic resources was seen almost entirely in terms of tree improvement and breeding programs that included activities such as plus-tree selection, progeny testing, seed orchard establishment, clonal plantations, and advanced generation breeding. Such programs were aimed at producing 'genetically improved' seedlings for expanding artificial forest regeneration programs. With increasing emphasis on implementing sustainable forestry practices, ecosystem management, and declining population numbers and sizes, the conservation of genetic resources

---

[1]Canadian Forest Service, Petawawa National Forestry Institute, Box 2000, Chalk River, Ontario K0J 1P0, Canada.

has become a priority issue in forest management. The maintenance of genetic diversity in both natural populations and breeding populations is also an important issue in tree improvement programs based on selective breeding and gene transformation. Conservation of genetic resources includes activities such as preserving biological diversity, establishing networks of protected areas, preparation of species status reports, and implementing recovery plans for rare, threatened (or vulnerable), and endangered populations.

The new emphasis on *in situ* gene conservation in forestry has also created a renewed emphasis on natural, as opposed to artificial, regeneration of the forest and the development and implementation of silvicultural (harvesting) systems that promote natural regeneration. The success of natural regeneration is predicted on maintaining population viability, or reproductive capacity, following harvesting. With the decline in population numbers and sizes in many forest tree species and fragmentation of the forest, the concept of minimum viable population (MVP) size may become increasingly important developing indicators (Table 1) for monitoring sustainable forestry practices and for maintaining population viability.

Table 1. Criteria and indicators of population viability in trees

| Criteria | Indicators |
|---|---|
| Reproductive capacity | Pollen and Seed yield |
| | Pollen and Seed quality |
| | Seedling growth performance |
| Genetic diversity | Inbreeding levels |
| | Heterozygosity |
| | Gene frequencies |
| | Gene flow |
| | Genetic drift |
| | Genetic structure |
| | Rare alleles |
| | Number of alleles per gene locus |
| | Proportion of polymorphic loci |
| Minimum viable population size | Absolute population size |
| | Spacing or spatial distribution (within population) |
| | Population fragmentation |

The concept of MVP size was first developed by wildlife biologists concerned with managing small animal populations to ensure their survival. In conservation biology, MVP size is viewed as a critical threshold population size below which a population's extinction becomes imminent. Analysis of MVP size is used in developing conservation strategies, designing ecological reserves, and for implementing species recovery plans for the restoration and protection of rare, threatened, and endangered animal species. An understanding of what constitutes the MVP for a species depends on the knowledge of species life history, ecological relationships, and specific threats to its survival.

The MVP size (and structure) is that which will maintain the population through innate population dynamics, processes, and requirements and endure a variety of external calamities. Although this definition expresses the general idea, it does not provide indicators or guidelines for sustainable forest management or for predicting population persistence. Shaffer (1981) has provided a more precise definition: MVP size is the smallest isolated population having a 99 per cent chance of survival for 1000 years (or 95% over a 100 years) despite random demographic, environmental, and genetic effects, or natural catastrophes. The emphasis here is on the ability of the MVP size to predict the persistence time or the probability of survival of a population. While such definitions attempt to provide some predictive value, they are based on precise biological and ecological information about the species and also on many assumptions about essentially stochastic and unpredictable events.

To be useful to operational forest conservation and management, a definition of MVP size should be based on indicators affecting population viability and survival. These indicators (Table 1) must be measurable so that population viability can be monitored and the impacts of forest harvesting can be assessed and managed through silvicultural operations. For managing natural populations of forest trees, the MVP size is that which maintains: (i) reproductive capacity (seed quality, seed quantity, seedling growth performance); (ii) propagule dispersal ability; and (iii) evolutionary potential or genetic diversity (heterozygosity, allelic diversity, and adaptive variation).

The objectives of MVP size analysis in forestry are: (i) to identify the relationship between population parameters (such as absolute population size, spacing or spatial distribution within the population, and fragmentation) and measures of population viability (i.e., reproductive success and genetic diversity); and, (ii) to use this information to develop recovery plans for rare, threatened, and endangered tree species, and to establish criteria, indicators, and management guidelines for the development of forestry practices that maintain population viability. These objectives embody the twin goals of sustainable forestry: ecological sustainability and sustainability of the timber supply. Ecological sustainability may be attained largely through maintenance of population viability.

## 2. THREATS TO POPULATION SURVIVAL

Population viability is dependant on several general types of threats to population survival: (i) environmental degradation; (ii) natural catastrophes; (iii) environmental stochasticity; (iv) genetic stochasticity; and, (v) demographic stochasticity (Shaffer, 1981). Environmental degradation describes deterministic events such as the introduction of pests, diseases, competitors, and the long-term climatic changes associated with glacial events, increased levels of $CO_2$ in the atmosphere, pollution, urbanization, agricultural development, etc.

Natural catastrophes such as floods, fires, and droughts that can destroy whole populations are essentially stochastic events. Environmental stochasticity describes the temporal and often cyclical variation in habitat parameters such as epidemics of diseases, pests, and competitors that can reduce populations to critical levels over one or several generations. Trees may be less susceptible to local extinction for reasons of environmental stochasticity because of their long life spans. For instance, poor pollination conditions associated with unfavourable spring weatner conditions or pest epidemics can reduce reproductive capacity over the short-term (Mosseler *et al.*, 1992b), but such stochastic events are less likely to affect population survival over the longer term.

Environmental degradation, natural catastrophes, and environmental stochasticity affect populations regardless of size. However, population viability analysis is primarily concerned with the effects of small population size on survival, since small populations are much more likely to become extinct (Shaffer, 1987). Genetic and demographic stochasticity describe threats peculiar to small populations. By integrating MVP size information into forestry practices, the genetic and demographic processes that threaten small population survival can be mitigated and managed through relatively small changes in current forestry practices. Maintaining population numbers above genetically and demographically definable thresholds will become a central theme of sustainable forestry, particularly with less common or rare species and with those characterized by small population size.

Genetic stochasticity describes the loss of genetic diversity related to the combined effects of genetic drift and inbreeding in small populations. Population genetics theory suggests that losses of genetic diversity through genetic stochasticity may represent a longer-term threat to small populations of long-lived species like trees. Most often, small populations go extinct for demographic reasons related to reproductive failure before any genetic effects become noticeable (Lande, 1988). Demographic stochasticity describes chance events affecting the reproductive success or mortality rates of a finite number of individuals for non-genetic reasons. In small populations of animal species, a single failed breeding season can spell disaster for a population. Obviously, the loss of genetic diversity in such situations is a moot point. The extinction of the heath hen (*Tympanuchus cupido*) (Shaffer, 1981) has a well documented history that demonstrates how a succession of threats to survival resulted in the extinction of this bird in 1932. Genetic and demographic processes related to small population size played a major role in this extinction which could have been predicted as early as 1908 based on MVP theory.

### 2.1 Population Genetics and Genetic Stochasticity

Genetic stochasticity describes changes in gene frequencies associated with small or finite population size. These genetic changes are a sampling property of small populations. For instance, when a population is largely destroyed by a natural catastrophe such as fire leaving only a few survivors, the surviving population may represent only a small sample of the genetic variation of the original population. Likewise, a new population of trees that arises from a small sample of seeds dispersed by a bird far enough from the parental tree population to restrict gene flow (i.e., a founder event), represents only a limited sample of the ancestral gene pool and may result in the random fixation of only a small proportion of the total genetic variation contained in the parental population. This process is referred to as genetic drift.

Genetic drift is the process responsible for the loss of genetic diversity (allelic variation) in finite or small populations. This process can be envisioned by imagining a large, isolated population or gene pool that is suddenly reduced to a small number of survivors following a natural catastrophe such as fire. Over the course of the next generation a new population arises from a very limited sample of the gene pool based on only a few survivors. This limited sample of the gene pool can represent only a small fraction of the total genetic variation contained in the original population prior to the population bottleneck caused by the fire. The results of such a small sample of surviving genotypes (or genetic drift) are: (i) a loss of genetic diversity (allelic variation) within this population, and (ii) possibly inbreeding depression if some of the surviving genes are mildly deleterious (Nunney and Campbell, 1993).

If population numbers do not recover quickly following a genetic bottleneck, the loss of genetic diversity can be compounded through inbreeding which results in a further erosion of genetic diversity in individuals through increases in homozygosity. Alleles are more likely to be lost in small, inbreeding populations that are subject to genetic drift (Namkoong, 1989).

Species that normally occur in large, highly outcrossed, heterozygous populations may experience inbreeding depressions related to expression of deleterious and/or lethal recessive genes that would normally be hidden by the heterozygous condition. Inbreeding depression may be expressed as a loss of fitness that accompanies increasing homozygosity (Charlesworth and Charlesworth, 1987). In trees, reduced fitness results from reduced viability and fecundity and is usually expressed as various morphological abnormalities such as chlorophyll deficient mutations, abnormal stem, leaf, and branch morphology, etc.

When large, outcrossing populations such as trees decline suddenly to a few individuals, reduced viability and fecundity results from increased matings among closely related individuals. In small populations the combination of inbreeding and genetic drift can greatly reduce the average fitness and genetic variation in a population and lead to the demise of populations for strictly genetic reasons (Lande, 1988). Many controlled breeding experiments with plants and animals have shown that lines propagated by continuous brother-sister mating or controlled self-fertilization become sterile or inviable causing populations to collapse after several generations through expression of deleterious, recessive genes.

Allelic variation at specific gene loci (location on a chromosome) can be identified using various types of molecular markers. These molecular markers can be differentiated by different types of molecular sieving techniques based on the molecular weight and/or electrostatic charge of proteins, enzymes, DNA fragments, etc. and used to calculate allele frequencies in a population. Using the Hardy-Weinberg formula, $1 = p^2 + 2pq + q^2$, where p and q represent allele frequencies at a gene locus, the expected proportion of genotypes (homozygotes versus heterozygotes) can be calculated for a population mating at random (see any introductory genetics text). The level of inbreeding can be inferred by comparing the expected heterozygosity (He) with the observed heterozygosity (Ho) to derive the inbreeding coefficient, F, according to the formula: $F = (He - Ho)/He$ (Hedrick, 1985). Knowledge of the inbreeding coefficient and the degree of heterozygosity provides useful information on population genetic processes that affect the genetic diversity of a population and the rate at which genetic diversity is being eroded.

Animal breeders have observed that as the inbreeding coefficient approaches 0.5–0.6, severe inbreeding depression occurs through reductions in viability and fecundity. As this inbreeding depression threshold is approached, a population may be headed for extinction from genetic causes alone (Soule, 1980). Setting the inbreeding coefficient at 0.6, we can use the formula: $F = 1 - (1-1/2Ne)t$, where t = number of generations, to find the length of time until inbreeding depression may be expected to result in serious population decline. An effective population of 50 would reach this threshold of F = 0.6 after about 90 generations. The length of time it takes to reach this inbreeding depression threshold varies with the generation time of the species. A population of 50 mice might take 40 years to reach this threshold, whereas a population of 50 deer might take 200 years. A population of 50 jack pine might take 2–3000 years assuming a fire cycle of 25 years, or 6000 years if the fire cycle were doubled, etc.

The long generation time of most tree species suggests that trees only reach such thresholds after several thousands of years. Therefore, genetic diversity in trees may be more likely to survive such processes as a result of recent human intervention in the landscape. However, once a tree species has lost genetic variation through inbreeding and genetic drift it would require many thousands of years to recover this variation. Red pine, *Pinus resinosa*, is a tree species that shows unusually low levels of genetic variation (Fowler and Morris, 1977; Mosseler *et al.* 1992a). This genetic diversity may have been eroded following genetic drift and prolonged, mild inbreeding in small populations (Mosseler, 1992) that may have followed a post-glacial bottleneck (Fowler and Morris, 1977) or perhaps a succession of such bottlenecks over the course of the Pleistocene.

Red pine has not recovered this variation during the present interglacial period—a period that has now lasted 12–15,000 years—despite significant increases in population numbers following glacial retreat. Given the periodicity of glacial cycles and the number of generations required to recover from a genetic bottleneck (Nei *et al.*, 1975), it appears unlikely that long-lived trees such as red pine recover their genetic diversity once it has been lost.

Based on population genetics theory and empirical observations, the genetic minimum viable population size can be determined. The genetic MVP size is the genetically effective population size (Ne) that minimizes inbreeding, inbreeding depression, and loss of genetic diversity (Gilpin, 1991). The genetically effective population size is an important (yet elusive) concept in population genetics that is based on several large assumptions (such as random mating, equal sex ratio, equal progeny per family, non-overlapping generations, etc.). For practical purposes, the genetically effective population can be equated with the number of mating individuals in the population.

The rate of loss of heterozygosity through inbreeding is perhaps the most commonly used and important measure of the loss of variation within populations (Soule, 1980). Based on their experiences with inbreeding depression in animals, breeders have developed the 1 per cent rule of inbreeding which maintains that inbreeding at a rate of 1 per cent per generation will avoid serious inbreeding depression and is thus permissible over the short-term. The loss of heterozygosity can be calculated as: 1 – 1/2Ne per generation; where Ne is the genetically effective population size (Hedrick, 1985). This formula suggests that inbreeding can be kept at a manageable level of 1 per cent per generation by ensuring that a genetically effective population size of 50 mating individuals is maintained (Ewens *et al.*, 1987).

While a 1 per cent reduction in heterozygosity per generation for inbreeding may be a good practical guide for short-term conservation of genetic diversity, this number may need to be modified as better genetic information on specific populations of interest is obtained. A highly heterozygous population may carry a high genetic load of deleterious, recessive genes that may increase susceptibility to inbreeding depression (Park and Fowler, 1984). In contrast, a highly homozygous population that has experienced historically higher levels of inbreeding may carry a relatively low number of deleterious and lethal recessive genes and be much less susceptible to inbreeding depression (Fowler, 1965).

While a minimum number of 50 mating individuals may protect against inbreeding depression in the short-term, 500 individuals has been suggested as the minimum long-term genetically effective population size because at population sizes of less than 500, genetic variance is lost more quickly than it can be renewed through mutation (Franklin, 1980). If 500 is the real genetically effective population size and only 25 per cent of the population is mating, then the MVP may increase to several thousand reproductively mature adults (Nunney and Campbell, 1993). For long-term conservation of forest tree populations MVP sizes of several thousand reproductively mature individuals may be required. Unfortunately, the genetically effective population size is usually much smaller than the censused population, simply because not all the individuals in a population are either reproductively mature or mating. Observations in animal populations show that often only 25 per cent of the censused adults are reproductively active in any generation. Seed orchard studies indicate similar deviations from panmixis (Adams and Birkes, 1989).

The genetic effects of small population size can be summarized as follows: in small populations, homozygosity increases because of inbreeding, allele frequencies drift randomly because of sampling variance, and alleles may be lost. Population isolation through fragmentation may limit gene flow that might otherwise counter the combined effects of inbreeding and genetic drift. However, the numbers presented as genetically effective minimum viable population sizes are tentative at best. They are based on population genetic theory and depend on a number of difficult assumptions that need to be verified through information on the genetics and life history characteristics of the species.

### 2.2 Breeding Systems

Although self-fertilization is the most extreme form of inbreeding and can lead to rapid declines in heterozygosity over several generations, milder forms of inbreeding through matings with close relatives are normal. Most tree species have evolved breeding systems that prevent or mitigate the effects of self-fertilization under natural conditions. Among the angiosperm (deciduous) trees the occurrence of selfing is limited or prevented through breeding systems based either on genetic self-incompatibility or dioecy (see Richards, 1986).

In dioecious species the sexes are separated among different individuals, thereby precluding self-fertilization. Willow (*Salix*), poplar (*Populus*), and ash (*Fraxinus*) trees are either male or female. However, dioecious breeding systems are less common in trees than monoecious or other forms of bisexuality where self-fertilization is at least theoretically possible. To minimize the occurrence of self-fertilization many bisexual angiosperms have evolved genetic self-incompatibility systems relying on genetic self-incompatibility alleles to prevent selfed pollen from germinating on the female flower of the same plant.

Gymnosperms (conifers) are monoecious, carrying both male and female structures on the same individual, and they are fully self-compatible and self-fertile. The spatial separation of female and male reproductive structures within the tree crown helps to minimize (but not prevent) self-pollination and self-fertilization. There are few physiological barriers to self-fertilization in conifers. Conifers minimize the effects of self-fertilization through the mechanism of polyembryony in which each ovule or seed forming structure contains several egg cells or archegonia, each of which can be fertilized independently of other fertilization events within the same ovule (see Owens and Blake, 1985). Under the system of polyembryony, some embryos will result from self-fertilization and others will result via cross-fertilization. However, self-fertilized embryos will often abort or be outcompeted by the more vigorous cross-fertilized embryos. In the absence of adequate cross-pollination and cross-fertilization, such as may be expected in small populations or isolated trees, high amounts of empty seeds may form and the seed that develops may produce degenerate seedlings as a result of inbreeding depression.

### 2.3 Propagule Dispersal and Gene Flow

The dispersal of pollen and seed from one relatively isolated population to another promotes the flow of genes between populations. Such gene migration can have a profound effect in reversing the effects of genetic drift in small, isolated populations. Gene flow is a powerful evolutionary force capable of counterbalancing the adverse effects of inbreeding and genetic drift in small populations by infusing new genetic variation into the population. It has been estimated that as few as one immigrant every one or two generations is enough to counteract the combined effects of inbreeding and genetic drift in small populations (Slatkin, 1985).

Pollen and seed dispersal normally follow a strongly leptokurtic (reverse J-shaped curve) and skewed distribution (Adams, 1993; Grant, 1980) from a point source or parent tree (Fig. 1) with only a very minute fraction of pollen or seeds dispersed beyond several hundred metres from the parent tree (Di-Giovanni and Kevan, 1991). Dispersal of seed from a red pine mutant (Fig. 2) in western Newfoundland showed a striking relationship between prevailing winds and seed dispersal. Most of the seeds fell within about 40 m of the parent with very few mutant progonies found beyond 100 m from the parent.

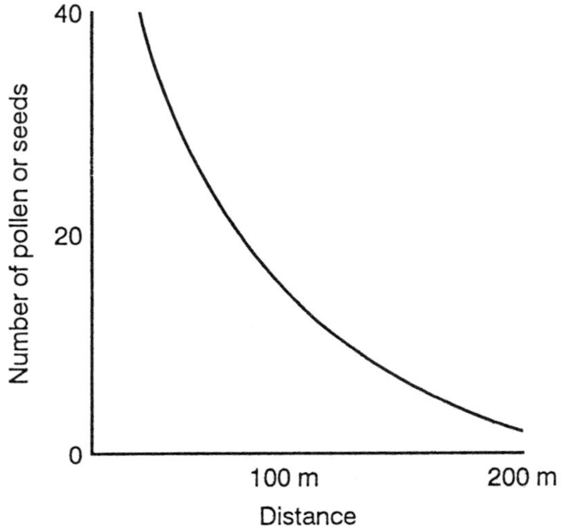


Fig. 1. Generalized leptokurtic dispersion of pollen and seed from a parent tree.

Fig. 2. A morphological mutation in red pine (centre) in the midst of a normal or wildtype population. The mutation has provided an unique opportunity to study long- distance seed dispersal in a tree species.

Efficient dispersal is critical to the survival of highly subdivided metapopulations such as those of red pine. Red pine is dependant on dispersal to a continually shifting mosaic of suitable habitats prepared by disturbances related to fire to locate a habitat suitable for seed germination. Metapopulation species must balance local extinction with recolonization of newly available, suitable habitats. Wind dispersal is limited in space and cannot be relied upon to facilitate recolonization events (Fig. 1).

A long-distance dispersal mode is essential if newly available, suitable habitats are to be reached. Animals and birds provide such a dispersal mechanism and may be a critical, if largely unrecognized, component in the survival of many metapopulation trees (Furnier *et al.*, 1987). Vander Wall and Ball (1977) reported avian dispersal distances of more than 20 km for conifer seeds. Such long-distance seed dispersal has been documented for a morphological mutant in a metapopulation of red pine located in western Newfoundland, Canada. Figure 2 shows a mutant red pine in the midst of a population of normal or 'wild type' trees several km from the point source or mother-of-all-mutants. The most likely dispersal agents in this case are the red crossbills (*L. curvirostera*) which are native to Newfoundland and which forage on red pine seeds. While crossbills are opportunistic feeders, and will switch from spruces to pines depending on cone crop availability, the red crossbill is most commonly associated with the cones of eastern white pine and red pine (Dickerman, 1987). Dickerman (1987) has attributed the near extinction of a subspecies of red crossbill, *L. curvirostra neogaea*, that was particularly well adapted to feeding on eastern white pine cones to the post-settlement destruction of white pine that had occurred throughout north eastern North America by 1900.

Supporting evidence for the effectiveness of bird dispersal comes from the rates of migration following glacial retreat. Tree species migration rates were much higher than the rate of seed dispersal by wind alone. Average tree migration rates have been estimated at 10–45 km per century (Huntley and Birks, 1983) up to 200 km per century (Ritchie and MacDonald, 1986) to explain the geographical ranges of most northern tree species (Davis *et al.*, 1986). Such migration rates strongly suggest a highly motile dispersal vector (see review by Schwartz, 1992).

Connectivity of populations in a patchy environment has a strong bearing on the persistence or extinction of small populations of animals (Fahrig and Merriam, 1985). Movement of animals, or plant propagules, among subpopulations prolongs the persistence of the metapopulation. Models presented by Roff (1974a,b) show that, in the absence of dispersal between subpopulations of a metapopulation, the metapopulation is unstable and will become extinct in a comparatively short time.

### 2.4 Demographic Stochasticity

The likelihood of population extinction for purely genetic reasons is remote. Small populations normally collapse for demographic reasons related either to abnormal mortality rates or to reproductive failure (Lande, 1988). Demographic stochasticity describes chance events in the survival and reproductive success of finite (small) populations (Shaffer, 1981). In animal populations these non-genetic effects have been referred to as Allee effects. The Allee effect is a low-density extinction threshold related to the demographic (mating and survival) requirements of a species and describes demographic processes in which individuals in small populations experience diminished viability and reproductive success for social, behavioural, or environmental reasons linked to the necessity to maintain some threshold number or density. Allee effects may be caused by a breakdown in social interactions and behaviour related to activities such as group defense against predators or competitors; density-dependant mating success (i.e. the difficulty of finding a suitable mate in a small population); or through chemical modifications of the environment that promote survival, reproduction, etc. Demographic MVPs tend to be in the same range (Gilpin and Soule, 1986) or slightly less than the minimum number of 50 individuals presented as the genetic MVP by Franklin (1980).

Are there responses in plant populations similar to the Allee effect? Observations suggest that population size has an important effect on pollination success and may be expected to have an important effect on the behaviour of pollinators and seed dispersers. Assuming that foraging behaviour by animals is opportunistic and therefore related to resource availability or population size, small and isolated populations may be less attractive to foraging animals.

Conifers are wind-pollinated and pollen dispersal distances are relatively short, with most pollen falling within 100–200 m of a tree (Fig. 1). Under normal conditions of stand density, enough pollen may be available to overcome the adverse effects of self-pollination and self-fertilization on seed yield and quality through mechanisms such as polyembryony. However, trees in small, isolated, sparsely populated patches may be expected to experience increased self-fertilization resulting in reductions in numbers filled seed/cone and seedling vigour (Fig. 3). A similar positive correlation has been demonstrated between stand density and seed yield (Fig. 4). Therefore, pollination and fertilization success in trees is very much density-dependant, and thus may be similar to the Allee effects described in many animal populations.

## 3. APPROACHES TO IDENTIFYING MVP SIZES FOR TREES

There are several approaches to identifying MVP sizes.

By observing the biogeographical distribution patterns of species occurring in insular or patchy environments or those that are adapted to living in small populations, an approximation of MVP size may be inferred. However, not all species occur in patchy environments and, in many cases, habitats and landscapes have been so seriously disrupted that this approach has obvious limitations.

Simulation models have been developed to determine MVP based on biological requirements. Such simulations have been used to assess the probability of survival of populations of a given size over different time spans. While

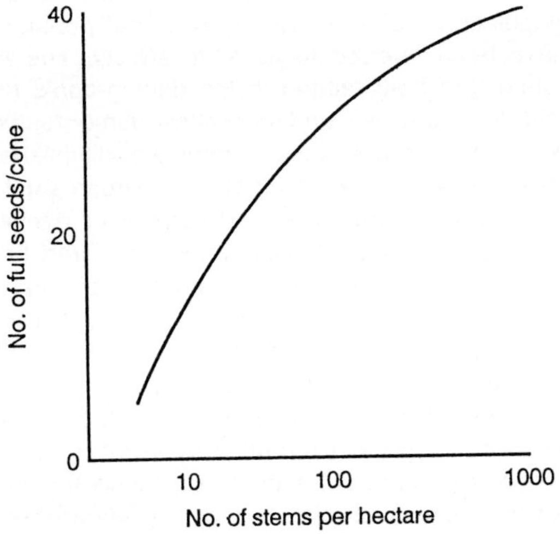


Fig. 3. Generalized relationship between population size and seed yield per cone (based on observations with white spruce, *Picea glauca*).

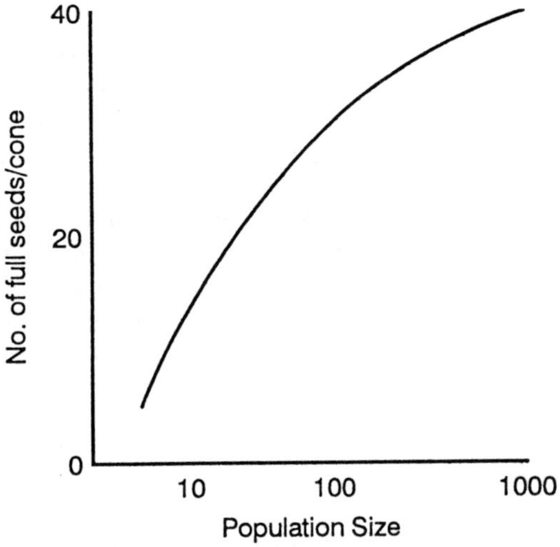


Fig. 4. Generalized relationship between population density and seed yield per cone (based on observations with red pine, *Pinus resinosa*).

these models offer predictive capability, they are also based on many assumptions about essentially stochastic events. This approach would probably be of limited interest or usefulness in developing criteria and indicators for sustainable forestry practices.

The integration of ecological information, life history traits, normal fire cycles and fire relations, age to reproduction, lifetime fecundity, age structure, sex ratios, seed dispersal mechanisms, density relationships, pollination requirements, genetic load, and pest relations could yield some notions about MVP sizes for trees. Much of the ecological information required for such simulations is available for many of the commercially important tree species. These simulation models might also be used to evaluate the effects of the various types of threats (demographic, genetic, environmental stochasticity, natural catastrophes, etc.) and point to the limiting factors for survival.

A third approach to determining MVP sizes could be based solely on the minimum genetically effective population size, based on population genetics theory. Given adequate genetic information, realistic models defining minimum genetically effective population size can be developed. Population genetics theory alone suggests that the number of mating individuals required would be the range of 50 to 500. However, ensuring that long-term evolutionary potential is maintained may require substantially larger populations (Soule, 1980). These recommendations are based on very general, basic principles of population genetics theory and need to be validated with more detailed information on genetic variation, genetic structure, historical levels of inbreeding, genetic load, the nature of inbreeding depression, life history traits, and on the reproductive biology of a species. While much of this information is available for many of our commercially important tree species, very little information exists for many of the less common, less commercially important, trees that are at greatest risk. In the absence of such information genetically based minimum viable population size estimates are imprecise and may not be very useful in developing conservation strategies, establishing protected areas network for population conservation, or for implementing species recovery plans. Furthermore, these genetic models do not consider the demographic requirements of species.

A fourth option in developing indicators for MVP size is to create or locate isolated populations of various sizes and monitor their performance in terms of maintaining genetic diversity and reproductive success. Several study areas have been identified in eastern Canada where sets of isolated populations of varying size can be found within a limited geographical area. This approach is being used to study the effects of small population size in white pine, *Pinus strobus* L., and white spruce, *Picea glauca* (Moench) Voss. The experimental design used to study MVP size for these species consists of three populations in each of the following six population size classes: isolated single trees, populations with less than 10 trees, populations with 15 to 25 trees, 40 to 60 trees, 100 to 200 trees, amd populations with more than 500 trees. Seed yields, seed quality, and seedling growth performance are being quantified and related to population size. Levels of inbreeding and genetic diversity can be estimated using molecular genetic assays.

In small populations we expect and can test for the following population characteristics related to population size: (i) loss of additive genetic variance; (ii) increased inbreeding and homozygosity; (iii) expression of deleterious alleles; and, (iv) reduced reproductive capacity and viability. Through these studies we hope to develop indicators for establishing minimum viable population sizes for several tree species.

Until these MVP size studies are completed, population genetics theory and preliminary empirical observations suggest that, in fragmented landscapes, a metapopulation in which the sizes of individual populations (subpopulations) are maintained at several hundred reproductively mature trees, at densities of at least 10 trees per species per hectare, may provide reasonable, preliminary MVP size criteria for maintaining the viability of tree populations.

## ACKNOWLEDGMENTS

The support of the Ontario Ministry of Natural Resources, the Southern Ontario Forest Genetics Association, the Eastern Ontario Model Forest Association, and the Canadian Forest Service is gratefully acknowledged. Joy Lavereau is gratefully acknowledged for the preparation of figures.

## REFERENCES

Adams, W.T. 1993. Gene dispersal within forest tree populations. *New Forests* **6**: 217–240.

Adams, W.T. and Birkes, D.S. 1989. Mating patterns in seed orchards. *In*: Proc 20th South. For. Tree Improv. Conf., Charleston, SC. 75–86.

Charlesworth, D. and Charlesworth, B. 1987. Inbreeding depression and its evolutionary consequences. *Annu. Rev. Ecol. Syst.* **18**: 237–268.

Davis, M.B., Woods, K.D., Webb, S.L. and Futyma, R.P. 1986. Dispersal versus climate: Expansion of *Fagus* and *Tsuga* into the Upper Great Lakes. *Vegetatio* 67: 93–103.

Dickerman, R.W. 1987. The "Old Northeastern" subspecies of Red Crossbill. *Am. Birds* **41**: 189–194.

Di-Giovanni and Kevan, P.G. 1991. Factors affecting pollen dynamics and its importance to pollen contamination: a review. *Can. J. For. Res.* **21**: 1155–1170.

Ewens, W.J., Brockwell, P.J., Gani, J.M. and Resnick, S.I. 1987. Minimum viable population size in the presence of catastrophe. *In*: M.E. Soule (Ed.) Viable Populations for Conservation. Cambridge University Press, Cambridge, U.K. 59–68.

Fahrig, L. and Merriam, G. 1985. Habitat patch connectivity and population survival. *Ecology* **66**: 1762–1768.

Fowler, D.P. 1965. Effects of inbreeding in red pine, *Pinus resinosa* Ait. II. Pollination studies. *Silvae Genet.* **14**: 12–23.

Fowler, D.P. and Morris, R.W. 1977. Genetic diversity in red pine: evidence for low genic heterozygosity. *Can. J. For. Res.* **7**: 343–349.

Franklin, I.R. 1980. Evolutionary change in small populations. *In*: M.E. Soule and B.A. Wilcox (Eds) Conservation Biology: An Evolutionary-Ecological Perspective. Sinauer Associates, Sunderland, MA. 135–149.

Furnier, G.R., Knowles, P., Clyde, M.A. and Dancik, B.P. 1987. Effects of avian seed dispersal on the genetic structure of whitebark pine populations. *Evolution* **41**: 607–612.

Gilpin, M.E. 1991. The genetic effective size of a matapopulation. *Biol. J. Linn. Soc.* **42**: 165–175.

Gilpin, M.E. and Soule, M.E. 1986. Minimum viable populations: processes of species extinction. *In*: M.E. Soule (Ed.) Conservation Biology: The Science of Scarcity and Diversity. Sinauer Associates, Sunderland, MA. 19–34.

Grant, V.G. 1980. Gene flow and the homogeneity of species populations. *Biol. Zbl.* **99**: 157–169.

Hedrick, P.W. 1985. Genetics of Populations. Jones and Bartlett Publishers Inc., Boston.

Huntley, B. and Birks, H.J.B. 1983. An atlas of past and present pollen maps for Europe: 0–13,000 years ago. Cambridge University Press, Cambridge. U.K.

Lande, R. 1988. Genetics and demography in biological conservation. *Science* **241**: 1455–1460.

Mosseler, A. 1992. Life history and genetic diversity in red pine: implications for gene conservation in forestry. *For. Chron.* **68**: 701–708.

Mosseler, A., Egger K.N. and Hughes, G. 1992a. Lack of genetic diversity in *Pinus resinosa* confirmed by random amplified polymorphic DNA markers. *Can. J. For. Res.* **22**: 1332–1337.

Mosseler, A., Roberts, B.A. and Tricco, P. 1992b. The effects of fir coneworm, *Dioryctria abietivorella* (Lepidoptera: Pyrallidae), on reproductive success in small, isolated populations of red pine, *Pinus resinosa* Ait. *For. Ecol. Mgmt.* **53**: 15–27.

Nei, M., Maruyama, T. and Chakraborty, R. 1975. The bottleneck effect and population variability. *Evolution* **29**: 1–10.

Namkoong, G. 1989. Population genetics and the dynamics of conservation. *In*: L. Knutson and A.K. Stoner (Eds) Biotic Diversity and Germplasm Preservation, Global Imperatives. Kluwer Academic Publ., Boston, MA. 161–181.

Nunney, L. and Campbell, K.A. 1993. Assessing minimum viable population size, demography meets population genetics. *Trends Ecol. Evol.* **8**: 234–239.

Owens, J.N. and Blake, M.D. 1985. Forest tree seed production. Can. For. Serv., Inf. Rep. PI-X-53.

Park, Y.S. and Fowler, D.P. 1984. Inbreeding in black spruce (*Picea mariana* (Mill.) B.S.P.): self-fertility, genetic load, and performance. *Can. J. For. Res.* **14**: 17–21.

Richards, A.J. 1986. Plant Breeding Systems. George Allen & Unwin, London, U.K. 529 pp.

Ritchie, J.C. and MacDonald, G.M. 1986. The pattern of post-glacial spread of white spruce. *J. Biogeog.* **13**: 527–540.

Roff, D.A. 1974a. Spatial heterogeneity and the persistence of populations. *Oecologia* **15**: 245–258.

Roff, D.A. 1974b. The analysis of a population model demonstrating the importance of dispersal in a heterogeneous environment. *Oecologia* **15**: 259–275.

Schwartz, M.W. 1992. Modelling effects of habitat fragmentation on the ability of trees to respond to climate warming. *Biodiv. and Conserv.* **2**: 51–61.

Shaffer, M.L. 1981. Minimum population sizes for species conservation. *Bioscience* **31**: 131–134.

Shaffer, M.L. 1987. Minimum viable populations: coping with uncertainty. *In*: M.E. Soule (Ed.) Viable Populations for Conservation. Cambridge University Press, Cambridge, U.K. 69–87.

Slatkin, M. 1985. Gene flow in natural populations. *Ann. Rev. Ecol. Syst.* **16**: 393–430.

Soule, M.E. 1980. Thresholds for survival: maintaining fitness and evolutionary potential. *In*: M.E. Soule and B.A. Wilcox (Eds) Conservation Biology: An Evolutionary- Ecological Perspective. Sinauer Associates, Sunderland, MA. 151–169.

Vander Wall, S.B. and Ball, R.P. 1977. Coadaptations of the Clark's Nutcracker and the pinon pine for efficient seed harvest and dispersal. *Ecol. Monogr.* **47**: 89–111.

# 14

# Genetic Diversity in East-Asian *Pinus* Species

*Zin-Suh Kim*[1] *and Seok-Woo Lee*[2]

**ABSTRACT**

The allozyme and RAPD marker literature was reviewed to obtain estimates of the level and distribution of genetic diversity in 10 East-Asian pine species. These values were compared with similar estimates for other tree species, particularly those for pine trees in Europe and North America. This analysis indicated that East-Asian pine species had the higher levels of genetic diversity than temperate and tropical trees as well as pine trees of Europe and North America. The mean number of alleles per locus overall 10 East-Asian pine trees was 2.5 and the mean observed and expected heterozygosities were 0.205 and 0.211, respectively. On an average, *Diploxylon* pines showed the higher levels of genetic diversity than *Haploxylon* pines. Genetic variation at polymorphic loci was partitioned such that most (96%) of the diversity was found within the population, while a smaller fraction (4%) accounted for population differentiation, indirectly indicating that gene flow among Asian pine tree populations is high enough to counteract the effect of genetic drift.

## 1. INTRODUCTION

Evolutionary theory shows that genetic diversity is essential for the long-term survival of species. Without genetic diversity, species cannot adapt to environmental changes and are more likely to become extinct. Measures of the levels and distribution of genetic diversity within species, within and among populations, therefore, have been of considerable interest (Hamrick and Godt, 1989;

[1]Department of Forest Resources, Korea University, Seoul 136–701 Korea.

[2]Present address: Forest Genetics Research Institute, P.O. Box 24, Suwon 441-350 Korea.

Hamrick, 1994). In recent years, the difficulties of estimating parameters such as the proportion of polymorphic loci and/or heterozygosity that faced every population geneticists have been alleviated as a result of the availability of biochemical (isozyme) and molecular (RFLPs and RAPDs) techniques that allow the identification and analysis of several single-gene loci. Today, it is possible to obtain estimates of genetic diversity in populations of many plant species (Hamrick and Godt, 1989).

The genus *Pinus* dominated the forest vegetation during most of the Mesozoic era, and are still widely distributed in the Northern Hemisphere, from the timberline in sub-arctic lowlands to high mountains of subtropical and montane, tropical regions (Mirov, 1967). They grow in a variety of sites from sea level to 4000 m in elevation and account for as much as 70 per cent of all wood land areas.

The classification of the genus *Pinus* varies according to different scientists. As many as 105 species are recognized by Mirov (1967) while only 92 are listed by Farjon (1984). In most classifications, the genus is divided into two subgenera: *Haploxylon* (Strobus) and *Diploxylon* (Pinus), and these further into sections and subsections (Farjon, 1984). The total number of *Pinus* species recognized from Asia differs among taxonomists. According to Mirov (1967), there are approximately 24 species in Asia, of which 11 belong to *Haploxylon*, and 13 to *Diploxylon* subgenera. The distribution patterns of *Haploxylon* and *Diploxylon* species in Asia are different. *Haploxylon* pines have discontinuous distributions. The ranges of individual species are relatively limited and seldom overlapped. On the other hand, *Diploxylon* pines usually have large continuous and overlapping distributions.

Despite of several decades of intensive research, our knowledge about the patterns and levels of genetic variation among and within different *Pinus* species is still rather scarce. Many species, especially those occurring in Asia have not been studied to date. In this study, an attempt was made to provide new insights into the level and patterns of genetic diversity in some East-Asian *Pinus* species by reviewing the allozyme and DNA marker literature.

## 2. GENETIC MARKERS USED IN POPULATION STUDIES OF FOREST TREES

The description of the population genetic structure and its dynamics are based on the analysis of the gene and/or the genotype frequencies. Thus, population genetic studies require stable and reproducible genetic markers which show sufficient variation in the material analyzed. Due to difficulties in inferring genotypes from phenotypes, morphological characters and secondary compounds such as flavonoids and terpenes fail to be candidates for genetic markers (Crawford, 1983).

In contrast, allozymes possess one distinct advantage over other markers as they permit easy assay of a large number of individuals and population for many characters (Wheeler and Guries, 1987). In spite of certain limitations, the equation between allozyme phenotype and genotype remains reasonably well-defined. Therefore, in the past two decades allozyme markers have been widely used in genetic analysis of various organisms.

In the last few years, molecular genetic approaches such as analysis of RFLPs (restriction fragment length polymorphisms), DNA fingerprinting, and RAPDs (randomly amplified polymorphic DNAs) marker system have been applied in forest genetics, opening new possibilities for studies of the nuclear and organelle genome. The greatest advantage of DNA markers is that they are not the products of transcription or translation and can thus be viewed as providing pure genetic information, i.e., genotype = phenotype (Nienhuis *et al.*, 1987). Theoretically, the number of potential DNA markers is almost unlimited and as a method for detecting variation, DNA analysis is estimated to be much more powerful than isozyme electrophoresis (Clegg *et al.*, 1984). The use of DNA markers in forest genetics has been contemplated early (Brown and Moran, 1981). However, it was only recently that studies utilizing DNA markers have been made in conifers (Szmidt and Wang, 1991).

## 3. SPECIES STUDIED

East-Asian diploxylon pine species appear to be less differentiated than their counterparts from North America. Notably all diploxylon species native to East-Asia belong to one subsection *Sylvestris*. In contrast, North American species from this subgenus show considerable diversity and are subdivided into several subsections (Farjon, 1984).

*Pinus sylvestris*, the most widely distributed species, grows throughout northern Eurasia from Scotland to northern China. The species is noted for its immense phenotypic variability and a systematic division is still unclear (Molotkov and Patlaj, 1991). Two geographic varieties, var. *mongolica* (Litvinov) and var. *sylvestriformis* (Takenouchi) are recognized at the eastern limit of the *P. sylvestris* distribution. The var. *mongolica* occurs in the mountainous areas of extreme northern China. The var. *sylvestriformis* occurs in a very limited region in the Baekdu mountain of Korea (*Changbaik* in Chinese) where it grows at elevations between 800 and 1600 m, partly overlapping with *P. densiflora* (Sieb. et Zucc.) which occurs below 900 m (Cheng and Fu, 1978). It does not overlap, however, with the distribution of the var. *mongolica* which is confined to the northeastern extremes of China. The systematic position of the var. *sylvestriformis* is not settled but there has been a general agreement among taxonomists that it is morphologically intermediate between var. *mongolica* and *P. densiflora* (Cheng and Fu, 1978).

*P. densiflora* is widely distributed in Korea, Japan, eastern Manchuria and on the Santhung Peninsula in China (Mirov, 1967). *P. thunbergii* grows mainly in South Korea along its coastlines and also occurs along the coasts of three main islands of Japan (Mirov, 1967). In Korea, its natural range overlaps with the distribution of *P. densiflora* and consequently natural hybridization may happen in which two species occur sympatrically. In certain regions, some scientists reported the presence of natural hybrid swarms showing variable hybridity (Lee, 1994).

*P. tabulaeformis* is a widespread species occurring in the northern and central parts of China. *P. yunnanensis* has its distribution in the southwestern part of China (Mirov, 1967; Farjon, 1984). Some taxonomists believe that the two species intercrossed in the Yunnan and Sichuan region in China as early as Tertiary (Mirov, 1967) and formed a natural hybrid species, *P. densata* (Mirov, 1967; Farjon, 1984). Today, *P. densata* occurs at high mountain elevations between 2700 and 3900 m where neither of the two putative parental species can normally grow (Wang *et al.*, 1990).

There are five haploxylon pine species in East-Asia. The three species, *P. koraiensis, P. pumila* and *P. sibirica* fall taxonomically in subsection *Cembrae*. *P. bungeana* belongs to subsection *Gerardianae* and *P. parviflora* to subsection *Strobi*. *P. sibirica* is widely distributed in Eurasia from the Ural Mountains through western and central Siberia to northern Mongolia—an east-west distance of about 4000 km. It overlaps the range of *P. pumila* on the eastern portion of its distribution near Lake Baikal in Siberia.

Japanese stone pine, *P. pumila* grows in northern Siberia and in sub-alpine parts of Japan, Korea and Manchuria. It extends north almost to the Arctic Ocean (70°N), west to Mongolia and to the Lake Baikal area, and south to Korea and Honshu, Japan. It grows from low elevations in the north to high elevations in the south. It commonly forms thickets just below barren tundra and tops of mountains or lowlands in the extreme north. Like Siberian stone pine, it extends nearly 4000 km from east to west and 3000 km from north to south.

Korean pine, *P. koraiensis*, occurs throughout Korea and eastern Manchuria into southeastern Siberia as well as on the islands of Honshu and Shikoku in Japan. It tends to grow in more maritime conditions and lower mountains than its neighbor—the Japanese stone pine. Its geographic range overlaps that of the Japanese stone pine, but the species occupy different ecological niches. Korean pine, unlike its counterparts, grows in association with hardwoods where near-maritime climates prevail.

The geographic distributions of the reviewed East-Asian *Pinus* species is given in Fig. 1 A and B. These descriptions are based primarily on those of Critchfield and Little (1966) and Mirov (1967). The species studied, their taxonomic position and the origin of plant materials collected for the researches reviewed in the present study are given in Table 1.

## 4. LEVELS OF GENETIC DIVERSITY IN EAST-ASIAN PINES

The genetic variation of a species and populations is perhaps the most fundamental piece of information for the species that requires management. The most commonly used measures of intrapopulational variation are the per cent of polymorphic loci (P), the number of alleles per locus (A/L), the effective number of alleles per locus ($n_e$), and observed and expected heterzygosities ($H_o$ and $H_e$, respectively).

Levels of intrapopulational allozyme variation have been the subject of several reviews (Hamrick and Godt, 1989; Hamrick, 1994). Although each

A

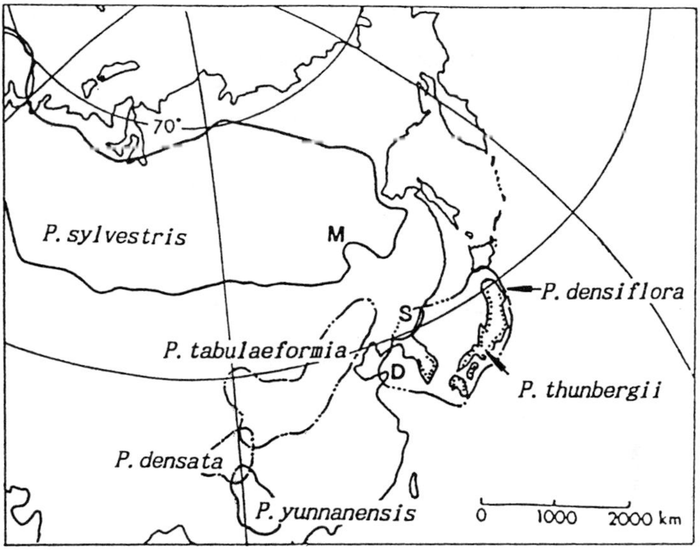


B

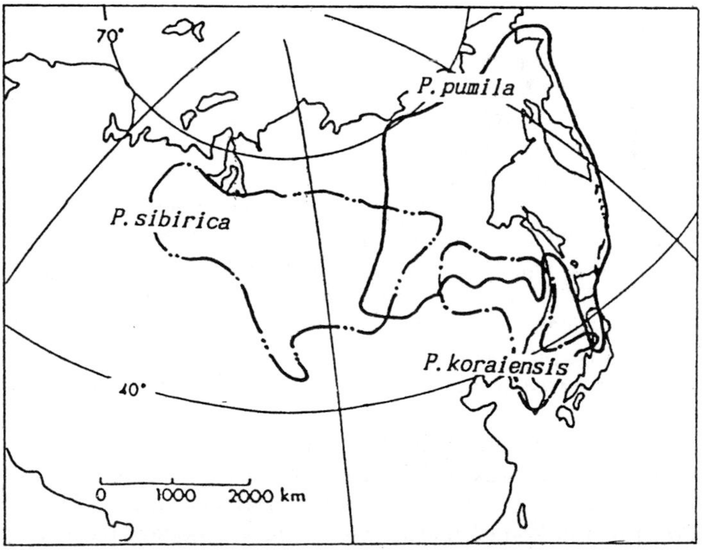


Fig. 1. Geographic distributions of the investigated *Diploxylon* (A) *Haploxylon* (B) pine speices (after Mirov, 1967). M: *P. sylvestris* var. *mongolica*, S: *P. sylvestris* var. *sylvestriformis* D: *P. densiflora*.

Table 1. List of Asian *Pinus* species included in this study

| Subgenus | Section | Subsection | Species | Origin* |
|---|---|---|---|---|
| *Diploxylon* | *Pinus* | *Sylvestres* | *P. densata* | China |
| | | | *P. densiflora* | Korea, Japan |
| | | | *P. sylvestris*, | |
| | | | var. *mongolica* | China |
| | | | var. *sylvestriformis* | China |
| | | | *P. tabulaeformis* | China |
| | | | *P. thunbergii* | Korea, Japan |
| | | | *P. yunnanensis* | China |
| *Haploxylon* | *Strobus* | *Cembrae* | *P. koraiensis* | Korea, Russia |
| | | | *P. pumila* | Russia |
| | | | *P. sibirica* | Russia |

*Countries from which plant materials were collected for the researches reviewed in the present study.

review used different criteria to include studies, the general conclusions are similar; plant species generally maintain relatively high amounts of genetic variation within populations. In their review of over 400 species Hamrick and Godt (1989) found that plant species has 50.5 per cent of their loci polymorphic, 1.96 alleles per locus, and a mean heterozygosity per individual of 0.149 on an average.

Woody plants have been found to contain a high level of isozyme variation within populations than other groups of plants (Hamrick and Godt, 1989). This is probably due to their longevity, predominant outcrossing, broad range, and potential for extensive gene flow, all of which contribute to large effective population size. In general, species that are widespread, long-lived, primarily outcrossed by wind-pollination, have high lifetime fecundities and are charateristic of the later stages of succession maintain higher levels of intrapopulational variation than species with other combinations of traits. Among the tree species, temperate tree species, which represent mostly wind-pollinated genera have higher levels of genetic diversity ($P_s$=65.2%; $P_p$=50%; $H_{es}$ = 0.171; $H_{ep}$=0.146; $P_s$ and $P_p$ = percentage of loci polymorphic within species and within populations, respectively; $H_{es}$ and $H_{ep}$ = mean heterzygosity within species and within populations, respectively) than predominately animal-pollinated tropical species ($P_s$=50.6%; $P_p$=36.9%; $H_{es}$=0.160; $H_{ep}$=0.125) (Hamrick, 1994).

In conifers, the average expected heterozygosity ($H_e$) over 20 species (mainly *Pinus* species) was 0.207, but varied greatly between species, from 0 in *Pinus resinosa* to 0.341 in *Picea abies* (Hamrick *et al.*, 1981). Similarly, within European and North American *Pinus* species, genetic diversity was very variable between species, from 0 in *P. torreyana* to 0.362 in *P. teada* with the average of 0.174 (Ledig, 1986). Additionally, according to the review of Goncharenko *et al.* (1993b), the value of $H_e$ ranged from 0 in *P. torreyana* to 0.270 in *P. oocarpa* with the average of 0.132 over 25 *Pinus* species.

Table 2. Mean values for the percentage of polymorphic loci (P), average number of alleles per locus (A/L), observed and expected heterozygosities ($H_o$ and $H_e$, respectively) in 10 Asian pine species

| Species | No. of pop. (seed source) | No. of loci Investigated | A/L | P+ | $H_o$ | $H_e$ |
|---|---|---|---|---|---|---|
| *Diploxylon* | | | | | | |
| *Pinus densata* | 1 (China)[10)] | 13 | 2.5 | 61.5 | .179 | .210 |
| *P. densiflora* | 6 (Japan)[9)] | 14 | 3.5 | 64.3 | .255 | .275 |
| | 25 (South Korea)[4)] | 23 | 2.4 | 66.3 | .258 | .262 |
| | 10 (South Korea; RAPD)[3)] | 31 | – | 95.2 | .521 | .395 |
| *P. sylvestris,* | | | | | | |
| var. *mongolica* | 4 (China)[9)] | 14 | 2.9 | 54.3 | .184 | .187 |
| var. *sylvestriformis* | 5 (China)[9)] | 14 | 3.8 | 71.4 | .254 | .287 |
| *P. tabulaeformis* | 1 (China)[10)] | 13 | 2.8 | 53.8 | .165 | .195 |
| *P. thumbergii* | 22 (Japan)[7)] | 14 | 3.9 | – | – | .240 |
| | 13 (South Korea)[6)] | 27 | 2.2 | 55.3 | .214 | .212 |
| *P. yunnanensis* | 1 (China)[10)] | 13 | 2.2 | 46.2 | .158 | .169 |
| Mean | | | 2.9 | 59.1 | .208 | .225 |
| *Haploxylon* | | | | | | |
| *P. koraiensis* | 8 (South Korea)[5)] | 23 | 2.0 | 61.4 | .200 | .208 |
| | 3 (Russian Far East)[8)] | 17 | 1.6 | 43.2 | .137 | .131 |
| *P. sibirica* | 8 (Siberia)[2)] | 20 | 1.8 | 45.0 | .173 | .176 |
| | 10 (Siberia)[8)] | 19 | 1.8 | 46.2 | .162 | .158 |
| *P. pumila* | 5 (Sakhalin)[1)] | 22 | 2.5 | 68.0 | .288 | .255 |
| | 4 (North of Kamchatka Peninsula)[8)] | 20 | 2.4 | 60.0 | .247 | .249 |
| Mean | | | 2.0 | 54.0 | .201 | .196 |
| Total Mean | | | 2.5 | 56.6 | .205 | .211 |

**References:** 1) Goncharenko *et al.*, 1993a; 2) Goncharenko *et al.*, 1993b; 3) Kim, 1995; 4) Kim and Lee, 1995; 5) Kim *et al.*, 1994; 6) Lee, 1994; 7) Miyata and Ubukata, 1994; 8) Politov and Krutovskii, 1992; 9) Szmidt and Wang, 1993; 10) Wang *et al.*, 1990.
+, locus has been considered polymorphic if the frequency of the most common allele has not exceeded 95 per cent.

In East-Asian pines, the mean number of alleles per locus (A/L) ranged from 1.6 in *P. koraiensis* from Russian Far East to 3.9 in *P. thunbergii* from Japan and the overall mean value for 10 species was 2.5 (Table 2). The polymorphic loci (0.95 level) ranged from 43.2 per cent in *P. koraiensis* from Russian Far East to 71.4 per cent in *P. sylvestris* var. *sylvestriformis* and the mean value for 10 pines was 56.6 per cent. The observed heterozygosities ($H_o$) ranged from 0.137 in *P. koraiensis* from Russian Far East to 0.288 in *P. pumila* with the avearge of 0.205. The mean expected heterozygosities ($H_e$)

ranged from 0.131 in *P.koraiensis* from Russian Far East and to 0.282 in *P. sylvestris* var. *sylvestriformis* with the average of 0.211. Out of 10 Asian pines reviewed here, *P. koraiensis* from Russian Far East has the lowest genetic diversity.

At the species level, geographic range is the best predictor of levels of allozyme variation (Hamrick and Godt, 1989). Endemic species have a low genetic diversity whereas regionally distributed and widespread species maintain a high level of genetic diversity. This is due to the fact that species with wide geographic ranges may have a history of large, continuous populations that are less susceptible to loss of genetic variation owing to genetic drift. Endemic species, on the other hand, might be expected to consist of smaller, more ecologically limited populations that have experienced population bottlenecks during their evolutionary history. Our allozyme literature supported this suggestion very well. Namely, among *Diploxylon* pines, *P. densiflora*, the more widespread species maintained greater genetic diversity ($H_e$) than more geographically restricted species (see Fig. 1A and Table 2) with the exception of *P. sylvestris* var. *sylvestriformis*. The high level of genetic diversity of this variety may be due to the past historical hybridization between var. *mongolica* and *P. densiflora* as described above. Szmidt and Wang (1993) provided the genetic evidences supporting this suggestion. In that study, they reported that var. *sylvestriformis* harbours substantial admixtures of allozymes from var. *mongolica* and *P. densiflora* and further showed the evidence of introgression character of var. *sylvestriformis* by analysis of cpDNA (chloroplast DNA) variation. Similarly the higher diversity in *P. densata* as compared to *P. tabulaeformis* and *P. yunnanensis* may be the result of hybridization between two genetically distinct parental populations (*P. tabulaeformis* and *P. yunnanensis*).

In *Haploxylon* pines, geographically more widespread species, *P. pumila* had the highest level of genetic diversity. Interestingly, *P. koraiensis* from South Korea had greater genetic diversity than that from Russian Far East (Table 2). Although the differences in electrophoretical procedures and isozyme loci investigated in two studies prevented the accurate comparison, it is likely that the amount of genetic variation of *P. koraiensis* in South Korea is much more than that in the Russian Far East. This result seems to support the hypothesis that *P. koraiensis* expanded to the far eastern region of Russia from the south as late as postglacial times (the Holocene) (Mirov, 1967). In other words, *P. koraiensis* grew only south of the present border of Russia during the Pleisotcene (Kim *et al.*, 1994).

*Diploxylon* pines showed higher level of genetic diversity (A/L=2.9; $H_o$=0.208; $H_e$=0.226) than *Haploxylon* pines (A/L=2.0; $H_o$=0.201; $H_e$=0.196). As mentioned earlier, this may be due to the distinctiveness of the distribution pattern of two subgenera. That is to say, *Haploxylon* pines have discontinuous distribution and the ranges of individual species are relatively limited while *Diploxylon* pines usually have large continuous and overalapping distributions (Critchfield and Little, Jr., 1966; Mirov, 1967).

The greater genetic diversity was observed at the RAPD markers ($H_o$=0.521; $H_e$=0.395) than that of allozyme markers ($H_o$=0.258; $H_e$=0.262) in *P. densiflora* from South Korea. It is generally known that the level of genetic diversity at DNA marker systems is higher than that of allozymes. This is due to the differences in biochemical and/or molecular characters between two marker systems. For more detailed reviews, see Pogson *et al.* (1995), Szmidt *et al.* (1996), and Lee *et al.* (1977).

## 5. DISTRIBUTION OF GENETIC DIVERSITY WITHIN AND AMONG POPULATIONS

There are two commonly used measures for population differentiation. Wright's (1951) $F_{ST}$ statistic is a measure of variance in allele frequecies among populations relative to the stadardized variance based on mean allele frequencies ($F_{ST}= \sigma^2/pq$). It is calculated on each allele at a locus. On the other hand, Nei's (1973) hierarchial genic diversity statistics also can be used to partition variation within and among populations. His $G_{ST}$ statistic is the genic diversity due to variation among populations ($D_{ST}$) divided by the total diversity ($H_T$); $G_{ST}=D_{ST}/H_T$.

Woody plant species, generally, have a high proportion of their total genetic diversity within populations than other plant (herbaceous) species (Hamrick and Godt, 1989). This is undoubtedly due to the fact that most tree species are outcrossing, whereas a large proportion of herbaceous species are self-pollinated.

Hamrick and Godt (1989) demonstrated that selfing species generally have $G_{ST}$ values above 0.50 while outcrossing tree species have mean $G_{ST}$ value below 0.10. On the other hand, temperate woody species, because of the large number of wind-pollinated species, have a mean $G_{ST}$ value of 0.099, whereas the $G_{ST}$ value of tropical trees (most of them are animal-pollinated trees and have geographically distant and/or isolated individuals) is higher (0.135) (Hamrick, 1994). However, the $G_{ST}$ value for tropical trees is still low relative to that of many other herbaceous plant species. This indicates that gene flow among populations of tropical tree species may be high.

The $G_{ST}$ ($F_{ST}$) values for East-Asian pines ranged from 0.008 in *P. sylvestris* var. *mongolica* to 0.073 in *P. thunbergii* from Japan and the overall mean value for 7 species was 0.039 (Table 3). This value is smaller than that (0.095) of all woody plant species as well as that (0.099) of temperate woody species (Hamrick, 1994).

Gene flow plays a critical role in determining the genetic structure of populations. Theoretical studies have demonstrated that even low levels of gene flow can weaken the effects of local and directional selection (Ellstrand, 1992). The mean $F_{ST}$ value can be used to calculate the number of migrants per generation indirectly ($N_m$, where N is the population size and m is the rate of migration; $F_{ST}=1/(4Nm + 1)$, Wright, 1951). In addition to this method, Slatkin (1985) has developed an indirect method of estimating gene flow. Hamrick (1994) calculated Nm values for several groups of plant species using both indirect procedures. The two methods of estimating gene flow gave similar results. Mean estimates of Nm based on the Slatkin procedure ranged from 0.065 for selfing species to 5.38 for outcrossed wind-pollinated species. Mixed-mating and out-

Table 3. Genetic diversity within and among populations of 10 Asian pine species and, gene migration values (Nm) based on Wright's (1951) estimate

| Species | No. of pop. (seed source) | $H_T$ | $H_S$ | $D_{ST}$ | $G_{ST}$ | Nm |
|---|---|---|---|---|---|---|
| *Diploxylon* | | | | | | |
| *Pinus densata* | 1 (China) | – | – | – | – | – |
| *P. densiflora* | 6 (Japan)[9] | 0.321 | 0.298 | 0.024 | 0.058 | 4.06 |
| | 25 (South Korea)[4] | 0.292 | 0.281 | 0.115 | 0.038 | 6.16 |
| | 10 (South Korea; RAPD)[3] | 0.442 | 0.385 | 0.058 | 0.129 | 1.67 |
| *P. sylvestris,* | | | | | | |
| var. *mongolica* | 4 (China)[9] | 0.237 | 0.235 | 0.002 | 0.008 | 31 |
| var. *sylvestriformis* | 5 (China)[9] | 0.349 | 0.338 | 0.011 | 0.026 | 9.37 |
| *P. tabulaeformis* | 1 (China) | – | – | – | – | – |
| *P. thunbergii* | 22 (Japan)[7] | 0.259 | 0.240 | 0.019 | 0.073 | 3.17 |
| | 13 (South Korea)[6] | 0.255 | 0.245 | 0.011 | 0.044 | 5.43 |
| *P. yunnanensis* | 1 (China) | – | – | – | – | – |
| *Haploxylon* | | | | | | |
| *P. koraiensis* | 8 (South Korea)[5] | 0.239 | 0.225 | 0.014 | 0.049 | 5.07 |
| | 3 (Russian Far East)[8] | – | – | – | 0.40* | 6.00 |
| *P. sibirica* | 8 (Siberia)[2] | – | – | – | 0.041 | 5.85 |
| | 10 (Siberia)[8] | – | – | – | 0.025* | 9.75 |
| *P. pumila* | 5 (Sakhalin)[1] | – | – | – | 0.043 | 5.56 |
| | 4 (North of Kamchatka Peninsula)[8] | – | – | – | 0.021* | 11.65 |
| Total Mean | | – | – | – | 0.039 | 8.59 |

**References:** 1), Goncharenko *et al.*, 1993a; 2), Goncharenko *et al.*, 1993b; 3), Kim, 1995; 4) Kim and Lee, 1995; 5), Kim *et al.*, 1994; 6), Lee, 1994; 7), Miyata and Ubukata, 1994; 8) Krutovskii *et al.*, 1992; 9), Szmidt and Wang, 1993.
* $F_{ST}$ value

crossed animal-pollinated species had intermediate Nm values. Our reviews are in accordance with those of above reports (Table 3). Namely, the mean Nm value for 7 Asian pines was 8.59, indicating that gene flow was large enough to limit differentiation due to genetic drift.

The predominantly outcrossing mating system and wind-pollination found in most forest trees, especially in pine trees, were considered to be among the major forces responsible for the above results. In fact, studies of pollen flight have shown that majority of pollen falls within a short distance of the parent trees; but also, some pollen can be blown by wind to considerable distances (Koski, 1970). Thus, although most of the pollen produced by a tree is likely to fertilize near the neighbors, the small amount of pollen that travels great distance can be responsible for gene flow between widely separated populations. Gene flow alone is not, however, the possible cause of the lack of microgeographic diversity, i.e., the lack of interpopulation differentiation. Studies of other plant species have shown that genetic differentiation among subpopulations can occur despite great amounts of gene flow (Bradshaw, 1972). Another cause of the lack of differentiation may be population history.

## 6. CONCLUSION

The present study indicates that the level of intrapopulational allozyme variation in East-Asian pine trees is relatively high. Consequently, it is likely that the amount of genetic variation of East-Asian pines is more than that of Europe and North America although the differences in electrophoretical procedures, isozyme loci investigated, and the number of tree species reviewed prevented the accurate comparison in two regions. In general, widely spread plant species with large ranges have high levels of genetic variation. Our allozyme literature supports this suggestion very well. *Diploxylon* pines which have large, continuous and overlapping distributions showed higher levels of genetic diversity than *Haploxylon* pines having discontinuous distribution and relatively limited ranges. Additionally, within each subgenera, geographically more widespread species, *P. densiflora* in *Diploxylon* and *P. pumila* in *Haploxylon* showed greater genetic diversity than more geographically restricted species.

East-Asian pine species have a low degree of genetic differentiation among populations like other conifers. Namely the mean $G_{ST}$ value over 7 East-Asian pines was 0.039. This value is smaller than that (0.095) of all woody plant species as well as that (0.099) of temperate woody species (Hamrick, 1994). East-Asian pines also have a high Nm value (the number of migrants per generation, 8.59) showing the gene flow is large enough to limit genetic differentiation between populations owing to genetic drift, etc. Besides the Nm value for East-Asian pine trees is higher than that for 16 Europe and North American pines (3.41).

Because there has been a lack of knowledge on the level of genetic diversity in pine tree species based on DNA markers, the accurate comparison of genetic diversity at DNA level with that of allozyme level is not simple at present. However, it seems that the genetic variation at DNA level is higher than that of allozyme level. Further studies are needed to provide more evidences on this issue.

Although several studies on the genetic diversity of Asian pine trees have been accomplished in recent years, our knowledge about the patterns and levels of genetic variation of Asian *Pinus* species is still rather scarce. Especially the genetic information for the pine trees occuring in West- and South-Asia such as *P. gerardiana, P. griffithii, P. khasya* and *P. merkusii* does not exist at all. For more detailed studies on the genetic diversity and structure of the Asian *Pinus* tree species, the population genetic studies for West- and South-Asian pines should be started as soon as possible.

**REFERENCES**


Bradshaw, A.D. 1972. Some evolutionary consequences of being a plant. *Evol. Biol.* **5**: 25–47.

Brown, A.H.D. and Moran, G.F. 1981. Isozymes and genetic resources in forest tree. *In*: M.T. Conkle (Ed.) Proc. Symp. North American Forest Trees and Insects. USDA For. Serv. General Tech. Rep. PSW-48. 1–10.

Cheng, W.C. and Fu, L.G. 1978. Chinese Flora. Science Press 7, 203–280 (in Chinese).

Clegg, M.T., Brown, A.H.D. and Whitfield, P.R. 1984. Chloroplast DNA diversity in wild and cultivated barley: implications for genetic conservation. *Genet. Res. Camb.* **43**: 339–343.

Crawford, D.J. 1983. Phylogenetic and systematic inferences from electrophoretic studies. *In*: S.D. Tanksley and T.J. Orton (Eds) Isozymes in Plant Genetics and Breeding. Part A. Elsevier, Amsterdam. 257–287.

Critchfield, W.B. and Little (Jr), E.L. 1966. Geographic Distribution of the Pines of the World. Misc. Publ. 991. Washington DC, Department of Agriculture, Forest Service. 97 pp.

Ellstrand, N.C. 1992. Gene flow among seed plant populations. *In*: W.T. Adams, S.H. Strauss, D.L. Copes and A.R. Griffin (Eds) Population Genetics of Forest Trees. Kluwer Academic Publishers, Dordrecht. 241–257.

Farjon, A. 1984. Pines: Drawings and Descriptions of the Genus *Pinus*. E. Brill/Dr. Backhuys, Leiden, The Netherlands. 204 pp.

Goncharenko, G.G., Padutov, V.E. and Silin, A.E. 1993a. Allozyme variation in natural populations of Eurassian pines. I. Population structure, genetic variation, and differentiation in *Pinus pumila* lPall. Regel from Chukotsk and Sakhalin. *Silvae Genetica* **42**: 237–246.

Goncharenko, G.G., Padutov, V.E. and Silin, A.E. 1993b. Allozyme variation in natural populations of Eurassian pines II. Genetic variation, diversity, differentiation, and gene flow in *Pinus sibirica* Du Tour in some lowland and mountain populations. *Silvae Genetica* **42**: 246–253.

Hamrick, J.L. 1994. Genetic diversity and conservation in tropical forests. *In*: Proc. Inter. Symp. Genetic Conser. and Production of Trop. For. Tree Seed. June 14–16, 1994. Chiang Mai, Thailand. 1–9.

Hamrick, J.L., Mitton, J.B. and Linhart, Y.B. 1981. Levels of genetic variation in trees: Influence of life history characteristics. *In*: M.T. Conkle (Ed.) Proc. Symp. North American Forest Trees and Insects. USDA For. Serv. General Tech. Rep. PSW-48. 35–41.

Hamrick, J.L. and Godt, M.J.W. 1989. Allozyme diversity in plants. *In*: A.H.D. Brown, M.T. Clegg, A.L. Kahler and B.S. Weir (Eds) Population Genetics, Breeding and Germplasm Resources in Crop Improvement. Sinauer Press, Sunderland, MA. 43–63.

Kim, Y.Y. 1995. Genetic Variation of Ten Natural Population of *Pinus densiflora* in Korea Based on RAPD Marker Analysis. Ph.D. Thesis (in Korean), Seoul National University. 115 pp.

Kim, Z.S. and Lee, S.W. 1995. Genetic diversity of three native *Pinus* species in Korea. *In*: Ph. Baradt, W.T. Adams and G. Muller-Starck (Eds) Population Genetics and Genetic Conservation of Forest Trees. SPB Academic Publishing, The Netherlands. 211–218.

Kim, Z.S., Lee, S.W., Lim, J.H., Hwang, J.W. and Kwon, K.W. 1994. Genetic diversity and structure of natural populations of *Pinus koraiensis* (Sieb. et Zucc.) in Korea. *For. Genet.* **1**: 41–49.

Koski, V. 1970. A study of pollen dispersed as a mechanism of gene flow in conifers. *Commun. Inst. Forest Fenn.* **70**: 1–78.

Krutovskii, K.V., Politov, D.V. and Altukhov, Y.P. 1992. Genetic differentiation and phylogeny of stone pine species based on isozyme loci. Proc. Inter. Work. Subalpine Stone Pines and Their Environment: The Status of Our Knowledge. St. Moritz, Swizerland, September 5–11, 1992. 19–30.

Ledig, F.T. 1986. Heterozygosity, heterosis, and fitness in outbreeding plants. *In*: M.E. Soule (Ed.) Conservation Biology: The Science of Scarcity and Diversity. Sinauer Associates, Sunderland, Mass. 77–104.

Lee, S.W. 1994. Genetic Diversity and Structure of Natural Populations of *Pinus thunbergii* in Korea. Ph.D. Thesis, Korea University, 137 pp.

Lee, S.W., Kim, Y.Y., Hyun, J.O. and Kim, Z.S. 1997. Comparison of genetic variation in *Pinus densiflora* natural populations by allozyme and RAPD analysis. *Korean J. Breed.* **29**: 72–83 (in Korean).

Mirov, N.T. 1967. The Genus *Pinus*. New York, Roland Press Company. 602 pp.

Miyata, M. and Ubukata, M. 1994. Genetic variation of allozymes in natural stands of Japanese black pine. *J. Jpn. For. Soc.* **76**: 445–455 (in Japanese).

Molotkov, P.I. and Patlaj, I.N. 1991. Systematic position within the genus *Pinus* and intraspeciefic taxonomy. *In*: M. Giertych and C. Matyas (Eds) Genetics of Scots Pine. Akademiai Kiado, Budapest. 31–39.

Nei, M. 1973. Analysis of gene diversity in subdivided populations. *Proc. Natl. Acad. Sci.* USA **70**: 3321–3323.

Nienhuis, J., Helentjaris, T., Slocum, M., Ruggero, B. and Schaefer, A. 1987. Restriction fragment length polymorphism analysis of loci associated resistance in tomato. *Crop Science* **27**: 797–803.

Pogson, G.H., Mesa, K.A. and Boutilier, R.G. 1995. Genetic population structure and gene flow in the Atlantic cod *Gadus morhua:* a comparison of allozyme and nuclear RFLP loci. *Genetics* 139: 375–385.

Politov, D.V. and Krutovskii, K.V. 1992. Allozyme, polymorphism, heterozygosity, and mating system of stone pines. Proc. Inter. Workshop on Subalpine Stone Pines and Their Environment: The Status of Our Knowledge. St. Moritz, Switzerland, September 5–11, 1992. 36–50.

Slatkin, M. 1985. Rare alleles as indicators of gene flow. *Evolution* **39**: 53–65.

Szmidt, A.E. and Wang, X.-R. 1991. DNA markers in forest genetics. *In*: G. Müller-Stark and M. Ziehe (Eds) Genetic Variation in European Populations of Forest Trees. Sauerlander's Verlag Frankfurt am Main. 79–94.

Szmidt, A.E. and Wang, X.-R. 1993. Molecular systematics and genetic differentiation of *Pinus sylvestris* (L.) and *P. densiflora* (Sieb. et Zucc.). *Theor. Appl. Genet.* **86**: 159–165.

Szmidt, A.E., Wang, X.-R., and Lu, M.Z. 1996. Empirical assessment of allozyme and RAPD variation in *Pinus sylvestris* (L.) using haploid tissue analysis. *Heredity* 76: 412–420.

Wang, X.-R., Szmidt, A.E., Lewandowski, A. and Wang, Z.-R. 1990. Evolutionary analysis of *Pinus densata* Masters, a putative tertiary hybrid. 1. Allozyme variation. *Theor. Appl. Genet.* **80**: 635–640.

Wheeler, N.C. and Guries, R.P. 1987. A quantitative measure of introgression between lodgepole and jack pines. *Can. J. Bot.* **65**: 1876–1885.

Wright, S. 1951. The genetical structure of populations. *Ann. Eugen* **15**: 323–354.

# 15

# Principles and Problems in Conservation of Tree Genetic Resources

*Sunil Puri*[1]

**ABSTRACT**

The necessity of conserving the forest tree-genetic resources existing in natural populations is now well recognized. Conservation of genetic diversity is the responsibility of tree breeders and should be regarded in breeding strategies as being as important as the production of improved material. Managing the genetic resources of trees requires knowledge on the diversity and distribution of genes in a population. *In situ* and *ex situ* techniques are discussed in order to conserve and manage the genetic resources. It is emphasized that *in situ* and *ex situ* methods needs to be taken as complementary, not opposing, methodologies. *In situ* conservation provides the opportunity to preserve the broadest range of species, but *ex situ* collections may be more appropriate when access to specific or threatened populations is desired. The paper briefly reviews the problems of conservation of genetic resources by *in situ* and *ex situ* methods. Some recent developments in the field of genetic resource conservation are examined in a historical perspective, focusing on continuing programs, trends and needs in the field of plant genetic resources.

## 1. INTRODUCTION

Genetic variation, accumulated in all living organisms during some three thousand millions of biological evolution, constitutes the genetic resources of our planet. This diversity provides a buffer against climatic and other environmental changes, and is thus essential for maintaining the stability and biological balance of the biosphere. The value of genetic variability of tree species,

---

[1]Department of Forestry, Indira Gandhi Agricultural University, Raipur 492 012, India.

and its uses, in tree improvement has only been recognized recently. This variability is today exposed to many threats, linked in particular with the depletion of forest cover in the tropics. As our landscape becomes more dissected by land uses that fragment plant and animal populations, gene flow between isolated populations may be interrupted to the point where evolutionary forces such as genetic drift and inbreeding may begin to accelerate losses of genetic variation within populations (Gilpin, 1991). This illustrates the importance of gene conservation in trees. Sound conservation strategies carried out as an integral part of genetic improvement, are a prerequisite for continued and sustainable genetic gains in the future.

## 2. GENETIC VARIABILITY

The natural variability existing within species is the result of complex interactions among various factors, like mutations, response to diversity of habitat, breeding system, degree of outbreeding, hybridization, size of population, isolation, etc. This variability has always been the main safeguard system of living organisms, a mechanism created by nature. It constitutes a buffer against changes in the environment and climate. Genetic variability also constitutes the raw material for tree breeding. The higher the variability inside a population, the better the chances to select families and individuals with desirable characteristics.

Genetic variation in natural forest populations is not uniformly distributed. Population genetic structure is described by the partitioning of genetic variation within and between populations of a species. In most outcrossed species, e.g., conifers with large continuous distribution, most of the genetic variation resides within the population (Hamrick and Godt, 1990). Small population size, restricted gene flow, inbreeding, and life history features such as the highly specific site/habitat requirements that result in populations fragmentation tend to increase genetic differences between populations. Gibson and Hamrick (1991) opined that the cycles of local extinction and colonization that characterize some metapopulation species tend to exhibit more genetic differentiation between populations.

Genetic drift through founder events (the establishment of a new population from a limited gene pool in an area from which the species was previously absent) is more likely to allow new genetic variants to become established, whereas in species with more continuous distributions, new genetic variants are more likely to be eliminated through hybridization with the more common alleles in the large population (Hartl, 1980). Genetic drift and founder events thus become important determinants of populations genetic structure in genetically variable species. The loss of populations thus possess unique variation in the form of rare alleles (van Treuren *et al.,* 1991) may be important to the evolution of the species and for genetic improvement through selective breeding (Mosseler, 1992).

Outcrossing species passing through a genetic bottleneck may become inbred through mating among close relatives over several generations, and rapidly lose heterozygosity and variation (Nei *et al.,* 1975). According to simulations presented by Nei *et al.* (1975), it could require thousands of generations to recover lost genetic diversity. Genetic bottlenecks are of particular concern in long-lived, long-generation organisms like trees where thousand of generations translate into million of years. Such time frames may not pormit the recovery of genetic variation needed to adapt to rapidly changing environments. Outcrossed tree species could evolve self-pollinating mating systems as a response to reductions in population size as a result of population fragmentation.

Self pollination and mating among close relatives in small populations erode genetic variation within populations through loss of heterozygosity (Selander, 1983), but also ensures the ability of isolated individual trees to recolonize areas following catastrophic disturbances such as fire. This ability is of obvious adaptive value in pioneer species. However, the long-term survival of a species depends on adaptive responses that are predicted on the presence of sufficient genetic diversity to overcome environmental challenges. Since the rate of adaptation through natural selection is based on the amount of genetic variation in a species, it is reasonable to assume that a loss of genetic variation may have serious longer-term consequences in a species facing rapid environmental changes like global warming (Harrington, 1989).

## 3. CONSERVATION OF VARIABILITY

In this paper, the concept of conservation is used as defined in the World Conservation Strategy: The management of human use of genetic resources so that they yield the greatest sustainable benefit to present generations, while maintaining their potential to meet the needs and aspirations of future generations (IUCN, 1980). The principles of protecting genetic diversity are not confined to either our century or to our civilization. Conservation of forest and animal resources *in situ* was mandated by official decrees in parts of India and China as early as 700 B.C. (Swaminathan, 1983). Plant introduction and *ex situ* conservation activities in these fields are documented from the times of the ancient Egyptians, before 1000 B.C. The various factors that led to the development of conservation biology as a scientific discipline is reviewed by Soule (1986). Undoubtedly the most powerful factor is the 'extinction spasm' (Myers, 1988) that has resulted from non-sustainable use of natural resources, which in turn is a consequence of massive human population growth.

As stated earlier, the genetic variation within and among species is an inherent feature of the evolution of forests and it must be considered in developing any conservation strategy. Breeding can create greater diversity among populations and can enhance the utility of the genetic resource by managing advanced generations of diverse breeding populations. When conserving trees *in situ,* it may be necessary to incorporate large areas of land to conserve the gene pool adequately. Merely counting number of tree does not provide effective population sizes of species, and merely counting species is inadequate for determining the genetic resources of key tree species.

Knowledge of the requirements for perpetuating tree species is generally meagre, and ability to organize conservation programs is low. As a result, conservation is often reduced to preserving areas in centers of species diversity in the hope that genetic diversity and differentiation are also conserved. Clearly, this pragmatic approach is necessary, but by itself, it is an insufficient step in genetic conservation and only adequate as a short-term contingency measure while more satisfactory conservation strategies are developed.

For most species, however, genetic variation is not well conserved, and certainly, not all significant variation is included in established genetic conservation or breeding programs. Further, for scores of species, ecogeographical surveys are still needed, at least to target populations for breeding. Such surveys are also needed for continued monitoring of the distribution of genetic variation to trigger warnings about the need for management interventions. If the sampling problem is solvable, then an array of management techniques exist that differ not only in the details of their execution but also in the conditions under which they are necessary or particularly useful.

At one extreme of simplicity, a species may exist in a state of homogeneity for all gene loci so that any sample of sufficient size would capture all alleles. In such situations the breeding can be straight forward, based on a single selection objective. Such a situation may exist for a few species whose natural variation may be very low. Also, for genetically depauperate species, that is, species in which little useful genetic variation exists, any equivalent size sample is as sufficient as any other sample. In such cases, simple storage and propagation programs are sufficient.

For almost all tree species, however, experimentation shows that genetic variation is high. But not all species have to be developed for all uses; hence, if the objectives are limited, finite conservation programs can be more readily defined. Some species exist within secure collections that contain a wide sample of the extant genetic variation and little further collection is needed, although better maintenance may be required. If species are classified according to the objectives of a forest management program, those whose values lie exclusively in nonproduction functions can only be managed *in situ* and are primarily reproduced by natural regeneration. For most of these species, no direct management interventions are feasible, but some forms of forest management (by regulating removal of trees or by preventive maintenance) can affect populations sizes and structures, as well as their genotypic distributions, and thereby maintain the genetic variation needed for population viability and general evolution of the species. It is also possible that introducing populations of key species into reclamation areas or stand clearings could affect the evolution of the local ecosystem.

For most of the species whose values are unknown, conserving genetic variation also depends on maintaining *in situ* stands. The adequacy of such programs for conserving nonproduction functions would therefore be the primary focus for these species. Although some of these species might eventually be found amenable to production forestry and some will be found to have traits of use for timber, medicinal, or other products, their interim maintenance will largely depend on the quality of *in situ* programs. Seed storage may be a feasible means of conserving sampled variation, and it may be necessary for species in endangered habitats. The cost of sampling, collecting, and storing more than a few hundred or thousand species may be too high, however, to justify allocating scarce funds for this purpose. Moreover, storage methods are not known for seeds of most species.

## 4. *IN SITU* CONSERVATION

It can be defined as the conservation of ecosystems and natural habitats and the maintenance and recovery of viable populations of species in their natural surroundings and, in the case of domesticated or cultivated species in the surroundings where they have developed their distinctive properties. *In situ* conservation allows species to continue to evolve. In general, *in situ* conservation methods share three characteristics (Food and Agriculture Organization, 1984):

* All growth phases of a target species are maintained largely within the ecosystem in which they originally evolved.
* Land use of the sites (e.g., agroforestry) is limited to those activities that will not have detrimental effects on habitat conservation objectives.
* Regeneration of target species occurs without human manipulation, or intervention is confined to short-term measures to counter detrimental factors resulting from adjacent land use or from fragmentation of the forest. Examples of manipulation that may be necessary in heavily altered ecosystems are artificial regeneration using local seed and manual weeding or controlled burning to suppress competing species temporarily.

In principle, *in situ* conservation is on a common ground with nature conservation, but there are at least three important differences: *first* nature conservation aims at protecting the entire flora within certain habitats, communities, ecosystems, but it is not concerned with protecting the intraspecific variability of component species; *second, in situ* conservation is generally compatible with the managed production of goods and services, in addition to being compatible with activities such as watershed management and erosion control; and finally habitats, communities, ecosystems can be easily identified, while the identification of genetic variability generally has to be experimentally proven.

Key requirements of *in situ* conservation of threatened or endangered genetic resources are the estimation and design of minimum viable population areas for a target species. To ensure conservation of substantial genetic diversity within a species, multiple reserves must be created, the exact number and size of which will depend on the distribution of the genetic diversity of the selected species. The promotion of the continued maintenance and function of an ecosystem under *in situ* conservation depends on the understanding of several ecological interactions, particularly the symbiotic relationships among plants, pollinators, seed dispersers, fungi associated with tree roots, and the animals that live in the ecosystem.

An effective *in situ* program for genetic conservation has several key aspects: identification of gene pools, selection of specific sites, acquisition and design of the layout and administration of the reserves to ensure the availability of germplasm for use, and management of the reserves in perpetuity. Consideration of the needs of local people must also be emphasized, because *in situ* conservation techniques can rarely if ever be carried out without the collaboration of the locally affected people. Thus, adjunct programs that provide instruction in the purpose and use of conservation areas are often indispensable, and research is needed on the design of programs and social support structures that can contribute to maintaining *in situ* stands.

Because *in situ* stands often provide services to various interests, coordination among those interests must also be included in program development plans. This will often require that site selection criteria include ease of management and minimal disruption of local uses. For managed areas, sites must be integrable with multiple local uses and accessible for management and collection activities (Palmberg, 1988). For many tree species, for example, controlled harvesting or other moderate disturbances are not necessarily threats to viability.

*In situ* conservation presents many advantages (FAO/UNEP 1984):

i. It usually allows a wider sampling of the variability, which increases the statistical chances of capturing valuable alleles.
ii. It is particularly well suited to species which are difficult to establish or regenerate outside their natural habitat.
iii. It ensures, to a certain extent, protection of associated species: considering the great diversity of tropical tree and shrub species, it would not be feasible to undertake specific conservation efforts focused on each single species. Priority will be given for such action to species currently utilized or of potential utilization (the number of which is considerably less than the number of unutilized species). However, many species with still unknown potential will also be conserved as a side benefit, wherever *in situ* conservation of economically important species is carried out.
iv. It does not a *priori* exclude certain forms of utilization and even commercial exploitation of some products of the forest ecosystem. *In situ* conservation of wild species does not necessarily imply conservation of the whole ecosystem nor of specific individuals, and therefore, it is not incompatible with certain forms of exploitation. A satisfactory solution would consist in adopting and developing a multipurpose management concept taking into account the capacity of the forest to provide a variety of goods and services, while at the same time, conserving the genetic diversity of priority plant species, which can, for example, be important timber tree species, or wild relatives of food and cash crops.
v. It allows the study of species in their natural ecosystems: morphological and ecological characteristics and environmental conditions can thus be related to genetic variation leading to better evaluation and utilization.

vi. It renders possible and optimal utilization of existing protected areas: there is presently around the world a network of national and regional parks and protected areas of various types, having as objective the conservation of floristic communities, habitats of ecoystems.

A limiting factor for *in situ* conservation of genetic resources in tropical countries is the difficulty of demarcating permanent forest reserves and regulating activities in natural forests. In this respect, the difficulties are more or less the same as those met in the development of forest management. Conservation and management are closely linked and conservation of the genetic diversity of forest species can only progress within the framework of a forest management policy.

The possibilities for translating these concepts into practice are strongly constrained by the diversity of funding sources for conservation activities and by the generally low levels of funds available. Moreover, many agencies, whether their programs are coordinated or not have different conservation objectives. Hence, no global agenda for species inclusiveness exists. Only one-third of the biosphere reserves have been inventoried, even for trees; many other designated areas are not sufficiently well protected to ensure the security of species thought to be contained within their borders, and almost none is scientifically managed to maintain species diversity or genetic variation of the constituent species. In addition, no broad agreement exists on what is expected of local people or governments with respect to the conservation agency. Hence, the agency may confront lack of infrastructure support, indifference, or even an adversary relationship with different segments of the public and among sectoral users. The potential conservation utility of these programs has not been realized and may not be for many years.

## 5. *EX SITU* CONSERVATION

The conservation of components of biological diversity outside their natural habitats, in facilities such as botanical gardens and gene banks. While not a substitute for conservation in the wild, *ex situ* techniques complement *in situ* efforts by safeguarding populations of endangered species, increasing public awareness of the value of biodiversity and providing materials for basic and applied scientific research needed to improve management techniques.

In contrast to *in situ* methods, *ex situ* methods include any of those practices that conserve genetic material outside the natural distribution of the parent population, and they may use reproductive material of individuals or stands located beyond the site of the parent population. *Ex situ* methods and materials include gene banks for seed or pollen and clonal banks, arboreta, and breeding populations (Bonner, 1985). They also include active collections involving shorter-term, temporary storage to distribute materials for evaluation and screening, as well as working collections for breeding.

The most common form of *ex situ* conservation of trees is the living stand. Such stands are frequently started from a single-source seed collection and are maintained for observational purposes. The size of the stands may range from specimens in botanical gardens and arboreta, to a few ornamental trees on small plots, to larger units with scores of trees.

Seed storage, another *ex situ* conservation method, refers to storage of intact seeds in a controlled environment. Under controlled temperature and moisture conditions, stored seed of some species remain viable for decades. This technique is the mainstay of germplasm conservation of agriculturally important species, and it is starting to be used for conserving rare tree species. When the viability of stored seeds decreases, the usual procedure is to regenerate the sample in the field. This procedure is impractical for tree species, however, because of the long vegetative period before trees produce seeds (up to 20 or more years), but alternative strategies can be developed. A system of regeneration stands can be organized, for example, to ensure the continuous availability of sexually mature samples, and vegetative materials can be held in juvenile condition by hedging and other technique and then allowed to mature quickly when needed. Coordinated sets of materials can then be kept available for any set of stored genotypes.

Maintenance of living stands as field gene banks is another *ex situ* method, but its use is currently restricted to highly selected genotypes of species that are of commercial importance, such as those in breeding programs in which grafting or rooted cuttings can be developed into mature reproductive materials. Hence, at present, such trees are hardly to be considered conservation collections. With the use of cuttings, genetic variation in cloning ability is often seen. Cuttings are useful for preserving specific genotypes, obtaining rapid regeneration, and saving genotypes faced with destruction that cannot otherwise reproduce.

Tissue culture also has the potential to provide a secure conservation method. The technique involved micropropagation (whether meristems, embryos, or other). It requires large investments in development, but if cryogenic storage is developed it provides a secure conservation method. The concept of *in vitro* gene banks is being tested. However, tissue culture is still in the experimental stages for most tree species.

Cryogenic storage, the preservation of biological material suspended above or in liquid nitrogen at temperatures from −150 °C to −196 °C, has been used for many years as a means of keeping animal semen for breeding purposes. This technology is relatively new to seed storage, and hence, the time limits for storage of true orthodox seeds have not yet been determined. Cryogenic storage of genera with small seeds, such as *Eucalyptus,* may be cost-effective, and the technology promises less genetic damage than conventional seed storage. However, storage of recalcitrant seeds, costs for larger-seeded species, susceptibilities to mechanical breakdowns, and regeneration remain formidable problems to be overcome.

## REFERENCES

Bonner, F.T. 1985. Technologies to Maintain Tree Germplasm Diversity. Prepared for the Office of Technology Assessment, U.S. Congress, Washington, D.C.

FAO/UNEP, 1984. Final Report. FAO/UNEP Project on the Conservation of Forest Genetic Resources. Rome. 171 pp.

FAO, 1984. *In Situ* conservation of Genetic Resources of Plants: The Scientific and Technical Base. FORGEN/MISC/84/1. Rome, Italy. 58 pp.

Gibson, J.P. and Hamrick, J.L. 1991. Genetic diversity and structure in *Pinus pungens* (Table Mountain Pine) populations. *Can. J. For. Res.* **21:** 635–642.

Gilpin, M.E. 1991. The genetic effective size of a metapopulation. *Biol. J. Linn. Soc.* **42:** 165–175.

Hamrick, J.L. and Godt, M.J.W. 1990. Allozyme diversity in plant species. *In*: A.D.H. Brown, M.T. Clegg, A.L. Kahler and B.S. Weir (Eds) Plant Populations Genetics, Breeding and Genetic Resources. Sinauer Associates. Inc., Sunderland, MA. 43–63.

Harrington, J.B. 1989. Climatic change: a review of causes. *Can. J. For. Res.* **17**: 1313–1339.

Hartl, D.L. 1980. Principles of Populations Genetics. Sinauer Assoc., Inc., Sunderland, MA.

IUCN, 1980. World Conservation Strategy. Prepared by the International Union for Conservation of Nature Resources (IUCN) in collaboration with World Wildlife Fund (WWF), the United Nations Environment Programme (UNEP), FAO and UNESCO. IUCN, Gland, Information Folder.

Mosseler, A. 1992. Life history and genetic diversity in red pine implications for gene conservation in forestry. *Forestry Chronicle* **68**: 701–708.

Myers, N. 1988. Tropical forests and their species: going, going ........? *In*: E.O. Wilson (Ed.) Biodiversity. Nat. Acad. Press, Washington, D.C. 28–35.

Nei, M., Maruyama, T. and Chakraborty, R. 1975. The bottleneck effect and population variability. *Evolution* **29**: 1–10.

Palmberg, C. 1988. Plant Genetic Resources: Their Conservation *In Situ* for Human Use. Rome, Italy. FAO.

Selander, R. 1983. Evolutionary consequences of inbreeding. *In*: C.M. Schonewald-Cox, S.M. Chambers, B. MacBryde, and W.L. Thomas (Eds) Genetics and Conservation. Benjamin/Cummings Publishing Co., Inc., London. 201–215.

Soule, M.E. 1986. Conservation biology and the "real world". *In*: M.E. Soule, (Ed.) Conservation Biology. Sinauer Assocs., Sunderland, MA. 1–12.

Swaminathan, M.S. 1983. Genetic conservation: microbes to man. Presedential address at the XV International Congress of Genetics, New Delhi, 12–22 Dec. 1983. 33 pp.

van Treuren, R., Bijlsma, R., van Delden, W. and Ouborg, N.J. 1991. The significance of genetic erosion in the process of extinction. I. Genetic differentiation in *Salvia pratensis* and *Scabiosa columbaria* in relation to population size. *Heredity* **66**: 181–189.

# D. VEGETATIVE PROPAGATION

# 16

# Application of Biotechnology in Forest Trees—Clonal Multiplication of Sandalwood, Rosewood, Eucalypts, Teak and Bamboos by Tissue Culture in India

*G. Lakshmi Sita*[1] *and B.V. Raghava Swamy*[2]

**ABSTRACT**

Forest tree tissue culture has witnessed tremendous progress during the last decade. Forest genetics and tree improvement research in India is hardly four decades old. Indian scientists have contributed substantially to the biotechnology of trees during the last decade, and developed successful technologies for many of the tropical trees. Authors examine the problems in conventional tree improvement programs and the role of tissue culture in forestry followed by case-studies of successfully micropropagated trees like sandalwood, teakwood, rosewood, eucalypts and bamboos, discussing the need for the application of tissue culture.

**ABBREVIATIONS**

MS: Murashige and Skoog's medium; WPM: Woody Plant Medium; mWPM: Modified Woody Plant Medium; NAA: α-naphthalene acetic acid; IAA: indole-3-acetic acid; IBA: indole-3-butyric acid; BAP: 6-benzylaminopurine; KIN: Kinetin; IPA: indole-3-propionic acid; DBH: Diameter at breast height.

---

[1]Department of Microbiology & Cell Biology, Indian Institute of Science, Bangalore 560 012, India.

[2]Monsanto Company, CSIC Complex, Indian Institute of Science Campus, Bangalore 560 012, India.

## 1. INTRODUCTION

The need of planting stock for reforestation is continuously increasing due to increase in world use of wood products. There is an urgent need to improve the quality and quantity of the forest trees to meet the demands of rising population. The new biotechnologies namely cell and tissue culture combined with recombinant DNA technology seem to have opened up possibilities of obtaining a large number of propagules with improved quality through genetic engineering in trees. They not only help in the rapid mass multiplication of existing stocks, but also in the conservation of important elite and rare trees which are threatened by extinction. Production of short duration trees with rapid turnover is one of the foremost priorities to increase the biomass production. In the following pages, problems involved in conventional breeding are outlined followed by the role of tissue culture in forest tree improvement. Early developments in tree tissue culture research and its application in some economically important forest trees is also discussed.

## 2. PROBLEMS IN CONVENTIONAL METHODS OF PROPAGATION AND BREEDING

Tree improvement by conventional methods of propagation and breeding is slow and time consuming. Extensive work has been done in agricultural crops by conventional methods. Whereas very little is done on tree improvement. Trees belonging to horticultural and plantation crops have been considerably improved over the centuries, since they were brought under cultivation. Forests are often left to regenerate naturally or are artificially regenerated by seeding or planting seedlings. In either instance, forests receive minimum cultivation during their lives compared to agronomic crops which have undergone innumerable selective modifications. On the other hand, forest trees suffer a 10,000 year deficiency in applied selection pressure targeted (Haissig *et al.*, 1987) to human needs. As a result, natural and artificial regeneration of forest seeds are produced from natural stands of wild type ancestors. Present day forest trees are quite heterozygous and are imitations of nature designed trees for her needs. Breeding programs are hampered due to long duration, polyploidy, complex pollination mechanisms, polygenic controls of desirable characters, self sterility favoring heterozygous state, lack of selection methods and natural barriers of interspecific crosses, etc. (Burley, 1987).

Biotechnology comprising tissue culture and recombinant DNA technology seems to be the answer to overcome some of the problems in tree improvement.

## 3. TISSUE CULTURE AND ITS APPLICATIONS

The process of culturing single cells, tissues and organs is collectively described as tissue culture. Plant tissues are usually cultured aseptically on a synthetic medium containing a carbon source, a mixture of inorganic nutrients supplemented with plant growth hormones which bring about various developmental activities in *in vitro*. The idea of culturing plant cells was conceived as early as 1902 by Haberlandt. But it took nearly 55 years to demonstrate the ideas conceived by Haberlandt. With the development of suitable media like Murashige and Skoog (1962), foundations for commercial tissue culture were laid out. Murashige (1974) formulated basic principles and developed the concept of four important dovclopmental stages namely:

*Stage-1:* Explanting or the establishment of live and growing plant material in culture.

*Stage-2:* Multiplication of the propagule in culture.

*Stage-3:* Establishment of rooted plants, hardening and plantlets survival in the soil.

*Stage-4:* The planting into soil and special treatment required for initiating rapid growth and development.

The three different types of propagule multiplication that are possible through tissue culture are: enhanced axillary bud breaking, production of adventitious shoots, and somatic cell embryogenesis. Enhanced axillary bud breaking perhaps nets the lowest multiplication rate. Sometimes higher shoot numbers have been reported. Adventive shoots have a greater potential in multiplication as shoots may arise from any area of the recultured inoculum. Somatic cell embryogenesis has potentially the greatest multiplication rate and produces a complete tiny plantlet similar to a seedling produced from a zygotic embryo. There are, however, many problems that must be resolved before this system will be commercially feasible. Also several factors contribute to the successful commercialization of a species. A few examples are the tissue (genotype source, history), media (minerals, hormones and other organics supporting agents), environment (light, temperature, gases and vessels), timing (subculture period, dosage), and interactions between the above factors.

Possible tissue culture technologies suitable for tree improvement are:

1. Clonal Propagation:
   a) Micropropagation from axillary and terminal meristems from selected superior trees.
   b) Adventitious shoot development from explants either directly or indirectly.
   c) Induction of somatic embryogenesis and subsequent development of plantlets.
2. Production of haploids by anther/pollen, ovule/ovary culture for reducing breeding time.
3. Production of triploids by endosperm culture and subsequent production of polyploids.
4. Protoplast fusion and gene transfer.
5. Induction and selection of useful mutants at the cell level for disease resistance, salt resistance, etc.

Modification of single cells is the end research for microorganisms. But in plants, any transformation done at single cell stage are meaningless until the technology for the development of single cells to whole plant is available. Thus further advances in tissue culture are indispensable if genetic engineering is to be useful for the improvement of forest trees.

Major findings on the application of tissue culture for forest trees include sandalwood (Lakshmi Sita *et al.*, 1979; Lakshmi Sita *et al.*, 1980; Lakshmi Sita, 1991), eucalypts (Lakshmi Sita and Vaidyanathan, 1979; Lakshmi Sita and Shobharani, 1985; Lakshmi Sita, 1993), rosewood (Lakshmi Sita *et al.*, 1986; Raghava Swamy *et al.*, 1992; Lakshmi Sita and Raghava Swamy, 1993), mulberry (Lakshmi Sita and Ravindran, 1991), cashew and redsanders (Lakshmi Sita *et al.*, 1992). Some of these will be discussed along with other important trees like teak and bamboos.

## 4. SANDALWOOD (*SANTALUM ALBUM* LINN.)

Sandalwood is one of the important trees of commercial value. The annual world requirement of sandal oil is about 200 tons which is equal to ten thousand tons of wood. Only ten per cent of this is met from the natural resources. Sandalwood production has come down considerably during the last decade. One of the reasons attributed is the spike disease caused by mycoplasma and the losses caused by it are alarming. Progress in the study of spike disease is hampered due to lack of accurate information about the causative agent. Since 1969 it has been known that the disease is not caused by virus but by a self duplicating microorganism that resembles the mycoplasma. Application of antibiotic gives only temporary remission. Presently available treatments are neither adequate nor economically justified for field application. It has been suggested to have a program for breeding strains of sandal inherently resistant to the disease. However, no experimentally proved resistant strains have been reported so far, but there are reports of apparently healthy and disease free trees occurring in otherwise heavily infected strands (Srimathi *et al.*, 1981). One possible approach in solving the problem is to have suitable methods of vegetative propagation of disease free sandal plants. Cloning by conventional or *in vitro* techniques is especially valuable for propagation of heterozygous, sexually incompatible genotypes.

The laboratory in the Department of Microbiology of the Indian Institute of Science has initiated tissue culture studies in 1976 to develop clonal propagation methods for superior selected sandal trees. Emphasis was on mature tree explants since clonal propagation from seedlings is not desirable as their quality is not known and progeny may not necessarily be the same as that of the parent (Bonga, 1977). Callus cultures were established from explants obtained from mature trees. Viable plantlets were obtained by the method of somatic embryogenesis from callus cultures. Different stages in the growth of tissue cultured sandalwood are shown in Figs. 1, 2 and 5. Plantlets thus obtained were established in the field. Several hundred plantlets were established

Fig. 1. Somatic embryogenesis in sandalwood.

in polybags and some were given to the Forest Department of Karnataka to establish in the field.

Normally sandal seedlings grow rapidly when well protected and are about 20–30 cm in height at the end of the second year. Our observations indicate that the selected and clonal tissue cultured plants perform better than seed raised trees. It has been observed that the tissue cultured sandal trees have flowered in three years. Early flowering is an advantage in seed orchards. Tissue cultured plants have grown to 3 m height in two years. After about 8 years the growth in terms of girth and height is same as that of 50–60 years (at the base only). The comparison between natural plantation and tissue cultured plants are shown in Tables 1, 2 and 3. The core samples taken showed the formation of 5 cm of heartwood, compared to 7 cm in natural plantations. This information suggests that it may be possible to reduce the harvesting period in sandalwood from 50 years to 20 years atleast with selection and good management practices.

## 5. ROSEWOOD (*DALBERGIA LATIFOLIA* ROXB.)

*Dalbergia latifolia* Roxb. is an important leguminous timber tree of great commercial value. Rosewood is widely distributed in India, from Sikkim in the sub-

Fig. 2. Plantlets developed from somatic embryos in sandalwood.

Table 1. Rate of growth of natural sandal trees

| Age (Years) | Mysore Plantations | | Javadi & Yelagiri Hill Plantations, Tamil Nadu | |
|---|---|---|---|---|
| | Mean girth (cm) | Height (m) | Mean girth (cm) | Height (m) |
| 10 | 13.2 | 2.1 | 7.9 | 1.9 |
| 20 | 30.4 | 4.0 | 23.9 | 4.6 |
| 30 | 43.1 | 5.5 | 43.0 | 6.3 |
| 40 | 53.3 | 6.8 | 62.2 | N.A. |
| 50 | 60.9 | 8.1 | 74.9 | N.A. |

N.A.: Not available

Table 2. Performance of tissue cultured sandal trees

| Age (years) | Girth (cm) | Height (m) |
|---|---|---|
| 2 | 23 | 3.04 |
| 4 | 51 | 4.57 |
| 7 | 61 | 6.09 |
| 8 | 66 | 7.62 |

Table 3. Measurement of core samples

| Characters | Tissue cultured tree | Natural sandal elite tree |
|---|---|---|
| Age | 7 years | 50 years |
| Core sample | 8 cm | 11 cm |
| Heart Wood | 5 cm | 7 cm |
| Sap Wood | 3 cm | 4 cm |
| Girth | 61 cm | 60 cm |

Himalayan tract to Southern most parts of India. The best growth of this species is found in the moist tropical deciduous forest and in semi-evergreen forests along the Western ghats. This luxury timber has been in the world market for centuries commanding high price in national and international markets. Rosewoods are native to India, and are slow growing. These trees once widespread are nowhere abundant now, and all the natural stands are fast disappearing.

Conventional propagation by grafts and rooted cuttings is slow and time consuming. Seed propagation is not satisfactory as the percentage of germination is very low. Rapid propagation of superior trees of good form, cylindrical bole, narrow crown and disease-free trees is of utmost importance. With a view to develop tissue culture techniques for propagation of 'elite' rosewood trees, three approaches were undertaken, namely (1) induction of organogenesis through shoot and leaf callus culture, (2) induction of single and multiple shoots through mature axillary meristems of 60–80 year-old elite trees, and (3) induction of somatic embryogenesis from immature zygotic embryos. Cloning of mature trees (60–80 year-old) was achieved through mature axillary meristems, organogenesis and somatic embryogenesis. Different stages of tissue cultured rosewood plants are shown in Figs. 3, 4 and 6.

Fresh, green, mature axillary nodal segments were collected in the sprouting season. The season is very critical, since the axillary buds are only active from March to June in a year. Induction of single and multiple shoots was obtained from nodal explants of trees on MS basal medium supplemented with BAP (1.0 mg/l) and NAA (0.05 mg/l) or IAA (0.5 mg/l). Multiplication of shoots was obtained on MS (reduced major elements) or WPM supplemented with BAP (1.0 mg/l) and KIN (0.5–1.0 mg/l). Excised shoots were rooted on half-strength MS with IBA (2.0 mg/l) to obtain complete plantlets. The regenerated plantlets have been acclimatized and successfully transferred to the soil. Tissue cultured rosewood trees initiated through this method are now in the field for the past three years. For more details on the axillary bud break and others, refer Raghava Swamy *et al.* (1992).

Organogenesis from shoot and leaf callus cultures was successfully achieved (Lakshmi Sita *et al.*, 1986; Lakshmi Sita and Raghava Swamy, 1993). Compact callus was initiated on MS basal medium supplemented with 2,4-D (1.0 mg/l), NAA (5.0 mg/l), BAP (1.0 mg/l) and 10 per cent coconut water. High frequency (15–20 shoots/g callus) regeneration of shoot bud differentiation was obtained on MS (3/4 reduced major elements) or WPM (Lloyd and

Fig. 3. Tissue cultured rosewood plants.

McCown, 1981) supplemented with BAP (5.0 mg/l) and NAA (0.5 mg/l). Leaf abscission and shoot tip necrosis was controlled using mWPM. About 90 per cent of the excised shoots rooted in mWPM supplemented with 2.0 mg/l IBA and 1.0 mg/l caffeic acid. The *in vitro*-raised rooted plantlets were hardened for successful transplantation to soil. The transplanted plants were exposed to various humidity conditions and 80 per cent transplant success was achieved.

## 6. EUCALYPTS

The natural distribution of *Eucalyptus* species is largely restricted to Australia, with a limited occurrence of the species of minor importance in New Guinea, Timore, Java and Philippines. It was first introduced in India as a garden tree

Fig. 4. Rosewood plantlets established in pots.

in 1790 on Nandi Hills in Karnataka State. The wood is hard and durable. It is used as a timber and fuel wood. The leaves of blue gum (*E. globulus*) yield eucalypt oil and of rose gum (*E. citriodora*) are used mainly for the manufacture of citriodora oil. However, there is a lot of variation from tree to tree. It is important for the grower to have uniform plantations to project total biomass or essential oil content.

Tissue culture studies on *Eucalyptus* were initiated nearly two decades ago. Excellent reviews were published on *Eucalyptus* giving details on different tissue culture approaches (Durand Creswell *et al.*, 1982; Lakshmi Sita, 1993). *E. territicornis, E. grandis, E. citriodora, E. globulus, E. camadulensis* and *E. torreliana* are the most economically important species cultivated in India. Though, organogenesis and somatic embryogenesis through callus cultures have been reported successfully in some *Eucalyptus* species, the technique has not yet reached the stage of commercialization. Micropropagation through enhanced axillary branching is the most successfully exploited technique in *Eucalyptus*.

### 6.1 Micropropagation Through Enhanced Axillary Branching

The principle of enhanced axillary branching is as follows: Each leaf has an axillary bud in its axil, which has the potential to develop into a shoot. In

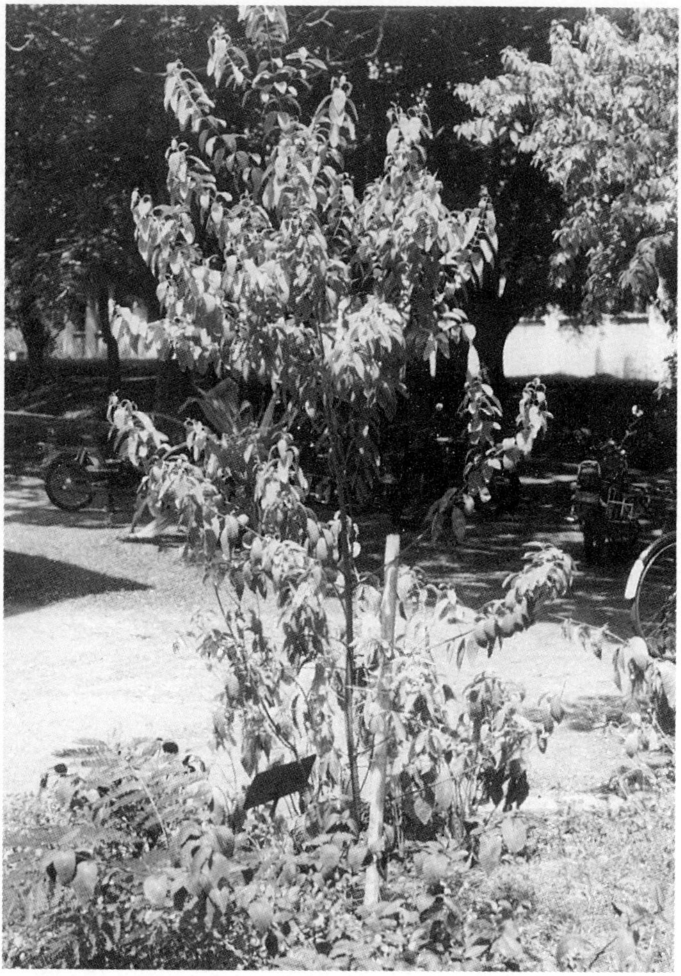

Fig. 5. Well established tissue cultured sandal tree.

nature, these buds remain dormant for various periods, depending on the growth patterns and environmental conditions. However, by culturing nodal segments on media containing appropriate concentrations of cytokinins, it is possible to break this dormancy and subsequent development of multiple shoots from nodal segements of aseptic seedlings or mature axillary meristems. The shoot cultures produced by the above method, without involving callus phase, are the stocks for clonal propagation with a high multiplication rate and sufficient genetic stability.

Successful micropropagation techniques have been developed in *E. grandis* (Lakshmi Sita and Shobharani, 1985), *E. citriodora* (Gupta *et al.*, 1981; Lakshmi Sita and Vaidyanathan, 1979), *E. territicornis* (Mascarenhas *et al.*,

Fig. 6. Well established tissue cultured rosewood tree.

1982), *E. camadulensis* (Gupta *et al.*, 1983), *E. globulus* (Gupta and Mascarenhas, 1987) and *E. torreliana* (Gupta *et al.*, 1983). Field performance of micropropagated *E. citriodora* trees have been reported by Gupta *et al.* (1991). The concentration of total oil, citronellal and citronellol in 1- and 3-yr old micropropagated plants was similar to that in the parent tree. In seedling-derived plants however, it has taken 3–4 years for concentration to attain the same level. Tissue cultured grown trees of *E. territicornis* showed greater height, diameter and biomass value than control trees. The biomass yields of tissue culture grown plants of *E. territicornis* at 11, 34, 52 and 60 months were 200, 34 16, 6 per cent, respectively, more than the controls.

The paper and pulp industry in India is interested in the clonal propagation of *Eucalyptus* species. Laboratories have been set up by Tata Tea and Co., Harihar Polyfribres, Unicorn Biotechnology, Bhadrachalam Paper Mills and South India Viscose based on the technology developed in this country.

## 7. TEAK (*TECTONA GRANDIS* LINN.F.)

*Tectona grandis* Linn.f., commonly called the teak, is a deciduous and tropical hardwood timber tree indigenous to South East Asia (India, Burma, Thailand and Indonesia). Teak is well adapted to moist, dry and semi-moist sites, but also flourishes well in a fairly moist, warm, tropical climate. It reaches larger dimensions in the moist areas of west coast than in the drier parts of the Indian Peninsula. Teak is well known for its sterling wood qualities and hence enjoys the reputation of being high class timber.

Due to high degree of variation in progeny and several constraints in its natural and artificial regeneration, there is a demand for rapid multiplication of selected clones. Micropropagation of teak has been successfully achieved using apical buds (Gupta *et al.*, 1980; Mascarenhas *et al.*, 1987). The protocols for micropropagation of teak were described in detail by Mascarenhas *et al.* (1987). Also, Mascarenhas *et al.* (1993) reviewed teak micropropagation with further refinements of their previous work, both in media composition, reduction in the number of stages of micropropagation and statistically designed comparative field trials conducted on tissue cultured raised teak trees at National Chemical Laboratory (NCL), Pune. The following culture media were used for micropropagation of teak:

MS-1: MS + KIN (0.15 mg/l) + BAP (0.15 mg/l). MS-1 was used for initiation and proliferation of shoot cultures.

MS-2: Half strength MS liquid medium provided with a filter paper support, and mixture of auxins each at 2 mg/l (IAA + IBA + IPA).

MS-3: Half strength MS liquid medium with a filter paper support. MS-2 and MS-3 were used for *in vitro* rooting of shoots.

In a recent review article on field performance of micropropagated teak trees, Gupta *et al.* (1991) described that the trees from tissue culture grew significantly faster than those from seedlings, but by 5th year there was no significant difference in height increment or diameter at breast height (DBH) of the two stock types. However, teak plantlets derived from tissue culture flowered in the 3rd year, whereas 7 to 10-years are normally required to flower (Gupta *et al.*, 1991). Early flowering is an advantage in seed orchards for the production of superior seeds. Commercial laboratories are now routinely mass producing teak plants from elite varieties.

## 8. BAMBOO

Bamboo form the single most important item of forest produce used by the rural communities in Asia and the Pacific. Its use as a long fibre raw material in the pulp and paper industry is well known and is one of the much sought after raw material in the tropics. Their use in housing, agricultural and horticultural pursuits, basket making, fish industry, transport system both on land and water, handicrafts and production of edible shoots etc., is well recognized. There are about 75 genera and 1250 species of bamboo widely distributed all over the world. The most prominent in India are *Bambusa, Melocenna* and *Dendrocalamus*. Bamboo cover about 12.8 per cent of the total forest area of the country (Bahadur and Verma, 1980).

In spite of its great importance, bamboo resources are dwindling and there is an urgent need to improve and increase plantations. Propagation of bamboo is by seeds or vegetatively. Viability of the seed is limited to one year. Traditional methods of propagation are said to be inadequate to increase the desired levels of production. In view of the constant demand and the scarcity of the material and the problems associated with conventional methods of propagation, development of effective *in vitro* techniques for different bamboo species has become a necessity.

Successful *in vitro* culture was demonstrated in the 80s and a complete protocol for micropropagation was published by Mehta *et al.* (1982). Since then many micropropagation methods for different bamboo species were reported (Nadgir *et al.*, 1984; Dekkers and Rao, 1989; Saxena and Bhojwani, 1993). Micropropagation of bamboo has been attempted both from the seed/seedling and mature explants. Although considerable success has been achieved with embryonic tissue, only limited progress was seen in the adult tissues. Forced axillary shoot multiplication is the most desirable method for commercial application. Nadgir *et al.* (1984) multiplied the shoots derived from seedlings through forced axillary shoot multiplication method in *Dendrocalamus strictus*, and estimated that nearly 10,000 plants could be obtained from a single embryo every year. In *Bambusa glaucescens* excised axillary buds were used to obtain multiple shoots on a medium supplemented with 5 mg/l BAP, 1 mg/l NAA and 3 g/l activated charcoal (Banik, 1987). In *B. tulda*, the rooting frequency was 92 per cent from the shoots derived from seedling material. Similarly, the shoots obtained from seedling explants of *Dendrocalamus strictus* rooted with ease, but those from mature explants were found to be difficult to root, and only 20 per cent rooting was obtained when treated with IBA (1 mg/l) for 4 days in dark followed by their transfer to 1/2 strength MS basal medium (Nadgir *et al.*, 1984). However, the same group (Nadgir *et al.*, 1984) was unable to root the shoots of *B. arundinacea* and *B. vulgaris* by using the same treatment. Saxena and Bhojwani (1993) reported a complete protocol for *Dendrocalamus longispathus* from a 4 year old tree through forced axillary branching.

The available information on bamboo tissue culture indicates a great potential for tissue culture. Somatic embryogenesis (Rao *et al.*, 1985) obtained from seedling explants and induction of *in vitro* flowering are other significant discoveries which opened up new avenues of research. Both these results have been obtained from seedling explants. Reliable application of these findings to elite material would be highly significant as controlled flowering would not only allow breeding improved varieties of bamboo, but can also provide an everlasting source of bamboo seed production which is a rare feature in nature. As on today reliable protocols from adult plants of bamboo are not available, but we are not far from it!

## 9. CONCLUSION

Micropropagation has been achieved in a number of woody species. Success and progress of a technology is need based. Due to the increase in demand of wood based products, more technological and financial inputs are needed. The current awareness has led to tremendous investments by the government and the private agencies in developing commercially feasible technologies for most economically important trees like teakwood, rosewood, sandalwood, eucalypts and bamboo. Already commercial laboratories are using the technology developed by national laboratories. Atleast three commercial laboratories are producing teak plants from elite material by micropropagation techniques. Several entrepreneurs are mass producing eucalyptus species for the paper and pulp industry. Sandalwood and rosewood also have attracted the attention of the industry in view of their highly priced timber. Two laboratories have been set up for commercialization. There is tremendous awareness among progressive farmers who are now willing to grow some of the economically important trees discussed in this review. In addition, other economically important fruit trees like banana are now grown routinely by micropropagation techniques. The progress in the application of tissue culture for clonal multiplication of tropical fruit trees is some what slow compared to the counterparts in temperate countries. Though papaya is not a tree, is also being multiplied by tissue culture. Extensive research is being conducted in oil palms, but is yet to reach the level of commercialiazation. Fuel woods like bamboo and subabul will soon be commercialiazed by the private industries. In subabul (*Leucaena leucocephala* L.), techniques for quality of the wood are developed in an author's laboratory (unpublished). These are supposed to be giving furniture quality wood in 7–8 years time. On the whole, tree tissue culture has come of age. Tissue culturists are working in almost all the tree crops.

It is for the foresters to take interest in this exciting area. Before clonal material is regenerated by tissue culture, it would be desirable to consult geneticists/breeders for inclusion of pedigree material in the tree improvement programs by tissue culture. In the next phase, production costs, genetic fidelity, the performance of *in vitro* regenerated plants will determine the future of micropropagation in clonal forestry. Although the true to type plants are the desired goal of clonal forestry programs, micropropagation may not always yield high fidelity and clonal regenerants. A spin off from tissue culture is somaclonal variation, which offers opportunities for selection of new useful variants. Although several other biotechnological approaches like, anther culture, protoplast culture and genetic transformation are available, they need more expertise and time to reach the goals of tree improvement. Micropropagation is comparatively simple for foresters to adapt and as a first step, phenotypically superior trees can be multiplied. In view of the awareness of disappearing forests, the current trend of biotechnology for mass propagation of elite trees will soon become reality and help in afforestation.

## REFERENCES

Bahadur, K.N. and Verma, J. 1980. Country Report India. *In*: G. Lenard and A. Chouinard (Eds) Proc. Workshop on Bamboo Research in Asia. Singapore, IDRC, Ottawa, Canada. 19–46.

Banik, R.L. 1987. Techniques of bamboo propagation with special reference to pre-rooted and pre-rhizomed branch cuttings and tissue culture. *In*: A.N. Rao (Ed.) Recent Research on Bamboos. Chinese Acad. For. and IDRC, Canada. 160–169.

Bonga, J.M. 1977. Application of tissue culture in forestry. *In*: J. Reinert and Y.P.S. Bajaj (Eds) Plant Cell Tissue and Organ Culture. Springer-Verlag, Berlin. 93–108.

Burley, J. 1987. Application of biotechnology in forestry and rural development. *Common. For. Rev.* **66**: 357–367.

Dekkers, A.J. and Rao, A.N. 1989. Tissue culture of four bamboo genera. *In*: A.N. Rao and A.M. Yusoff (Eds) Proc. Seminar on Tissue Culture of Forest Species. FRI, Malaysia and IDRC, Singapore. 83–90.

Durand-Cresswell, R., Boulay, M. and Franclet, A. 1982. Vegetative propagation of *Eucalyptus*. *In*: J.M. Bonga and D.J. Durzan (Eds) Tissue Culture in Forestry. Martinus Nijhoff, Dordrecht. 158–181.

Gupta P.K. and Mascarenhas, A.F. 1987. Eucalyptus. *In*: J.M. Bonga and D.J. Durzan (Eds) Cell and Tissue Culture in Forestry. Case Histories: Gymnosperms, Angiosperms and Palms. Vol. 3. Martinus Nijhoff, Dordrecht. 385–399.

Gupta P.K., Mascarenhas, A.F. and Jagannathan, V. 1981. Tissue culture of forest trees—clonal propagation of mature trees of *Eucalyptus citriodora* Hook by tissue culture. *Plant Sci. Lett.* **20**: 195–201.

Gupta P.K., Mehta, U.J. and Mascarenhas, A.F. 1983. A tissue culture method for rapid propagation of *Eucalyptus camadulensis* and *E. torreliana* from mature trees. *Plant Cell Rep.* 2: 296–299.

Gupta P.K., Nadgir, A.L., Mascarenhas, A.F. and Jagannathan, V. 1980. Tissue culture of forest tree-clonal multiplication of *Tectona grandis* (Teak) by tissue culture. *Plant Sci. Lett.* **17**: 259–268.

Gupta P.K., Timmis, R. and Mascarenhas, A.F. 1991. Field performance of micropropagated forestry species. *In Vitro Cell. Dev. Biol.* **27**P: 159–164.

Haissig, B.E., Nelson, N.D. and Kidd, G.H. 1987. Trends in the use of tissue culture in forest improvement. *Bio/Technology* **5**: 52–59.

Lakshmi Sita, G. 1986. Sandalwood (*Santalum album*). *In:* Y.P.S. Bajaj (Ed.) Biotechnology in Agriculture and Forestry. Vol. 2 Trees. Springer-Verlag, Berlin. 363–374.

Lakshmi Sita, G. 1991. Performance of tissue cultured plants of sandalwood. *Curr. Sci.* **61**: 794.

Lakshmi Sita, G. 1993. Micropropagation of *Eucalyptus*. *In*: M.R. Ahuja (Ed.) Micropropagation of Woody Plants. Kluwer Academic Publishers, Dordrecht. 263–280.

Lakshmi Sita, G., Chattopadhyay, S. and Tejavathi, D.H. 1986. Plant regeneration from shoot callus of Rosewood (*Dalbergia latifolia* Roxb.). *Plant Cell Reports* **5**: 266–268.

Lakshmi Sita, G., Raghava Ram, N.V. and Vaidyanathan, C.S. 1979. Differentiation of embryoids and plantlets from shoot cultures of sandalwood. *Plant Sci. Lett.* **15**: 265–271.

Lakshmi Sita, G., Raghava Ram, N.V. and Vaidyanathan, C.S. 1980. Triploids from endosperm cultures of sandalwood by experimental embryogenesis. *Plant Sci. Lett.* **20**: 63–69.

Lakshmi Sita, G. and Raghava Swamy, B.V. 1993. Regeneration of plantlets from leaf disc cultures of rosewood: Control of leaf abscission and shoot tip necrosis. *Plant Sci.* **88**: 107–112.

Lakshmi Sita, G. and Ravindran, S. 1991. Gynogenic plants from ovary cultures of mulberry. *In*: J. Prakash and R.L.M. Pieriek (Eds) Horticulture: New Technologies and Applications. Kluwer Academic Publishers, Dordrecht. 225–229.

Lakshmi Sita, G. and Shobharani, B. 1985. *In vitro* propagation of *Eucalyptus grandis* L. by tissue culture. *Plant Cell Rep.* **4**: 63–65.

Lakshmi Sita, G., Sreenatha, K.S. and Sujatha, S. 1992. Plantlet production from shoot tip cultures of red sandalwood. *Curr. Sci.* **62**: 532–535.

Lakshmi Sita, G. and Vaidyanathan, C.S. 1979. Rapid multiplication of *Eucalyptus* by multiple shoot production. *Curr. Sci.* **48**: 350–352.

Lloyd, G. and McCown, B.H. 1981. Commercially-feasible micropropagation of mountain laurel, *Kalmia latifolia*, by use of shoot tip culture. *Proc. Int. Plant Prop. Soc.* **30**: 421–427.

Mascarenhas, A.F., Hazra, S., Potdar, U., Kulkarni, D.K. and Gupta, P.K. 1982. Rapid clonal multiplication of mature forest trees through tissue culture. *In*: A. Fujiwara (Ed.) Plant Tissue Culture. Proc. 5th Int. Cong. Plant Tissue Cell Culture. Tokyo, Japan. 719–720.

Mascarenhas, A.F., Kendurkar, S.V., Gupta, P.K., Khuspe, S.S. and Agarwal, D.C. 1987. Teak. *In*: J.M. Bonga and D.J. Durzan (Eds) Cell and Tissue Culture in Forestry. Case Histories: Gymnosperms, Angiosperms and Palms. Vol. 3. Martinus Nijhoff, Dordrecht. 300–315.

Mascarenhas, A.F., Kendurkar, S.V. and Khuspe, S.S. 1993. Micropropagation of teak. *In*: M.R. Ahuja (Ed.) Micropropagation of Woody Plants. Kluwer Academic Publishers, Dordrecht. 247–262.

Mehta, U., Rao, I.V.R. and Mohan Ram, H.Y. 1982. Somatic embryogenesis in bamboo. *In*: Plant Tissue Culture. Jpn. Assoc. Plant Tissue Culture, Tokyo. 109–110.

Murashige, T. 1974. Plant propagation through tissue cultures. *Ann. Rev. Plant Physiol.* **25**: 135–165.

Murashige, T. and Skoog, F. 1962. A revised medium for rapid growth and bioassay with tobacco tissue cultures. *Physiol. Plant.* **15**: 473–497.

Nadgir, A.L., Phadke, C.H., Gupta, P.K., Parsharami, V.A., Nair, S. and Mascarenhas, A.F. 1984. Rapid multiplication of bamboo by tissue culture. *Silvae Genet.* **33**: 219–223.

Raghava Swamy, B.V., Himabindu, K. and Lakshmi Sita, G. 1992. *In vitro* micropropagation of elite Rosewood (*Dalbergia latifolia* Roxb.). *Plant Cell Rep.* **11**: 126–131.

Rao, I.U., Rao, I.V.R. and Narang, V. 1985. Somatic embryogenesis and regeneration of plants in the bamboos, *Dendrocalamus strictus*. *Plant Cell Rep.* **4**: 191–194.

Saxena, S. and Bhojwani, S.S. 1993. *In vitro* clonal multiplication of 4-year old plants of bamboo, *Dendrocalamus longispanthus* Kurz. *In vitro Cell. Dev. Biol.*: 135–142.

Srimathi, R.A., Kulkarni, H.D. and Venkatesan, K.R. 1981. Selection of sandal (*Santalum album* L.) for spike resistance and qualities. *In*: H.C. Govindu, K. Maramorosch, S.P. Raychaudri and V. Muniyappa (Eds) Mycoplasma and Allied Pathogens of Plants, Animals and Human Beings. Univ. Agric. Sci., Bangalore. 46–49.

# 17

# Application of Tissue Culture Techniques in Tree Improvement

*Manoj Kumar*[1], *M. Reddy*[1] *and B.S. Nadagoudar*[1]

**ABSTRACT**

In forestry, the commercial application of tissue culture is still in its infancy. Apart from tissue culture technique involving micropropagation for the rapid clonal propagation of elite and plus trees, the somaclonal variation coupled with *in vitro* cell selection, has tremendous potential to select trees for desirable traits, such as disease resistance, drought tolerance, salt tolerance, etc. Somaclonal variation and its application in tree improvement are discussed in this paper.

## 1. INTRODUCTION

Considerable progress has been made over the last two decades on the development of tissue culture methodologies for trees (Bonga and Durzan, 1982). In India although tissue culture began in 1960s, only in recent years there has been an increasing interest in commercializing *in vitro* propagation of forest trees, especially by the pulp and paper industries (Mascarenhas and Muralidharan, 1989; Gurumurti *et al.*, 1992). Of the several plant tissue culture techniques the somaclonal variation (any genetic variability brought under *in vitro* culture conditions) coupled with *in vitro* selection to select trees for desirable traits, such as salt tolerance, drought tolerance, frost resistance, disease resistance, etc. and rapid clonal multiplication of such trees, have tremendous potential.

[1]Department of Forestry, University of Agricultural Sciences, Dharwad 580 005, India.

## 2. SOMACLONAL VARIATION

The term 'somaclonal variation' was coined by Larkin and Scowcroft (1981) to describe the variation displayed amongst the plants derived from any form of cell cultures. Bajaj (1990) used the term in a broad sense to include variability in cell and callus cultures as well as changes induced by other *in vitro* systems and techniques. Earlier such changes were considered undesirable and were, therefore, discarded as main emphasis was on clonal propagation and genetic stability of the cell cultures. Spontaneous variability in morphogenetic pattern in two subcultures derived from a single cell line in *Citrus grandis* observed by Chaturvedi and Mitra (1975) was perhaps the first in woody species. Lester and Barbee (1977) observed a wide range of variation in height, number of branches, leaf traits and chromosome number in callus derived plants in several clones of black poplar (*Populus nigra*) and Euramerican poplar (*Populus X euramericana*).

### 2.1 Causes of Somaclonal Variation

Various types of changes in cell culture, such as genetic, developmental or epigenetic and physiological, may be derived either from changes already existing in the explant or induced *in vitro* by the culture media and environment (Bajaj, 1990). The source of tissue is an important factor in somaclonal variation and different tissues can give rise to different amount of variability. Somaclonal variation arises most noticeably, when cell growth is allowed to progress in a disorganized manner. Cell suspensions and protoplast cultures are most prone to instability because of their high degree of disorganization, while meristem—tip culture remains free from somaclonal variation (Karp, 1991). The instability in culture is also reported due to prolonged culture time and frequency of the sub-culture.

The plant growth regulators contribute to somaclonal variation in the induction of epigenetic changes. Auxins and cytokinins, which are known to promote cell division, cause morphological (Varga *et al.*, 1988) and chromosomal (Bayliss, 1980) abnormalities.

### 2.2 Detection of Somaclonal Variation

The somaclonal variants are detected using morphological, cytogenetical, genetical and biochemical methods.

Morphological characters have long been the means of studying genetic variability in population and species. In order to determine accurately the value and genetic basis of somaclones, sexual progeny should be examined. For this selfing of regenerants is done and simple Mendelian segregation is studied. However, some of the chromosomal rearrangements such as deletions, inversion, etc. cannot be easily detectable unless cytological studies are made. The above methods are either tedious or time consuming, particularly in trees, biochemical tests involving isozyme electrophoresis and RFLP/RAPD marker techniques can be successfully used to shorten delays (Kane *et al.*, 1992).

### 2.3 Significance of Somaclonal Variation

Spontaneous genetic variation and mutuation breeding have traditionally been used to develop new plant varieties. More than 337 varieties have been produced as a result of mutagenesis (Singh, 1990). Although mutation breeding is valuable in new variety development, it has significant limitations over recently originated somaclonal variation which operates at a cellular level. In contrast to spontaneous mutations *in vivo*, *in vitro* generated variation seems to occur more frequently, and is detected more easily because variants can be readily spotted in a limited space and in a short time. Somaclonal variation can be profitably utilized in crop improvement since it reduces the time required for releasing the new variety by at least two years compared to mutation breeding and by three years in comparison to the backcross method of gene transfer (Singh, 1990).

### 2.4 Application of Somaclonal Variation

Unfortunately somaclonal variation has to date been described for many more herbaceous than woody species and no somaclonal tree has yet been put to commercial use. By employing appropriate cultural conditions it is possible to generate somaclonal variation in trees. Though forest trees are highly heterozygous—the average level of heterozygosity is twice that in herbaceous plants (Zobel and Talbert, 1984), they do require somaclonal variation for improvement under the changing environmental conditions. The somaclonal approach can also be exploited for recovery of newer genotypes with faster growth, short rotation cycle, disease resistance, salt tolerance, drought tolerance, frost tolerance, etc. Since conventional methods take longer time to breed and select such genotypes in trees, the somaclonal approach can offer opportunities for isolation of newer genotypes at a relatively faster rate.

## 3. *IN VITRO* SELECTION

One of the most important objective of tree improvement is to reduce damage by disease and insect pests and to produce strains that are well suited to grow in adverse environments. But any breeding program with trees is expensive and of long term. Thus, *in vitro* selection technique can be used in identifying plants which are resistant or tolerant to stresses produced by phytotoxins from pathogens, herbicides, cold temperature and also to salinity and water stress conditions. *In vitro* selection usually involves subjecting a population of cells to a suitable selection pressure, recovering any variant lines which have developed resistance or tolerance to the stress, and then regenerating plants from the selected cells (Smith and Drew, 1990). This approach presumes that tolerance operating at the unorganized cellular level can act, to some degree of effectiveness, in the whole plant. If the tolerance has genetic basis then the trait can be transferred to other plants.

### 3.1 Application of *in vitro* Selection

In India, about 7 million ha of land is salt affected and another 15–20 million ha is on the verge of conversion. Such lands can be reclaimed by growing salt tolerant plants. However the determination of 'absolute tolerance' under *in vivo* conditions is impossible because of both the complex interactions between the plant system and the environmental factors. Recent developments in *in vitro* technology offer a meaningful tool for determining the tolerance and also screening and developing salt tolerant genotypes (Bajaj, 1990). Like most other agronomic traits, salt tolerance seems to be under genetic control (Sumaryati *et al.*, 1992). The usual method for selecting salt tolerant plants through cell cultures is to incorporate lethal levels of salts, say sodium chloride, into growing medium and isolate resistant cells visually. Similarly the cell lines resistant to drought stress can be selected by exposing callus to a medium containing PEG (polyethylene glycol). The genetic studies of the selfed progenies revealed that the PEG resistant trait is controlled by a single dominant gene. Direct selection of cell lines for drought resistance is difficult, selection for over production of proline is suggested as proline over production is observed in response to stress.

Tissue culture techniques are used for development of disease resistant plants. Most of the fungi and disease causing organisms act by releasing toxins into the plant system. Direct selection using toxins into the media is the most common method employed for selection in cell culture. The usual technique is to place pieces of culture tissues on a medium containing near lethal concentration of the toxin, and select the fast growing viable sectors of tissue from the remainder of the cultured material killed by the toxin (Vidhyasekaran *et al.*, 1990). A second method to isolate disease resistant cells is to inoculate spores or mycelium onto the culture media and isolate the resistant cells that grow (Miller *et al.*, 1984). Hyper-sensitive resistance to blister rust was displayed by sub-cultured callus of sugar-pine (*Pinus lambertiana*) thus making it possible to test disease resistance under *in vitro* conditions (Diner *et al.*, 1984). The technique has also been used to produce and select clones of hybrid poplar resistant to *Septoria musiva* (Ostry and Skilling, 1988).

The *in vitro* selection techniques can be exploited judiciously provided there is a reproducible system for regenerating a large number of plants from unstressed cells. Also, the tolerance to the stress should operate both at the cellular and the whole plant level so that there is a greater chance of recovering desirable plants. Furthermore, new technologies should not replace the conventional ones but can be valuable adjuncts to the time honoured forest tree breeding and improvement practices.

## 4. MICROPROPAGATION

Micropropagation is an invaluable aid in rapid clonal multiplication of superior genotypes having desired traits using tissue culture techniques. It can be considered an extension of the more traditional methods of plant propagation,

Table 1. Status of forest tree tissue culture of angiosperms in India

| Species | Stage/Age of Parent Tree | Explant | Method | Response/ Result | Reference(s) |
|---|---|---|---|---|---|
| *Acacia auriculiformis* | SL | AXB | OR | PL | Mittal *et al.*, 1989 |
| | SD | COT | SE | PL | Das *et al.*, 1993 |
| *A. nilotica* | MT | NS, INS | OR | PL | Mathur & Chandra, 1983 |
| *A. nilotica* subsp. *indica* | SL | CN | OR | PL & S | Dewan *et al.*, 1992 |
| *Albizzia amara* | SL (10-12d) | HC | OR | PL & S | Tomar & Gupta, 1988b |
| *A. lebbeck* | MT | AN | AG | PL (Haploid) | Gharyal *et al.*, 1983 |
| | SL (10d) | HC, RT, COT | SE, OR | PL | Upadhyay & Chandra, 1983 |
| | SL (10-25d) | HC, LF, INS | SE | PL & S | Rao & De, 1987a |
| *A. lucida* | SL | HC | OR | PL | Tomar & Gupta, 1988b |
| *A. richardiana* | SL | HC | SE, OR | PL & S | Tomar & Gupta, 1988a. b |
| *Anacardium occidentale* | SL | CN | OR | PL & FP | D'Silva & D'Souza, 1992 |
| *Anogeissus pendula* | SL | CN, ECNS | OR | PL & S | Joshi *et al.*, 1991 |
| *Azadirachta indica* | MT (15yr) | LF | SE | PL | Narayan & Jaiswal, 1985 |
| | SD | COT | SE | PL & S | Muralidharan & Mascarenhas, 1987a |
| | MT | AN | AG | PL | Gautam *et al.*, 1993 |
| *Bauhinia purpurea* | MT (15-18yr) | SS | SE | PL & S | Kumar, 1992 |
| *B. variegata* | MT | NS | OR | PL & S | Mathur & Mukunthakumar, 1992 |
| *Cinnamomum zeylanicum* | SL, SD | SD, NS, ST, HC, COT | OR, (MS) | PL | Rai & Chandra, 1987 |
| *Commiphora wightii* | ET | NS | OR | PL & S | Barve & Mehta, 1993 |
| *Dalbergia latifolia* | SL | RT, HC, LF, SS, COT | SE | PL | Anand & Bir, 1984 |
| | MT | LF, SS | SE | CL | Anand & Bir, 1984 |
| | MT (5-6yr) | INS | SE | PL | Rao, 1986 |

(Contd)

Table 1 *Contd.*

| Species | Stage/Age of Parent Tree | Explant | Method | Response/ Result | Reference(s) |
|---|---|---|---|---|---|
| | ET (60-80 yr) | INS, NS, AXB | SE, OR | PL & FP | Lakshmi Sita & Raghava Swamy, 1992 |
| | ET (60-80yr) | LF | SE | PL & S | Lakshmi Sita & Raghava Swamy, 1993 |
| *D. sissoo* | SL | RT | SE, OR | PL | Mukhopadhyay & Mohan Ram, 1981 |
| | MT | NS | OR (MS) | PL | Datta *et al.*, 1983 |
| | MT (30-50yr) | AXB | OR | PL & S | Dawra *et al.*, 1984 |
| | ET | CAM | CS | PL | Kumar *et al.*, 1991 |
| *Duboisia myoporoides* | MP (3yr) | LF | SE | PL & S | Kukreja *et al.*, 1986 |
| *Eucalyptus camaldulensis* | MT (12-15yr) | NS | OR | PL & FP | Gupta *et al.*, 1983 |
| | SL | LF | OR | PL & S | Muralidharan & Mascarenhas, 1987b |
| *E. citriodora* | MT | NS | OR (MS) | PL & FP | Gupta, *et al.*, 1981 |
| | SD | EMB | SE | PL & S | Muralidharan & Mascarenhas, 1987a, b |
| | SD | EMB | SE | PL & S | Muralidharan *et al.*, 1989 |
| *E. globulus* | SL | CN, HC | OR (MS) SE | PL & CL | Rajkumar & Ayyappan, 1992 |
| *E. grandis* | MT (5yr) | NS | OR (MS) | PL | Lakshmi Sita & Shobha Rani, 1985 |
| | J & MT | NS | OR (MS) | PL | Rao & Venkateshwara, 1985 |
| *E. tereticornis* | ET (8-10yr) | AXB | SE, OR | PL & S | Das & Mitra, 1990 |
| *E. torelliana* | MT (12-15yr) | NS | OR | PL & S | Gupta *et al.*, 1983 |
| *Ficus religiosa* | MT (20yr) | SS | SE, OR | PL | Jaiswal & Narayan, 1985 |
| *Legerstroemia flos-reginae* | MT(4 & 30 yr) | NS | OR (MS) | PL & FP | Paily & D'Souza, 1986 |

*(Contd)*

Table 1 *Contd.*

| Species | Stage/Age of Parent Tree | Explant | Method | Response/ Result | Reference(s) |
|---|---|---|---|---|---|
| *Leucaena leucocephala* | SL (14d) | CN, NS | OR | PL & FP | Dhawan & Bhojwani, 1985 |
| | MT (9m) | NS | OR | PL & S | Dhawan, & Bhojwani, 1985 |
| | SL | ST, NS | OR (MS) | PL | Dhawan & Bhojwani, 1987 |
| *Mitragyna parvifolia* | MT (40yr) | AXB, APB | OR (MS) | PL & FP | Roy *et al.*, 1988 |
| *Morus alba* | MT | ST | OR (MS) | PL | Tewary & SubbaRao, 1990 |
| *M. indica* | MT (10yr) | AXB, LF | OR | PL | Mahatre *et al.*, 1985 |
| *M. nigra* | MT (12yr) | ST, NS | OR | PL & FP | Yadav *et al.*, 1990a |
| *Parkinsonia aculeata* | MT | NS | OR | PL & S | Mathur & Mukunthakumar, 1992 |
| *Peltophorum pterocarpum* | MT | AN | AG | PL (Haploid) | Rao & De, 1987b |
| *Populus alba* | | LF, NS, INS | OR (MS) | MS | Mehra & Cheema, 1985 |
| *P. ciliata* | MT (40yr) | LF | SE | PL & S | Cheema, 1989 |
| *Prosopis cineraria* | SL | HC | OR | PL & S | Goyal & Arya, 1981 |
| | ET (4.5yr) | NS | OR | PL & S | Kackar *et al.*, 1991 |
| | PT | SS | OR | PL & S | Shekhawat *et al.*, 1993 |
| *P. juliflora* | SL | APB,INF,HC, CN | SE | CL | Nandwani & Ramawat, 1991 |
| | MT (10yr) | NS | SE, OR | PL & S | Nandwani & Ramawat, 1991 |
| *P. tamarugo* | SL | HC, CN | SE, OR | PL | Nandwani & Ramawat, 1992 |
| *Pterocarpus santalinus* | SL | NS, ST, COT | SE, OR | CL, MS | Sarita *et al.*, 1988 |
| | SL | ST | OR | PL & S | Lakshmi Sita *et al.*, 1992 |
| *Putranjiva roxburghii* | SD | END | SE | PL | Srivastava, 1973 |
| *Salix babylonia* | MT (15yr) | NS | OR (MS) | PL & S | Dhir *et al.*, 1984 |
| *Santalum album* | MT (22-25yr) | NS, INS | CL | PL & FP | Lakshmi Sita, 1986 |

*(Contd)*

Table 1 *Contd.*

| Species | Stage/Age of Parent Tree | Explant | Method | Response/ Result | Reference(s) |
|---|---|---|---|---|---|
| | SD | END | SE | PL(Triploids) | Lakshmi Sita, 1986 |
| | SD | END | SE | PL | Bapat & Rao, 1992 |
| | SL | HC | SE | PL | Bapat & Rao, 1992 |
| | PT (65yr) | ST | OR | CL | Manoj Kumar, 1994 |
| | MT (10yr) | NS | OR | MS | Manoj Kumar, 1994 |
| | SL (60d) | NS, HC, COT | OR | MS | Manoj Kumar, 1994 |
| *Sapium sebiferum* | MT | NS | OR (MS) | PL & FP | Kotwal *et al.*, 1983 |
| *Sesbania bispinosa* | SL | COT, LF | SE | PL | Sinha & Mallick, 1991 |
| *S. grandiflora* | SL | HC | SE, OR | PL | Khattar & Mohan Ram, 1983 |
| | SL | HC, COT | SE, OR | PL & FP | Shanker & Mohan Ram, 1990 |
| *Syzygium aromaticum* | SL | NS | OR | PL | Mathew & Hariharan, 1990 |
| *S. cuminii* | SL | NS, ST | OR | PL & S | Yadav *et al.*, 1990b |
| *Tamarindus indica* | SL | ST | OR | PL & S | Kopp & Nataraja, 1990 |
| | SL | COT | OR | PL & S | Jaiswal & Gulati, 1991 |
| *Tecomella undulata* | SL | APB,AXB,LF, INS | SE, OR | PL | Raj Bhansali, 1993 |
| | MT (10-15yr) | APB, AXB | OR | PL | Raj Bhansali, 1993 |
| *Tectona grandis* | SL | ST,HC,COT, RT | OR | PL & S | Gupta *et al.*, 1980 |
| | ET (100yr) | APB, AXB | OR | PL & S | Gupta *et al.*, 1980 |

AG – Androgenesis
AN – Anther
APB – Apical/Terminal bud
AXB – Axillary bud
CAM – Cambial tissue
CL – Callus
CN – Cotyledonary node
COT – Cotyledon
CS – Cell suspension
ECNS – Epicotylydonary node and shoots
EMB – Embryo
END – Endosperm
ET – Elite tree
FP – Field planting
HC – Hypocotyl
INF – Inflorescence
INS – Internodal segment
J – Juvenile
LF – Leaf
MP – Mature Plant
MS – Multiple shoot
MT – Mature tree
NS – Nodal segment
OR – Organogenesis
PL – Plantlet
PT – Plus tree
RT – Root
S – Soil transfer
SD – Seed
SE – Somatic embryogenesis/ Regeneration via callus
SL – Seedling
SS – Stem segments/bits
ST – Shoot tip

wherein shoot tips, buds and nodal segments of desired elite plants are cultured on appropriate medium to get multiple shoots. These shoots are subcultured repeatedly until many plants are produced all having the genetic characteristics of the original plant.

Up to 1975, tissue culture of hardwoods involved the production of callus, which was not very suitable for plant propagation as it encountered genetic instability. Currently organ cultures are being used for the propagation of plants (Chalupa, 1987). Using micropropagation, it is possible to exploit total genetic variance rather than just the additive portions (Timmis *et al.*, 1987). That is, asexual reproduction through direct regeneration allows the multiplication of elite full-sib families or superior individuals in a family, that exhibit significant gain due to non-additive gene effects. Furthermore, tissue culture could allow exploitation of the genetic variance within a given generation through the cloning of outstanding individuals for testing and mass propagation while conventional breeding allows genetic gain in subsequent generations (Thorpe *et al.*, 1991).

The progress made in tree culture of angiosperms in India has been tabulated in Table 1. Most of the success reported involved the use of excised embryos and seedlings part as explants. The reason for this choice was that by the time trees were old enough for evaluation, they were often recalcitrant in culture. It has been reported that, generally the rooting percentage, survival and growth, all declined, particularly when the parent plants were more than ten years old. However, successful propagation of 100 year old teak (*Tectona grandis*) tree (Gupta *et al.*, 1980) and an estimated production of more than one lakh *Eucalyptus citriodora* plants from a single bud within a year period (Gupta *et al.*, 1981) are far more encouraging in the mass multiplication of genetically uniform plantlets from matured elite trees. The successful regeneration of plantlets from matured trees through micropropagation was also achieved in *Dalbergia sissoo* (Dawra *et al.*, 1984), *Eucalyptus grandis* (Lakshmi Sita and Shobha Rani, 1985), *Lagerstroemia flos-reginae* (Paily and D'Souza, 1986), *Mitragyna parvifolia* (Roy *et al.*, 1988), *Dalbergia latifolia* (Lakshmi Sita and Raghava Swamy, 1993). Thus, the application of the micropropagation technique to clonal propagation of trees has enormous potential and it is possible to achieve a multiplication rate running into millions per year from a single plant.

## REFERENCES

Anand, M. and Bir, S.S. 1984. Organogenetic differentiation in tissue cultures of *Dalbergia latifolia*. *Curr. Sci.* **53**: 1305–1307.

Bajaj, Y.P.S. 1990. Biotechnology in Agriculture and Forestry Vol. II Somaclonal Variation in Crop Improvement-I. Springer-Verlag, Berlin. 685 pp.

Bapat, V.A. and Rao, P.S. 1992. Biotechnological approaches for sandalwood (*Santalum album* L.) micropropagation. *Ind. For.* **118**: 48–54.

Barve, D.M. and Mehta, A.R. 1993. Clonal propagation of mature elite trees of *Commiphora wightii*. *Plant Cell Tissue Organ Culture* **35**: 237–244.

Bayliss, M.W. 1980. Chromosome variation in plant tissues in culture. *In*: I.K. Vasil (Ed.) Perspectives in Plant Tissue Culture. Int. Rev. Cytol. Suppl. 11A, Academic Press, New York. 133–144.

Bonga, J. M. and Durzan, D.J. 1982. Tissue Culture in Forestry. Martinus Nijhoff Pub., Dordrecht. 420.

Chalupa, V. 1987. European hardwoods. *In*: J.M. Bonga and D.J. Durzan (Eds) Cell and Tissue Culture in Forestry. Vol. 3. Martinus Nijhoff Pub., Dordrecht. 224–246.

Chaturvedi, H.C. and Mitra, G.C. 1975. A shift in morphogenetic pattern in citrus callus tissue during prolonged culture. *Ann. Bot.* **39**: 683–687.

Cheema, G.S. 1989. Somatic embryogenesis and plant regeneration from cell suspension and tissue culture of mature Himalayan poplar (*Populus ciliata*). *Plant Cell Rep.* **8**: 124–127.

Das, P.K., Chakravarti, V. and Maity, S. 1993. Plantlet formation in tissue culture from cotyledon of *Acacia auriculiformis* A. Cunn Ex. Benth. *Indian J. For.* **16**: 189–192.

Das, T. and Mitra, C.G. 1990. Auxins + $KNO_3$ induced regeneration of leguminous tree—*Leucaena leucocephala* through tissue culture. *Curr. Sci.* **54**: 248–250.

Datta, S.K., Datta, K. and Pramonik, T. 1983. *In vitro* clonal multiplication of mature trees of *Dalbergia sissoo*. *Plant Cell Tissue Organ Culture* **2**: 15–20.

Dawra, S., Sharma, D.R. and Chowdhury, J.B. 1984. Clonal propagation of *Dalbergia sissoo* Roxb. through tissue culture. *Curr. Sci.* **53**: 807–809.

Dewan, A., Nanda, K. and Gupta, S.C. 1992. *In vitro* micropropagation of *Acacia nilotica* subsp. *indica* Brenan. via cotyledonary nodes. *Plant Cell Rep.* **12**: 18–21.

Dhawan, V. and Bhojwani, S.S. 1985. *In vitro* vegetative propagation of *Leucaena leucocephala*. *Plant Cell Rep.* **4**: 315–318.

Dhawan, V. and Bhojwani, S.S. 1987. Hardening *in vitro* and morphological changes in the leaves during acclimatization of micropropagated plants of *Leucaena leucocephala* (Lam) de Wit. *Plant Sci.* **53**: 65–72.

Dhir, K.K., Angrish, R. and Bajaj, M. 1984. Micropropagation of *Salix babylonia* through *in vitro* shoot proliferation. *Proc. Indian Acad. Sci.* (*Plant Sci.*) **93**: 655–660.

Diner, A.M., Mott, R.L. and Amerson, H.V. 1984. Cultured cells of white pine show genetic resistance to axenic blister rust hyphae. *Science* **224**: 407–408.

D'Silva, I. and D'Souza, L. 1992. *In vitro* propagation of *Anacardium occidentale* L. *Plant Cell Tissue Organ Culture* **29**: 1–6.

Gautam, V.K., Nanda, K. and Gupta, S.C. 1993. Development of shoots and roots in anther derived callus of *Azadirachta indica* A. Juss—a medicinal tree. *Plant Cell Tissue Organ Culture* **34**: 13–18.

Gharyal, P.K., Rashid, A. and Maheswari, S.C. 1983. Production of haploid plants in anther cultures of *Albizzia lebbeck* L. *Plant Cell Rep.* **2**: 308–309.

Goyal, Y. and Arya, H.C. 1981. Differentiation in cultures of *Prosopis cineraria* Linn. *Curr. Sci.* **50**: 468–469.

Gupta, P.K., Mascarenhas, A.F. and Jagannathan, V. 1981. Tissue culture of forest trees: Clonal propagation of mature trees of *Eucalyptus citriodora* Hook. by tissue culture. *Plant Sci. Lett.* **20**: 195–201.

Gupta, P.K., Mehta, U.J. and Mascarenhas, A.F. 1983. A tissue culture method for rapid clonal propagation of mature trees of *Eucalyptus torelliana* and *Eucalyptus camaldulensis*. *Plant Cell Rep.* **2**: 296–299.

Gupta, P.K., Nadgir, A.L., Mascarenhas, A.F. and Jagannathan, V. 1980. Tissue culture of forest trees: Clonal multiplication of *Tectona grandis* L. (Teak) by tissue culture. *Plant Sci. Lett.* **17**: 259–268.

Gurumurti, K., Balakrishnan, K.S., Staley Jagdess, S. and Jayachandran, C.K. 1992. Biotechnology in forestry in India. *In*: P.K. Khosla (Ed.) Status of Indian Forestry Problems and Perspective. Indian Society of Tree Scientists, Solan. 295–319.

Jaiswal, V.S. and Narayan, P. 1985. Regeneration of plantlets from the callus of stem segments of adult plant of *Ficus religiosa*. *Plant Cell Rep.* **4**: 256–258.

Jaiswal, P.K. and Gulati, A. 1991. *In vitro* high frequency regeneration of a tree legume *Tamarindus indica* (L). *Plant Cell Rep.* **10**: 569–573.

Joshi, R., Shekhawat, N.S. and Rathore, T.S. 1991. Micropropagation of *Anogeissus pendula* Edgew.—An arid forest tree. *Indian J. Exp. Biol.* **29**: 615–618.

Kackar, N.L., Solanki, K.R., Singh, M. and Vyas, S.C. 1991. Micropropagation of *Prosopis cineraria. Indian J. Exp. Biol.* **29**: 65–67.

Kane, E.J., Wilson, A.J. and Chourey, P.S. 1992. Mitochondrial genome variability in *Sorghum* cell culture protoclones. *Theor. Appl. Genet.* **83**: 799–806.

Karp, A. 1991. On the current understanding of somaclonal variation. *In*: B.J. Miflin (Ed.) Oxford Surveys of Plant Molecular and Cell Biology Vol. 7. Oxford University Press. 1–58.

Khattar, S. and Mohan Ram, H.Y. 1983. Organogenesis and plantlet formation *in vitro* in *Sesbania grandiflora. Indian J. Exp. Biol.* **21**: 252–253.

Kopp, M.S. and Nataraja, K. 1990. *In vitro* plantlet regeneration from shoot tip cultures of *Tamarindus indica* L. *Indian J. For.* **13**: 30–33.

Kotwal, M., Gupta, P.K. and Mascarenhas, A.F. 1983. Rapid multiplication of *Sapium sebiferum* by tissue culture. *Plant Cell Tissue Organ Culture* **2**: 133–139.

Kukreja, A.K., Mathur, A.K. and Ahuja, P.S. 1986. Morphogenetic potential of foliar explants in *Duboisia myoporoides* R. Br. (Solanaceae). *Plant Cell Rep.* **5**: 27–30.

Kumar, A. 1992. Micropropagation of a mature leguminous tree—*Bauhinia purpurea. Plant Cell Tissue Organ Culture* **31**: 257–259.

Kumar, A., Tandon, P. and Sharma, A. 1991. Morphogenetic responses of cultured cells of cambial origin of a mature tree—*Dalbergia sissoo* Roxb. *Plant Cell Rep.* **9**: 703–706.

Lakshmi Sita, G. 1986. Sandal wood (*Santalum album* L.). *In*: Y.P.S. Bajaj (Ed.) Biotechnology in Agriculture and Forestry. Vol. 1 Trees I. Springer-Verlag, Berlin. 363–374.

Lakshmi Sita, G. and Raghava Swamy, B.V. 1992. Application of cell and tissue culture technology for mass propagation of elite trees with special reference to Rosewood (*Dalbergia latifolia* Roxb.). *Indian For.* **118**: 36–47.

Lakshmi Sita, G. and Raghava Swamy, V.V. 1993. Regeneration of plantlets from leaf disc cultures of rosewood; control of leaf abscission and shoot tip necrosis. *Plant Sci.* **88**: 107–112.

Lakshmi Sita, G. and Shobha Rani, B. 1985. *In vitro* propagation in *Eucalyptus grandis* by tissue culture. *Plant Cell Rep.* **4**: 63–65.

Lakshmi Sita, G., Sreenatha, K.S. and Sujata, S. 1992. Plantlet production from shoot tip cultures of red sandalwood (*Pterocarpus santalinus* L). *Curr. Sci.* **62**: 532–535.

Larkin, P.J. and Scowcroft, W.R. 1981. Somaclonal variation—a novel source of variability from cell cultures for plant improvement. *Theor. Appl. Genet.* **60**: 197–214.

Lester, D.T. and Barbee, J.G. 1977. Within clone variation among black poplar trees derived from callus cultures. *For. Sci.* **23**: 122–131.

Mahatre, M., Bapat, V.A. and Rao, P.S. 1985. Regeneration of plants from the culture of leaves and axillary buds in mulberry (*Morus indica* L.). *Plant Cell Rep.* **4**: 78–80.

Manoj Kumar, M. 1994. Genetic Divergence, Isozyme Pattern and Micropropagation Studies in Sandal wood (*Santalum album* L.). M.Sc. Thesis. Tamil Nadu Agric. Univ., Coimbatore, India. 192pp.

Mascarenhas, A.F. and Muralidharan, E.M. 1989. Tissue culture of forest trees in India. *Curr. Sci.* **58**: 606–613.

Mathew, M.K. and Hariharan, M. 1990. *In vitro* multiple shoot regeneration in *Syzygium aromaticum. Ann. Bot.* **65**: 277–279.

Mathur, I. and Chandra, N. 1983. Induced regeneration in stem explants of *Acacia nilotica. Curr. Sci.* **52**: 882–883.

Mathur, J. and Mukunthakumar, S. 1992. Micropropagation of *Bauhinia variegata* and *Parkinsonia aculeata* from nodal explants of mature trees. *Plant Cell Tissue Organ Culture* **28**: 119–121.

Mehra, P.N. and Cheema, G.S. 1985. Differential response of male and female Himalayan poplar (*Populus ciliata*) and *P. alba in vitro. Phytomorphology* **35**: 151–154.

Mittal, A., Agarwal, R. and Gupta, S.C. 1989. *In vitro* development of plantlets from axillary buds of *Acacia auriculiformis*—a leguminous tree. *Plant Cell Tissue Organ Culture* **19**: 65–70.

Miller, S.A., Davidse, L.C. and Maxwell, D.P. 1984. Expression of genetic susceptibility, host resistance, and non-host resistance in Alfalfa callus tissue innoculated with *Phytophthora megasperma. Phytopathology* **74**: 345–348.

Mukhopadhyaya, A. and Mohan Ram, H.Y. 1981. Regeneration of plantlets from excised roots of *Dalbergia sissoo. Indian J. Exp. Biol.* **19**: 1113–1115.

Muralidharan, E.M., Gupta, P.K. and Mascarenhas, A.F. 1989. Plantlet production through high frequency somatic embryogenesis in long term cultures of *Eucalyptus citriodora. Plant Cell Rep.* **8**: 41–43.

Muralidharan, E.M. and Mascarenhas, A.F. 1987a. *In vitro* morphogenesis in *Azadirachta indica* A. Juss. and *Eucalyptus citriodora* Hook F. *In*: Abst. International Workshop on Tissue Culture and Biotechnology of Medicinal and Aromatic Plants, CIMAP, Lucknow. 13.

Muralidharan, E.M. and Mascarenhas, A.F. 1987b. *In vitro* plantlet formation by organogenesis in *Eucalyptus camaldulensis* and by somatic embryogenesis in *E. citriodora. Plant Cell Rep.* **6**: 256–260.

Nandwani, D. and Ramawat, K.G. 1991. Callus culture and plantlets formation from nodal explants of *Prosopis juliflora* (Swartz) Dc. *Indian J. Exp. Biol.* **29**: 523–527.

Nandwani, D. and Ramawat, K.G. 1992. High frequency plantlets regenerations from seedling explants of *Prosopis tamarugo. Plant Cell Tissue Organ Culture* **29**: 173–178.

Narayan, P. and Jaiswal, V.S. 1985. Plantlet regeneration from leaflet callus of *Azadirachta indica. J. Tree Sci.* **4**: 65–68.

Ostry, M.O. and Skilling, D.D. 1988. Somatic variation in resistance of *Populus* to *Septoria musiva. Plant Disease* **72**: 724–727.

Paily, J. and D'Souza, L. 1986. *In vitro* clonal propagation of *Lagerstroemia flos-reginae* Retz. *Plant Cell Tissue Organ Culture* **6**: 41–45.

Rai, V.R.S. and Chandra, K.S.J. 1987. Clonal propagation of *Cinnamomum zeylanicum* Breyn by tissue culture. *Plant Cell Tissue Organ Culture* **9**: 81–88.

Raj Bhansali, R. 1993. Bud culture for shoot multiplication and plantlet formation of *Tecomella undulata* (Rohida), a woody tree of the arid zone. *Trop. Sci.* **33**: 1–8.

Rajkumar, R. and Ayyappan, P. 1992. *In vitro* multiplication of *Eucalyptus globulus* Labill. *J. Tree Sci.* **11**: 34–40.

Rao, K.S. 1986. Plantlets from somatic callus tissue of East Indian Rosewood (*Dalbergia latifolia*). *Plant Cell Rep.* **5**: 199–201.

Rao, K.S. and Venkateshwara, R. 1985. Tissue culture of forest trees: Clonal multiplication of *Eucalyptus grandis. Plant Sci.* **40**: 51–55.

Rao, P.V.L. and De, D.N. 1987a. Tissue culture propagation of tree legume *Albizia lebbek* (L.) Benth. *Plant Sci.* **51**: 263–267.

Rao, P.V.L. and De, D.N. 1987b. Haploid plants from in *vitro* anther culture of the leguminous tree, *Peltophorum pterocarpum* (DC) K. Hayne (copper pod). *Plant Cell Tissue Organ Culture* **11**: 167–177.

Roy, S.K., Rahman, S.K.L. and Datta, P.C. 1988. *In vitro* propagation of *Mitragyna parvifolia* Korth. *Plant Cell Tissue Organ Culture* **12** (75): 75–80.

Sarita, P., Bhatnagar, S.P. and Bhojwani, S.S. 1988. Preliminary investigations on micropropagation of a leguminous timber tree *Pterocarpus santalinus. Phytomophology* **38**: 41–45.

Shankar, S. and Mohan Ram, H.Y. 1990. Plantlet regeneration from tissue cultures of *Sesbania grandiflora. Curr. Sci.* **59**: 39–43.

Shekhawat, N.S., Rathore, T.S., Singh, R.P., Deora, N.S. and Rao, S.R. 1993. Factors affecting *in vitro* clonal propagation of *Prosopis cineraria*. *Plant Growth Regulation* **12**: 273–280.

Sinha, R.K. and Mallick, R. 1991. Plantlets from somatic callus tissue of the woody legume *Sesbania bispinosa* (Jacq.) W.F. Wight. *Plant Cell Rep.* **10**: 247–250.

Singh, B.D. 1990. Plant Breeding: Principles and Methods. Kalyani Publishers, New Delhi. 496–509.

Smith, M.K. and Drew, R.A. 1990. Current applications of tissue culture in plant propagation and improvement. *Aust. J. Plant Physiol.* **17**: 267–289.

Srivastava, P.S. 1973. Formation of triploid plantlet in endosperm culture of *Putranjiva roxburghii*. *Z. Pflanzenphysiol.* **69**: 270–273.

Sumaryati, S., Negrutiu, I. and Jacobs, M. 1992. Characterization and regeneration of salt and water stress mutants from protoplast culture of *Nicotiana plumbaginifolia* (Viviani). *Theor. Appl. Genet.* **83**: 613–619.

Tewary, P.K. and Subba Rao, G. 1990. Multiple shoot formation through shoot apex culture of mulberry. *Indian J. For.* **13**: 109–111.

Thorpe, T.A., Harry, I.S. and Kumar, P.P. 1991. Application of micropropagation to forestry. *In*: P.C. Debergh and R.H. Zimmerman (Eds) Micropropagation. Kluwer Academic Publishers, Netherlands. 311–336.

Timmis, R., Abo El-Nil, M.M. and Stonecypher, R.W. 1987. Potential genetic gains through tissue culture. *In*: J.M. Bonga and D.J. Durzan (Eds) Tissue Culture in Forestry. Martinus Nijhoff, Dordrecht. 198–215.

Tomar, U.K. and Gupta, S.C. 1988a. Somatic embryogenesis and organogenesis in callus of a tree legume—*Albizia rechardiana* King. *Plant Cell Rep.* **7**: 198–215.

Tomar, U.K. and Gupta, S.C. 1988b. *In vitro* plant regeneration of leguminous tree (*Albizzia* spp.). *Plant Cell Rep.* **7**: 385–388.

Upadhyay, S. and Chandra, N. 1983. Shoot and plantlet formation in organ and callus culture of *Albizzia lebbeck*. *Ann. Bot.* **52**: 421–424.

Varga, A., Thoma, L.H. and Bruinsma, J. 1988. Effects of auxins of epigenetic instability of callus-propagated *Kalanchoe blossfeldiana* Poelln. *Plant Cell Tissue Organ Culture* **15**: 223–231.

Vidhyasekaran, P., Ling, D.H., Borromeo, E.S., Zapata, P.J. and Mew, T.W. 1990. Selection of brown spot-resistant rice plants from *Helminthosporium oryzae* toxin-resistant calluses. *Ann. Appl. Biol.* **117**: 515–523.

Yadav, U., Lal, M. and Jaiswal, V.S. 1990a. Micropropagation of *Morus nigra* L. from shoot tip and nodal explants of mature trees. *Scientia Horti.* **44**: 61–67.

Yadav, U., Lal M. and Jaiswal, V.S. 1990b. *In vitro* micropropagation of the tropical fruit tree *Syzygium cuminii* L. *Plant Cell Tissue Organ Culture* **21**: 87–92.

Zobel, B. and Talbert, J.T. 1984. Applied Forest Tree Improvement. John Wiley and Sons, New York. p. 505.

# 18

# Mass Clonal Propagation of Tropical Forest Trees for Improvement in Timber Yield and Quality

*M. Kamaluddin*[1]

**ABSTRACT**

The article considers practical aspects of clonal selection and propagation with particular emphasis on selection process of mature trees, their propagation and establishment in hedge beds. Productivity and management of stock plants, and the method of mass propagation by cuttings are described. Genetic diversity and deployment strategy of clonal plantations are considered.

## 1. INTRODUCTION

Mass clonal propagation of tropical forest trees is a recent development. Current emphasis on operational planting has been on the use of rooted stem cuttings. When a number of rooted cuttings are obtained from a single individual, a clone is formed, in which all the newly formed plants are genetically identical. When they are planted out, a greater uniformity can result from eliminating genetic variation. At the same time, an increased benefit is obtained through capture of both additive and non-additive genetic variation. Consequently, clonal propagation makes use of almost all the genetic gain which can be achieved by skilful selection and/or breeding.

The technique allows production of a large and continuous supply of planting stock. This, when includes superior individuals, can result in large genetic

[1]Institute of Forestry and Environmental Sciences, University of Chittagong, Chittagong 4331, Bangladesh.

gains. By selection of superior trees from wild populations or clones derived from them, it is often possible to achieve rapid improvements in yield and quality in excess of those made by provenance selection (Leakey, 1990a). A substantial improvement has been obtained in timber yield and quality for eucalypts in Congo and Brazil (Leakey, 1987; Zobel and Ikemori, 1983), *Gmelina arborea* in Malaysia (Wong and Jones, 1986), and *Triplochiton scleroxylon* in Nigeria (Leakey, 1987, 1990a). In addition to timber yield and quality, the clonal option allows to select clones for disease resistance, site adaptability and wood properties (Zobel and Ikemori, 1983). The spectacular success of clonal technique for the species encourages its wider application for others.

Forest tree improvement is possible through selection and propagation of superior trees, but a large gain is likely to occur in species which have considerable genetic variation in traits of forestry interests.

## 2. SELECTION OF SUPERIOR TREES

Selection of superior genotypes is an important element of the clonal technique. Wild population of many tropical forest trees has been subject to heavy dysgenic selection by loggers and now threatens the status of the gene resource of superior genotypes. Selection of superior individuals from the wild population should be done in stands that have a large proportion of good trees and that have not been subjected to logging operations.

Generally, plantations are preferable to natural stands for selection of superior individuals. In plantations, provenance or progeny trials, all trees are exactly the same age and spacing among trees is more uniform. This approach certainly ensures some genetic gain because dominant phenotypes in plantations, provenance or progeny trials are strongly determined by competitive forces between trees.

The main aim of the selection is to increase selection differential which results in greater gain. Selection differential may be affected by the selection method applied. Two selection methods, independent culling and base index (Cotterill and Dean, 1990), were examined with data from 16, 18, 20 and 22-year old plantations of *Dalbergia sissoo* (Haque and Kamaluddin, 1995) for growth and quality traits. Sectional area was used as growth trait, and stem straightness (1 to 6 score) and clear bole length as form traits. Clear bole length (m) indicates the self-pruning capacity of individual trees growing in a plantation of uniform site. Stem straightness and clear bole length were combined with the expectation that the higher the straightness score and clear bole length, better the tree in form traits. Although both the selection methods displayed substantial differential in the selected traits, the base index method exhibited larger selection differential in sectional area, clear bole length and standing volume per tree than the independent culling method.

When trees are selected within natural or planted stands, the chosen trees are usually felled or otherwise stimulated to induce the formation of easily rootable coppice-type shoots from near the base of the trunk. The derived clones are then re-evaluated in field trials.

## 3. PROPAGATION OF SELECTED INDIVIDUALS

Propagation of mature trees by cuttings is difficult without felling mainly because producing rootable materials in mature and large trees is difficult. However, semi-juvenile materials can be produced with the onset of spring by stimulating dormant buds to sprout on the trunk of mature trees. Such an approach has been found successful in the old trees of *Dalbergia sissoo* (Kamaluddin *et al.*, 1994). Some of the branches originating from the tree trunk were cut as closely as possible to the trunk to induce formation of epicormic shoots on the trunk. Dormant buds sprouted within 2 weeks. Six weeks after the appearance of the new shoots, they were collected, moistened and put into a fold of a banana leaf to avoid desiccation while transporting to the nursery. The cuttings were set into a propagator after 48 hours of collection. Percentage rooting of cuttings ranged from 80 to 95, but the number of roots per cutting was less than those for cuttings collected from nursery grown seedlings.

## 4. ESTABLISHMENT OF HEDGE BEDS

The rooted cuttings of the mature trees (Kamaluddin *et al.*, 1994) were established in nursery beds at a planting density of 10–12 stock plants per square meter bed area and grown there for one year when they were topped at a height of 30 cm above ground level to produce new shoots. The shoots were harvested at 6-week intervals. Rejuvenation of the shoots of three clones were examined by studying their rooting ability, growth rate and growth habit, and comparing the data with those from seedling cuttings of five families (Kamaluddin and Haque, in preparation). Within 18 months of experimentation, three important conclusions have been drawn:

(a) there are no significant differences between clonal and seedling cuttings in respect of percentage rooting, steckling per cent, growth rate and growth habit at the first harvest; the capacity of root production in the clonal cuttings increases at the second harvest (Fig. 1).
(b) the shoots produced by hedging are orthotropic; and
(c) there are substantial clonal/family variations in rooting ability of cuttings and growth of stecklings.

Morphologically, vigorous vegetative growth and orthotropic growth habit of hedge shoot indicate their rejuvenation. Serial propagation of the hedge shoots and their establishment in new hedge beds enhance the rejuvenation process and stability of the stockplants.

## 5. PRODUCTIVITY OF STOCKPLANTS

Success of a mass clonal propagation program for a species depends on the production of rootable cuttings per stockplant or per unit hedge-bed area at a given time. Early in a clonal programme, harvesting shoots from the stockplant

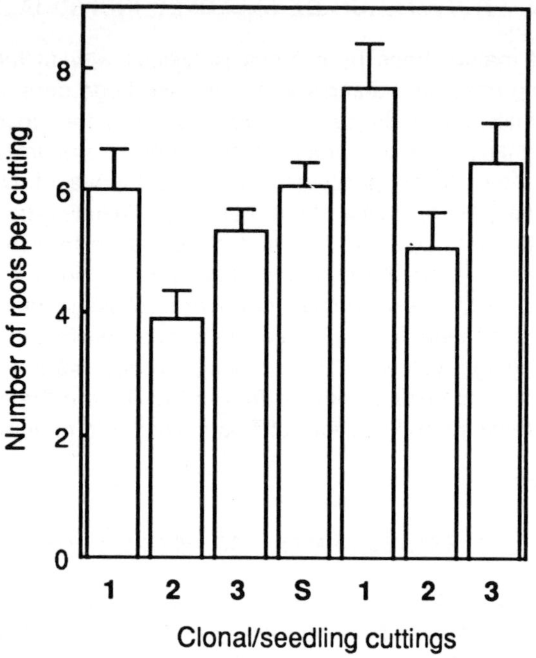


Fig. 1. Root production in cuttings collected from young stockplants of three clones of *D. sissoo*. The numbers, 1, 2, 3, indicate clone number and 'S' stands for seedling cuttings of a tested family; the bars for the clones on the left are for the data of the first harvest and on the right for the data of the second harvest.

can begin from 4 to 6 months since establishment of the stockplants. However, when the program is well established, the stockplants should be topped when their stem diameter at the base is between 8–12 cm, in eucalypts for instance (Eldridge *et al.*, 1993).

Since different clones are genetically different, shoot production capacity is likely to vary from clone to clone. Working with a few clones, the author did not find a significant clonal variation in shoot production capacity for *Dalbergia sissoo*. But the height at which the stockplant was topped was important. The stockplants topped at 30 cm above ground produced a higher number of rootable cuttings (2-node cuttings, 10–12 cm long) than those topped at 10 cm above ground (Fig. 2).

Stockplant diameter is also related with the cutting production. In *Dalbergia sissoo*, clonal stockplants of 18 mm diameter class (diameter at the base) produced more rootable cuttings than those of 10 mm diameter class (Fig. 3). Kantarli (1993) also observed such a relationship between sapling diameter and number of shoots produced when *Hopea odorata* saplings were hedged. All, except one or two young shoots, can be harvested at a time for cuttings. The retained shoots are allowed to grow to nourish the roots and subsequently cut for use as cuttings. Removal of all the shoots at a time may be detrimental

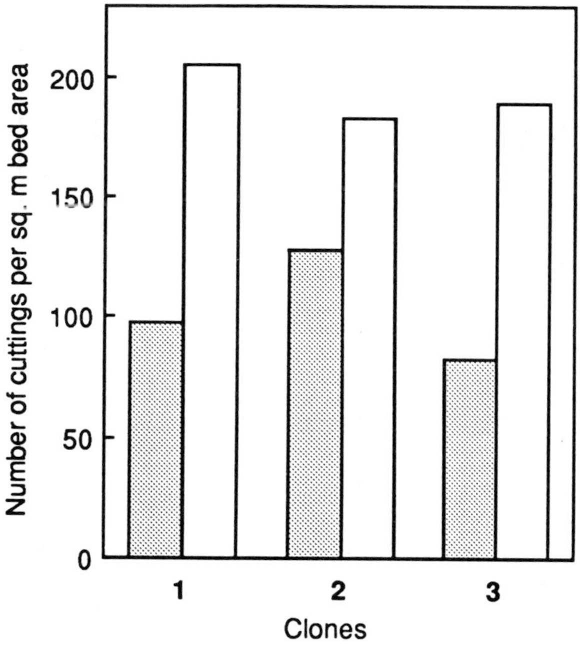


Fig. 2. Cutting (2-node) production of one-year old stockplants of three clones of *D. sissoo*, when topped at 10 cm above ground (shaded) and 30 cm above ground (clear).

for certain species. For example, complete decapitation of stockplants of *Dalbergia sissoo* by removing all the shoots resulted in the death of many stockplants.

Normally, two harvests of shoots can be made in a season from each stockplant. For *Azadirachta indica*, it is possible to harvest shoots from each managed stockplant at three weeks intervals, whereas for *Dalbergia sissoo* the harvesting interval has to be at least six weeks. About 180–200 double-node cuttings per square meter bed area can be obtained from one-year old stockplants of *D. sissoo* (Fig. 2) whereas only about 90 tip shoot cuttings can be got from *A. indica* stockplants of the same age.

## 6. MANAGEMENT OF STOCKPLANTS

To operate a clonal propagation program for supplying stecklings at an operational scale, a large number of shoots must be available for cuttings. Performance of the cuttings depends on management of the stockplants. Stockplants grown under low irradiance enhance rooting of cuttings (Leakey and Storeton-West, 1992). Shading affects both the amount and quality of light received by the shoots of stockplants. Both these factors independently affect the physiology, morphology and rooting ability of cuttings (Hoad *et al.*, 1990). Nutrient

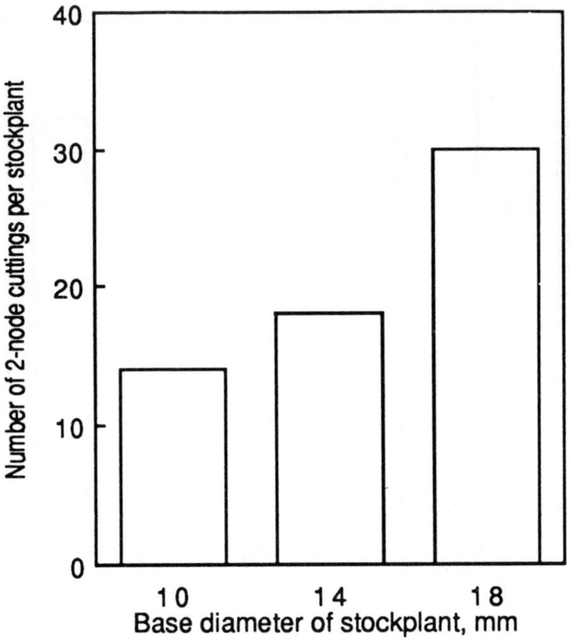


Fig. 3. Cutting production of one-year old stockplants of *D. sissoo* by base diameter of stockplants topped at 30 cm above ground.

status of the stockplant interacts with the effects of light and shading, with shading and high nutrients combining to enhance rooting (Leakey and Storeton-West, 1992).

Nutrient deficiencies are detrimental to productivity of stockplants and rooting of cuttings. De Souza and Felker (1986) suggest application of fertilizers rich in nitrogen and low in phosphate, potassium and other nutrients to stimulate stem nitrogen and maintain high rootability of cuttings. Soil moisture is also important because water stress adversely affects sprouting following decapitation (Leakey and Ladipo, 1987).

Considering the need for low irradiance, retention of soil moisture and maintenance of soil fertility, stockplants can be planted and maintained in such a way that all these requirements are well satisfied. This can be done by planting and establishing stockplants with a suitable nurse plant in a mixed form with the provision of artificial mulching in between the plants. Nitrogen-fixing leguminous species with light-shading property and the leaves of which decompose rapidly and most importantly which can be grown easily is a good choice as nurse plant. The nurse plants will provide shade and retain fertility of the soil by sustained supply of nutrients particularly nitrogen from decomposed nodules and leaf litter. Artificial mulching will retain the soil moisture and also improve moisture retention capacity and aeration of the soil.

# 7. PROPAGATION METHOD

## 7.1 Propagation Unit

Requirements of propagation environment for root initiation in leafy cuttings are those that minimize physiological stress in the cuttings. The propagation systems so far developed for mass propagation of forest trees are mist and non-mist. The technology of mist spraying is successful, but it is vulnerable to power cuts, interruptions of water supply and mechanical breakdown.

A low-cost, non-mist propagator, described by Kamaluddin and Ali (1994), has been found suitable for successful propagation of several forest tree species including *Azadirachta indica, Chickrassia velutina, Baccaurea ramiflora, Eucalyptus camaldulensis, Dalbergia sissoo* and hybrid of *Acacia mangium* × *A. auriculiformis*. The propagator and the overhead shading reduce air temperature, provide high humidity and hence lower the transpiration losses of the cuttings in the propagator.

## 7.2 Cutting Preparation

For many tropical forest trees, several cuttings are produced from each shoot usually 2-node cuttings (with four leaves per cutting), but sometimes 1-node cuttings (with two leaves). No difference is found between 2-node and 1-node cuttings of *Dalbergia sissoo* in respect of rooting of cuttings and growth of rooted cuttings (data not presented). In some cases, as in *Azadirachta indica* tip cuttings exhibit better rooting and growth of the rooted cuttings than those taken subsequently from the same shoot.

Leaves in each cutting is usually trimmed to half to reduce transpiration losses. Rooting ability in leafy cuttings is sometimes related to the production of reflux-soluble carbohydrates, apparently derived from current photosynthesis while cuttings are in a propagation unit (Leakey and Storeton-West, 1992). In an experiment with *Dalbergia sissoo*, deleterious effect of sub-optimal leaf area on rooting of cuttings was observed (data not presented). This indicates that cuttings of the species need additional photosynthate for rooting and have a critical requirement for leaf area for photosynthate during propagation period. Current photosynthesis in some species may be of little importance for root formation in leafy cuttings when the cuttings contain sufficient carbohydrate reserves to satisfy rooting demand (Kantarli, 1993).

Leakey and Coutts (1989) studied the leaf water potential of cuttings with different leaf area during propagation under intermittent mist for *Triplochiton scleroxylon* and demonstrated a deleterious effect of larger leaf area on rooting of cuttings resulting from decreased leaf water potential. In an experiment with *Azadirachta indica* in a non-mist propagator, no significant difference in rooting of cuttings between the cuttings with different leaf area was observed (Kamaluddin and Ali, 1996). It was concluded that the deleterious effect of larger leaf area might be minimized by the less fluctuation and high humidity of the non-mist propagator.

Removal of axillary shoots from the cuttings before setting into the propagator is important. It is observed in several species that when the cuttings are taken from unbranched shoots, the shoots developed from the axillary buds of the cuttings are orthotropic. If axillary shoots are retained in the cuttings, they exhibit plagiotropic growth habit. When the axillary shoots are removed at the time of cuttings preparation, orthotropic shoots are developed from accessory buds of the cuttings (Leakey, 1990b).

## 7.3 Rooting Hormone

Indole-3yl-butyric acid (IBA) is a widely used root-forming auxin for increasing rooting of cuttings. The applied auxin not only improves percentage rooting but also increase the number of roots and the speed of rooting. In cuttings with a high level of endogenous auxin content, applied auxin inhibits rooting, while conversely in cuttings with a low endogenous auxin content, the applied auxin causes significant increase in rooting response. Differing responses to auxin between species are well known, but there can also be variation in auxin preference within a species (Leakey *et al.*, 1982). Before the operational use of a clone, it is important to determine the degree of rooting response and the auxin treatment that maximizes rooting and growth of rooted cuttings.

The most conspicuous effect of auxin treatment is the increase in root number per cutting. It is generally accepted that more roots per cutting indicate a better root system and greater vigor. In an experiment with *Dalbergia sissoo* (data not presented), though IBA treatment increased the number of roots, there was no direct relationship between the root number and the growth of the rooted cuttings. All the roots formed per cutting did not develop as macroroots. Only few roots (2–4) per cutting developed as macroroots, and extensively branched and rebranched forming a well developed root system. There was no significant difference in root dry weight between the control and IBA-treated cuttings because the root biomass was mostly influenced by dry weight of macroroots rather than the number of roots per cutting and hence no increase in the growth of rooted cuttings as a result of auxin effects of increased root numbers per cutting was observed.

Nevertheless, IBA treatment is not always required to produce quality stecklings. In most of the cases, when fully rejuvenated materials are used, 'tap root type' macroroots (2–4 per cutting) are produced and the stecklings exhibit orthotropic growth habit and a growth similar to that of seedlings.

## 7.4 Treating with Fungicide

Fungicidal treatment is a common practice to prevent cuttings from fungal attack. Cuttings are immersed briefly in a solution of fungicide (2 g Diathan M45 per liter of water), rinsed and kept under shade for 5–10 min in open air before treating with hormone. Some species like *D. sissoo, Chickrassia velutina* and *Gmelina arborea* do not require fungicidal treatment.

## 7.5 Root Formation, Weaning and Aftercare

Choice of rooting medium is important because rooting success depends on the proper balance of aeration and moisture within the medium. Rooting medium of coarse sand mixed with gravel (0.1–0.3 cm) has been found suitable for rooting of cuttings in the non-mist propagator. The cuttings are set into the propagator after treatment and watered immediately after planting. Normally, no further watering is required before transfer of the rooted cuttings from the propagator. The propagator is opened briefly twice, once in the morning and once in the afternoon, to facilitate gas exchange.

Root initiation normally takes place within 2–4 weeks after setting into the propagator. When the cuttings are well rooted, the propagator is kept open at night for the first two days of weaning and then in the morning and in the afternoon for the next two days, and finally for another two or three days under overhead shade. This gradual exposure enhances root lignification and acclimation process of the rooted cuttings. Finally, the rooted cuttings are transferred to polythene bags filled with soil mixed with compost or decomposed cow dung at 3:1 proportion by volume. The transferred cuttings are kept under light shade for 3–5 days before exposure to regular sunlight.

Depending on the fertility of the soil, periodic fertilization of NPK may be needed to support the growth of stecklings. In Bangladesh, the stecklings are usually fertilized with 12-12-12 NPK in solution at fifteen days intervals starting from seven days of transfer. The solution is prepared by dissolving one teaspoonful of fertilizer in 20 liters of water. Normally, it takes two to three months from rooting of the cuttings until the planting stock is ready for field planting.

## 8. GENETIC DIVERSITY AND DEPLOYMENT STRATEGY

Sufficient variation within a production program must be maintained to accommodate a wide variety of environmental and biotic conditions even within a single planting region. Use of diverse genotypes is an effective way of increasing genetic diversity. Genetic diversity can be more efficiently maintained in the clonal technique by selecting highly productive, but unrelated clones and planting them either in a form of intimate mixture or in a mosaic of pure stands.

A mosaic of monoclonal stands rather than an intimate mixture of 20–30 unrelated clones is likely to be a better deployment strategy. When a small area (few ha or less) is planted with a single clone, the variation within the plantation is less than when a mixture of clones is planted. If individual clones fail, the problem can be readily recognized in the mosaic plantations and these clones can be removed and replaced. It is necessary to have a large number of clones in a clone bank, even though only a few clones will be in use at a given time. When some are eliminated from the planting program, new ones will be added on.

## REFERENCES

Cotterill, P.P. and Dean, C.A. 1990. Successful Tree Breeding with Index Selection. CSIRO, Australia. 80 pp.

De Souza, S.M. and Felker, P. 1986. The influence of stockplant fertilization on tissue concentrations of N, P and carbohydrates and the rooting of *Prospis alba* cuttings. *For. Ecol. Mgmt.* **16**: 181–190.

Eldridge, K., Davidson, J., Harwood, C. and Van Wyk, G. 1993. Eucalypt Domestication and Breeding. Clarendon press, Oxford. 288 pp.

Haque, M.N. and Kamaluddin, M. 1994. Growth and standing volume of *Dalbergia sissoo* and selection methods for its genetic improvement. *Chittagong University Studies (Science)* **19**: 121–126.

Hoad, S.P., Maclellan, A.J. and Leakey, R.R.B. 1990. Vegetative propagation of *Eucalyptus grandis* W. Hill ex Maiden. Final Report (1990) to Shell Research Ltd., Inst. Terrestrial Ecology, Scotland. 77 pp.

Kamaluddin, M. and Ali, M. 1994. A technique for mass propagation of neem by juvenile stem cuttings. Tree Breeding and Propagation News 3, UNDP/FAO Regional Project RAS/91/004, Laguna, Philippines.

Kamaluddin, M. and Ali, M. 1996. Effects of leaf area and auxin on rooting and growth of rooted stem cuttings of neem. *New Forests* **12**: 11–18.

Kamaluddin, M., Ali, M. and Bhuiyan, M.K. 1994. Effects of leaf retention and auxin applications on rootability of green stem cuttings from mature trees of *Dalbergia sissoo*. *Annals For.* **12**: 142–146.

Kantarli, M. 1993. Vegetative propagation of dipterocarpus by cutting in ASEAN region. Review Paper No. 1, ASEAN- Canada Forest Tree Seed Centre Project, Saraburi, Thailand. 58 pp.

Leakey, R.R.B. 1987. Clonal forestry in the tropics—a review of developments, strategies and opportunities. *Common. For. Rev.* **66**: 61–75.

Leakey, R.R.B. 1990a. The domestication of tropical forest trees by cloning: a strategy for increased production and for conservation. *In*: D. Werner and P. Muller (Eds) Fast Growing Trees and Nitrogen Fixing Trees. Gustav Fischer Verlag, Stuttgart, Trees. 22–31.

Leakey, R.R.B. 1990b. Nauclea diderrichii: rooting of stem cuttings, clonal variation in shoot dominance, and branch plagiotropism. *Trees* **4**: 164–169.

Leakey, R.R.B., Chapman, V.R. and Longman, K.A. 1982. Physiological studies for tropical tree improvement and conservation: factors affecting root initiation in cuttings of *Triplochiton scleroxylon* K. Schum. *For. Ecol. Mgmt.* **4**: 53–66.

Leakey, R.R.B. and Coutts, M.P. 1989. The dynamic of rooting in *Triplochiton scleroxylon* cuttings: their relation to leaf area, node position, dry weight accumulation, leaf water potential and carbohydrate composition. *Tree Physiol.* **5**: 135–146.

Leakey, R.R.B. and Ladipo, D.O. 1987. Selection for improvement in vegetatively propagated tropical hardwoods. *In*: A.J. Abbot and R.K. Atkin (Eds) Improvement of Vegetatively Propagated Plants. Academic Press, London. 324–336.

Leakey, R.R.B. and Storeton-West, R. 1992. The rooting ability of *Triplochiton scleroxylon* cutting: the interaction between stockplant irradiance, light quality and nutrients. *For. Ecol. Mgmt.* **49**: 133–150.

Wong, C.Y. and Jones, N. 1986. Improving tree form through vegetative propagation of *Gmelina arborea*. *Common. For. Rev.* **65**: 321–324.

Zobel, B. and Ikemori, Y.K. 1983. Vegetative propagation in Eucalyptus. *In*: L. Zsuffa, R.M. Rauter and C.W. Yeatman (Eds) Proc. Nineteenth Meeting of the Canadian Tree Improvement Association, Toronto, Canada. 136–144.

# 19

# Selection of Superior *Eucalyptus* Trees for Industrial Requirements

*K. Gurumurthi,*[1] *R.K. Verma*[2] *and N. Preetha*[3]

**ABSTRACT**

The paper describes the method for selection of superior trees of *Eucalyptus*, their improvement and mass multiplication through tissue culture. The technique for selection is based on the Congo Brazilian method. The rejuvenation and multiplication of mature trees were done using young shoots or emerging axillary buds. MS medium supplemented with Biotin (0.1 mg/l), Cal.D. Pantothenate (0.1 mg/l) and the Cytokinin BAP (0.1 mg/l) and Kinetin (0.1 mg/l) were found to be effective for shoot initiation in *E. tereticornis*. A detailed protocol for mass multiplication is given. In order to produce quality seeds it is essential that clones are subjected to multilocational trial and $D^2$ analysis.

## 1. INTRODUCTION

The tree improvement strategies are time consuming when conventional breeding principles are followed. The approaches like provenance trial, progeny trial, seedling seed orchard, and clonal seed orchard are essential steps that need to be followed in an organized tree improvement program. At the same time strategies need be developed to bring about rapid improvement in yields on a short term basis. The present paper describes the methodology that can be followed for rapid tree improvement of fast growing tree species on a short

---

[1]Plant Biotechnology Division, Institute of Forest Genetics and Tree Breeding, Coimbatore 641 002, India.

[2]Central Forest Organization, JK Corporation Ltd., Raygada 765 006, India.

[3]Department of Life Sciences, Goa University, Goa, India.

term basis. It is realized that there can be shortcomings in this approach and therefore it should be practized in consonance with regular tree improvement programs. This approach relies on selecting superior performers from the available population and bringing them together through macropropagation strategies followed by genetic assessment and development of strategies for improved planting stock production, both as seed and clonal stock.

## 2. METHOD FOR SELECTION OF SUPERIOR PERFORMERS

The approach involves selecting plants from normal plantation consisting an area of around 50–100 ha. Initially, it is necessary to collect data on the total area, seed source, topography, survival percentage, soil nutrients, humidity, maximum-minimum temperatures and mean monthly rainfall. Other relevant information may also be collected. To illustrate it further, let us assume a 3–4-year old eucalypt plantation in an area of 100 ha with spacing of 2 × 2 m and 60 per cent survival. The total plants in the area will be approximately, 1,50,000. If the selection intensity is maintained at 1:3000, it is possible to select approximately 50 plants from the population. The selection intensity needs to be determined at the field level. Selection intensity and the performance of plantations must be treated as inversely correlated. In other words, if the performance of the plantation is uniformly good, the selection ratio will be less. If the performance of the plantation is highly variable then the selection ratio can be increased. For instance, in a good performing plantation the selection pressure can be maintained at 1:5000, whereas in a poorly performing plantation, the selection pressure can be reduced to 1:3000. The performance of the plantation needs to be assessed in terms of the coefficient of variation for the desired character(s). Often, under tropical moist conditions of our region, coefficient variation for any character is known to vary from 50–80 per cent (Gurumurti and Bhandari, 1987) which itself is an indicator of high genetic variability. It is essential to sample the plantation and determine the coefficient variation for desired character(s) appropriately. If the coefficient variation for various characters is less than 20 per cent, the possibility of genetic variation is very much reduced. Thus, with 80 per cent coefficient variation selection of 1:2000 and with 50 per cent CV 1:5000 is advocated.

Determining the selection ratio in a population determines the number of plots to be selected in an area for selection of plants. Thus, in a 100 ha area with tree population of 1,50,000 and a selection intensity of 1:3000 the number of plants to be selected is 50. Therefore, 50 plots should be laid out with each plot size of 20 × 20 m in the plantation. While laying out the plots, it is essential to study the topography and avoid border plants, depressions, elevations on the banks of streams, ponds, temporary water collection sources, rocky zones, sandy areas and other unusual features. It is advisable to lay plots at random avoiding the above cited areas. With spacing of 2 × 2 m in a 20 × 20 m plot and 60 per cent survival, around 60–80 plants are enumerated for height, diameter and frustum volume. Finally using methods outlined in the following pages one plant in each plot may be selected based on the phenotypic criteria.

## 3. METHOD FOR SELECTION OF SUPERIOR TREES IN THE PLOT

One of the problem with phenotypic selection of individual trees is the variability among trees caused by micro-enviornmental variation, i.e., differences among trees within a field caused by variation in soil type, fertility, moisture and so forth. When trees are selected for higher yield, they might all come from one section of the field where the fertility is greatest, even though the individuals may not be superior genetically. In such situations using of Grid Design (Gardner, 1961), with suitable modification, can minimize the soil heterogeneity effect on the performance of individual trees. In this technique the whole field under screening is divided into manageable size of grids. The trees are selected and marked with red paint. Whether intended or not, the selection of trees for one trait will inevitably result in changes in other traits. It is because of some type of correlation exists between the selected and other traits. If correlation exists, then correlated responses must be expected and the breeder may choose to influence them genetically, selecting trees on the basis of their performance in the several traits. Therefore, phenotypic selection is followed by construction of a multiple trait selection index for each individual selected tree. To construct the multiple trait selection index main bole volume is considered as the principal trait and its correlation with other traits like height, CDM, DBH and frustum volume is estimated (Searle, 1961) as follows:

$$\text{Correlation (r)} = \frac{\text{Cov} \cdot X_1\ X_2}{\sigma_x \cdot \sigma_x}$$

Where, $\text{Cov} \cdot X_1\ X_2$ = Covariance of $X_1$ and $X_2$

$\sigma_x$ = SD of $X_1$ trait

$\sigma_x$ = SD of $X_2$ trait

*Main Bole Volume:* Main bole volume is calculated by the equation following Chaturvedi and Khanna (1982).

$$\text{Main Bole Volume} = \frac{sl}{3} \text{ in cm}^3$$

Where, $s = (CDM/2)^2 \times \pi$ in $cm^2$; $l$ = height of the tree in cm.

*Frustum Volume:* Volume of the frustum can be calculated by the equation given by Chaturvedi and Khanna (1982)

$$\text{Frustum volume} = \frac{S_1 + S_2 + \sqrt{S_1 \cdot S_2}}{3} \times 130 \text{ in cm}^3$$

Where, $S_1 = (CDM/2)^2 \times \pi$ in $cm^2$

$S_2 = (DBH/2)^2 \times \pi$ in $cm^2$

Index for each character was calculated by multiplying the observed value of that with the correlation coefficient of the trait with the main bole volume.

The selection index is calculated by adding all the five values for each tree. The equation can thus be written as,

$$\text{Selection index (SI)} = X_1R_{1,5} + X_2R_{2,5} + X_3R_{3,5} + X_4R_{4,5} + X_5R_{5,5}$$

Where, $X_1$, $X_2$, $X_3$, $X_4$ and $X_5$ are height, CDM, DBH, frustum volume and main bole volume respectively, and $R_{1,5}$, $R_{2,5}$, $R_{3,5}$, $R_{4,5}$ and $R_{5,5}$ are the correlation coefficients (Weightage) of height, CDM, DBH, frustum volume and main bole volume.

After calculating selection index for all the initially marked trees, final selection was carried out. The trees with higher selection index within a grid are selected. Composite soil samples from each of the plot can be collected for analysis. In this approach comparison is made among the plants within the plot and no comparison is made of plants between the plots. Thus, the selection takes into consideration the heterogenity of the population and soil and at the sametime avoids the topographic and microclimate variations. The plants thus selected are utilized for propagation.

## 4. METHOD FOR CLONAL MULTIPLICATION

The selected superior trees are coppiced 15–20 cm above the ground level in the last week of February. Cuttings of two to three node length are made and kept in Stockosorb, a water holding compound or simply floated on clean water mixed with fungicide. Cuttings should be transported to the propagation complex. On arrival, they are clipped into single node cuttings and treated with 0.05 per cent mercuric chloride to avoid any fungal growth. Subsequently, they are dip smeared in growth hormone, e.g., with 2000 or 4000 ppm Indole Butyric Acid. Treated cuttings are planted in pre-soaked saturated vermiculite filled in root trainers (10 × 1.5"). Cuttings must be placed inside a mist chamber with 85 per cent relative humidity (RH). Usually root initiation begins after seven to ten days of planting. After root initiation, exogenous supply of nutrients may be provided in the form of one fourth of the normal strength of Hoagland solution, once a week. Later (25–30 days) rooted propagules should be hardened.

Vegetatively propagated clones are planted in the clone bank zone. Each clone is planted in single row of 5 to 10 ramets at a spacing of 2 m in single plant plot design. Before planting, soil is replaced with the mixture of sand: soil: FYM (2:1:1) to ensure better establishment of clones and uniformity for comparative assessment.

## 5. METHOD FOR PERFORMANCE ASSESSMENT

The effectiveness of selection for a trait depends on the relative importance of genetic and non-genetic factors in the expression of phenotypic differences among individual clones. The heritability of a character has major impact on the methods chosen for tree improvement. Single plant selection may be effective for a character with high heritability and relatively ineffective for a character which has low heritability. Heritability in broad sense ($h^2$) is calculated as:

$$\text{Heritability } (h^2) \text{ (per cent)} = V_g/V_p \times 100$$

Where, $V_g$ and $V_p$ are genotypic and phenotypic coefficient of variance respectively.

The objective of any tree improvement program is to improve genetic performance of a cultivar or clone. This requires a comparison of an amount of genetic improvement that can be achieved using alternative improvement methods with the available resources. The concept of genetic gain is based on the change in mean performance of a population that is realised, with each cycle of selection. One cycle includes establishment of seedling population selection of superior genotypes and utilization of the selected genotypes as parents form a new population for the next selection. The genetic advance at 5 per cent selection intensity is calculated for each character following Johnson *et al.* (1955).

$$\text{Genetic Advance (GA)} = K.h^2.\sqrt{V_p}$$

Where, K = selection differential (at 5 per cent selection intensity, K = 2.06)

$h^2$ = Heritability

$\sqrt{V_p}$ = Phenotypic standard deviation

The expected genetic advance per cent of mean can be calculated as under:

$$\text{Genetic Advance (\% of mean)} = \frac{GA}{\text{mean}} \times 100,$$

where, GA = Genetic Advance

## 6. METHOD FOR ESTIMATION OF GENETIC DIVERGENCE

The aim of tree improvement is to provide material of high genetic quality for propagation. There are several ways by which superior material can be propagated. The most important one being harvesting seeds from clonal seed orchards and vegetative propagation of outstanding clones for direct use in plantations. The genetic quality of seed harvested from a clonal seed orchard depends on the genetic make up of clones and layout of clonal seed orchard. It is an established fact that clones which are genetically distant produce more vigorous seed by intercrossing when planted together. To assess the genetic distance of clones from each other, Mahalanobis's $D^2$ (genetic divergence) method is used.

*$D^2$ Analysis:* The original mean values (X's) are transformed into uncorrelated variable (Y's). All possible n(n-1)/2 $D^2$ is calculated as sum of the squares of these deviation as follows:

$$D^2 = V - V^2 = \sum (Y - Y^2)^2$$

The Tocher method (Rao, 1952) is followed for grouping of clones in different clusters. In this method, two clones with the smallest distance from each other are considered first to which a third clone having smallest average $D^2$ value from the first two population is added. Then the fourth and so on till an increase in average $D^2$ exceeds significant level. This is followed by the second cluster with the lowest average $D^2$ value of remaining clones. Thus, the process is continued till all the clones are included in one or the other cluster. After formation of clusters, the average inter- and intra-cluster divergence is worked out taking into consideration all the component $D^2$ values possible among the members of the two clusters being considered. The square root of the $D^2$ values gives the distance (D) between the clusters.

Based on the average D values, the following ratings for distance as close, medium and highly divergent given under is adopted (Surendran, 1982).

| Category | D values |
|---|---|
| Closely related (c) | ≤ 3.0 |
| Moderately divergent (M) | > 3.0 |
| Highly divergent | ≥ 6.0 |

Canonical analysis is also carried out to determine the genetic divergence and to confirm the group constellations arrived by $D^2$ statistics. The relative importance of the characters and determining the principal component of variability are also observed by use of canonical analysis (Rao, 1952).

In the first step canonical vector is obtained by column total of 4 × 4 dispersion which are obtained from mean values of uncorrelated variable matrix by the highest value of the set, with this trial vector each row of the matrix is multiplied. This newly derived vector is a better approximation than the trial one. The operations are repeated until stable values are obtained. After obtaining stable values of the vector, the standardized values of first vector ($V_1$) are computed by dividing element of the stable values by the square root of their sum of squares. The first canonical root is derived from the highest value in the last approximation of vector,

i.e., = $\sqrt{\text{highest value in the last stage approximation}}$.

To obtain the second vector ($V_2$), a reduced matrix was derived by eliminating the product with appropriate power $X_j^{th}$ element of the first vector from the (ij) the element of matrix A with appropriate power. The process of choosing a trial vector and finding better approximation is repeated on the reduced matrix. The second canonical root is obtained from the highest column total in last approximation of vector ($V_2$).

Estimation of 'Z' values are required in plotting the various populations in two dimensional graph

$[Z_1] = [Y][V_1]$

$[Z_2] = [Y][V_2]$

where, [Y] are the mean transformed values and $[V_1]$ and $[V_2]$ are the first vector and second vector, respectively.

Using the method outlined above tree improvement strategies have been developed for casuarina and eucalypts at Institute of Forest Genetics and Tree Breeding, Coimbatore. By adopting the selection strategies mentioned in the earlier pages 33 clones of eucalypts have been brought into the clone bank. The technique used is outlined in ICFRE information bulletins (Verma *et al.*, 1994; Ashok Kumar *et al.*, 1994). Based on the $D^2$ and cannonical analysis, the cluster was developed for eucalypts which is given in Figs. 1 and 2.

The techniques for selection of eucalypt plants along with propagation techniques, as outlined above, is based on the Congo Brazilian method. In our experience not all the coppiced plants respond to rooting. Rejuvenation through tissue culture and developing micropropagation techniques was attempted. The selected clones were maintained under culture conditions either as continuous multiplication culture or as subdued cultures so that necessary plantlets of the desired stock can be generated and transferred to the field for further multiplication by vegetative means. In this approach it is essential that callus is avoided or discouraged to maintain the purity of the genetic stock.

## 7. METHOD FOR MULTIPLICATION OF BUDS FROM ADULT TREES

Either the shoot or axillay buds of genetically proven superior trees can be selected. Cloning mature tissues *in vitro* is adversely affected by maturation phenomenon and reduced rooting ability. For rejuvenation of superior performers to produce identical clones of eucalypts, following methods are suggested:

1. The time of collection of bud materials should synchronize with the period of active vegetative growth.
2. Only young and just emerging buds should be selected.
3. The terminal part of a tree being ontogenically most mature, collection of axillary bud materials from the lower branches are preferred (Plageotropy is a risk).
4. The shoots arising from the meristem of lignotubers are juvenile and serves a good source material.
5. The axillary buds from coppice shoots also provides juvenile material and can be used as explant source.
6. Adult trees can be ringed and the emerging epicormic buds can be used as explants.

The buds are collected as nodal cuttings along with leaves at the time of bud break. The buds being tender are washed with 70 per cent alcohol for 2

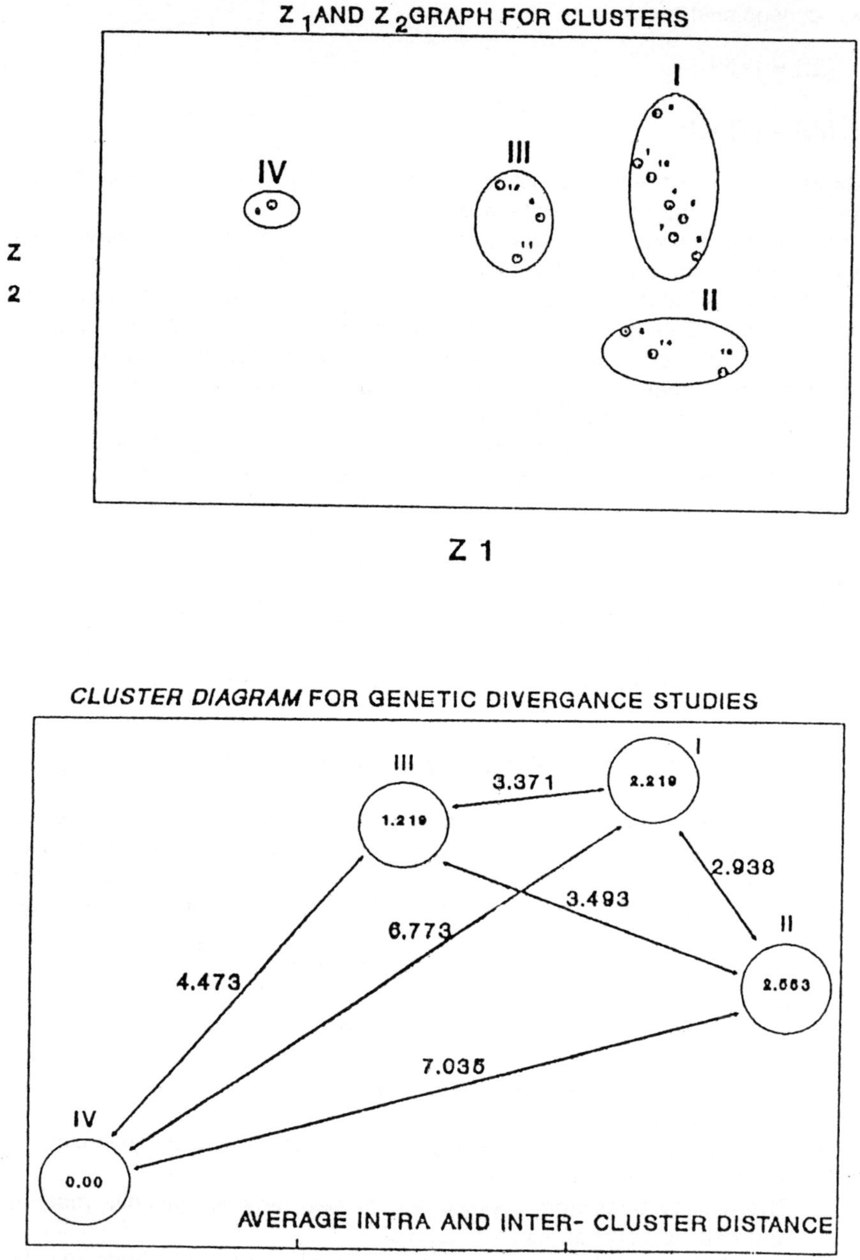


Fig. 1. Genetic divergence analysis for *Eucalyptus tereticornls*.

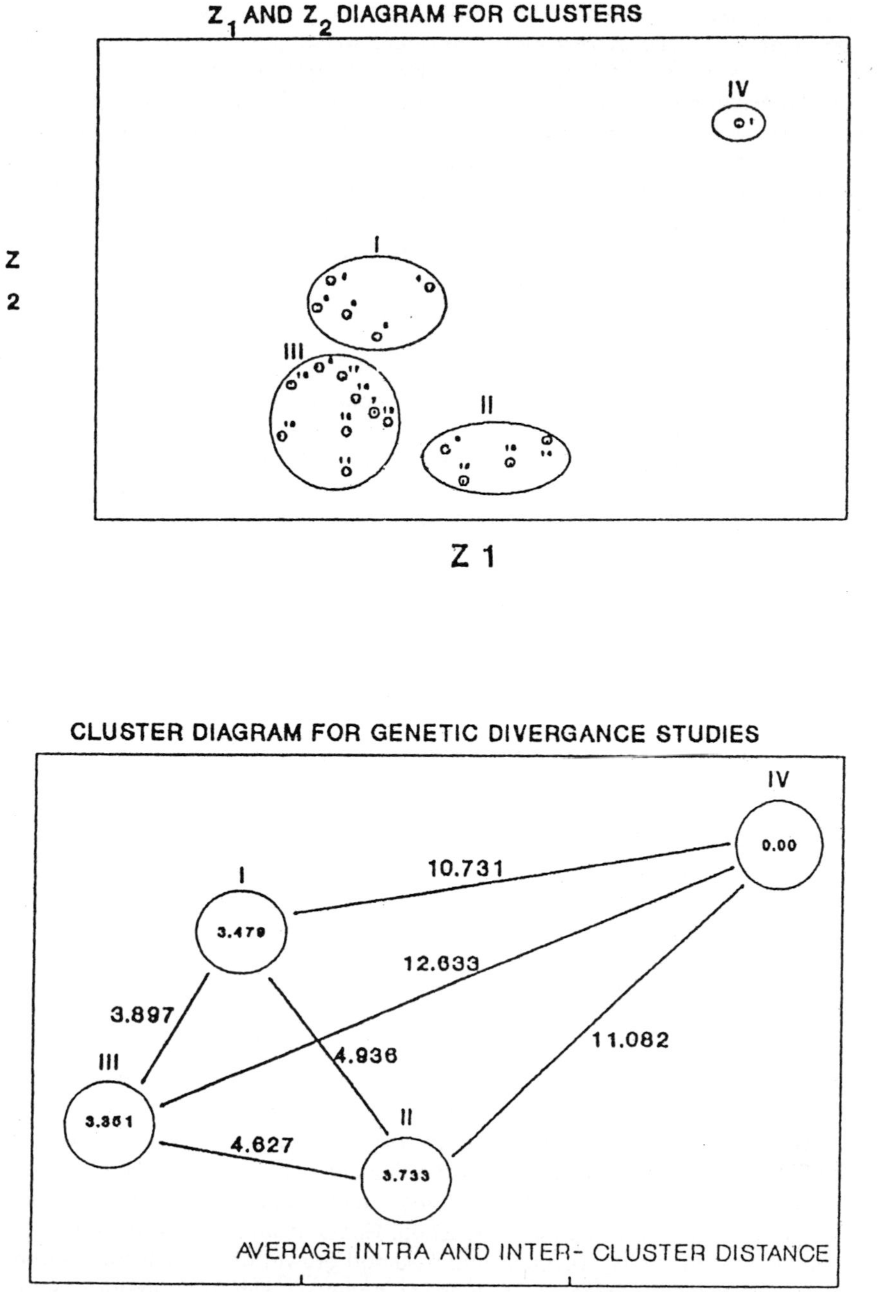


Fig. 2. Genetic divergence analysis for *Eucalyptus camaldulensis*.

minutes followed by 0.1 per cent $HgCl_2$ for 4 minutes and with sterile water under aseptic conditions. The surface moisture should be removed by a blotting paper. Care should be taken to remove the damaged tissue ends.

MS medium supplemented with Biotin (0.1mg/l), Cal.D. Pantothenate (0.1 mg/l) and the cytokinin BAP (0.1 mg/l) and Kinetin (0.1 mg/l) was found to be suitable for shoot initiation in *E. tereticornis*. The major problem encountered was the exudation of phenols into the medium. This can be overcome to a great extent by changing the medium within one week of culture. The cultures are maintained at 24 °C and 12 hrs photoperiod. The initial explant develops into 5–8 shoots within 40–45 days. Subculturing in groups of 2–3 shoots in the same medium results in proliferation to form 5–10 shoots of 3–4 cm height within 30 days. Axillary bud proliferation can be promoted by removal of the apical bud. Gupta *et al.* (1981) reported a two step multiplication route whereby the cultures were maintained at a lower concentration of cytokinin BAP 0.1 mg/l and kinetin 0.5 mg/l.

The protocol developed is quantified in terms of the number of multiple shoots induced per bud and the average length of the shoots. The MS medium (Table 1) was found to be suitable for both initiation and maintenance of cultures due to the high rate of multiplication and the development of healthy well grown shoots, and 40 per cent of the explants showed shoot initiation.

Table 1. Tissue culture stragegy for multiplication using buds from 15–20 year old plants

| Stage of culture | Media | No. of shoots/ explant | Time course of multiplication (Days) | Response (%) |
|---|---|---|---|---|
| Shoot initiation | MS + Kin (0.1 mg/l) + BAP (0.1 mg/l) | 5–8 | 40–50 | 40 |
| Shoot multiplication | MS + Kin (0.1 mg/l) + BAP (0.1 mg/l) | 5–10 | 30 | |
| Rooting | MS 1/2 strength + IBA (1 mg/l) + Rutin (0.5 mg/l) + Quercetin (0.5 mg/l) | | 20 | 70 |

Root initiation occurs in the presence of a lower concentration of nutrients in Whites liquid medium. The multiple shoots of 3–4 cm are separated by excision at the base and kept on a filter paper bridge in the medium taking care that the shoot base is dipped in the medium. The liquid medium is supplemented with IBA (1 mg/l), Rutin (0.5 mg/l) and Quercetin (0.5 mg/l). Within 15–20 days 70 per cent rooting is obtained. Roots initiated in the presence of auxins fail to grow in its presence and resumed growth only when transferred to a medium without auxins. Rooting ability increases with the number of subcultures. Repeated subculturing in the presence of high concentration of BAP is beneficial for rejuvenation of buds from mature trees. Carefully remove the rooted plants from the medium without damaging the root system. Transfer these to polybags containing sterile sand, soil and vermiculite (1:1:1). Cover the plants with polythene bags or polytunnels sprayed with water to maintain high humidity and place in double net shade house.

Within 15–20 days the plants acclimatize and transplanted to bags containing soil: compost (1:1 v/v) and kept in a single net shade house. After 4–6 weeks the plants develop new and healthy leaves and can be planted in the field with regular watering. During field planting care should be taken to avoid attack by root pathogens and if any, a fungicide treatment is recommended. In our institute a technique was followed by which the pits were filled with a mixture of red soil, sand and manure and drenched with 0.1 per cent copper fungicide. A clone bank consisting of propagules derived from a single elite tree of *Eucalyptus tereticornis* has been established. The tissue culture raised plants were found to show uniform growth.

Lakshmi Sita (1993) attempted induction of callus from cotyledons and hypocotyl of 5 day old seedlings of *E. citriodora*. MS media supplemented with NAA and 2,4-D (1–5 mg/l) induced callus. The callus showed differentiation into green protuberance from which shoots developed in a medium supplemented with 1 mg/l Zeatin and 0.2 mg/l IAA. These shoots rooted when transferred to 1 mg/l IAA. Callus initiation was also obtained by the same authors from shoots of 10–15 year old elite trees of *E. citriodora* on MS media supplemented with 1 mg/l 2,4-D. Differentiation into embryoid occurred on MS medium supplemented with 0.3 mg/l BA and 1 mg/l GA.

Thus, rejuvenation of mature eucalypts is possible by working out a careful strategy right from stock plant selection to field planting. It is evident from results that the major determining factors are the selection of the bud material and the concentration of hormone in the medium.

## 8. QUALITY SEED PRODUCTION AND NETWORK METHOD FOR RAPID TREE IMPROVEMENT

The $D^2$ analysis reveals the amplitude of genetic variation among the population of selected clones. It is essential that clones are subjected to multilocational trial and $D^2$ analysis is carried out along with commercial analysis for every location and industrial end use. The clones which continue to show almost same genetic distance in different locations can distinctively be classified as genetically apart. Such clones can be multiplied on a large scale and planted together in a determined design for production of quality seeds. The seeds then can be used for raising improved planting stock. The plantation can also be carefully utilized for further improvement.

Using the above approach at 20–25 determined locations, clone banks can be raised by selecting from the population around the locations. Having assessed the clones for 2 years, they should be moved to different locations for multilocation trial in the third and fourth year. The results obtained by the fifth year, i.e., data for fifth year in the initial location and the data for third year for multilocation trial would determine the clones to be identified for the industry and development of clonal seed orchards. From year six, clonal seed orchard will be developed and by year eight proven quality seeding material will be available for multiplication and for further improvement. During the intervening period, the promising clones can be mass propagated on a large scale with appropriate management using block plantation approach; thus, concomitant approach for propagation and quality seed production can be developed and the tree improvement approach would start evolving by itself.

Simultaneously, controlled breeding program need to be practiced for materials which are genetically superior and the small quantity of seeds obtained can be multiplied on a large scale using a combination of tissue culture and vegetative propagation methods. Finally, it is essential that various biotechnological approaches are integrated into the tree improvement program suitably to achieve more rapid gains.

## REFERENCES

Ashok Kumar, Jayachandran, C.K., Venkataramanan, K.S., Ganesan, M., Balasubramanian, A. and Gurumurthi, K. 1994. Production of high yielding varieties of *Casuarina equisetifolia.* ICFRE Technical Bulletin, IFGTB, Coimbatore, India.

Chaturvedi, A.N. and Khanna, L.S. 1982. Forest Mensuration. International Book Distributors, Dehra Dun. 404 pp.

Gardner, C.O. 1961. An evaluation of the effect of mass selection and seed irradiation with thermal neutrons on yield of corn. *Crop Sci.* **1**: 241–245.

Gupta, P.K., Mascarenhas, A.F. and Jagannathan, V. 1981. Tissue culture of forest trees—clonal propagation of mature trees of *Eucalyptus citriodora* Hook by tissue culture. *Plant Sci. Lett.* **20**: 195–201.

Gurumurti, K. and Bhandari, H.C.S. 1987. Clonal forestry for high yielding biomass production systems. *In*: J.P. Mittal (Ed.) Proc. Nat. Conf. Energy Production Agri. and Food Processing. Indian Soc. Agri. Engineers, New Delhi. Monograph Series **1**: 306–321.

Johnson, H.K., Rabinson, H.F. and Comstock, R.E. 1955. Estimates of genetic and environmental variability in soybeans. *Agron. J.* **47**: 314–318.

Lakshmi Sita, G. 1993. Micropropagation of *Eucalyptus. In*: M.R. Ahuja (Ed.) Micropropagation of Woody Plants. Kluwer Academic Publishers, Dordrecht. 263–280.

Rao, C.R. 1952. Advanced Statistical Methods in Biometric Research. John Wiley & Sons Inc., New York. 256 pp.

Searle, S.R. 1961. Phenotypic, genotypic and environmental correlations. *Biometrics* **17**: 474–480.

Surendran, C. 1982. Evaluation of Variability, Phenotypic Stability, Genetic Divergence and Heterosis in *Eucalyptus tereticornis* Sm. Ph.D. Thesis, Tamil Nadu Agri. Uni., Coimbatore.

Verma, R.K., Ravi, N., Jayachandran, C.K., Ganesan, M., Ashok Kumar, Balasubramanian, A. and Gurumurthi, K. 1994. Hedge Orchards for Clonal Forestry. ICFRE Technical Bulletin, IFGTB, Coimbatore, India.

# E. BIOTECHNOLOGY

# 20

# Genetic Transformation in Conifers

*Yinghua Huang*[1] *and C.G. Tauer*[1]

## ABSTRACT

Genetic transformation refers to the genetic change that occurs in a cell or genome following incorporation of new genetic material by gene transfer or direct DNA uptake. Recent developments in gene transfer technology and their applications to forest species have extended to forest genetics and tree improvement programs and represent potential new dimensions. Transformation systems based on recombinant DNA and gene transfer technologies have already been developed for a few conifer species such as European larch and white spruce and are under development for other conifers. In this paper, a recent review of development of the state-of-art technologies for genetic manipulation of forest trees is presented and progress towards genetic engineering of conifers is discussed.

## 1. INTRODUCTION

Over the last several decades, forest genetics and tree improvement programs have made considerable progress. Recombinant DNA and genetic engineering techniques have the potential to supplement traditional tree breeding programs. These techniques allow the transfer of foreign gene(s) to plant cells and stable integration into the plant genome (i.e., chromosomes). If the introduced gene is intact, and constructed with appropriate regulatory sequences, the gene product will be synthesized by the transformed cell. Further, the transformed cells can be induced to form a whole plant which carries the new gene(s) contributing to genetic improvement. Some potentials of genetic engineering for tree improvement include bypassing the long time period required to reach

[1]Department of Forestry, Oklahoma State University, Stillwater, Oklahoma 74078, USA.

reproductive maturity, making desired changes without many cycles of selection and backcrossing, utilizing valuable foreign genes that do not exist in the breeding population of a given species, and selectively adding single gene(s) of interest into the target genome while maintaining the genetic composition responsible for the superior phenotype.

The technology of gene transfer in plants is rapidly developing and has become an important tool to both modify genetic composition and to study the regulation of gene expression. A variety of novel gene transfer approaches have been explored during the past several years, including non-vector and vector-mediated systems (Potrykus, 1991). Some of the new technologies have been successfully applied to conifer transformation although most conifer species are considered to be generally recalcitrant for both transformation and regeneration. Although genetic engineering in coniferous species is just in its infancy, emerging success and practical application in genetic transformation have been reported (Huang *et al.*, 1993a). These initial achievements have already proven that genetic transformation will make an inestimable contribution to tree improvement.

This chapter presents an overview of the development of gene transfer techniques for conifer transformation to the present, summarizes the general methods for analyses of transformed plant tissues, and presents a review of progress in regeneration of transgenic conifers. Finally, this paper discusses possible future developments that may enhance conifer genetic engineering studies and that may have an impact on genetic improvement of conifers.

## 2. DEVELOPMENT OF TRANSFORMATION TECHNOLOGIES

Transformation is a permanent genetic change induced in a cell following incorporation of new DNA. The formation of new combinations of heritable material can be achieved by traditional breeding techniques and practices, or by genetic engineering. Genetic engineering of plants usually implies direct genetic manipulation of plant cells at the cellular or molecular level, adding new genes to the plant's genome or replacing certain genes with other genes from other sources using recombinant DNA technology. The modern techniques developed for genetic engineering include vector-mediated systems based on *Agrobacterium* plasmids or viral vectors, and non-vector systems (direct gene transfer), such as biolistics (particle bombardment), microinjection, electroporation (electrical pulse treatment), chemical poration (polyethylene glycol-mediated osmotic DNA insertion), liposome fusion, and protoplast fusion.

### 2.1 *Agrobacterium* Systems

The first practical, most successful and widely used method for genetic engineering of plants relies on *Agrobacterium*-mediated genetic transformation systems. *Agrobacterium* are plant pathogenic organisms which cause tumoric diseases on infected host plants. The exploration of this gene vector system has developed from an understanding of the molecular basis of its pathogenesis. *Agrobacterium tumefaciens* and *A. rhizogenes* harbor an additional (nonchromosomal) genetic component, called the Ti (for tumor-inducing) or Ri (for root-inducing) plasmid. This virulent plasmid (about 200 kb) is the disease-causing agent because it carries the phytohormone biosynthesis genes, which are located on a T-DNA (for transferred DNA) region (Hooykaas and Schilperoort, 1992). During infection, *Agrobacterium* inserts its T-DNA into the plant cells, and these inserted DNA fragments are then integrated into the plant chromosomes. The transferred hormone genes then replicate and express along with the plant's DNA so that the elevated levels of phytohormones cause tumorous growth with abnormal patterns, such as crown galls or prolific root masses. However, the genes causing tumorous phenotype can be removed by deleting them from the T-DNA without loss of DNA transfer and integration functions. In order to develop the *Agrobacterium* plasmid as a gene vector for genetic engineering of plants, researchers have genetically engineered the T-DNA by replacing the oncogenic (tumor causing) genes with useful genes. In this way, the first genetically engineered plants expressing functional foreign genes were produced using tobacco. Thereafter, Ti and Ri plasmids, the natural gene vectors, have become an important tool for genetic engineering of plants.

Since the early literature suggested that many gymnosperms appear to be good hosts for *Agrobacterium tumefaciens* (De Cleene and De Ley, 1976), it is logical to develop the *Agrobacterium-mediated* transformation system for genetic engineering of conifers. Sederoff *et al.* (1986) tested 19 virulent *A. tumefaciens* strains on young seedlings of loblolly pine and found two strains able to induce crown galls on infected explants. Although gene integration was not demonstrated in the symptomatic tissues, opine production in the galls implied that the opine biosynthase genes were transferred and expressed in the pine cells. Similar results were obtained in *Larix decidua* (Diner and Karnosky, 1987). These preliminary tests drew research attention to the development of gene vectors for transformation of conifer species. Thereafter, much research effort was focused on three major areas: (1) screening potential *Agrobacterium* strains to develop transformation systems for species of interest, (2) examining factors affecting successful transformation, and (3) developing systems for both transformation and regeneration. As a result of these research efforts, conifer transformation using *Agrobacterium* systems has quickly advanced (Ellis *et al.*, 1989; Huang *et al.*, 1991a,b; 1993b). And most important, the first transgenic conifer, European larch, has been produced using the *A. rhizogenes*-mediated transformation system (Huang *et al.*, 1991a,b).

In the early experiments conducted with wild-type *Agrobacterium* strains, indicative (phenotypic) evidence such as gall formation and phytohormone autotrophic growth was used to assay gene transfer and gene expression. With the advances in vector development, binary vectors (gene constructs containing target gene, selective marker and appropriate promoter located on an additional plasmid capable of autonomous replication in *Agrobacterium* cells) were incorporated with the natural *Agrobacterium* system. Using *Agrobacterium* containing a binary vector carrying the NPT II gene, transfer and expression of the foreign DNA in a conifer was detected through DNA analysis of the transformed kanamycin resistant callus (Dandekar *et al.*, 1987).

Application of the *Agrobacterium*-mediated genetic transformation systems is being extended to many other conifer species (Table 1), but currently success in the recovery of transformed plants has been limited in conifers.

The *Agrobacterium*-mediated genetic transformation system has been the most widely used and efficient method of gene transfer in plants and has many advantages over other gene transfer methods. Since *Agrobacterium* achieves DNA transfer via a complete system including the *vir* function unit and the T-DNA border(s), this system is simple, and gives a relatively high transformation frequency. The inserted gene is generally stable in the recipient plants and is co-transmitted to their progeny with the chromosomes. One disadvantage with this system is the limited host range of *Agrobacterium*. However, its host-range in conifers has been greatly extended by reevaluation, and it will continue to be explored.

### 2.2 Particle Bombardment or Biolistics

The development of the gene gun (particle bombardment or biolistics) is another approach to foreign DNA insertion that has recently received considerable attention. This physical method involves acceleration of DNA-coated heavy microparticles (microprojectiles) for directly delivering foreign DNA into plant cells and tissues (McCabe *et al.*, 1988). Recently, it has also been used for delivering foreign DNA into the conifer genome as well as for studying the expression of foreign genes in conifer cells (Table 1). Microprojectile-mediated gene transfer has been reported in several conifer species; however, stable integration with this method has only been shown in a few cases, such as in *Picea abies* (Robertson *et al.*, 1992), and *Picea glauca* (Ellis *et al.*, 1993; Bommineni *et al.*, 1993). Microprojectile-mediated transient gene expression is an apparent rapid procedure for testing the effect of promoters and other regulatory sequences (Duchesne and Charest, 1992; Newton *et al.*, 1992).

The biolistics system has advantages and potential for general applicability: it is easy to handle, and it delivers DNA into many cells each shot, targeting every type of cell and even intact tissues. But integrative transformation events from biolistic experiments are of relatively low frequency and the technique is inefficient in yielding stable transformation (Potrykus, 1991).

### 2.3 Other DNA Delivery Systems

In addition to the two gene transfer systems described above, a great variety of alternative approaches have been explored for direct gene transfer. Electroporation has recently emerged as a predominant method for protoplast transformation. This method involves the application of a high-voltage electrical pulse to a solution containing a mixture of protoplasts and foreign DNA. Electroporation facilitates the movement of DNA molecules into plant cells through transient openings in the plasmolemma (protoplast membrane) caused by the electrical pulse treatment (Fromm *et al.*, 1986). For protoplasts, it has been one of several techniques for gene transfer in plants. Following electroporation, transient expression of reporter genes has been observed in several conifers (Bekkaoui *et al.*, 1988, 1990; Charest *et al.*, 1991). Microin-

Table 1. Conifers in which gene transfer and expression studies have been reported

| Species | Common name | Explant | Method | Foreign gene | Integration/ Expression | Reference |
|---|---|---|---|---|---|---|
| **Agrobacterium** | | | | | | |
| *A. alba* | Silver fir | sd | At | wtd | nt | 16 |
| *A. cephalonica* | Creek fir | st | At | wtd | nt | 64 |
| *A. concolor* | White fir | st | At | wtd | nt | 64 |
| *A. firma* | Momi fir | st | At | wtd | nt | 64 |
| *A. holophyla* | Needle fir | st | At | wtd | nt | 64 |
| *A. nordmanniana* | Nordmann fir | sd | At | wtd | nt | 1,13,16 |
| *A. procera* | Noble fir | sd | At/Ar | wtd | nt | 51 |
| *Araucariaceae bidwillii* | Bunya-bunya | tr | At | wtd | nt | 60 |
| *Chamaecyparis lawsoniana* | Lawson cypress | tr | At | wtd | nt | 59 |
| *Cunninghamia lanceolata* | China fir | st | At | wtd | nt | 64 |
| *Cupressus arizonica* | Arizona cypress | sd | At | wtd | nt | 63 |
| *C. benthamii* | Mexican cypress | sd | At | wtd | nt | 63 |
| *C. bakeri* | Modoc cypress | sd | At | wtd | nt | 63 |
| *C. duttoni* | | sd | At | wtd | nt | 63 |
| *C. forbesii* | Tecate cypress | sd | At | wtd | nt | 63 |
| *C. goveniana* | | | | | | |
| *C. knightiana* | Mexican cypress | sd | At | wtd | nt | 63 |
| *C. macnabiana* | Piute cypress | sd | At | wtd | nt | 63 |
| *C. macrocarpa* | Monterey cypress | sd | At | wtd | nt | 63 |
| *C. nevadensis* | Piute cypress | sd | At | wtd | nt | 63 |
| *C. pygmea* | Mendicino cypress | sd | At | wtd | nt | 63 |
| *C. sargentii,* | | | | | | |
| *C. sempervirens* | Italian cypress | sd | At | wtd | nt | 63 |
| *C. thurifera,* | | | | | | |
| *Juniperus communis* | var. Hibernica | sd | At | wtd | nt | 63 |
| *J. phoenecia* | Phoenician juniper | sd | At | wtd | nt | 63 |
| *J. procera* | African pencil cedar | sd | At | wtd | nt | 63 |
| *J. virginiana* | Red cedar | sd | At | wtd | nt | 63 |

***(Contd)***

Table 1. ***(Contd)***

| Species | Common name | Explant | Method | Foreign gene | Integration/ Expression | Reference |
|---|---|---|---|---|---|---|
| *Larix decidua** | European larch | Ap/cot/ hyp | Ar/At | aroA/Bt luc/nptII | stab | 34,36,37, 38,39,40, 58 |
| *L. laricina* | Tamarack | drs | Ar | wtd | nt | 50 |
| *Libocedrus decurrens* | Incense cedar | sd | At | wtd | nt | 61,66 |
| *Picea abies* | Norway spruce | sd | At/Ar | wtd | nt/stab | 1,13,14,33, 48 |
| *P. engelmanii* | Engelmann spruce | sd | At | wtd | nt | 24 |
| *P. glauca* | White spruce | sd | At | wtd | nt | 24 |
| *P. sitchensis* | Sitka spruce | sd | At | wtd | nt | 24 |
| *Pinus banksiana* | Jack pine | drs/sd | At | wtd | nt | 18,50 |
| *P. contorta* | Lodgepole pine | sd | At/Ar | wtd | nt | 45,48, |
| *P. echinata* | Shortleaf pine | sd | At/Ar | ipt | stab | 42,43,44 |
| *P. eldarica* | Afghan pine | sd | At | wtd | nt | 66 |
| *P. elliottii* | Slash pine | sd | At/Ar | wtd | nt | 42,43,44, 65,66 |
| *P. jeffreyi* | Jeffrey pine | sd | At | wtd | nt | 65,66 |
| *P. lambertiana* | Sugar pine | tcs/sd | At | nptII/wtd | stab | 46,65,66 |
| *P. monticola* | Western white pine | drs | Ar | wtd | nt | 50 |
| *P. nigra* | Austrian pine | ? | At | GUS | trans | 53 |
| *P. palustris* | Longleaf pine | sd | Ar | wtd | nt | 19 |
| *P. pinaster* | Maritime pine | rtc | At | wtd | nt | 32 |
| *P. ponderosa* | Ponderosa pine | sd | At/Ar | wtd | nt | 51,65,66 |
| *P. radiata* | Monterey pine | tcs/sd/ rtc | At | wtd | nt | 7,32,65,66 |
| *P. sylvestris* | Scots pine | rtc/sd | At/Ar | wtd | nt | 1,32,48,65, 66 |
| P. taeda | Loblolly pine | sd | At/Ar | wtd/ipt | nt/stab | 1,42,43,44, 57,65,66 |
| *P. virginiana* | Virginia pine | sd | At/Ar | wtd | stab | 42,43,44, 65,66 |
| *P. taeda* x *P. elliottii* | Hybrid | sd | At/Ar | ipt | stab | 42,43,44 |
| *Podocarpus elongatus* | | st | At | wtd | nt | 64 |
| *Pseudotsuga menziesii* | Douglas-fir | tcs/sd | At/Ar | nptII/wtd | stab/trans | 17,24,51,65 |

***(Contd)***

Table 1. ***(Contd)***

| Species | Common name | Explant | Method | Foreign gene | Integration/ Expression | Reference |
|---|---|---|---|---|---|---|
| *Sciadopitys verticillata* | Umbrella pine | st | At | wtd | nt | 64 |
| *Sequoiadendron gigantea* | Giant sequoia | st | At | wtd | nt | 64 |
| *Sequoia sempervirens* | Coast redwood | st | At | wtd | nt | 1,64 |
| *Taxus baccata* | English yew | ms | At/Ar | wtd | stab/nt | 30,35,64 |
| *T. brevifolia* | Pacific yew | ms | At/Ar | wtd | stab/nt | 30,35,54, 64 |
| *T. baccata* x *cuspdata* | Taxus x media | sd | At | wtd | nt | 30,64 |
| *Thuja dolobrata* | Hiba arborvitae | sd | At | wtd | nt | 63 |
| *T. occidentalis* | American arborvitae | sd | At | wtd | nt | 16,63 |
| *T. orientalis* | Oriental arborvitae | sd | At | wtd | nt | 63 |
| *T. plicata* | Western red cedar | sd | At | wtd | nt | 63 |
| *Thujopsis dolobrata* | False arborvitae | sd | At | wtd | nt | 63 |
| *Torreya californica* | California nutmeg | st | At | wtd | nt | 64 |
| *Tsuga heterophylla* | Western hemlock | sd | At/Ar | wtd | nt | 51 |
| **Particle Bombardment** | | | | | | |
| *Chamaecyparis nootkatensis* | Yellow cypress | pln | pb | GUS/nptII | trans | 31 |
| *Larix decidua* | European larch | ec | pb | GUS | trans | 22 |
| *Larix* x *eurolepis* | Hybrid larch | ec | pb | GUS/ nptII | trans | 12,20,21 |
| *L. laricina* | Tamarack | ec | pb | GUS/luc | trans | 12 |
| *Larix* x *leptoeuropae* | Hybrid larch | ec | pb | GUS | trans | 22 |
| *Larix* x *leptolepis* | Japanese larch | ec | pb | GUS | trans | 22 |
| *Picea abies* | Norway spruce | ec/ze/ pln | pb | GUS/luc/ nptII | trans/stab | 5,15,49,52, 55,71 |
| *P. glauca** | White spruce | ec | pb | GUS/ nptII/BT | trans/stab | 8,12,25,26 |
| *P. mariana* | Black spruce | ec/pln | pb | GUS/ nptII | trans | 9,12,20,21, 31 |

***(Contd)***

Table 1. ***(Contd)***

| Species | Common name | Explant | Method | Foreign gene | Integration/ Expression | Reference |
|---|---|---|---|---|---|---|
| *P. rubens* | Red spruce | ec | pb | GUS/ nptII | trans | 12 |
| *Pinus banksiana* | Jack pine | pln | pb | GUS/ nptII | trans | 31 |
| *P. contorta* | Lodgepole pine | pln | pb | GUS/ nptII | trans | 31 |
| *P. elliottii* | Slash pine | emb | pb | GUS | trans | 35 |
| *P. pinaster* | Maritime pine | pln | pb | GUS | trans | 49 |
| *P. radiata* | Monterey pine | ec | pb | GUS | trans | 10,28,69 |
| *P. sylvestris* | Scots pine | cal/sc/ bud | pb | GUS | trans | 2,3 |
| *P. taeda* | Loblolly pine | cot/ste | pb | GUS | trans | 47,56,67 |
| *Pseudotsuga menziesii* | Douglas-fir | cot | pb | GUS | trans | 27 |
| *Taxus cuspidata* | Japanese yew | ste | pb | GUS | trans | 23 |
| *Tsuga heterophylla* | Western hemlock | pln | pb | GUS/ nptII | trans | 31 |
| **Electroporation/ Peg-mediated** | | | | | | |
| *Larix* x *eurolepis* | Hybrid larch | pt | ep | cat/GUS/ nptII | trans | 11 |
| *Picea glauca* | White spruce | pt | ep | cat/GUS | trans | 4,5 |
| *P. mariana* | Black spruce | pt | ep | cat/GUS | trans | 5,68 |
| *Pinus banksiana* | Jack pine | pt | ep | cat/GUS | trans | 5,68 |
| *P. radiata* | Monterey pine | pt | ep | GU/luc | trans | 10 |
| *P. taeda* | Loblolly pine | pt | ep | luc | trans | 29 |
| *Pseudotsuga menziesii* | Douglas-fir | pt | ep | luc | trans | 29 |
| *Picea glauca* | White spruce | ? | mi | GUS | trans | 72 |
| *P. glauca* | White spruce | pt | peg | cat/GUS | trans | 70 |

**Reference:** 1, Ahuja 1988; 2, Aronen *et al.* 1994; 3, Aronen *et al.* 1995; 4, Bekkaoui *et al.* 1988; 5, Bekkaoui *et al.* 1990; 6, Bercetche *et al.* 1993; 7, Bergmann & Stomp 1992; 8, Bommineni *et al.* 1993; 9, Bommineni *et al.* 1994; 10, Campbell *et al.* 1992; 11, Charest *et al.* 1991; 12, Charest *et al.* 1993; 13, Clapham & Ekberg 1986; 14, Clapham *et al.* 1990; 15, Clapham *et al.* 1995; 16, DeCleene & DeCley 1976; 17, Dandekar *et al.* 1987; 18, Diner & Karnosky 1987; 19, Diner & Soliman 1993; 20, Duchesne & Charest 1991; 21, Duchesne & Charest 1992; 22, Duchesne *et al.* 1993; 23, Ellis (unpublished data); 24, Ellis *et al.* 1989; 25, Ellis *et al.* 1991; 26, Ellis *et al.* 1993; 27, Goldfarb *et al.* 1991; 28, Gonzales *et al.* 1993; 29, Gupta *et al.* 1988; 30, Han *et al.* 1994; 31, Hay *et al.* 1994; 32, Hawes & Pueppke 1987; 33, Hood *et al.* 1990; 34, Huang 1993; 35, Huang jection and macroinjection, the injecting of DNA into single plant cells, successfully established for transformation of animal cells, are being adapted for transformation of plant cells (Crossway *et al.*, 1986). These micromanipulation techniques have the capacity to deliver foreign DNA into intact regenerable cells and may avoid the inherent difficulties of plant regeneration from protoplast and cell cultures. Polyethylene glycol-mediated direct DNA uptake and transient expression have been observed in spruce protoplasts (Wilson *et al.*, 1989). Other vectorless gene transfer systems have also been explored for plant genetic manipulation, such as liposome-mediated DNA delivery and pollen-mediated gene transfer (Potrykus, 1991). Pollen transformation is especially promising because plants are easily regenerated from zygotes. In addition, other types of biological vector systems are plant DNA and RNA viruses. However, for some technical reasons, such as difficulty in the cloning of viruses, little practical application has been made of these viral vector systems.

Although most of the above mentioned non-vector methods need further development for practical application, they show promise as plant genetic engineering systems. As summarized in Table 1, some of these non-vector techniques have been successfully applied to transformation of tree species (Bekkaoui *et al.*, 1988; Charest *et al.*, 1991; Wilson *et al.*, 1989). These few examples demonstrate their potential for introduction of foreign DNA into woody plant cells and tissues. However, these systems are still under study because of many limiting factors. For instance, incorporation of foreign DNA into a plant genome is sometimes unstable, or cell/protoplast culture systems are required but regeneration of whole plants after transformation is not yet possbile.

---

(unpublished data); 36, Huang & Karnosky 1991a; 37, Huang & Karnosky 1991b; 38, Huang *et al.* 1991a; 39, Huang *et al.* 1991b; 40, Huang *et al.* 1993a; 41, Huang *et al.* 1993b 42, Huang & Tauer 1993; 43, Huang & Tauer 1994; 44, Huang & Tauer 1995; 45, Lindroth *et al.* 1993; 46, Loopstra *et al.* 1990; 47, Loopstra *et al.* 1992; 48, Magnussen *et al.* 1994; 49, Martinussen *et al.* 1995; 50, McAfee *et al.* 1993; 51, Morris *et al.* 1989; 52, Newton *et al.* 1992; 53, Ordas *et al.* 1993; 54, Plaut-Carcasson *et al.* 1993; 55, Robertson *et al.* 1992; 56, Sargent *et al.* 1993; 57, Sederoff *et al.* 1986; 58, Shin *et al.* 1994; 59, Smith 1935; 60, Smith 1936; 61, Smith 1937; 62, Smith 1938; 63, Smith 1939; 64, Smith 1942; 65, Stomp *et al.* 1988; 66, Stomp *et al.* 1990; 67, Stomp *et al.* 1991; 68, Tauatorus *et al.* 1989; 69, Walter *et al.* 1994; 70, Wilson *et al.* 1989; 71, Yibrah *et al.* 1994; 72, Attree (unpublished data).

**Abbreviations :** ap, apex; Ar, *Agrobacterium rhizogenes*; aroA, glyphosate resistance gene; At, *Agrobacterium tumefaciens*; Bt, Bacillus thuringiensis (insecticidal gene); cal, callus/calli; cat, chloramphenicol acetyltransferase; cot, cotyledon; drs, derooted seedling; ec, embryogenic culture; ep, electroporation; GUS, beta-glucuronidase; hyp, hypocotyl; ipt, isopentenyl transferase (cytokinin biosynthesis gene); luc, firefly luciferase; mi, microinjection; ms, stem from mature tree; nptII, kanamycin resistance gene; nt, not tested; pb, particle bombardment; peg, polyethylene glycol-mediated; pln, pollen; pt, protoplast; rtc, root cap cell; sd, seedling; st, small tree; stab, stable integration/expression; ste, stem; tcs, tissue- culture-derived shoot; tr, tree; trans, transient expression; wtd, wild-type T-DNA; ze, zygotic embryo.

## 3. ANALYSIS OF TRANSFORMED PLANT CELLS

### 3.1 Phenotypic (indicative) Evidence

#### 3.1.1 Tumorigenesis

Unlike many plant bacterial pathogens which cause cell wilting and/or necrosis, agrobacterial infection results in hypotrophic growth of the host cells (Huang *et al.*, 1993a,b). Crown gall and hairy root are characterized by rapid and unlimited cell proliferation following *Agrobacterium* invasion through fresh wounds. Tumorigenesis on infected plant tissues is the typical symptom of successful infection by *Agrobacterium*. Differential pathological symptoms develop at inoculation sites depending on the specific bacterial strains used. In general, plant cells infected by *A. tumefaciens* grow as disorganized tumorous masses (crown gall), while a cluster of roots (hairy root) develop following infection by *A. rhizogenes* (Huang *et al.*, 1993b). Altered tumor morphology has also been reported, such as crown gall teratomas, abnormal shoots with deformed leaves and shortened nodules, or normal-looking shoots (Huang *et al.*, 1991a,b). In nature, infection by *Agrobacterium* usually occurs at the ground level near the junction of the stem and root since *Agrobacterium* inhabits the soil. In laboratory conditions, axenic explants are first wounded with a sterile hypodermic needle or scalpel blade and then aseptically inoculated with freshly prepared bacterial cultures. In the case of oncogenic (tumor causing) *Agrobacterium*, characteristic symptoms, i.e., tumors or roots, develop at the inoculation sites and often become visible within three-week cocultivation under the high humidity conditions of *in vitro* culture.

#### 3.1.2 Hormone Autotrophic Growth

Development of tumorigenic and rhizogenic symptoms is the direct result of the expression of T-DNA-encoded phytohormone genes in the plant cells. These genes specify the biosynthesis of the hormones (auxin and cytokinin) which disturb the natural balance of endogenous phytohormones, and lead to neoplastic growth of the transformed tissues or to root development. Therefore, crown galls (tumors) and hairy roots are hormone-autotrophic due to the self-supplied hormone from the expression of the stably integrated hormone genes. *In vitro* cultures of tumors and roots continue to grow and proliferate on hormone-free medium after excision from parental explants.

#### 3.1.3 Resistance to Selective Agents

Modern transformation vectors often carry a dominant marker gene designed to enable transformed cells to survive in a culture medium containing a normally toxic level of the associated selection agent, usually an antibiotic or herbicide. The gene coding for neomycin phosphotransferase type II (NPT II) is commonly used to construct plant gene vectors, facilitating selection of transformed cells and plants with the antibiotic kanamycin. Kanamycin selection has proved useful as a selective agent for transformed cells and tissues from several conifers, including larch, spruce, pine and Douglas-fir (Dandekar *et al.*, 1987; Ellis *et al.*, 1993). New types of selectable markers are also being used which confer herbicide resistance to the plant, such as resistance to the herbicide glyphosate or phosphinothrincin (Comai *et al.*, 1985). A mutant bacterial gene (*aroA*) encoding the enzyme enolpyruvylshikimate-3-phosphate (EPSP) synthase, which detoxifies the herbicide glyphosate (Roundup), was introduced into the larch genome, enabling larch cells to survive the glyphosate selection process (Huang, 1993). Thus, resistant lines have been selected by growth in the presence of the herbicide. Selection and growth of putatively transformed plant cells on selective medium provide initial phenotypic evidence of genetic transformation.

However, it is known that the indicative evidences described above are unreliable in some cases. For instance, spontaneous variants with increased resistance to some chemicals can be induced or selected due to somaclonal variation in plant tissue culture. Also, false positives or artifacts in phenotypic assay may occur due to cross-protection effects and other reasons. Therefore, molecular and biochemical evidence is essential to confirm the integration and expression of transferred genes in the host cells.

### 3.2 Molecular (biochemical) Evidence

#### 3.2.1 Gene Integration

Foreign DNA transferred to plant cells by one of the techniques described above is usually integrated into the nuclear plant genome, although it is not necessary for the transferred DNA to be integrated into the host chromosome for expression. Transient expression of a gene temporarily existing within the plant cell is often seen in non-vector mediated transformation, such as particle bombardment. Without stable integration, which is essential for genetic manipulation, the transferred foreign DNA cannot remain permanently in the cell and will not be transmitted to the progeny with predictable properties. Targeted integration is probably based on a homologous recombination process. In most cases, foreign DNA sequences are randomly integrated at a single locus, either as one copy or as a cluster of tandem copies. However, simultaneous multiple insertions into two or more different sites on different chromosomes have been observed. To claim stable transformation, it is necessary to provide convincing data from molecular analysis.

The integration of foreign DNA into a plant genome can be determined via Southern analysis or DNA amplification using the polymerase chain reaction (PCR). Southern analysis, based on complementary hybridization between DNA molecules, allows the number of copies and nature of the integration of specific genes or DNA regions to be determined by autoradiography (Southern, 1975). When genomic DNA isolated from putatively transformed plant tissues is probed with a radioactive-labeled DNA fragment made from an internal sequence of the introduced gene, a resultant hybridization signal serves as evidence for the presence of that particular DNA sequence in the recipient genome. Due to the large size of conifer genomes, a clear signal for single or low copies of transferred DNA requires long film exposure, up to 7–10 days; therefore, a very clean background is critical (Huang, 1993). PCR is another powerful technique for confirming foreign DNA insertion in transformed plant cells. Primers can be designed to amplify a specific DNA sequence (i.e., a part of the inserted gene) in transformed cells, thus, amplification of DNA of the expected size from DNA of the putatively transformed plants is considered evidence that the transferred gene or DNA region exists in the genome of the transformed plants. This DNA analysis procedure requires a very small amount of plant tissue and a large number of samples can be analyzed rapidly. Compared to Southern analysis, however, this technique cannot produce more information on the copy number of inserts or the patterns of DNA integration. Also, contamination can result in false positives. In fact, the ultimate proof of stable integration is a positive Southern analysis on transformed plant offspring.

### 3.2.2 Gene Expression

Whether the transferred genes function in the recipient cells depends on the expression of the foreign gene in the cellular system of the host. Molecular and biochemical evidence for the expression of the inserted gene(s) can be obtained via northern analysis, western blotting or enzyme assays. Northern analysis (e.g., RNA blotting) is a technique similar to Southern blotting but the analysis is performed at the RNA level. This method is used to detect the presence of a specific RNA product of a correct size which is transcribed from the inserted gene. Western blotting allows detection of the anticipated translation products (proteins). Both northern and western blottings can provide quantitative measurements. In some cases when intact genes are used, enzyme assays can be performed, which produce more detailed information about the expression of a particular gene and confirm the production of a functionally active gene-specific protein.

Several reporter genes developed for transformation systems facilitate identification of transformants at the early stage. These reporter genes have been useful for primary screening of conifer transformation (Huang and Tauer, 1994). Several reporter genes, including the *cat* gene coding for a bacterial chloramphenicol acetyltransferase, the *luc* gene for firefly luciferase, and the *lacZ* gene encoding beta-galactosidase have been developed for enzyme assays of gene expression in transformed plants. To date, however, the most widely used reporter gene in plant transformation is the *E. coli gus* gene coding for beta-glucuronidase (Jefferson, 1987). The *gus* gene has proved its usefulness for accurate assay in genetic transformation and gene expression studies of conifers (Ellis *et al.*, 1993; Huang, 1993).

Proof of integrative transformation normally includes (1) parallel analyses of treatments and controls, (2) a tight correlation between phenotypic and molecular (DNA analysis) data, and (3) a method allowing discrimination between true transformants and false positives in the evaluation of the data (Potrykus, 1991). Southern analysis must contain the predicted signals in high-molecular-weight DNA including hybrid fragments between the foreign gene and host DNA, and evidence for the absence of contaminating DNA fragments or identification of such fragments.

## 4. REGENERATION OF TRANSGENIC TREES

A transgenic plant is the final product of the plant genetic engineering process. Without regeneration the value of transformation is limited. There are several steps to achieve the final goal of producing transgenic plants, including introducing DNA into target cells/tissues, selecting stable transformants, and regenerating the whole transgenic plants. The last step is the key to complete the whole program of tree genetic engineering, but it is also the bottleneck through which recalcitrant species must proceed. For many species, systems for efficient *in vitro* regeneration are well established. Shoot organogenesis and somatic embryogenesis are the two principal methods of plant regeneration in *in vitro*. Regeneration of transgenic plants in many agricultural and horticultural crop species is now routine; however, there has been limited success in regenerating tree species from transformed tissues. So far, regeneration of transgenic plants has only been successful in two conifer species, *Larix decidua* (Huang *et al.*, 1991a,b) and *Picea glauca* (Ellis *et al.*, 1993).

### 4.1 Shoot Organogenesis From *Agrobacterium*-transformed Larch Tissues

The recovery of transgenic plants requires an appropriate regeneration system compatible with the transformation method. A 'leaf disc' procedure by Horsch *et al.* (1985) was modified for various types of larch tissues. In larch, various explants tested showed differential responses to inoculation with different *Agrobacterium* vectors (Huang *et al.*, 1993b). Tumorous characteristics also varied with inoculation sites on a given seedling. In response to infection by *A. rhizogenes* 11325 vector, inoculation made to wounds in the lower hypocotyl induced hairy roots or root clusters, whereas inoculation of the apex and upper hypocotyl developed shoot buds or shooty teratomas. The same treatment to the apex and upper hypocotyl wounds with *A. rhizogenes* A4pARC8 resulted in only multiple roots. In addition, the frequency of tumor formation was dependent on the tissue inoculated. While hypocotyls are very responsive to inoculation with oncogenic *Agrobacterium*, no symptoms of infection developed on cotyledons and radicles. Due to mixed cell populations within tissues/organs, some cells are competent for transformation but not for regeneration, while others are more competent for regeneration than transformation. It is possible that there are some synchronous cells which have the competence for both gene transfer and regeneration. Thus, the results obtained from these early tests indicated that the upper hypocotyl and shoot apex, with the potential for shoot morphogenesis, were good target materials for the transformation experiments.

Beyond cell competence for differentiation and regeneration, tumorigenesis morphology in some larch tissues was dependent on the specific bacterial strain and/or plasmid employed. Therefore, our other strategy for producing transgenic plants was the development of vectors. Generally, due to the tumorigenesis properties of oncogenic *Agrobacterium* plasmids, plant regeneration is difficult when the transformed cells were driven by wild bacterial strains. The expression of the wild-type plasmid *onc* genes (*tms1, tms2,* and *tmr* loci) causes the continuous production of auxins and cytokinins in the tumorous tissues resulting in the repression of shoot development and the inhibition of plant regeneration. Thus, binary vectors with the oncogenes deleted were utilized to avoid the problems of the unlimited production of phytohormone, allowing plant regeneration from the transformed cells.

Identifying suitable *Agrobacterium* strains/vectors and appropriate plant material are the two most important components in developing systems for regenerating transgenic plants from transformed cells. A variety of strains of both *A. rhizogenes* and *A. tumefaciens* were screened as potential vectors for transformation of European larch. We identified *A. rhizogenes* strain 11325, harboring the oncogenic nopaline type plasmid pRi11325, as the best in producing regenerable shoot buds at inoculation sites (Diner and Karnosky, 1987; Huang *et al.*, 1991a, b). We believe that adventitious buds induced by *Agrobacterium* infection have a special type of tumor characteristic. It is likely that hormone production in transformed cells is a key to shoot bud differentiation. A reasonable assumption is that the T-DNA of plasmid pRi11325 may contain mutant genes producing a shooty type of tumor. Suppression of the neoplastic state of the transformants could take place, resulting in the development of transformed shoots. This phenomenon has been reported in tobacco transformation (Wullems *et al.*, 1981). Alternatively, at the early stage of adventitious-bud differentiation, the transformed cell might be organized by neighboring normal plant cells in response to the hormone imbalance in the tumorous cells according to the morphogenetic mechanism described by Otten *et al.* (1981). Therefore, several binary vectors (chimeric constructs), pCGN1133 containing the CaMV 35S-NPTII-aroA, pWB139 containing CaMV 35S-NPTII-Bt, and pYH102 containing CaMV35S-CaMV35S-cat were separately introduced into the 11325 cells, resulting in an excellent system for developing transgenic larch plants. The cotransferred genes from pRi11325 and the binary vector have been detected in the transgenic larch plants.

Adventitious shoot buds were developed at the inoculation sites on young seedlings within 20–30 days after inoculation with the virulent *A. rhizogenes* strain 11325. The shoot buds appeared to originate from meristematic cells rather than vascularized tissues. These cells differentiated into bud primordia, possibly due to endogenous hormone stimulation following expression of bacterial hormone genes by these transformed cells. Then the bud primordia developed into shoot buds and subsequently into shoots. The system developed in this study represents a novel strategy for plant transformation and subsequent regeneration using the virulent Ri plasmid of *A. rhizogenes.*

For plantlet development, adventitious shoot buds, 3–4 weeks old, were excised and placed on hormone-free solid GD medium with 3% sucrose for two or three weeks for shoot development. Actively growing shoots were subcultured at either 2 or 4-week intervals, and cycled through GD medium with charcoal, then shoot-elongation medium (LMG) consisting of Litvay mineral salts plus 10 mM glutamine and 1% sucrose (Litvay *et al.*, 1981), and finally back to hormone-free GD medium for additional shoot elongation. Healthy, elongated (1–2 cm in length) shoots were rooted and transplanted to plastic

3"-square pots filled with a soilless mix (peat/perlite/vermiculite, 1:1:1). These plants were kept in a mist chamber for about three weeks before being moved into the greenhouse environment.

Selection of transformants was first performed at an early stage. The excised short shoots were grown directly on the GD medium containing 40 mg/l kanamycin sulfate if the shoots were induced by the binary vectors carrying the *nptII* gene. A second kanamycin selection was carried out at the stage of rooting shoots in order to screen for any shoots that may have escaped the first kanamycin selection. Putatively transformed plantlets with the *nptII-gene* were subjected to the rooting media supplemented with kanamycin.

Transformed shoots were readily rooted on root-initiation medium after short exposure to a low level of auxin (0.1 mg/l IBA). Phenotypically, the transgenic larch plants looked like normal tissue culture plantlets. The classical teratomic fashion with wrinkled leaves and thickened and shorter stems, associated with *Agrobacterium*-transformed regenerants did not appear in larch transformants. However, the presence of pRi11325 T-DNA and genes placed in the gene vectors was verified in these tranformed plantlets by Southern hybridization analysis. Transgenic larch plants containing two agronomically important genes, the Bt insect toxin gene and the *aroA* gene conferring resistance to the herbicide glyphosate, have been produced using the *Agrobacterium* transformation system (Shin *et al.*, 1994).

A successful *Agrobacterium*-mediated transformation system is comprised of two stages: stable transformation of plant cells and efficient regeneration of transformed plants. The system developed for *Larix*, using wild *Agrobacterium rhizogenes* alone or as a binary vector together with the Ri-plasmid as a helper, facilitates plant cell transformation followed by shoot bud initiation and subsequent recovery of transformed plants, which is more straightforward than plant regeneration after transformation. This simple and reliable system has proven an excellent model system for genetic engineering in European larch. Further, this *A. rhizogenes*-mediated transformation system is a unique way for recovery of transformants in a conifer species.

### 4.2 Somatic Embryogenesis from Bombarded *Picea* Tissues

To achieve regeneration of transformed white spruce (*Picea glauca*), tissues were subjected to particle bombardment using microparticles coated with DNA. Following bombardment, the cell cultures containing chimeric constructs were placed on embryogenic induction medium for reinitiation of embryogenic cultures, and were then exposed to antibiotic selection for transformed cells. Finally, putatively transformed embryos containing the foreign DNA were redifferentiated from the embryogenic callus. Transformed white spruce plants have recently been obtained using the above described particle acceleration method (Ellis *et al.*, 1993), but it has not been possible to produce transgenic white spruce plants with the *Agrobacterium*-mediated transformation systems. Transgenic white spruce plants containing the *Bt cryIA* endotoxin gene expressed it at a low, sublethal level.

### 4.3 Factors Influencing *In Vitro* Regeneration

Selecting transformed cells from a large population of untransformed cells is dependent on the expression of a selectable marker gene in the host cell, providing the cells with resistance to the selective agent. The ability of cells to survive this selection process is very important in the development of a transformation system for a given species. The most widely used marker for stable transformation to date is the neomycin phosphotransferase (NPT II) gene that confers host cells resistance to kanamycin. For cells transformed by a binary vector containing the *npt II* gene, kanamycin selection can be conducted at various stages such as cell multiplication, shoot development or root induction, or continued throughout the entire process of transformant development. The timing of antibiotic resistance selection has been shown to be critical to a high efficiency in production of transformed plants. Early selection will favor the competition of transformed over untransformed cells, in fact, early selection will help to ensure the stabilization of foreign genes in the host genome and reduce deletion of introduced genes during the process of cell division. However, in conifers as well as some other species, most tissues are very sensitive to this antibiotic and hence plating at a fairly low density on selective media is a necessary precaution to avoid 'cross-detoxification' effects and the problems caused by polyphenol production from the large proportion of dying, non-transformed cells.

Wounding and cocultivation with *Agrobacterium* are the prerequisites for the DNA transfer process mediated by *Agrobacterium*. However, both treatments caused so much damage to target cells that most infected cells do not survive this process. In particular, cotyledon explants are seriously damaged by co-cultivation with *Agrobacterium*. Cell recovery from the wound-inoculation process can be improved by a careful inoculation method, appropriate cocultivation time, and frequent transfer of explants onto fresh media. Favorable conditions for cell redifferentiation would enhance plant regeneration from transformed cells following transformation. Inclusion of a selection agent such as an antibiotic to the growth medium is required in order to select transformed cells from a mixed cell population. Unfortunately, transformed pine cells appear to be inhibited directly by synthetic antibiotics and indirectly by secretions from the surrounding dead tissues. These chemical stresses can be reduced by delaying exposure to the selection agent and frequent subculturing. We are testing various antibiotics to identify minimal concentrations of the agents which kills agrobacteria effectively and have no or minimal negative effect on plant cell growth and development in conifers.

### 4.4 Choice of Explants for Transformation

Transformation without plant regeneration is of limited value. Therefore, the main objective of any DNA transfer procedure is to stably insert a gene into the nuclear genome of cells capable of giving rise to a whole transformed plant. Plant tissues are mixed populations of cells with competence for different responses. The relative composition of cell populations in tissues is determined by species, genotype, type of organ, developmental state, and even the developmental history of individuals. To design an experiment for a given species, we must first consider how to identify and use regenerable (e.g., competent for regeneration) cell types for transformation or to make a cell competent for both transformation and regeneration. In conifers it is difficult to do this, but several cell types are worthwhile target explants for transformation. Cultured cells able to differentiate into a plant via organogenesis or somatic embryogenesis are readily accessible for transformation. Immature embryos or organ meristem cells (e.g., apical meristems) are very promising because a plant can be obtained through continued development of the embryo or organ. Mature embryo or seed are candidates for transformation resulting in direct development of chimeric plants. In addition, gene transfer to pollen or DNA-coated pollen might give rise to a whole transformed plant via normal fertilization. In any case, to design an experiment for a given species, one must consider both the potential of target cells to develop into a whole plant and the availability of a tissue culture system for regeneration of plants from transformed cells or tissues.

## 5. APPLICATION OF GENE TRANSFER TO TREE IMPROVEMENT

Genetic engineering, like conventional tree breeding, aims at the use of superior genes or desired traits to genetically improve trees. Some valuable genes have already been isolated from other organisms and successfully transferred to many crop species as well as a few tree species. Some important examples include transfer of the bacterial *aroA* gene (detoxifying the herbicide glyphosate) from *Salmonella typhimurium* into a hybrid clone of *Populus* (Fillatti *et al.*, 1987) and European larch (Huang, 1993). The transgenic larch plants expressed the *aroA* gene-encoding 5-enolpyruvylshikimate-3-phosphate (EPSP) synthase and exhibited a high degree of tolerance to glyphosate after spray tests. The tolerance level observed in the transgenic larch plants (Shin *et al.*, 1994) was similar to that reported in transgenic tobacco, in which 0.5 kg/ha of the glyphosate was applied on the plants (Comai *et al.*, 1985), but this expression level was higher than that in transgenic hybrid poplar (Riemenschneider *et al.*, 1988), where treatment with 0.28 kg/ha glyphosate resulted in the death of transgenic poplar.

*Bacillus thuringiensis* is a bacterium with a *Bt* gene that synthesizes insecticidal proteinaceous crystals, known as commercial bio-insecticides, effective against more 50 lepidopteran pest species. The cloned *Bt* gene has been introduced into European larch (Huang and Karnosky, 1991a,b) and white spruce (Ellis *et al.*, 1993). The *Bt* insecticidal proteins expressed by transgenic larch were detected in Western blot analysis, and in feeding tests the transgenic plants show improved resistance to gypsy moth (*Lymantria dispar* L.), a lepidopteran-type insect (Shin *et al.*, 1994). In transgenic white spruce, feeding trials with spruce budworm (*Chorisoneura fumiferana*) suggest expression of the *Bt* endotoxin, although Western analysis has not demonstrated the presence of a protein corresponding to the *Bt* endotoxin (Ellis *et al.*, 1993).

In addition to the *aroA* and *Bt* genes, other genes already available are good candidates for gene transfer and may contribute to one of many tree breeding objectives, including disease resistance, environmental stress tolerance, improved wood quality, desired landscape and ornamental characteristics, and enhanced tree management and forest productivity. Enzymes encoded by wound-response genes that could be involved in pathogen resistance have been isolated from poplar (Davis *et al.*, 1991). Drought is one of the most important abiotic stresses limiting forest production. Stress-induced genes are under study through purification of mRNA induced in response to drought and salinity and by screening of genomic libraries using the mRNA-derived cDNA as probes (Chang *et al.*, 1994). Lignin is an important component of wood, but lignin content and structure greatly affect the pulping and bleaching processes in paper production. Several research projects are underway to study the regulation of lignin biosynthesis. Genes encoding o-methyltransferase (OMT) and cinnamyl alcohol dehydrogenase (CAD) have cloned from *Populus tremuloides* (Bugos *et al.*, 1991) and from *Pinus taeda* (O'Malley *et al.*, 1992). Up- and down-regulation of these genes could lead to modification in lignin content and composition. Thus, desired wood structure and quality might be designed via genetic engineering. Trees can be designed with more desirable ornamental characteristics, such as preferred shapes, sizes, and different colored flowers and leaves. In the past few years, much knowledge about the genetic determination of flower color has been gained at the molecular level. Genes controlling flower color have been identified and cloned, which opens the door to the development of new ornamental plant varieties (Mol *et al.*, 1989). Genetic engineering has also made it possible to improve flower longevity, produce more flowers, and modify plant architecture, such as dwarf and upright forms (Woodson, 1991). Certainly, additional useful genes will become available for our use. Transgenic germplasms having novel genes from a wide range of plants, bacteria and other biological systems would be an important supplement to conventional tree breeding for overcoming the specific limitations of existing species/genotypes and also to develop new improved genotypes with desired traits.

## 6. CONCLUSIONS

Although genetic engineering in forestry and woody ornamental species began only a few years ago, rapid and substantial progress in this research has already been made. Genetically engineered larch and spruce plants expressing agronomically important traits, i.e., herbicide and insect resistance, have been successfully produced. These early achievements demonstrate the feasibility of genetic engineering in conifer species and have advanced the application of gene transfer and molecular biology to conifer species. Now more research efforts have been directed toward the utilization and incorporation of DNA transfer technology into the existing tree improvement programs. It is expected that more transgenic conifers will be produced in next five years using one or several transformation systems.

In spite of the existence of a variety of transformation methods, there is no universal system suitable for all plant species. Choice of the most appropriate system will probably be on a case by case basis depending on target species, ease and availability of technology at a particular location, and research goals. For example, the *A. rhizogenes* system has already proven to be excellent vector systems for the production of transgenic plants in *Larix* (Huang *et al.*, 1991a,b), whereas a microprojectile-mediated DNA transfer method works best for *Picea* (Ellis *et al.*, 1993). No matter which system is chosen, a complementary technique of plant regeneration has to be available or developed for the system. The prerequisite of developing an *Agrobacterium*-based transformation system for a given species is the existence of a compatible relationship between *Agrobacterium* and the target plant. To exploit this relationship, it may be necessary to screen diverse bacterial strains on a number of genotypes. With microprojectile bombardment, the remaining challenge is to improve the frequency of stable integration. Again, more attention needs to be paid to the biology of explants before and after bombardment.

It is important to keep in mind that the successful application of genetic engineering in tree improvement requires several steps: isolation of desired genes from trees or other organisms, introduction of these genes into the tree genome, and regeneration of whole plants from genetically modified cells or tissues. Gene transfer and expression in transformed tissues have been reported in a great number of conifers. However, regeneration of transformed plants still remains a problem in most conifer species, as efficient regeneration methods do not exist. The lack of plant regeneration systems is currently limiting progress in genetic engineering of most conifers. Thus, regeneration is an area needing more research. At present, few valuable genes and promoters from trees have been isolated and characterized. Identification and evaluation of both useful genes and promoters should be a future research emphasis. This is probably the most important immediate task for forest molecular biologists in the next 5–10 years. Another critical area for future research is regulation of foreign gene expression in transgenic trees.

Again, it should be mentioned that genetic engineering and conventional tree breeding are complementary rather than competing techniques. Both are essential components in successful tree improvement programs. Therefore, traditional tree breeding methods and modern biotechnology can and should become fully integrated in tree improvement programs. It is also important to recognize that increased cooperation among multidisciplinary individuals or groups, would greatly enhance the possibility of success.

## ACKNOWLEDGEMENTS

Much of the information and data on white spruce transformation described above was adapted from Dr David Ellis' publications; therefore, the authors would like to acknowledge the considerable amount of his work discussed in this chapter.

## REFERENCES

Ahuja, M.R. 1988. Gene transfer in forest trees. *In*: J.W. Hanover and D.E. Keathley (Eds) Genetic Manipulation of Woody Plants. Plenum Publishing Corp., New York. 25–41.

Aronen, T., Haggman, H. and Hohtola, H. 1994. Transient *B*-glucuronidase expression in Scots pine tissues derived from mature trees. *Can. J. For. Res.* **24**: 2006–2011.

Aronen, T., Hohtola, A., Laukkanen, H. and Haggman, H. 1995. Seasonal changes in the transient expression of a 35S CaMV-GUS gene construct introduced into Scots pine buds. *Tree Physiol.* **15**: 65–70.

Bekkaoui, F., Dalta, R.S.S., Pilon, M., Tautorus, T.E., Crosby, W.L. and Dunstan, D.I. 1990. The effects of promoter on transient expression in conifer cell lines. *Theor. Appl. Genet.* **79**: 353–359.

Bekkaoui, F., Pilon, M., Laine, E., Raju, D.S.S., Crosby, W.L. and Dunstan, D.I. 1988. Transient gene expression in electroporated *Picea glauca* protoplasts. *Plant Cell Rep.* **7**: 481–484.

Bercetche, J., Dinant, M., Paques, M. and Matagne, R.F. 1993. Genetic transformation of embryogenic tissues of *Picea abies* by microprojectile bombardment. 5th Workshop of the IUFRO Working Party on Somatic Cell Genetics of Trees. October 18–22, 1993. Balsian, Spain, 51.

Bergmann, B.A. and Stomp, A.-M. 1992. Effect of host plant genotypes and growth rate on *Agrobacterium tumefaciens*-mediated gall formation in *Pinus radiata. Phytopatho.* **82**: 1457–1462.

Bommineni, V.R., Chibbar, R.N., Dalta, R.S.S. and Tsang, E.W.T. 1993. Transformation of white spruce (*Picea glauca*) somatic embryos by microprojectile bombardment. *Plant Cell Rep.* **13**: 17–23.

Bommineni, V.R., Dalta, R.S.S. and Tsang, E.W.T. 1994. Expression of *gus* in somatic embryo cultures of black spruce after microprojectile bombardment. *J. Expt. Bot.* **45**: 491–495.

Bugos, R., Chiang, V.L.C. and Campbell, W.H. 1991. cDNA cloning, sequence analysis and seasonal expression of lignin- bispecific caffeic acid/5-hydroxyferulic acid O-methyltransferase of aspen. *Plant Molecular Bio.* **17**: 1203–1215.

Campbell, M.A., Kinlaw, C.S. and Neale, D.B. 1992. Expression of luciferase and beta-glucuronidase in *Pinus radiata* suspension cells using electroporation and particle bombardment. *Can. J. For. Res.* **22**: 2014–2018.

Chang, S., Dias, M.A.D., Veeraragavan, P., Cairney, J. and Newton, R.J. 1994. Characterization and expression analysis of cDNA clones induced by environmental stress in loblolly pine. 6th Workshop of the IUFRO Working Party on Molecular Genetics of Forest Trees. May 20–23, 1994. Scarborough, Maine.

Charest, P.J., Calero, N., Lachance, D., Datla, R.S.S., Duchesne, L.C. and Tsang, E.W.T. 1993. Microprojectile-DNA delivery in conifer species: factors affecting assessment of transient gene expression using the beta-glucuronidase reporter gene. *Plant Cell Rep.* **12**: 189–193.

Charest, P.J., Devantier, Y., Ward, C., Jones, C., Schaffer, U. and Klimaszewska, K.K. 1991. Transient expression of foreign chimeric genes in the gymnosperm hybrid larch following electroporation. *Can. J. Bot.* **69**: 1731–1736.

Clapham, D. and Ekberg, I. 1986. Induction of tumours by various strains of *Agrobacterium tumefaciens* on *Abies nordmanniana* and *Picea abies. Scand. J. For. Res.* **1**: 435–437.

Clapham, D., Ekberg, I., Eriksson, G., Hood, E.E. and Norell, L. 1990. Within-population variation in susceptibility to *Agrobacterium tumefaciens* A281 in *Picea abies. Theoret. Appl. Genet.* **79**: 654–656.

Clapham, D., Manders, G., Yibrah, H.S. and von Arnold, S. 1995. Enhancement of short- and medium-term expression of transgenes in embryogenic suspensions of *Picea abies*. *J. Expt. Bot.* **46**: 655–662.

Comai, L., Facciotti, D., Hiatt., W.R., Thompson, G., Rose, R.E. and Stalker, D.M. 1985. Expression in plants of a mutant *aroA* gene from *Salmonella typhimurium* confers tolerance to glyphosate. *Nature* **317**: 741–744.

Crossway, A., Hauptli, H., Houck, C.M., Irvine, J.M., Oakes, J.V. and Perani, L.A. 1986. Micromanipulation techniques in plant biotechnology. *Biotechniques* **4**: 320–334.

Dandekar, A.M., Gupta, P.K., Durzan, D.J. and Knauf, V. 1987. Transformation and foreign gene expression in micropropagated Douglas-fir (*Pseudotsuga meziesii*). *Bio/Technology* **5**: 587–590.

Davis, J.M., Clarke, H.R.G., Bradshaw, H.D. and Gordon, M.P. 1991. Populus chitinase genes, structure, organization, and similarity of translated sequences to herbaceous plant chitinase. *Plant Molecular Bio.* **17**: 631–639.

DeCleene, M.D. and DeCley, J.D. 1976. The host range of crown gall. *The Botanical Rev.* **42**: 389–466.

Diner, A.M. and Karnosky, D.F. 1987. Differential responses of two conifers to *in vitro* inoculation with *Agrobacterium rhizogenes*. *European J. For. Patho.* **17**: 1–5.

Diner, A.M. and Soliman, K. 1993. *Pinus palustris* transformation by *Agrobacterium rhizogenes*. *In Vitro Cellular & Develop. Bio.* **29A**: 86A.

Duchesne, L.C. and Charest, P.J. 1991. Transient expression of the *B*-glucuronidase gene in embryogenic callus of *Picea mariana* following microprojection. *Plant Cell Rep.* **10**: 191–194.

Duchesne, L.C. and Charest, P.J. 1992. Effect of promoter sequence on transient expression of the *B*-glucuronidase gene in embryogenic calli of *Larix* X *eurolepis* and *Picea mariana* following microprojection. *Can J. Bot.* **70**: 175–180.

Duchesne, L.C., Lelu, M.-A., von Aderkas, P. and Charest, P.J. 1993. Microprojectile-mediated DNA delivery in haploid and diploid embryogenic cells of *Larix* spp. *Can. J. For. Res.* **23**: 312–316.

Ellis, D.D., McCabe, D.E., McInnis, S., Ramachandran, R., Russell, D.R., Wallace, K.M., Martinell, B.J., Roberts, D.R., Raffa, K.F. and McCown, B.H. 1993. Stable transformation of *Picea glauca* by particle acceleration. *Bio/Technology* **11**: 84–89.

Ellis, D.D., McCabe, D., Russell, D., Martinell, B. and McCown, B.H. 1991. Expression of inducible angiosperm promoters in a gymnosperm, *Picea glauca* (white spruce). *Plant Molecular Bio.* **17**: 19–27.

Ellis, D.D., Roberts, D., Sutton, B., Lazaroff, W., Webb, D. and Flinn, B. 1989. Transformation of white spruce and other conifer species by *Agrobacterium tumefaciens*. *Plant Cell Rep.* **8**: 16–20.

Fillatti, J.J., Sellmer, J., McCown, B., Haissig, B. and Comai, L. 1987. *Agrobacterium* mediated transformation and regeneration of *Populus*. *Mol. Gen. Genet.* **206**: 192–199.

Fromm, M.E., Taylor, L.P. and Walbot, V. 1986. Stable transformation of maize after electroporation. *Nature* **319**: 791–793.

Goldfarb, B., Strauss, S.H., Howe, G.T. and Zaerr, J.B. 1991. Transient gene expression of microprojectile-introduced DNA in Douglas-fir cotyledons. *Plant Cell Rep.* **10**: 517–521.

Gonzales, M.V., Vey, M., Ordas, R.J., Ancora, G. and Tavazza, R. 1993. Transient gene expression in cultured radiata pine cotyledons. 5th Workshop of the IUFRO Working Party on Somatic Cell Genetics of Trees. October 18–22, 1993. Balsian, Spain. 59.

Gupta, P.K., Dandekar, A.M. and Durzan, D.J. 1988 Somatic proembryo formation and transient expression of a luciferase gene in Douglas-fir and loblolly pine protoplasts. *Plant Sci.* **58**: 85–92.

Han, K.-H., Fleming, P., Walker, K., Loper, M., Chilton, W.S., Mocek, J., Gordon M.P. and Floss, H.G. 1994. Genetic transformation of mature *Taxus*, an approach to genetically control the *in vitro* production of the anticancer drug, taxol. *Plant Sci.* **95**: 187–196.

Hawes, M.C. and Pueppke, S.C. 1987. Correlation between binding of *Agrobacterium tumefaciens* by root cap cells and susceptibility of plants to crown gall. *Plant Cell Rep.* **6**: 287–290.

Hay, I., Lachance, D., von Aderkas, P. and Charest, P.J. 1994. Transient chimeric gene expression in pollen of five conifer species following microparticle bombardment. *Can. J. For.Res.* **24**: 2417–2423.

Hood, E.E., Clapham, D.H., Ekberg, I. and Johannson, T. 1990. T-DNA presence and opine production in tumors of *Picea abies* (L.) Karst induced by *Agrobacterium tumefaciens* A281. *Plant Molecular Bio.* **14**: 111–117.

Hooykass, P.J.J. and Schilperoort, R.A. 1992. *Agrobacterium* and plant genetic engineering. *Plant Molecular Bio.* **19**: 15–38.

Horsch, R.B., Fry, J.E., Hoffmann, N., Eichholtz, D., Rogers, S.G. and Fraley, R.T. 1985. A simple and general method for transferring genes into plants. *Science* **227**: 1229–1231.

Huang, Y. 1993. Genetic Engineering of *Larix decidua*: *Agrobacterium*-Mediated Gene Transfer and Regeneration of Transgenic Plants in European Larch. UMI Publishing Company, Ann Arbor, Michigan. 245 pp.

Huang, Y. and Karnosky, D.F. 1991a. A system for gymnosperm genetic transformation and regeneration: *Agrobacterium rhizogenes* and *Larix decidua*. *In Vitro Cellular & Develop. Bio.* **27**(3): 153A.

Huang, Y. and Karnosky, D.F. 1991b. Transfer and integration of *Bacillus thuringiensis* insecticidal gene into *Larix decidua*. Proc. Inter. Symp. on the Applications of Biotechnology to Tree Culture, Protection, and Utilization. Columbus, OH. 108.

Huang, Y. and Tauer, C.G. 1993. Another tool for gene transfer in pine species: *Agrobacterium rhizogenes*. *In Vitro Cellular & Develop. Biol.* **29** (3): 65 A.

Huang, Y. and Tauer, C.G. 1994. Integrative transformation of *Pinus taeda* L. and *P. echninata* Mill. by *Agrobacterium tumefaciens*. *For. Genet.* **1**: 23–31.

Huang, Y. and Tauer, C.G. 1995. Genetic transformation of southern pines: A summary of recent research. *In*: S. Wang and X. Jiang (Eds) Growth and Development Control and Biotechnology in Woody Plants. China Forestry Publishing House, Beijing. 41–60.

Huang, Y. Diner, A.M. and Karnosky, D.F. 1991a. *Agrobacterium rhizogenes*-mediated genetic transformation and regeneration of a conifer, *Larix decidua*. *In Vitro Cellular & Develop. Bio.* 201–207.

Huang, Y., Karnosky, D.F. and Tauer, C.G. 1993a. Applications of biotechnology and molecular genetics to tree improvement. *J. Arboriculture* **19**: 84–98.

Huang, Y., Shin, D.I. and Karnosky, D.F. 1991b. Evidence of *Agrobacterium*-mediated transformation in *Larix decidua*. *Woody Plant Biotech*. 233–235.

Huang, Y., Stokke, D.D., Diner, A.M., Barnes, W.M. and Karnosky, D.F. 1993b. Virulence of *Agrobacterium* on *Larix decidua* and their cellular interactions as depicted by scanning electron microscopy. *J. Expt. Bot.* **44**: 1191–1201.

Jefferson, R.A. 1987. Assaying chimeric genes in plants: the GUS fusion system. *Plant Mol. Biol. Rep.* **5**: 387–405.

Lindroth, A., Gronroos, R. and von Arnold, S. 1993. Transformation with *Agrobacterium* in lodgepole pine; *Pinus contorta* and genes specifically expressed during root initiation. 5th Workshop of the IUFRO Working Party on Somatic Cell Genetics of Trees. October 18–22, 1993. Balsian, Spain. 50.

Litvay, J.D., Johnson, M.A. and Verma, D. 1981. Conifer suspension culture medium development using analytical data from developing seeds. Institute of Paper Chemistry Technical Paper Series No. 115, Appleton, WI. 1–17.

Loopstra, C.A., Stomp, A.-M. and Sederoff, R.R. 1990. *Agrobacterium*-mediated DNA transfer in sugar pine. *Plant Molecular Bio.* **15**: 1–9.

Loopstra, C.A., Weissinger, A.K. and Sederoff, R.R. 1992. Transient gene expression in differentiating pine wood using microprojectile bombardment. *Can. J. For. Res.* **22**: 993– 996.

Magnussen, D., Clapham, D., Gronroos, R. and von Arnold, S. 1994. Induction of hairy and normal roots on *Picea abies, Pinus sylvestris*, and *Pinus cortorta* by *Agrobacterium rhizogenes. Scandinavian J. For. Res.* **9**: 46–51.

Martinussen, I., Bate, N., Weterings, K., Junttila, O. and Twell, D. 1995. Analysis of gene regulation in growing pollen tubes of angiosperm and gymnosperm species using microprojectile bombardment. *Physiol. Plantarum* **93**: 445–450.

McAfee, B.J., White, E.E., Pelcher, L.E. and Lapp, M.S. 1993. Root induction in pine (*Pinus*) and larch (*Larix*) spp. using *Agrobacterium rhizogenes. Plant Cell, Tissue and Organ Culture* **34**: 53–62.

McCabe, D.E., Swain, W.E., Martinell, B.J. and Christou, P. 1988. Stable transformation of soybean (*Glycine max*) by particle acceleration. *Bio/Technology* **6**: 903–926.

Mol, J., Stuitje, A., Gerats, A., van der Krol, A.R. and Jorgensen, R. 1989. Saying it with genes, Molecular flower breeding. *Trends in Biotech.* **7**: 148–153.

Morris, J.W., Castle, L.A. and Morris, R.O. 1989. Efficacy of different *Agrobacterium tumefaciens* strains in transformation of pinaceous gymnosperms. *Physiological and Molecular Plant Patho.* **34**: 451–461.

Newton, R.J., Yibrah, H.S., Dong, N., Clapham, D.H. and von Arnold, S. 1992. Expression of an abscisic acid responsive promoter in *Picea abies* following bombardment from an electric particle accelerator. *Plant Cell Rep.* **11**: 188–191.

O'Malley, D.M., Porter, S. and Sederoff, R.R. 1992. Purification, characterization and cloning of cinnamyl alcohol dehydrogenase in loblolly pine (*Pinus taeda* L.). *Plant Physiol.* **98**: 13–1371.

Ordas, R.J., Lopez, M.A., Pacheco, J.C., Manzanera, J.A., Bueno, A., Pardos, J.A. and Rodriguez, R. 1993. Possibilities to use *A. tumefaciens* as gene transfer vector in *Pinus nigra*. 5th Workshop of the IUFRO Working Party on Somatic Cell Genetics of Trees. October 18–22, 1993. Balsian, Spain. 52.

Otten, L., DeCreve, H. and Hernalsteens, J.P. 1981. Mandelian transmission of genes introduced into plants by the Ti plasmids of *Agrobacterium tumefaciens. Molecular and General Genetics* **183**: 209–213.

Plaut-Carcasson, Y.Y., Benkrima, L., Dawkins, M., Wheeler, N., Yanchuk, A. and Misra, S. 1993. Taxol from *Agrobacterium* transformed root cultures. *In* : S. Scher and B.S. Schwarzschild, (Eds) Proc. Inter. Yew Resources Conf. March 12–13, 1993. Berkeley, CA. 28.

Potrykus, I. 1991. Gene transfer to plants. *Ann. Rev. Plant Physiol.* **42**: 205–225.

Riemenschneider, D.E., Haissig, B.E., Sellmer, J. and Fillatti, J.J. 1988. Expression of a herbicide tolerance gene in young plants of a transgenic hybrid poplar clone. *In*: M.R. Ahuja (Ed.) Somatic Cell Genetics of Woody Plants. Kluwer Publishing Co., Dordrecht. 73–80.

Robertson, D., Weissinger, A.K., Ackley, R., Glover, S. and Sederoff, R.R. 1992. Genetic transformation of Norway spruce (*Picea abies*) using somatic embryo explants by microprojectile bombardment. *Plant Molecular Bio.* **19**: 925–935.

Sargent, W.A., Kodrzycki, R.J., Handley, L.W., Godbey, A.P., Loopstra, C.A. and Sederoff, R.R. 1993. Biolistic parameters for transient expression of loblolly pine cultures. *In Vitro Cellular & Develop.* Bio. **29** (3): 85A.

Sederoff, R., Stomp, A.-M., Chilton, W.S. and Moore, L.W. 1986. Gene transfer into loblolly pine by *Agrobacterium tumenfaciens. Bio/Technology* **4**: 647–649.

Shin, D.-I., Podila, G.K., Huang, Y. and Karnosky, D.F. 1994. Transgenic larch expressing genes for herbicide and insect resistance. *Can. J. For. Res.* **24**: 2059–2067.

Smith, C.O. 1935. Crown gall on conifers. *Phytopathol.* **25**: 894.

Smith, C.O. 1936. Crown gall on *Araucaria bidwillii. Phytopathol.* **26**: 400–401.

Smith, C.O. 1937. Crown gall on incense cedar, *Libocedrus decurrens. Phytopathol.* **27**: 844–849.

Smith, C.O. 1938. Crown gall on *Taxus baccata. Phytopathol.* **28**: 153–155.

Smith, C.O. 1939. Susceptibility of species of Cupressaceae to crown gall as determined by artificial inoculation. *J. Agri. Res.* **59**: 919–925.

Smith, C.O. 1942. Crown gall on species of Taxaceae, Taxodiaceae and Pinaceae, as determined by artificial inoculations. *Phytopathol.* **32**: 1005–1009.

Southern, E. 1975. Detection of specific sequences among DNA fragments separated by gel electrophoresis. *J. Mol. Bio.* **98**: 503–517.

Stomp A.-M., Loopstra, C., Sederoff, R., Chilton, S., Fillatti, J., Dupper, G., Tedeschi, P. and Kinlaw, C. 1988. Development of a DNA transfer system for pines. *In*: J.W. Hanover and D.E. Keathley (Eds) Genetic Manipulation of Woody Plants. Plenum Publishing Corp., New York. 231–241.

Stomp, A.-M., Weissinger, A. and Sederoff, R.R. 1991. Transient expression from microprojectile-mediated DNA transfer in *Pinus taeda. Plant Cell Rep.* **10**: 187–190.

Stomp, A.-M., Loopstra, C., Chilton, W.S., Sederoff, R.R. and Moore, L.W. 1990. Extended host range of *Agrobacterium tumefaciens* in the genus *Pinus. Plant Physiol.* **92**: 1226–1232.

Tauatorus, T.E., Bekkaoui, F., Pilon, M., Datla, R.S.S., Crosby, W.L., Fowke, L.C. and Dunstan, D.I. 1989. Factors affecting transient gene expression in electroporated black spruce (*Picea mariana*) and jack pine (*Pinus banksiana*) protoplasts. *Theoret. Appl. Genet.* **78**: 531–536.

Walter, C., Smith, D.R., Connett, M.B., Grace, L. and White, D.W.R. 1994. A biolistic approach for the transfer and expression of a *gusA* reporter gene in embryogenic cultures of *Pinus radiata. Plant Cell Rep.* **14**: 69–74.

Wilson, S.M., Thorpe, T.A. and Moloney, M.M. 1989. PEG-mediated expression of GUS and CAT genes in protoplasts from embryogenic suspension cultures of *Picea glauca. Plant Cell Rep.* **7**: 704–707.

Woodson, W.R. 1991. Biotechnology of floricultural crops. *HortScience* **26**: 1029–1033.

Wullems, G.J., Molendijk, L. and Schilperoort, R. 1981. Differential expression of crown gall tumor markers in transformant obtained after *in vitro Agrobacterium tumefaciens*-induced transformation of cell wall regenerating protoplasts derived from *Nicotiana tabacco. Proc. Natl. Acad. Sci. (USA)* **78**: 4344–4348.

Yibrah, H.S., Manders, G., Clapham, D.H. and von Arnold, S. 1994. Biological factors affecting transient transformation in embryogenic suspension cultures of *Picea abies. J. Plant Physiol.* **144**: 472–478.

# 21

# Molecular Markers: A Tool for Understanding the Relationship among Species of *Prosopis* (Leguminosae, Mimosoideae)

*B.O. Saidman*[1], *J.C. Vilardi*[1], *S. Montoya*[1], *M.J. Dieguez*[1] *and H.E. Hopp*[2]

**ABSTRACT**

Isozyme electrophoresis and RFLP techniques were applied to analyse the relationships among species of two sections, Algarobia and Strombocarpa, of the genus *Prosopis*. Isozymal studies allowed to estimate the genetic variability and among species differentiation in both sections. Mean heterozygosities and percentages of polymorphic loci are higher in species belonging to section Algarobia than in those of Strombocarpa. Both, isozymal and DNA analyses show that species of Strombocarpa are highly differentiated from each other, while in Algarobia the similarity among species is much higher. Most of the species of Algarobia studied so far hybridize frequently and are so similar isoenzymatically as to be considered a syngameon. In this complex the gene flow was estimated from the isozymal data. The results suggest that despite the frequent occurrence of fertile interspecific hybrids the effective gene flow is not significant among nominal species. The molecular relationships estimated here are compared with the morphological classification and the present results are also discussed in relation with the genetic system, the reproductive strategies and the evolutionary rates of morphological and biochemical traits in the species studied.

---

[1]Depto. Ciencias Biologicas, Fac. Cs. Exactas Y Naturales, Universidad de Buenos Aires, 1428 Buenos Aires, Argentina.

[2]Instituto de Biotencnologia, CICV-INTA Castelar, CC 77, (1708) Moron, Argentina.

## 1. INTRODUCTION

The rational exploitation of promisory species as well as the developing of programs for protecting endangered species require a deep knowledge of the biological characteristics, adaptive strategies and relationships among entities within the group considered. The genus *Prosopis* has been studied with growing interest in the last few years because it includes promising multipurpose species for reforestation of arid and semiarid regions, production of wood, charcoal, forage, human food, etc. Morphologically the genus is divided into five sections and some of them are subdivided into series (Burkart, 1976), but biochemical information is only fragmentary and isozymal studies are restricted to only two sections, Algarobia and Strombocarpa (Saidman, 1985, 1993; Saidman and Vilardi, 1987, 1993; Saidman *et al.*, 1996). In addition to isozyme studies, strong information about the relationships among species and the degree of variability within species may be obtained from the analysis of polymorphisms for DNA restriction fragment lengths (RFLPs). This approach has been applied only recently in *Prosopis* (Dieguez *et al.*, 1992) yielding sound results when analysed together with previous morphological and isozymal information.

The present work compiles the conclusions attained through the combination of isozymal and the first DNA polymorphism analyses to species of the sections Algarobia and Strombocarpa.

## 2. GEOGRAPHICAL DISTRIBUTION, TAXONOMIC PROBLEMS AND POPULATIONS SAMPLED

The genus *Prosopis* has a wide distribution which has been divided by Burkart (1976) into five sections, with two of them, Strombocarpa and Algarobia, subdivided into two and six series respectively. The genus occurs in most of the Argentine territory up to the 12 °C isotherm as the south distribution limit. The highest number of species occur in the phytogeographical provinces (Cabrera and Willink, 1973) of Monte, Espinal and Chaco (Fig. 1), which are important centers of species differentiation (Hunziker *et al.*, 1986).

The taxonomy of the South American 'algarrobos' (Sect. Agarobia) constitute a very interesting problem because, despite the important morphological differences, the species are very similar biochemically, and interspecific hybridization is very frequent in zones of sympatry. The distinction of some of the series established by Burkart (1976) may be perhaps questioned on the grounds of different lines of evidence from which one of the most remarkable is the unexpected high frequency of interseries interspecific hybrids (compared to intraseries) (see Hunziker *et al.*, 1986).

Isozyme studies (Saidman 1993; Hunziker *et al.*, 1986; Saidman and Vilardi, 1987, 1993) have shown relatively low degrees of genetic differentiation among seven species of this section, and the phenograms based on genetic distances (or identities) do not agree either with the expectations according to the Burkart's series. The observed identity values corresponded to that expected for sub- or semi-species and the available information suggests that the

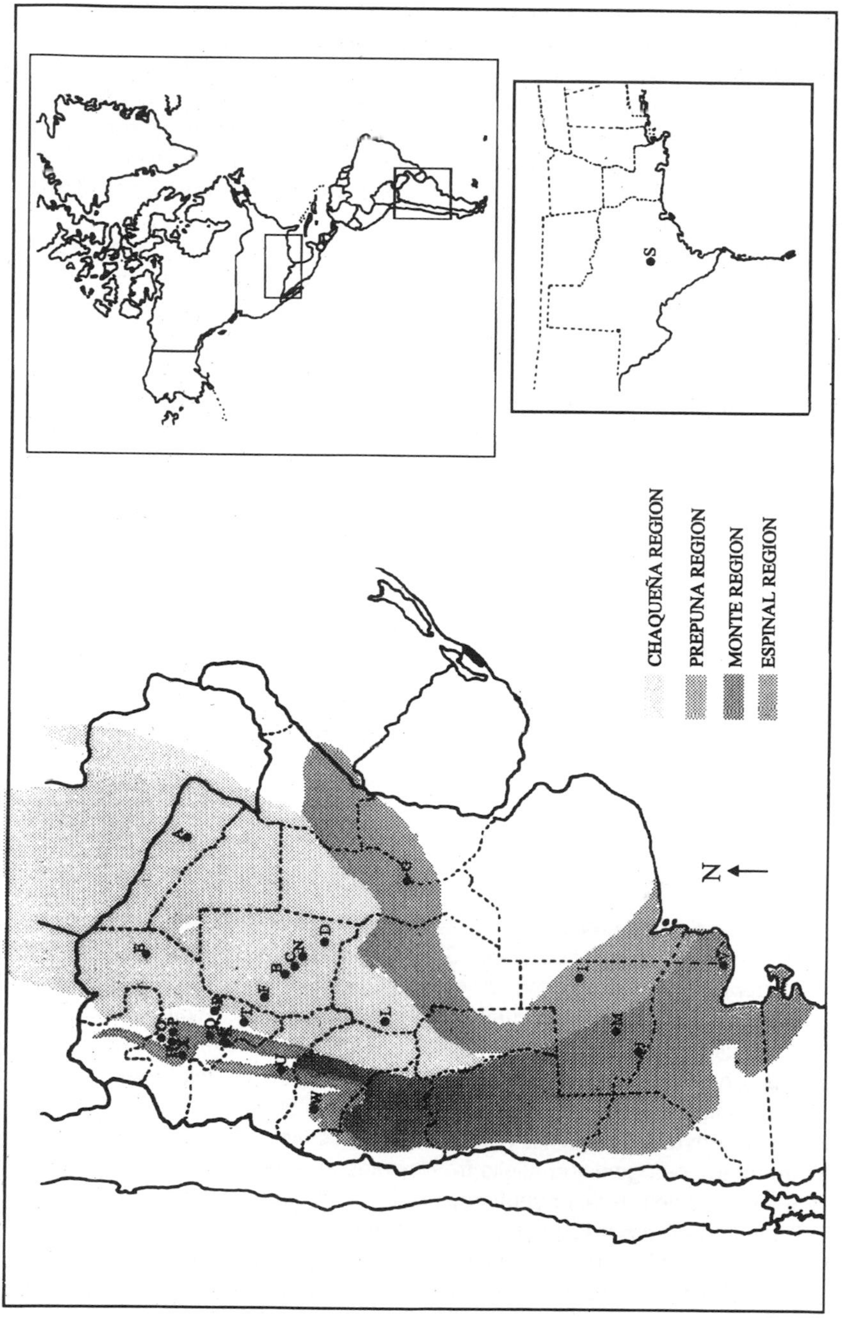


Fig. 1. Map showing the collection sites of populations analysed. The meaning of letters A-X are indicated in Table 1.

species so far studied of this section would constitue a syngameon (Saidman and Vilardi, 1993).

Contrary to the observations for Algarobia, hybridization is not a common feature within the Section Strombocarpa and their species are much more differentiated isoenzymatically from each other (Saidman *et al.*, 1996). There also seem to be differences between these two sections with respect to the reproductive system, the degree of variability and the adaptive strategy. The occurrence of differences in the genetic system of species belonging to these different sections is also suggested by the fact that no intersectional hybrids have been reported so far (Hunziker *et al.*, 1986).

The current research is oriented to solve different questions arising from the problems described above. These include those referred to the understanding of the internal dynamics of the Algarobia syngameon and the applicability of biological concepts of species to the entities belonging to this complex. As the genetic identity among nominal species in some cases is lower than intraspecific values, it is important analysing several populations of each species and sympatric populations of different nominal species to determine whether the interspecific hybridization is able to homogenize allelic frequencies. If this were the case, Nei's identity phenograms should reflect geographical patterns instead of specific status. Another question refers to the comparison of the within species genetic variability, among species genetic differentiation and the adaptive strategies between the sections Algarobia and Strombocarpa.

To solve these questions an extensive sampling of populations along the main centers of differentiation of this genus should be performed. Table 1 and Fig. 1 show the populations sampled and analysed up to now, representing an important portion of the distribution range in the New World.

## 3. THE CONTRIBUTION OF ISOZYME STUDIES

### 3.1 Section Algarobia

One remarkable characteristic of the Section Algarobia is the little specific differentiation at the isozymal level (Saidman and Vilardi, 1987, 1993). This fact is evident by the virtual absence of diagnostic loci for species identification and genetic distances ranging within the expected interval (Ayala *et al.*, 1974) from conspecific populations to semispecies. One of the advanced hypotheses for the observed genetic similarity among species is the high rate of interspecific hybridization and introgression taking place in wide areas of sympatry in the Chaco Phytogeographical Region. From this view, these proceses might be important in homogenizing allelic frequencies and reducing genetic differences between species. If this hypotheses is to be accepted, the question arises about the mechanisms maintaining the morphological discontinuities observed among the taxonomic species. An alternative though not necessarily excluding hypothesis (Saidman, 1985) is a dichotomy in the biochemical and morphological evolutionary rates.

Table 1. List of all *Prosopis* species and populations analysed so far for isozymal and/or DNA variation, along with their estimated variation.

| Section | Series | Species | | Population(=locality) | Collector | H(SE) | P(SE) |
|---|---|---|---|---|---|---|---|
| Algarobia | Ruscifoliae | *P. ruscifolia* | A | Dept. Patino, Formosa | R.A. Palacios | 0.13(0.04) | 38(11) |
| | | | B | Dept. Avellaneda, Sgo.Estero | BOS-JCV | 0.13(0.04) | 38(11) |
| | | | B | Herrera, Sgo.Estero | BOS-JCV | 0.26(0.05) | 61(10) |
| | | | C | Sarmiento, Sgo.Estero | BOS-JCV | 0.23(0.05) | 61(10) |
| | | | D | Pinto, Sgo. Estero | BOS-JCV | 0.25(0.05) | 61(10) |
| | | | E | Rivadavia, Salta | D.H.Vilardi | 0.24(0.05) | 62(10) |
| | | *P. hassleri* | A | Dept. Patino, Formosa | R.A. Palacios | 0.17(0.05) | 45(11) |
| | Chilenses | *P. nigra* | F | La Banda, Sgo.Estero | BOS-JCV | 0.21(0.05) | 48(11) |
| | | | G | Parana, Entre Rios | C.A.Naranjo | 0.22(0.05) | 48(11) |
| | | | H | La Merced, Salta | BOS-JCV | 0.25(0.05) | 57(10) |
| | | *P. caldenia* | I | Santa Rosa, La Pampa | S.Enus Zeiger-BOS | 0.20(0.05) | 48(10) |
| | | *P. flexuosa* | J | Cura-Co, La Pampa | S.Enus Zeiger-BOS | 0.23(0.05) | 50(11) |
| | | | K | Quilmes, Tucuman | BOS-JCV | 0.28(0.05) | 48(10) |
| | | | L | Chancani, Cordoba | A.Verga | – | – |
| | | *P. alpataco* | M | Chacharramendi, La Pampa | S.Enus Zeiger-BOS | 0.17(0.05) | 45(11) |
| | | *P. alba* | A | Dept. Patino, Formosa | R.A. Palacios | 0.17(0.05) | 45(11) |
| | | | N | Icano, Sgo. Estero | BOS-JCV | 0.19(0.05) | 48(10) |
| | | | H | La Merced, Salta | BOS-JCV | 0.18(0.05) | 39(10) |
| | | | O | Chicoana, Salta | BOS-JCV | 0.16(0.04) | 43(10) |
| | | | P | Sumalao, Salta | BOS-JCV | 0.18(0.04) | 44(10) |
| | | | Q | Curtiembres, Salta | BOS-JCV | 0.22(0.05) | 48(10) |
| | | | R | Trancas, Tucuman | A. Rabasa | 0.15(0.04) | 39(10) |
| | | *P. glandulosa* | S | Temple, Texas, USA | J. Evans | 0.19(0.05) | 47(10) |
| | | *P. chilensis* | L | Chancani, Cordoba | A. Verga | – | – |
| | | *P. chilensis aff.* | L | Chancani, Cordoba | A. Verga | – | – |
| | Sericanthae | *P. kuntzei* | T | Tacana, Tucuman | BOS-JCV | – | – |
| Strombocarpa | Strombocarpae | *P. strombulifera* | U | Copacabana, Catamarca | J.H. Hunziker | 0.05(0.03) | 13(7) |
| | | | V | Conesa, Rio Negro | A.D. Burghardt | 0.02(0.02) | 8(5) |
| | | *P. reptans* | B | Herrera, Sgo.Estero | BOS-JCV | 0.06(0.03) | 13(7) |
| | | | N | Icano, Sgo. Estero | BOS-JCV | 0.09(0.04) | 21(8) |
| | | *P. torquata* | W | Famatina, La Rioja | J.H. Hunziker-JCV | 0.08(0.04) | 18(9) |
| | | *P. pubescens* | S | Temple, Texas, USA | J. Evans | 0.03(0.03) | 7(7) |
| | Cavenicarpae | *P. ferox* | X | El Churcal, Salta | M. Pocovi-N-Acreche | 0.09(0.04) | 22(9) |

**Note:** H: mean heterozygosity, P: percent of polymorphic loci. Letters A-X indicate the location in the map of Fig. 1. Two populations, Avellaneda and Herrera, are very close to each other and are represented with the same letter(B).

One methodological approach to solve this question involves an extensive sampling including sympatric and allopatric species as well as different conspecific populations in order to determine whether the genetic distance between species is reduced in areas where hybridization is expected to occur more frequently.

Following this line a first interesting result was obtained when a *P. glandulosa* (mesquite) population from Temple, Texas was included in the phenogram based on 25 isoenzymatic loci (seven systems) with the previously studied South American Algarobia species (Gigena *et al.*, 1991) (Fig. 2). This species is a weedy shrub in desertic and semidesertic regions of North America, with a colonizing strategy similar to that of the South American *P. ruscifolia*, though morphologically is more similar to *P. flexuosa* (Burkart, 1976). In the phenogram based on Nei's genetic identities *P. glandulosa* associates with *P. ruscifolia* and, as previously observed (Saidman and Vilardi, 1987, 1993), the clustering obtained does not agree with Burkart's series. In this case, the high similarity between *P. glandulosa* and *P. ruscifolia* cannot be explained by hybridization since they are geographically isolated. The enzymatic relationships observed in this phenogram does not seem to agree with the geographical distribution either.

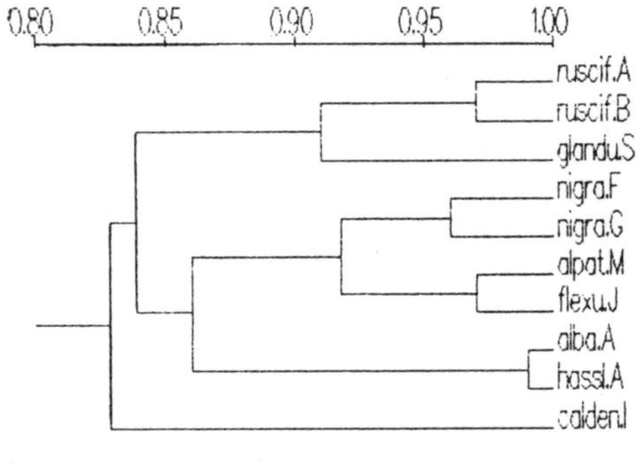


Fig. 2. Phenogram obtained through UPGMA from a matrix based on Nei's genetic identities of isozyme loci of populations of species belonging to section Agarobia, according to Gigena *et al.* 1991. ruscif. : *P. ruscifolia*, glandu.: *P. glandulosa*, nigra: *P. nigra*, alpat.: *P. alpataco*, flexu.: *P. flexuosa*, alba.: *P. alba*, hassl.: *P. hassleri*, calden.: *P. caldenia*. Letters after species name abbreviation represent population locations according to Table 1 and Fig. 1.

Another approach to determine whether hybridization does or does not imply effective gene flow among species was applied by Montoya *et al.* (1994) in a study of four populations of *P. ruscifolia*, six of *P. alba*, one of *P.nigra* and one of *P. flexuosa* by means of Wright's (1951) F statistics and Nei's genetic identities. Genetic variability (H = 0.15–0.28; P = 39–65%) did not differ statistically among populations and/or species. The phenogram based on genetic identities agrees with the specific status since conspecific populations are clustered (Fig. 3). Fst values estimated by the Nei and Chesser's (1983) method were highly significant for all variable loci when all populations were considered (Fst = 0.316). However, for conspecific populations Fst estimates were much lower (Fst = 0.065–068), and for some loci (Adh-1, Got-2, Est-2 and Prx-1 for *P. alba* and Amp-2 and 6Pgd-2 for *P. ruscifolia*) they were insignificant. The estimates of the gene flow obtained from Fst values (Fst = 1/(4Nm+1)) or from Slatkin's (1981, 1985) formula agreed and were insignificant (Nm < 1) among populations of different species even for sympatric or neighboring ones, while migration rates among conspecific populations were significant (about Nm = 3) (Montoya *et al.*, 1994).

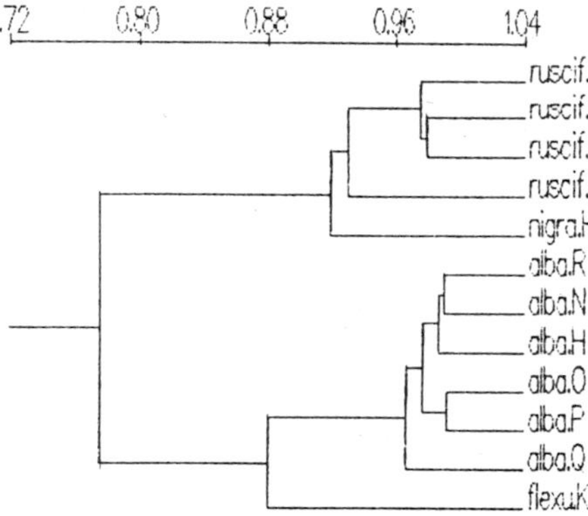


Fig. 3. Phenogram obtained through UPGMA from a matrix based on Nei's genetic identities of isozyme loci of populations of species belonging to section Agarobia, according to Montoya *et al.* (1994). ruscif.: *P. ruscifolia*, nigra: *P. nigra*, flexu.: *P. flexuosa*, alba.: *P. alba*. Letters after species name abbreviation represent population locations according to Table 1 and Fig. 1.

Though hybrids have been described for almost all possible pairwise combinations of these four species (see Hunziker *et al.*, 1986), the present results indicate that hybridization and introgression do not by themselves explain the high similarity among species of Algarobia since interspecific gene flow seems to be quite low.

### 3.2 Section Strombocarpa

The first isoenzymatic studies on species of this section referred to *P. strombulifera* and *P. reptans* (Saidman, 1985, 1993; Hunziker *et al.*, 1986; Saidman and Vilardi, 1993). They showed important differences from Algarobia with respect to the degree of variability and also suggested differences in the reproductive system. The high morphological and genetic similarities coupled with the allopatric distribution of these two taxa suggested that they could be subspecies instead of proper taxonomic species.

When more species were included in the analysis (*P. torquata, P. pubescens* and *P. ferox*) the differences with respect to Algarobia were more evident (Saidman *et al.*, 1996). The genetic variability was very low in all populations (Table 1) as compared with the Algarobia species. Diagnostic loci are abundant and all Strombocarpa species, but for the pair *P. strombulifera–P. reptans* are easily differentiated by their electrophoretic patterns. If *P. reptans* and *P. strombulifera* are considered subspecies as proposed above, the phenogram of Fig. 4 shows that between species identities are very low. When among species similarities are studied by principal component analysis (PCA) (Fig. 5) these tendencies are clearly shown. *P. reptans* and *P. strombulifera* populations are gathered as expected for conspecific ones, while the remaining populations are very dispersed (Saidman *et al.*, 1996).

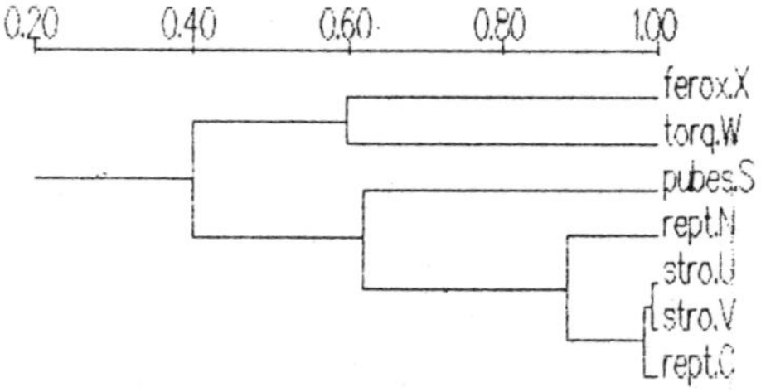


Fig. 4. Phenogram obtained through UPGMA from a matrix based on Nei's genetic identities of isozyme loci of populations of species belonging to section Strombocarpa, according to Saidman *et al.* (1995). ferox.: *P.ferox*, torq.: *P. torquata*, pubes.: *P. pubescens* rept.: *P. reptans*, stro.: *P. strombulifera*. Letters after species name abbreviation represent population locations according to Table 1 and Fig. 1.

Similarly to the results in Algarobia, in this section the isozymal studies do not agree with the expectations according to Burkart's series. In fact, *P. torquata* associates with *P. ferox* which belongs to Cavenicarpae instead of being clustered with those species of the series it belongs (Strombocarpae).

## 4. ANALYSIS OF DNA VARIATION AMONG SPECIES

An objective method which allows to study relationships among species and is not affected by environmental or developmental effects is based on the comparison of the length of DNA fragments obtained by the digestion with restriction endonucleases (RFLP) or by amplification of DNA fragments by the method of polymerase chain reaction (PCR). This technique allows comparison of the affinities among species for nuclear and organellar genes. Since these two kind of genes have different transmission systems, such a comparison may yield conclusions about the evolutionary mechanisms involved in the specific differentiation.

RFLP analysis of mitochondrial (mtDNA) and ribosomal DNA (rDNA) and PCR of a transcript spacer of rDNA have been applied to obtain the first results on the affinities among seven species of the sections Algarobia and Strombocarpa and a possible hybrid, *P. chilensis* aff., between *P. chilensis* and an unknown species (Dieguez *et al.*, 1992).

The RFLP analysis involved the use of one ribosomal (pTA71) and two mitochondrial (HJ13B4 and 16H12) probes coupled with the digestion with

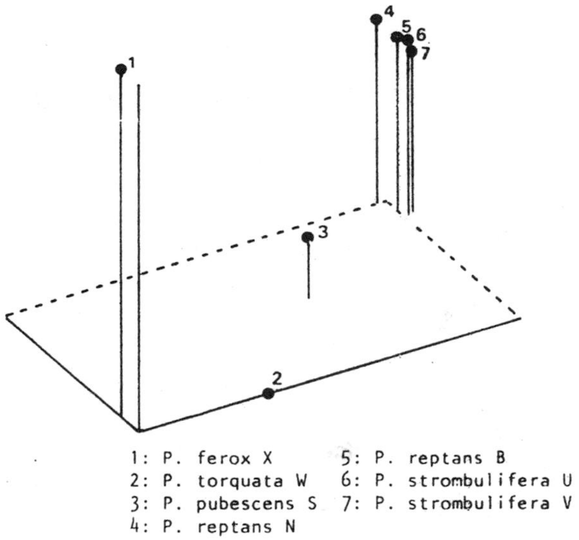


Fig. 5. Principal component analysis based on band presence- absence of the same isozyme loci analysed to obtain the phenogram of Fig. 4, according to Saidman *et al.* (1995). ferox.: *P. ferox*, torq.: *P. torquata*, pubes.: *P. pubescens*, rept.: *P. reptans*, stro.: *P. strombulifera*. Letters after species name abbreviation represent population locations according to Table 1 and Fig. 1.

seven restriction enzymes (EcoRI, BamHI, HindIII, BglII, TaqI, XbaI and MboI). For the PCR the primers used were ITS5 and ITS4 designed according to the sequence of the tomato ribosomal gene (Kiss *et al.*, 1989).

The total number of bands (fragments) analysed was 163 for mtDNA and 69 for rDNA (including RFLP and PCR). Band patterns allowed species identification. As the number of individuals per population analysed up to now is low, the data were coded as band presence (1) or absence (0) and a similarity matrix was obtained by the simple matching method (see Crisci and Lopez Armengol, 1983). From this matrix a phenogram by UPGMA was made. The information from rDNA (including RFLP and PCR techniques) and mtDNA fragments were analysed separately taking into account their differences in transmission systems.

In agreement with the expected from morphological criteria, the phenogram based on rDNA fragments (Fig. 6) shows the species of Section Algarobia associated in a cluster. Besides, *P. chilensis* is related with its presumptive hybrid *P. chilensis* aff. and both associate with *P. flexuosa*, the species belonging to the same series (Chilenses). *P. ruscifolia* (Series Ruscifoliae), which showed high isozymal similarity with the former, joins to that cluster, while *P. kuntzei* (Ser. Sericanthae) is more distant. This differentiation of Series Sericanthae from the other two is also consistent with preliminary isozymal studies (Pocovi, 1992) showing the same tendency.

Though *P. ferox* and *P.reptans* are clustered, they are not associated with the remaining studied species of Sect. Strombocarpae (*P. pubescens*). This

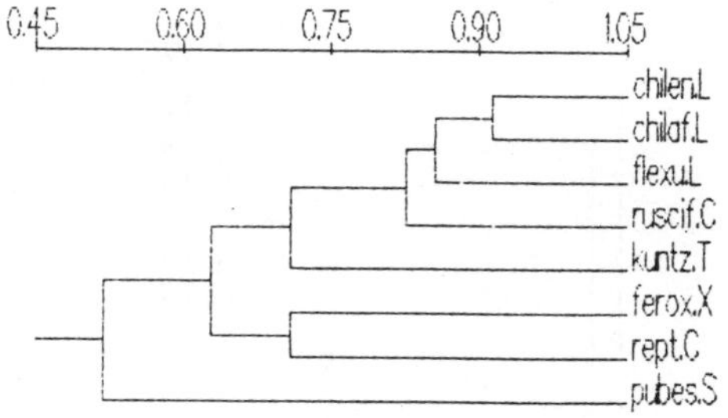


Fig. 6. Phenogram obtained through UPGMA from a simple matching similarity matrix obtained from the analysis of rDNA RFLP and PCR methods, according to Dieguez (1992) and Dieguez *et al.* (1992). ruscif.: *P. ruscifolia*, flexu.: *P. flexuosa*, chilen.: *P. chilensis*, chilaf.: *P. chilensis* aff., kuntz.: *P. kuntzei*, ferox.: *P. ferox*, pubes.: *P. pubescens*, rept.: *P. reptans*. Letters after species name abbreviation represent population locations according to Table 1 and Fig. 1.

may be the reflection of the high genetic differentiation among species detected by isozymal studies in this section.

The phenogram based on mtDNA (Fig. 7) is highly consistent with that obtained from rDNA, with the only difference in the position of *P. chilensis* aff., which in this case is more related to *P. flexuosa* than to *P. chilensis*. In order to explain this difference it is assumed that the cytoplasmic DNA of the hybrid *P. chilensis* aff. proceeds from a female parent closer to *P. flexuosa*.

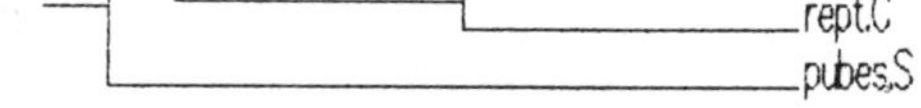

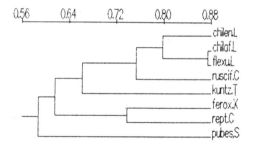


Fig. 7. Phenogram obtained through UPGMA from a simple matching similarity matrix obtained from the analysis of mtDNA RFLP method, according to Dieguez (1992) and Dieguez *et al.* (1992). ruscif.: *P. ruscifolia*, flexu.: *P. flexuosa*, chilen.: *P. chilensis*, chilaf.: *P. chilensis* aff., kuntz.: *P. kuntzei*, ferox.: *P. ferox*, pubes.: *P. pubescens*, rept.: *P. reptans*. Letters after species name abbreviation represent population locations according to Table 1 and Fig. 1.

## 5. CONCLUSION

Developing programs of germplasm conservation and controlled crosses to exploit benefical heritable characters requires a clear demarcation of species boundaries and the recognition of the existing isolating mechanisms between related groups. This purpose is far from a simple task since the very concept of species is very difficult to be defined in terms of universal applicability (for a wide discussion about the concept of species see Otte and Endler, 1989 and King, 1993).

The multidisciplinary approach is one of the most powerful ways to ascertain the relationships among species belonging to a particular group and bring trusted information to be applied for the rationale use of the biological diversity. In the genus *Prosopis* the joint analysis of morphological and biochemical data has yielded important conclusions about the relationships and the genetic systems in the sections Algarobia and Strombocarpa.

Several species of *Prosopis* are protogynous and some belonging to Algarobia were shown to be strict outcrossers and self-incompatible (Simpson, 1977; Simpson and Solbrig, 1977). The self-incompatibility would be consistent with the important isoenzymatic variability detected in species of Algarobia measured as per cent of polymorphic loci or mean heterzygosity (Table 1). The species of Strombocarpa however exhibit very little variabilities (Table 1) and this might be explained by the occurrence of at least partial selfing. This is supported by some evidences of autocompatibility in the species of this section (*P. tamarugo* and *P. torquata*) (see Hunziker *et al.*, 1986).

Based on morphological and chromatographical evidences, Palacios and Bravo (1981) proposed that a complex of species of Algarobia would constitute a syngameon. This was supported by the high genetic similarity observed among these species (Saidman, 1985; Hunziker *et al.*, 1986; Saidman and Vilardi, 1987, 1993). In the first studies on isozyme variability of *Prosopis*, Saidman (1985) and Saidman and Vilardi (1987) advanced two possible hypothesis to explain this similarity: a) the reproductive barriers among these species are weak, allowing hybridization and introgression to homogenize allelic frequencies; b) the evolutionary rates of morphological and molecular traits are different. The insignificant gene flow estimates among nominal sympatric species seems to be a support for the hypothesis b. As premating isolation is not well developed in some species of Alagarobia, the lack of gene flow among these species suggests the existence of more efficient postmating isolation mechanisms maintaining species boundaries within definite limits. Therefore, the entities involved in this syngameon might be considered species under the Templeton (1989) cohesive concept assuming demographically and/or ecologically rather than genetically cohesive mechanisms.

A likely hypothesis for the low evolutionary rate of isozymal markers is that many of the studied loci represent coadapted genes giving an adequate response to variable environmental stringencies, which are not to be altered without a loss in adaptedness. This hypothesis might also account to explain the higher similarity of *P. glandulosa* with *P. ruscifolia*, with which it shares a similar colonizing strategy, than with *P. flexuosa*, its most morphologically related species.

If isozyme loci in Algarobia were coadapted they would not be trusted as estimator of divergency times, because they would not be strictly neutral. However, the DNA analyses were consistent with isozymal studies in showing higher among species differentiation in Strombocarpa than in Algarobia. The latter seems to be a natural group and the phenograms obtained either from rDNA or mtDNA fragments were also consistent with the series defined by Burkart (1976). The lower affinity of *P. kuntzei* with the remaining species of Algarobia studied up to now is also supported by preliminar isozymal data (Pocovi, 1992). The apparent lack of hybrids between any species of Sericanthae with those of Ruscifoliae or Chilenses (see Hunziker *et al.*, 1986) suggests that the species of this series (*P. kuntzei* and *P. sericantha*) would not be component of the syngameon described for the former studied Algarobia species.

In the Section Strombocarpa isozymal homology between species is hardly demonstrable (diagnostic loci are abundant) and, according to DNA fragment based phenograms, *P. pubescens* is equally distanced from other species of Strombocarpa and those of Algarobia. The relationships among these species to each other and with respect to those of other sections need a deeper analysis.

The next step for a thorough phylogenetic study of the genus *Prosopis* involves the use of simultaneous molecular approaches including chloroplast, mitochondrial and nuclear DNA markers complementing and extending ongoing morphological and isozymal research. The results of such a multidisciplinary attack to the problem of the relationships among *Prosopis* species coupled with ecological studies referred to the role and requirements of the most promissory species should suggest the best strategies for their rationale exploitation and reforestation of particular arid and semiarid ecosystems.

## ACKNOWLEDGEMENTS

This work was carried out with the economical support of the International Foundation for Sciences (IFS), the Universidad de Buenos Aires and the Third World Academy of Sciences (TWAS) through grants to BOS. We wish to express our gratitude to Dr A.D. Burghardt, Dr J. Evans, Dr J.H. Hunziker, Dr C.A. Naranjo, Ing. Agr. R.A. Palacios, Dr A. Rabasa, Ing. Agr. A. Verga and Mr D.H. Vilardi who generously donated part of the materials analysed here. We are also indebted to Ing. Agr. Palacios for the taxonomic determination of the materials. The altruistic collaboration of Mr Fausto Romano from Transportes La Sevillanita in transporting population samples from Salta is greatly acknowledged. BOS and JCV are members of Carrera del Investigador Cientifico, Consejo Nacional de Investigaciones Cientificas y Tecnicas (CONICET, Argentina). HEH is member of Carrera del Investigador Cientifico, Comision de Investigaciones Cientificas (CIC) de la Provincia de Buenos Aires.

## REFERENCES

Ayala, F.J., Tracey, M.L., Hedgecock, D. and Richmond, R.C. 1974. Genetic differentiation during speciation process in *Drosophila. Evolution* **28**: 576–592.

Burkart, A. 1976. A monograph of the genus *Prosopis* (Leguminosae subfam. Mimosoideae). *J. Arnold Arboret.* **57**(3): 219–249.

Cabrera, A.L. and Willink, A. 1973. Biogeografia de America Latina. The General Secretariat of the Organization of American States, Washington, D.C.

Crisci, J.V. and Lopez Armengol, M.F. 1983. Introduccion a la teoria y practica de la taxonomia numerica. The general Secretariat of the Organization of American States, Washington, D.C. 132 pp.

Dieguez, M.J. 1992. Estudio de la variabilidad genetica, la evolucion y la taxonomia del genero *Prosopis* mediante marcadores moleculares. Seminario de Licenciatura, Departamento de Cs. Biologicas, Facultad de Cs. Exactas y Naturales, Universidad de Buenos Aires, Bs. As. 113 pp.

Dieguez, M.J., Saidman, B.O., Vilardi, J.C. and Hopp, H.E. 1992. Analisis de la relacion entre especies de *Prosopis* por medio de marcadores moleculares. Actas XIII Congr. Argent. Genetica, Pergamino, Buenos Aires. 15.

Gigena, A., Saidman, B.O. and Vilardi, J.C. 1991. Variabilidad genetica en *Prosopis glandulosa* (Leguminosae, Mimosoideae). Actas XXII Congr. Argent. Genetica, Catamarca. 22.

Hunziker, J.H., Saidman, B.O., Naranjo, C.A., Palacios, R.A., Poggio, L. and Burghard, A. 1986. Hybridization and genetic variation of Argentine species of *Prosopis*. *For. Ecol. Mgmt.* **165**: 301–315.

King, M. 1993. Species evolution the role of the chromosome change. Cambridge University Press, Cambridge. 336 pp.

Kiss, T., Kiss, M., Abel, S. and Solymosy, F. 1989. Nucleotide sequence of the 17 S-25 S spacer region from tomato rDNA. *Nucleic Acid Res.* **16**: 7179.

Montoya, S., Saidman, B.O., Vilardi, J.C. and Bessega, C. 1994. Diferenciaction y flujo genetico entre especies de la seccion Algarobia, Genero *Prosopis* (Leguminosae). Actas XXIV Congreso Argentino de Genetica, La Plata. 17.

Nei, M. and Chesser, R.K. 1983. Estimation of fixation indices and gene diversities. *Ann. Hum. Genet.* **47**: 253–259.

Otte, D. and Endler, J.A. 1989. Speciation and its consequences. Sinaver Associates Inc., Sunderland, Massachusetts. 679 pp.

Palacios, R.A. and Bravo, L.D. 1981. Hibridacion natural en *Prosopis* (Leguminosae) en la region chaquefia argentina. Evidencias morfologicas y cromatograficas. *Darwiniana* **23**: 3–35.

Pocovi, M.I. 1992. Estudios Isoenzimaticos en especies de *Prosopis* (Leguminosae subflia. Mimosoideae), Trabajo de Seminario de la Licenciatura en Cs. Biologicas, Fac. Cs. Naturales, Universidad Nacional de Salta, Salta, Argentiana. 102 pp.

Saidman, B.O. 1985. Estudio de la variabilidad alozimica en el genero *Prosopis*. Tesis de Doctorado. Facultad de Cs. Exactas y Naturales. UBA., Bs. As., Argentina.

Saidman, B.O. 1993. Las isoenzimas en el estudio de la variacion genetica y las afinidades entre especies de *Prosopis* (Leguminosae), Bol. Genet. Inst. Fitotec. *Castelar* **16**: 25–37.

Saidman, B.O. and Vilardi, J.C. 1987. Analysis of genetic similarities among seven species of *Prosopis* (Leguminosae: Mimosoideae). *Theoret. Appl. Genet.* **75**: 109–116.

Saidman, B.O. and Vilardi, J.C. 1993. Genetic variability and germplasm conservation in the genus *Prosopis*. *In*: S. Puri and P.K. Khosla (Eds) Nursery Technology of Forest Tree Species of Arid and Semiarid Regions. Winrock-Oxford & IBH Publishing Co. Pvt Ltd., New Delhi. 187–198.

Saidman, B.O., Vilardi, J.C., Pocovi, M.I. and Acreche, N. 1996. Isozyme studies in Argentine species of the section Strombocarpa, Genus *Prosopis* (Leguminosae). *J. Genetics* **75**: 139–149.

Simpson, B.B. 1977. Breeding systems of dominant perennial plants of two disjunct warm desert ecosystems. *Oecologia* (Berl.) **27**: 203–226.

Simpson, B.B. and Solbrig, O.T. 1977. Introduction. In: B.B. Simpson (Ed.) Mesquite. Its Biology in Two Desert Ecosystems. US/IBP Synthesis. Series 4. Dowden, Hutchinson and Ross Inc., Pennsylvania. 1–25.

Slatkin, M. 1981. Estimating levels on gene flow in natural populations. *Genetics* **99**: 323–335.

Slatkin, M. 1985. Rare alleles as estimators of gene flow. *Evolution* **39**: 53–65.

Templeton, A.R. 1989. The meaning of species and speciation: A genetic perspective. *In*: D. Otte, and J.A. Endler (Eds) Speciation and Its Consequences. Sinaver Associates Inc., Sunderland, Massachusetts. 3–27.

Wright, S. 1951. The genetical structure of populations. *Ann. Eugen.* **15**: 323–354.